Pioneers of Jazz

Frontispiece: Front row, left to right: Ollie "Dink" Johnson, James Palao, Norwood Williams. Back row: Eddie Vincent, Fred Keppard, George Baquet, Bill Johnson. [Palao family scrapbook]

Pioneers of Jazz

The Story
of the
Creole Band

Lawrence Gushee

OXFORD
UNIVERSITY PRESS

OXFORD
UNIVERSITY PRESS

Oxford University Press, Inc., publishes works that further
Oxford University's objective of excellence
in research, scholarship, and education.

Oxford   New York

Auckland   Cape Town   Dar es Salaam   Hong Kong   Karachi
Kuala Lumpur   Madrid   Melbourne   Mexico City   Nairobi
New Delhi   Shanghai   Taipei   Toronto

With offices in
Argentina   Austria   Brazil   Chile   Czech Republic   France   Greece
Guatemala   Hungary   Italy   Japan   Poland   Portugal   Singapore
South Korea   Switzerland   Thailand   Turkey   Ukraine   Vietnam

Published by Oxford University Press, Inc.
198 Madison Avenue, New York, New York, 10016

www.oup.com

First issued as an Oxford University Press paperback, 2010

Oxford is a registered trademark of Oxford University Press

Library of Congress Cataloging-in-Publication Data
Gushee, Lawrence.
   Pioneers of jazz : the story of the Creole Band / by Lawrence Gushee.
      p. cm.
   Includes bibliographical references and index.
   ISBN 978-0-19-973233-3
      1. Original Creole Orchestra.   2. Jazz musicians—Louisiana—New Orleans—Biography.   I. Title.
   ML421.O72G87 2004
   785'.2165'06076335—dc22   2004007643

9 8 7 6 5 4 3 2 1

Printed in the United States of America
on acid-free paper

To the memory of two Bills

William Manuel Johnson,
who lived it,

and William Russell,
who knew it was important

Preface

LONG OVERDUE THANKS to a maternal aunt for giving me, ca. 1943, a bunch of old records from the 1920s, including at least one by the Original Memphis Five. (I think I still have it someplace or other.) Be that as it may, I soon developed an interest in recorded jazz, by Benny Goodman, Duke Ellington, Louis Armstrong, and eventually a host of others. In high school I frequently made trips to the junk shops on Philadelphia's South Street, the main stem of the African-American community, and from time to time found recordings from the 1920s that tickled my fancy. For this I had only the guidance of *The Jazz Record Book*, Orin Blackstone's *Index to Jazz*, and the *Record Changer*. About the same time I received as a prize a copy of *Jazzmen* and also bought regularly *Metronome*, *Down Beat*, the *Record Changer*, and the under-appreciated *Jazz Record*. Far too young to be allowed into saloons or night clubs, I was nonetheless privileged to hear in person some of the oldest active jazz musicians—born before the turn of the century—including Sidney Bechet, Baby Dodds, and Bunk Johnson at Sunday afternoon concerts in the Academy of Music (fancy that!). All of this inclined me to appreciate the older jazz, although I also—thanks to *Metronome*—bought some of the earliest bebop recordings. Of course, wise after the fact, I now see clearly that in 1947 I should have been spending my afternoons with George Baquet rather than reading books and looking for old records.

After college and a couple of years of military service, I studied music theory and clarinet performance for some months in New York, and my apartment mate of the time won at auction a barely played copy of Doc Cook's "Spanish Mama" with its wonderful breaks by Freddie Keppard. It convinced me that the cliché that Keppard's few records were made when he was past his prime was pure hogwash. Be that as it may a few months later I was enrolled in a program of general musicological studies, where I eventually found a use for my schoolboy Latin by studying the music of the Middle Ages. As distant as this seems from the present undertaking, I owe to Leo Schrade some understanding of historical scholarship and the manner of interpreting documents that remain valid no matter the subject. So far as jazz went, I did no research but kept my hand in by playing clarinet and saxophone on a semiprofessional basis, then began to write jazz record reviews, most notably in the idealistic and short-lived *Jazz Review*. (These were mostly of contemporary or "modern" jazz.) Jazz was pigeonholed in a quite different part of my brain than other kinds of music, a state of affairs that persisted until 1978, when I was commissioned by Martin Williams, then of the Smithsonian Institution, to write liner notes for a reissue of the extant recordings of Freddie Keppard (and some that weren't by him, despite my attempts to persuade Martin to cut them).

There were so many loose ends regarding Keppard in those notes, especially his career with the Creole Band, that I found it impossible to close the file. During one of my first research trips to New Orleans in the late 1970s, Dick (Richard B.) Allen told me that a daughter of James Palao, the leader of the band, was living in Chicago. This was exciting news and I lost no time in making contact with Clotile Palao Glover (later Wilson), who introduced me to her ninety-plus-year-old mother, Armontine Carter Palao. Some of the information they shared with me was priceless because it was entirely personal. Little had to do with music or vaudeville, and often they learned things from me that were quite new to them. Be that as it may, these warm and generous people emboldened me to think that perhaps there was enough out there to write more than a short article or two.

Around 1980, German blues and jazz researcher Karl Gert zur Heide passed on to me third-hand photocopies of notes of a 1959 interview with the bassist and manager of the band, William Manuel Johnson. These notes cast so much light on the Creole Band that it now seemed that something more than "a short article or two" might truly be doable. At least it was enough to justify applying to the Guggenheim Foundation for a grant; this was viewed with favor. With both time and money (enough to buy the groceries and do some traveling) at hand, I drew up a "battle plan" and also continued to read extensively in both the general and theatrical newspapers of the time in order to establish a reliable itinerary. Proceeding at what seems to me now to have been a snail's pace, I wrote in 1987 a draft of an article dealing with the initial or pre-stages of the Creole Band. This was read at a national conference on black New Orleans music organized by Samuel A. Floyd, and was subsequently published in the journal of the Center for Black Music Research of Columbia College, Chicago.[1] Over the next few years materials slowly accumulated until by 1996 it seemed time (high time!) to begin to write.

To those on the outside, it sometimes seems that a college professor has limitless time for esoteric research. This is very far from the truth, thus any research support, however small, is precious. The Research Board of the University of Illinois, in addition to some material assistance for research trips, has also over the years funded a number of graduate research assistants: Rob Bird, Rebecca Bryant, Michael Corn, Ted Solis (I wonder if they ever thought a book would result from the sometimes bizarre tasks assigned to them) who helped with data entry and the ordering of newspapers on microfilm.

As the years passed, I gave talks on the Creole Band to meetings of professional societies and graduate students in musicology—first at York University, then at Rutgers, then to the New York chapter of the American Musicological Society. I blush to think how woefully tentative these initial efforts must have seemed; their chief role may have been to reveal how fragmentary my knowledge was. Finally, as the discovery of new sources slowed to a trickle then finally dried up, it seemed that it was time to put it all together.

The attentive reader will see that many absolutely priceless details regarding the early lives of Bill Johnson and Henry Morgan Prince have no source indicated. The person who collected these, and most generously and voluntarily passed them on to me, has emphatically insisted that his name not be mentioned. I hate to do it, not only because it violates the prime directive of scholarship—to clearly cite one's sources—but also because his dedication to the subject spurred me on to an effort that I might not otherwise have made. But, as they say, that's life.

I've singled out above a number of persons who have been especially influential over the years. My warm thanks to them all, as well as to others who have provided documents, advice, or encouragement over the years. They are (alphabetically) Lynn Abbott, Alden Ashforth, Gene Anderson, Pamela Arceneaux, Alma Freeman, Richard Hadlock, Thornton Hagert, Albert R. Kelly Jr., Brooks Kerr, Molly Kikuchi, Steven Lasker, James T. Maher, Mark Miller, Bruce Raeburn, William Russell, David Sager, Wayne Shirley, Fred Starr, John Steiner, and Steven Teeter. And especially to the person—who shall remain nameless— who said, "At least the discography will be short."

Sheldon Meyer of Oxford University Press has for more than thirty years fostered a prodigious list of distinguished publications in the history and esthetics of jazz. It seems almost that long that he's been on my track, most gently urging me to get something on paper that Oxford might publish. I'm also privileged to count myself among those for whom Jim (James T.) Maher has been an unflagging source of intellectual stimulus and moral support.

Above all, the Hogan Jazz Archive of Tulane University, directed by Bruce

Boyd Raeburn, and the Historic New Orleans Collection (holders of the William Russell Collection) comprise primary documents bearing on the history of ragtime and jazz in New Orleans. These unparalleled public collections are always welcoming to visitors and freely share their resources. To this short list must be added the collection of the New Orleans Jazz Club, now housed in the Old Mint as a branch of the Louisiana State Museum, and its curator, Stephen Teeter. Although the Institute of Jazz Studies of Rutgers University (Newark) is interested in New Orleans as part of a much larger picture, it still possesses documents of great importance. Its director, Dan Morgenstern, has given support and expressed interest in my researches over many years. His associates Ed Berger and Vincent Pelote have been of indispensable help on a number of occasions. I should also thank, even if they have rarely been of direct use in the present work, the Notarial Archives of Orleans Parish, with its historical section created and watched over by the incomparable Sally K. Reeves, and also the Louisiana Collection of the New Orleans Public Library, directed by Wayne Everard.

Documents of crucial importance in understanding the role of the band in the *Town Topics* revue were made available to me at that extraordinary collection, the Shubert Archive, even before it was formally open to the public. And special appreciation is due its curator Brigitte Kueppers and her successor Mary Ann Chach.

That the following expression of thanks comes in last place is not a way of indicating lesser importance; quite the contrary. Clearly, much of the documentation of the Creole Band's vaudeville peregrinations depended on the unstinting help of the interlibrary loan department of the University of Illinois Library in locating and ordering microfilm copies of local papers. But the newspaper library of the university library was also indispensable to the project.

My wife, Marion Sibley Gushee, has not only slogged through reams of my turgid prose and provided me a firm base for my scholarly research of all kinds, but she also has put up with a spouse whose mind was often on what happened ninety years ago. And our four children (Matt, Elizabeth, Sarah, and Rachel) grew up as their father spent countless hours hunched over a microfilm reader. Their curiosity as to what on earth I was up to will now, I trust, be satisfied.

Tradition would have it that at this point one begs the reader's indulgence— if not forgiveness—for the author's failings and errors, whether of commission or omission. I'm happy to embrace the tradition; additionally, let me point out that a work stitched together out of bits and pieces over a period of years is especially prone to repetitions and minor (I hope) contradictions. I do hope that through my efforts and those of my copy editor, most of these have been deep-sixed; those blemishes that remain will no doubt be brought to my attention by friend and foe alike. Rest assured that in the event of a revised edition, such things will be taken into account. Finally, one of my fantasies is that a reader in, for example, Los Angeles or Waterloo, Iowa, will remember an item in his or her family archive—a letter, newspaper article, photo, poster, program, ticket stub, and so forth—that bears on the history of the Creole Band, something that can also be included in the hypothetical revised edition.

By a stroke of scarcely believable luck, the presence of Bill Johnson and his band in California in 1908 no longer has to depend on the exegesis of uncertain reminiscences collected some 40 years after the fact. This is thanks to the extensive coverage by the Oakland Tribune of their hometown baseball club, the Oakland Oaks, a charter member of the Pacific Coast League, founded in 1903, with headquarters at Freeman's Park, a 7000 seat locale at 59th Street and San Pablo Avenue in North Oakland. The following is taken from three successive issues of the Tribune, from Saturday, 20 June, 1908, through Monday, 22 June, all likely from the pen of T.P. Magilligan. Apparently, the president of the Oakland Oaks, Ed Walter, heard a ragtime band called the "Creole Crushers" at a Thursday night contest of the presumably segregated West Oakland ball club. He hired them to play before the Oakland Oaks Sunday morning game and also between innings. Actually, there were two games between the Oaks and the Portland, Oregon, Athenians, one in the morning, the other in the afternoon.

Their Sunday appearance was described in loving sports-writerese in the Tribune's Monday evening edition, 22 June. I omit some of Magilligan's prose.

The morning's game was fraught with incidents that will tarry some in the memories of the fans. Music, attempted murder, mirth, frolic and baseball of the rip-snortin', buck-board kind marked the pre-luncheon affair.

Creole Crusher

For the edification of the assembled "Bugs" and "Bugines," Mr. W.M. Johnson's world-renowned Creole Orchestra shattered the air with melody and enlivened the proceedings. Mr. Johnson's Creoles put on tap a brand of rag time music that thrilled the bunch to their toes, and the chivalry and beauts cheered the musicianeers to the echo after each piece.

Mr. Johnson's got some band, bo. 'Taint organized none like dose raiglar regimental bands, nor does it worry itself by carrying music rolls. That orchestra includes and contains one snare drummer, greatest ever; one trombone artist, unrivalled; a cornet player, unmatched, a mandolin and guitar twanger and a bass viol, the latter three of which dispenses sounds dat shualey can set some feet to movin'.

An Obliging Orchestra

Mr. Johnsing and his Creoles are shualy an obligin' lot, for they toots a heep after dey starts 'er up, and keep a tootin' and a blowin' and scrapin' until the last fan ambles out of the park.

The rag that orchestra dispensed, free gratis to the fan, was of a new and weavy pattern. The gent with the trombone just cut holes in dat ole atmosphere, and when he got off to a runnin' staht in any one piece he always finished head up and tail out ahead of his companion pieces in the picture. The cornet boy also trifled some with his instrument, and when he put de gumbo stuff on dat New Orleans rag dey was some shakin of feet dat resembled yards of fire hose in the left field bleachers. The mandolin and guitar boys were dere wid dat shivery stuff, and when dey tinkled they s[h]ualy played music till de cows come home. The man wid de voil cut up some stuff dat was sharp as a razah and keen as a yen ho[k].

Music Makes Hit

. . . The ravishin' music of the Creoles seemed to turn the otherwise solid brains of Dangerous Danzig into curdled milk and that gent tried to commit murder on the person of a respected citizen in the bleachers back of first base [more follows].

Remarkably, on the same page is an account of the playing and singing of "Kid" North, known for his association with Ferd "Jelly Roll" Morton, as well as his commercial partnership with Bill Johnson in 1909 [see pages 75-77 below].

I leave it to the reader to follow up the important hints regarding musical style, such as the "new and weavy pattern" and further digging in various newspaper archives.

Contents

Pioneers of Jazz

Introduction

The Creole Band was *tremendous.* They really
played *jazz,* not just novelty and show stuff.
—Jelly Roll Morton to William Russell, ca. 1938

THIS HISTORY OF THE Creole Band offers itself as a narrative of the vaudeville career of the first jazz band to make its mark outside New Orleans. It will
also address the more general question of the beginnings of jazz as a national
music, and necessarily, if glancingly, deal with the beginnings in New Orleans.
An alert reader may already be muttering under his or her breath "what does
the author mean by 'jazz'?" and also, perhaps, "was it really a jazz band?" I beg
such an alert reader to permit me the use of these terms for the time being,
in exchange for my promise to answer these deceptively simple questions . . .
eventually. The epigraph above begs the questions, perhaps, but is invaluable
testimony from a musician whose mind and fingers had intimate knowledge
of both ragtime and jazz and also had a thorough acquaintance with vaudeville
tricks and hokum. He amply deserves being taken seriously.

While the chief purpose of the narrative is not to "set the record straight,"
I hope that it will do so, as well as introduce some degree of clarity into a subject that three generations of jazz writers have quite unintentionally muddled
almost beyond clarification. I also hope that the pioneering contribution of
some remarkable musicians will at last receive due credit, rather than being relegated to a brief and almost inevitably inaccurate footnote to the history of
early jazz.

Without pretending to go deeply into some important points concerning
the context in which the band operated, and some observations regarding the
ingrained traditions of jazz history writing, I nonetheless offer here my points
of view so that readers will know—as the contemporary vernacular has it—
"where I'm coming from." These observations are organized in four topics:

1. the history of musical exchanges between whites and blacks in the United States (a short version),
2. the development since roughly 1890 of a modern style of dancing,
3. the nature of vaudeville and the special problems facing musical groups operating in that now forgotten but once absolutely central institution, and
4. the various ways of writing jazz history and the questions answered and not answered; here will be included a few preliminary remarks on the history of recording popular dance music.

Musical Exchanges between African and European Americans

Many of those who might well remain on the fence regarding the geographical or chronological origin of "jazz" have no doubts as to *who* created it. Jazz, they are sure, is an African-American music. By this they mean the creation of persons of African or partly African descent and not of African-Americans and European-Americans. Point out to them that the instruments employed are European, that the harmony employed is European, and that the song forms that underlie virtually all jazz prior to 1960 are as well, and they will say that it's the supposedly African traits of blue notes or scales, the prominence of the 4/4 beat, the vocality of the instrumental voices, and the importance of improvisation that are the essential factors in jazz, the ones that make it part company with Europe. That much of the music of the Original Dixieland Jazz Band, as it became known through recordings in 1917–1918, is not improvised and not particularly vocal merely says to many that the music of the ODJB was not *really* jazz. To even continue this discussion with these assumptions is to follow a well-traveled and frustrating path, with traps of logic, philosophy, racial ideology, and politics everywhere one treads.

Let's take another path. First, let's take as a given that the borrowing and adaptation of European music by persons of African origin or ancestry have gone on since the eighteenth century at least. This has been pretty much a one-way street, due to the particular circumstances of coexistence of Africans and Europeans in the original colonies, and eventually the United States. Imagine an indigo plantation in Virginia. The owners might well have asked one or another of their slaves to provide dance music on the fiddle rather than send to Williamsburg or Richmond for European professionals. There's no reason to think that superficially they played anything other than what the imported professionals would have played—but with a particular attractive twist. We still might well deem it impossible or highly unlikely that the violin-playing son or piano-playing daughter of the house might pick up some African musical traits or habits. Still, music is free as the air, and at some point something in the slaves' music might well have left a mark on their masters' awareness or conception, if not the practice, of music.

But the plantation is only one place where African-American music-making went on. Let's imagine a city—say, nineteenth-century Philadelphia or New Orleans—in which black musicians, slave or free, might find steady employment by playing dance music. Their first hole card was that the dance hall owner didn't have to pay them as much as their Caucasian counterparts; their second, that they played the tunes of the day with an ear-tickling verve that made the dancers want to move. One assumes, nevertheless, that the repertory was a mix of traditional jig, reel, and country dance tunes and popular hits of the day (including potpourris from opera).

Meanwhile, over the course of the nineteenth century other kinds of music making showed that the European majority had been listening to the sounds of the minority, most notoriously the so-called Ethiopian minstrelsy, ubiquitous from the 1840s on. It strikes us as bizarre that the vast public should have preferred Caucasian "impressions" of African-Americans, such as Daddy Rice's version of Jim Crow's dance, to the genuine article. (It's not impossible, to be sure, that the interpretation of such a skilled performer would go over better on stage than the real thing.)

In the case of the Virginia Minstrels—Emmett, Brower, Whitlock, and Pelham—it seems to be unknown whether a specific African-American band of just that instrumentation (fiddle, banjo, tambourine, and bones) was their prototype. But it's clear that such small combos combining the most important European dance music instrument (the fiddle) with the African-derived banjo, with percussive noisemakers to be had in every kitchen or hearthside, were endemic in early nineteenth-century America.[2] Nevertheless, can we imagine that in 1843 New York a band of "real" African-Americans could have appeared on stage and garnered the kind of runaway success that the "fakes" did?

No, we cannot; this would have been too drastic a break with the deeply rooted tradition of Caucasian mimicry of the slaves entertainment. Eventually, after the Civil War, "real colored" minstrels began to appear in theaters and tents all over the United States and often found themselves obliged to imitate an imitation. This paradox makes us mindful of the functions of theater, sometimes offering up to audiences wonders and fancies, other times a mirror.

What is least likely to be remembered in all this is the prejudice, very common in the nineteenth century (and plausibly before), that the African was a simple child of nature, capable of heartfelt emotional expression and skillful and convincing mimicry but not true invention or creation, understood as accomplishments of the higher faculties. At least putting it this way is more complimentary than comparisons to the higher primates, understanding Africans to be, like their cousins, the chimpanzees, amazingly adept at "aping" the behavior of Europeans.[3]

In the nature of things as they were in mid-nineteenth century United States, black folk rarely had a chance to comment on this. Yet there is one exceptionally telling paragraph in an account of the 1869 New Orleans Mardi Gras festivities that appeared in a French language African-American newspaper. (The following translation is mine.)

> If there's something that must strike strangers who have never seen a masquerade in New Orleans, it's the large number of persons who were costumed in "negro" character. Our Caucasians have the gift of imitation in the highest degree, for most of them imitated the "negro" and especially the traditional "negro" such as he is represented to us . . . by the minstrels of the Olympic Theater, with a perfection that indicates amongst our cousins a great superiority.[4]

A commonly encountered theme in nineteenth-century writings is that we Americans had no national folk music, as, of course, many European countries had, except . . . the music of the slaves in the South. Needless to say, this offered something of a dilemma. In the European context, folk music was the product of a sturdy and greatly admired yeomanry. How could slaves, deprived on all sides of the legal rights of free men and by many considered little better than animals, be considered "us"?

Yet in the large repertory of nostalgic songs with a "plantation" setting, best remembered in the many songs of Stephen Foster, there was an exploitation of the enslaved African-American as a rural character of deep feeling, like a child prone to laughter or to tears. This was prior to the War of Secession / Civil War. After the war—and emancipation—black folk could speak and sing for themselves and contributed a wealth of songs embodying either plantation nostalgia ("Carry Me Back to Old Virginny") or a kind of jocular spirituality ("Oh, Dem Golden Slippers"), both songs by the African-American composer and minstrel performer James Bland.

Additionally, not a few examples of prewar "spirituals"—"Go Down Moses," "Swing Low, Sweet Chariot"—were converted from their unharmonized (and often emphatically rhythmed) "folk" form to quartet versions that made their way, along with the plantation songs, into college song collections. They remain to this day mainstays of the choral repertory and are accepted all over the world as American folk music, along with their snootier and often quite artful cousin, the solo concert spiritual.

This aspect of exchange between African-American and European-American music—or the *idea* of such music, since frequently there's nothing in the notes themselves that seems particularly African—is largely positive in a moral sense, for all that Ethiopian minstrelsy was regarded by many as a "low" form of entertainment. With the 1890s came a flood of dialect songs representing the urban Negro as a ne'er-do-well, a low-life gambler, and a deceiver of women. These so-called coon songs would be performed on stage by both black and white singers—the latter (and sometimes the former!) in blackface makeup. Among the earliest and most popular of these were "The Bully Song" and "Mr. Johnson, Turn Me Loose." The question of which of the hundreds, thousands of such songs embodied *musical* traits of African origin—even if distant and quite dilute—is a complicated one, but some certainly did, whatever the ethnicity of the composers.

At the same time, Americans began to hear on all sides syncopated compositions intended for dancing. There was the little remembered "Pas Ma La" of 1893–1894, followed by a flood from 1896 onward of cakewalks—understood to be an African-American dance in origin—and ragtime two-steps. Ragtime, whether as songs, piano music, or music for dancing, was also understood to be African-American, not only in origin but in its most authentic practice. It found its way onto phonograph records, as sheet music on the music racks of millions of pianos, and as orchestrations and arrangements for all kinds of ensembles, from "military bands" to mandolin and banjo clubs, to more ordinary dance bands.

Before the turn of the century all over the country, including the Deep South, African-American instrumentalists were making their mark as dance band players. This was a relatively low-status occupation, be it remembered, thronged with immigrants of every stripe. But where the Italian or German immigrant musician if sufficiently skilled could also hope to garner a post in a major wind band, such as Sousa's, a pit band in a large theater, or even a symphony orchestra (few though they were prior to 1900), no black musician ever did. No one had to explicitly draw the color line, it was simply in the nature of things.

We should hardly be surprised, then, that at their appearances in theaters from California to Massachusetts the Creole Band were singers of plantation songs, dancers, and comedians. They were simply demonstrating the inherent musicality of their "race," as well as doing what was expected in perpetuating an entertainment genre that went back a century.

Dancing

Henry Morgan Prince (1885–1969), from Alabama, was an all-round entertainer with a show business career reaching back to the turn of the century. In his tours with the Creole Band, he sang the plantation songs in quartet, but the core of his act was dancing. His role as "Uncle Joe" was standard fare demonstrating the ability of hot music to make old arthritic bones young again in dancing a "mean buck and wing."[5]

Where the *Oxford English Dictionary* pretty much strikes out on the term "buck-and-wing," with its earliest entry from 1895, Marshall and Jean Stearns in their much-lauded *Jazz Dance* cite Jim McIntyre, one of the most noted of latter-day minstrels, as having introduced "a syncopated buck-and-wing on the New York stage around 1880 (it did not become popular until later)."[6] Another old-time dancer whom they cite stated in a 1932 interview that the buck-and-wing was a "bastard dance, with a little of this and a little of that all mixed." The most we can conclude without making a doctoral dissertation of it is that it was neither the Irish jig (most recently highly visible in the show *Riverdance*), nor the clog, nor the shuffling Essence, all well known to nineteenth century audiences. Perhaps the most important thing is the association of buck-and-wing with syncopation.

In a review of Mabel Elaine (1893–1955), the blackface dancer who worked with the Creole Band for nearly five months in 1916, the noted critic Amy Leslie wrote admiringly that Mabel did "regulation old-time essence and double pat jig and buck and wing."[7] This youngster (twenty-three years old at the time of the review) had learned these dances at the feet of masters: she'd toured with the white minstrels McIntyre and Heath in their famous show *The Ham Tree*.

In any event, these stage dances aren't an essential part of the prehistory of jazz, which has primarily to do with social dancing. From the 1840s onward, any ball, whether in the Old World or the New, would have had as its mainstays the couple dances polka, waltz, and mazurka and the group dances lancers and quadrille. There were many others, to be sure, but these were the principal ones.

Around 1890 a simplified type of dance began to be adopted, the two-step, which by the end of the century was often danced (in the United States at least) to syncopated ragtime pieces. About this time there also began to appear in previously "polite" venues some rather risqué close dancing, with the partners plastered against each other rather than decorously side-by-side. Eventually, between about 1910 and 1915, the country as a whole began dancing or seeing danced various forms of close dances: the bunny hug and the grizzly bear, which are remembered, if only because of the quaint names; the turkey trot, which evolved from a close dance to the up-tempo one-step; the fox trot; and the exotic tango and maxixe. They were often referred to as "modern dancing." Although many of these were generally believed to have originated in the dance halls of San Francisco's Barbary Coast, some may have begun elsewhere, particularly in New Orleans.[8]

Sexy as the dances might have been when seen in the more liberal cabarets, not to speak of low-class dives, they were undoubtedly sanitized when taken up by professional society (or ballroom) dancers, of which the best recalled are Vernon and Irene Castle. But there were dozens of such couples, and seemingly overnight they began, ca. 1913–1914, to appear on vaudeville stages, accompanied frequently by on-stage bands composed of African-Americans. At the same time, dancers in cabarets—a relatively novel institution—often gyrated to the rhythms of black musicians.[9] These details are mentioned not to demonstrate that African-American musicians played dance music—they'd done so for two or three centuries—but they were beginning to have a public, even privileged, presence.

The relationship to New Orleans is this: while many of the earliest musicians we associate with ragtime played music as a part-time profession along with a variety of "day-jobs," a number of them, especially those who worked in dance halls catering to a transient or cosmopolitan public—such as those in the so-called District or Storyville—began to have music as their sole source of income. This required the development of a certain versatility along with note-reading ability in order to be able to play the latest hits from the New York publishers. The members of the Creole Band for the most part fitted this description; in other words they were far from being musical primitives or amateurs and consequently sufficiently "professional" to deal with the demand for polish and consistency of vaudeville.

Vaudeville

Vaudeville has negative connotations for many persons today: a particularly outrageous or corny joke may be met with "That's what killed vaudeville." And I've known some extremely knowledgeable conoisseurs to regard with disdain what they understand as vaudeville survivals in jazz performance. In one famous instance, this resulted in the unacknowledged removal on a modern reissue of the theatrical routines that prefaced a number of Jelly Roll Morton's Chicago recordings of 1926–1927. Of course, we all have a right to our opinion in matters of art; but this shouldn't lead to anachronistically imposing our latter-day taste and automatically dismissing as hambone corn or hokum anything performed on a vaudeville stage.

A few preliminaries are worth noting: we have lost the sense of the social implications of different kinds of theater, first of all the distinction between performance under canvas and that done indoors, whether in buildings built for stage performance or general-purpose halls pressed into service. Circuses and tent and medicine shows were ubiquitous and for some tiny towns the only kind of professional theater they could hope to see. Then between the late 1890s and the Great Depression there were the important distinctions between burlesque, vaudeville, tab shows, road shows, and legitimate theater, which operated in different ways and addressed different audiences.

OF THESE, VAUDEVILLE was the most pervasive and the most significant.[10] Much has been made of vaudeville as quintessential popular and topical entertainment, in which performer and audience were extraordinarily responsive one to the other. Obviously, the situations depicted and the views expressed were superficially mere entertainment; but they can also repay the student looking for deeper symbolism and social function.[11]

Taking a closer look at the organization of vaudeville in its heyday, ca. 1910–1920, there was real big-time vaudeville, typified by the Keith-Albee and Orpheum chains; small big-time vaudeville, as represented by Pantages and Loew; and real small-time vaudeville, in such regional chains as the Gus Sun or Butterfield Theaters centered in Ohio and Michigan, respectively. In the Middle West and around Chicago, there were not so much circuits as groups of theaters, owned by such as the Finn and Heiman interests but booked out of the Western Vaudeville Managers' Association offices in Chicago. There were besides in the larger cities tiny halls or storefront theaters that never received mention in the trade press.

A typical vaudeville program in the downtown theaters of larger cities seating between 1,500 and 2,000 might consist of nine, even ten, acts playing twice in a day (or three with a matinee). The price of admission in the most prestigious of these was a (relatively) astronomical one dollar for the best seats. (But two bits would admit you to the peanut gallery.) This was one end of a spectrum of possibilities. By the 'teens there were quite a few small-town and neighborhood theaters that combined motion pictures with three to five acts of vaudeville—so-called combination houses. The price of admission might typically be ten to thirty cents. Greedy theater owners also developed the practice of so-called continuous vaudeville, with the acts following one after the other without intermission or division into discrete shows. Under this regime, an act might have to perform four times in one day.

In much of the United States prior to air-conditioning, theaters were obliged to go dark between Memorial Day and Labor Day. To some extent this was compensated for by the large number of outdoor entertainment parks that once were found everywhere. But many vaudevillians enjoyed this enforced vacation, particularly if they had enough in the bank to tide them over.

To turn to the nature of the entertainment: the great preponderance of vaudeville acts were duos, although there were some solo acts and a few larger ensembles. An act often could claim no more than ten minutes or so, give or take a minute or two. This obviously put a premium on speed and snappy, highly polished delivery. Certain stars, for example Sophie Tucker, could be given thirty minutes or more, but this was quite exceptional and restricted to big-time vaudeville. Sometimes, however, a chain would book a large ensemble cast in what amounted to a mini musical comedy or drama. This would naturally also take up a good chunk of the time available and would reduce the total number of acts.

In any event, much of the art of presenting a vaudeville show was held to be in the clever positioning of acts for maximum effectiveness. In a nine-act show, the best slots were prior to intermission and next to the last position. The choice and positioning of acts was a matter of great interest to bookers, and reviews in the professional press very frequently comment on it.

Every theater would have a collection of stereotyped drops, thus vaudeville acts did not normally have much specific scenery, with novelty and color lent by costuming instead. If this were not so, the fact that the Creole Band traveled with "special scenery" would hardly have received the frequent comments it did. The music that accompanied virtually every act was rendered in the most pretentious theaters by orchestras of fifteen or more, in the most meager ones by a duo of piano and drums. Most of the music was probably read from publishers' stock orchestrations, although major stars might have special arrangements prepared. In this regard, one of the most intriguing survivals of the band's career is a fragment of what the Palao family understood as a cover for their music.

Certainly vaudeville had its share of acrobats, trained animals, hoop rollers, and such features redolent of the circus, but the mainstay was comedy and song, sometimes the two mixed together, with a fair amount of dancing. Most of the music was the product of the ever-churning Tin Pan Alley publishers, aided by an army of "pluggers" whose raison d'être was to place a song with as many important, or even unimportant, vaudevillians as possible. It's no exaggeration to say that the primary mode of dissemination of the popular song in the United States between 1900 and 1930 was the vaudeville stage.

Musical acts—that is, ones based on the playing of a collection of instruments—were pretty much obliged to have gimmicks, such as elaborate, often exotic, costumes or peculiar instruments, or to present their acts in a kind of choreography. The lesson that had to be learned was that the vaudeville audience was not there to be edified, as at a concert, but to be entertained. And music without words is not that entertaining by itself. This aspect of vaudeville was alive and well when dance bands began to appear on the vaudeville stage and found themselves obliged to impersonate Arabs, Eskimos, soldiers, sailors, and what have you.

FROM THE BUSINESS SIDE, vaudeville took full advantage of modern inventions: the telephone, the telegraph, the railroad, and the press release. Where burlesque still maintained an older practice of moving an entire company from one theater to the next, a vaudeville performance might present acts that had never appeared together, nor ever would again, with all the details arranged by virtuosos of permutation and combination in the central booking office.[12] The one major exception to this was the Pantages chain of theaters, stretching from Manitoba to California and eastward again to Kansas City, where the distances involved and the difficulties of travel during the winter months made it impractical to follow the normal practice. In the states surrounding the hub of Chicago, the dense rail net made it possible not only to combine acts in a variety of configurations but also to have them play split weeks, with the first half beginning on Monday (or sometimes Sunday), the second on Thursday, thus embracing the weekend. The same would hold true in the very largest cities, such as New York and Chicago.

While certain performers earned salaries in the many hundreds of dollars per week, the average vaudevillian was not spectacularly well paid, although better than most office and factory workers. In any event, the perks of living a seemingly glamorous life were enough to recommend it for many. The $75 per week that each of the members of the Creole Band earned (a rough average figure) was quite decent and, with seven members in the act costing all together some $500, enough to be prohibitive for many small-town theaters.

African-American acts in mainstream vaudeville were uncommon, certainly far fewer than their representation in the general population would indicate.

(For "mainstream" substitute "white" if you will.) Much of what they were allowed or expected to do drew on venerable minstrel routines, although there were a few notable exceptions, such as Fiddler and Shelton, whose appearances in full evening dress seem to have been much approved. So the Creole Band's reliance on the Uncle Joe routine and the singing of "My Old Kentucky Home" was almost to be expected, as also their wearing of southern farmhand costumes and their blackface makeup.[13] It was certainly novel and a bit odd dramaturgically for this to be combined with up-to-date ragtime or jazz. (There was beginning, by the way, to form in the first years of the twentieth century a collection of theaters for black patrons exclusively, which eventually were to be grouped in chains; one of the latest, the TOBA [Theater Owner's Booking Association], is often mentioned today in histories of black entertainment. This helped mitigate the fact that in some locales access to "white" theaters was made very difficult or impossible.)

A number of quite discriminatory business practices made the professional life of performers less than completely happy. Certainly, the terms of the standard contract were unfavorable to them, and their careers depended on following the dictates of personal managers and bookers, so as never to hear the dreaded "You'll never work in this town (or for this circuit) again." Alas, the Creole Band was to find itself in just that situation.

Perhaps due to their quarrel with agent Harry Weber—to be discussed below—the Creole Band never cracked true big-time vaudeville. For example, contrary to Jelly Roll Morton's assertion, they seem never to have played New York's Palace Theater. They were, nevertheless, an important act, especially after their appearance in *Town Topics,* a production of J. J. and Lee Shubert. They were well paid, traveled with special scenery, and were handled, at least for part of their career, by a major agent. My guess would be that they were seen and heard by more than a million Americans (including Canadians). We need to remember that contrary to the "personalism" that characterized vaudeville, they were not known as individuals but as a group.

A Word on Jazz Historiography

Not the least of the things for which I beg the reader's forgiveness is the use of the six-syllable word "historiography." I intend it to mean the history of writing jazz history. This section will discuss this topic especially as it applies to the interpretation of the historical role and importance of the Creole Band.

To start with, we should point out three fundamentally different points of view with regard to the beginnings of jazz.

1. Jazz began in New Orleans around the turn of the century, moved to Chicago, then to New York and Europe.
2. Jazz began (a) either someplace else or (b) more or less everywhere, more or less at the same time.
3. Jazz was "merely" a late form of orchestral ragtime played for dancing, and thus could have developed in different flavors in more than one place.
4. (This is really a subcategory of the third point.) "Jazz" was a name that happened to be applied in San Francisco, Chicago, and New York to ragtime dance music. Thus the beginnings of jazz are not so much the beginnings of a music but the beginnings of the use of a word.

Of these possibilities, the first is by far the predominant one, and those who hold to it credit the origin of the music to special conditions prevailing in New Orleans but not elsewhere.[14] My view is that there's something to be said for all of these. On occasion, as one of those jokes that's meant to tell the truth, I've said, "One thing for sure, New Orleans jazz began in New Orleans."

One of the salient oddities about discussions of the general question is that the subject under discussion, in other words "jazz," is undefined, it apparently being assumed that everyone's in agreement as to what "it" is. My guess is that a good many persons are in fact in tacit, if uninformed, agreement, the main points of which are, first, that jazz is a kind of conglomerate of a repertory and a way of playing that was first well represented on certain "classic" recordings of the period 1923–1928. Second, it's also assumed that the most important feature of this music is that it was spontaneously improvised. With the passage of time, this type of jazz and its "swing" progeny were relegated to the position of a forerunner, with the bebop recordings of 1944–1956 being a line of demarcation.

It seems clear that the first point is a result of the way in which the history of jazz was first written starting in the late 1930s, namely, by record collectors particularly enamored of these recordings of the 1920s and sometimes alienated by "swing" and its adolescent fans.[15] The second point is true to the extent that the framework of a jazz performance often permits spontaneous improvisation but fails to recognize how frequently what is played is very much the same from performance to performance.

Add to this the foregrounding of certain soloists deemed most innovative or creative and chiefly responsible for the stylistic development of the music, and we have a menu for the production of a jazz history that's spectacularly successful in avoiding what might be called esthetic or musical issues, not to speak of broader questions of social and economic history. In the last couple of decades, some important books have been written by persons fully qualified to discuss questions of musical technique and construction and sometimes with enough hands-on jazz experience to avoid the more idealistic blunders of the earliest writers. Even so, this deepening of discourse has rarely led to breaking down the parochial boundaries between the music and the broader context in which it lives. In this regard, the absence of African-Americans from the roster of writers on jazz has resulted in important distortions or evasions—not that being African-American automatically solves all problems of historical research, narrative, or interpretation.

The foundations of jazz history as they have been constructed by three generations of writers, scholars, and critics, and, more recently, technically descriptive analysts, center unequivocally on sound recordings. Accordingly, it's only to be expected that, in serious writing about jazz, discography has been primary, bibliography distinctly secondary, to the point that one suspects that an enduring tradition of writing on jazz is to downplay the importance of both primary published documents and the work of other writers. I exaggerate: in his epochal history of the Fletcher Henderson band, Walter C. Allen made use of every scrap of primary documentation he was able to find, albeit in the service of discography. One might say, however, that for the jazz historian the recording is analogous to the musical manuscript (or letter or archival document) for the academic musicologist examining the European musical past. If we didn't have them, there wouldn't be much to talk about, and even the anecdotes wouldn't make much sense.[16]

This fundamental bias must be one of the roots of the neglect of the Creole Band in the history of jazz, even now that more and more works of scholarship using as wide a possible range of sources have been written. Even so, considering the amount of speculative prose devoted to Charles "Buddy" Bolden—the alleged father of jazz who also left no recordings, even from his later career—the neglect is strange. Perhaps, after all, it's because their history unfolded outside New Orleans and in the context of show business.

THIS IS HARDLY the place to discuss all the musical features that one might identify as comprising "jazz." With one exception: a lot of reading and listening has led me to substitute the word and concept of "personalism" for "improvisation." It's of course not news that jazz is fundamentally learned and played by ear—although this doesn't mean that it can't be performed using musical notation in varying degree. Or rather, a musical performance does not happen as the accurate reproduction by one or more musicians of a written composition using a codified instrumental technique. Only the most naive would think that this rules out some degree of uncertainty or "personal interpretation" in the end result. But it's always clear that the music is Beethoven's, or Steven Sondheim's. There are of course jazz arrangements, but these demand players acquainted with the subtleties of jazz played by ear.

The jazz player in a deeply rooted sense "owns" what he plays, or the band owns it as a collective. "It's my music" or "It's our music," and while it can be written down with greater or lesser accuracy, some of the most essential properties can't really be transcribed, such as the fine nuances of rhythmic or melodic performance or instrumental timbre. Since you "own" it, there's no one to say that you can't change it or substitute an entirely different version if one occurs to you. Thus, improvisation is an effect rather than a cause.

IN NEW ORLEANS around the turn of the century and for some years thereafter, there was a sharp distinction between union musicians with relatively predictable and consistent "professional" instrumental technique and note-reading skills and ragtime musicians playing by ear. The two factions regarded each other with some disdain. A specific example that emerges in interviews of members of the Papa Jack Laine circle is the case of clarinetist Achille Baquet, who was seen by some as having lost his talent for ragtime or jazz performance because of his formal musical instruction from Santo Giuffre.

"Playing by ear" is a term that can mean quite different things. Many musicians the world over learn pieces from their teachers by rote, so that what they play is a pious replica of the original. And depending on the repertory or the culture, it may well be expected that the pieces always be played the same way. On the other hand, in other musical cultures, musicians pick up pieces by ear, sometimes written ones, and change them or simplify them in the process. In the case of many jazz performances, the players have in common a knowledge of a melody or a chord progression. What they play refers back to this common mental model that may never actually be heard.

Although for Caucasian dance musicians in New Orleans ca. 1900 there seems to have been something of a face-off between musical literacy and illiteracy—between the union professionals and the Laine crowd. African-American musicians, even though reasonably well paid for their efforts, needed any musical skills they could acquire in order to successfully compete. For them, the meaning of "ownership" of music went beyond individuality and should be considered as also imbued with all the intensity and emotional depth of a disenfranchised and often dispossesed social group. Nonetheless, those orchestras that read written arrangements often seem to have been admired.[17]

Whether the practice of playing dance music by ear was common ca. 1880 or before is as yet (and possibly for always) an unanswerable question: we didn't ask the right questions early enough. Likewise unanswerable is whether at that early date there existed alongside a written repertory a body of traditional or local tunes that might be trotted out as the night wore on and the dancers loosened up.

There's some testimony to this being the case around 1910, which is not surprising. Thus, a ragtime band wouldn't play hot ragtime all the time, as eventually became the norm, but only for certain numbers or certain occasions.

Another question we'd like to know more about than we do is whether the beginnings of jazz go along with a certain kind of instrumentation. A perusal of that amazing collection the *New Orleans Jazz Family Album* shows a profusion of seven-piece bands dating from about 1905 to 1920: violin, clarinet, cornet, trombone, string bass, guitar, and drums. But there's evidence that only after 1905 did the drum set gradually become a normal if not indispensable member of a dance band; and also that throughout the period much dance and entertainment music was provided by pianoless three- to five-piece bands without wind instruments, or with only one. We also know of early ragtime musicians who played the accordion, most notably Henry Payton.

These considerations, along with the five-piece instrumentation of the Original Dixieland Jazz Band, make one reluctant to identify any particular combination of instruments as a jazz or ragtime band, distinct from a dance band in general. So while we may be delighted with looking at the old photographs in R&S, we can't help asking "compared to what?" and want to see a collection of photographs of "ordinary" dance bands, and ones prior to 1905.

That we need to be aware of such questions is shown by the history of the African-American brass band in New Orleans. It seems that prior to 1920 they played mostly from written arrangements and only gradually both pared down their repertory and began playing largely by rote memory to produce that wonderfully richly textured ensemble sound known from recordings from the 1940s on.

The ordinary jazz aficionado might well lose patience with such abstruse matters, beloved though they may be by the historian or musicologist. And he or she might well settle for a legendary musical hero, larger than life, as the person who started it all. What's wrong with this, apart from the fact that one can argue that the ensemble is the primary force in the development of jazz, is that we have no way of choosing between those who credit Buddy Bolden with the invention of jazz and those who either choose someone else or think the whole idea of an individual starting it all is crazy. For my money, the time ca. 1905 was about right for the beginning of something new and important, which might be in large part the playing of "blues" or of blues-like "ratty" songs.

There is, I must admit, something comic about this search for objective criteria. Certainly for as long as I've been aware of the music—approximately 55 years—a person is a jazz musician if accepted by other jazz musicians. Admittedly, this is fundamentally circular but does embody something of great importance: namely, that one of the characteristics of jazz has been that it is under the control of those who play it more than it is of agents, record companies, club owners, audiences. My guess—I underline "guess"—is that this has been true since the 'teens at least, perhaps even before. This may mean, by the way, that jazz is such a small segment of the market for music that it can be ignored as a major source of income by the music business.

There are those to whom all speculation as to how a given person or band of the first two decades of the century may have sounded or how good they "really" were is a waste of time. Well, certainly, such speculations are arid alongside listening to a phonograph record. But it's not really a matter of either-or. We do have phonograph records of Keppard, Baquet, Louis Delille, Jimmie Noone, Bill Johnson, maybe even Eddie Vincent. If we accept the proposition that an individual's musical voice changes little or not at all once he attains mastery, then we can perhaps imagine something of what the overall sound was like.[18]

So, one answer to those who skeptically ask, "Was the Creole Band a jazz band at all?" or who comment, "Maybe if you heard them, you wouldn't like it," is that we can say something about how most of the musicians in the band sounded. Also, it was accepted as a jazz band by such as Jelly Roll Morton and Paul Howard, who even remembered some specifics about the way they played. (Once again, see Appendix 5.)

It seems all too obvious that the failure of writers on jazz to delve into the history of these musical pioneers was occasioned not by any lack of interest in their story but by the band's failure to make phonograph records. One might say that jazz writers have had no need to consider issues such as the ones mentioned above. They can rely on "ostensive definition," as though the answer to the question "what is jazz?" is to point at a record (or better yet, play it).

But were they a prototype in some concrete sense? Mabel Elaine, the pert blackface dancer who toured with the Creole Band to great applause for nearly five months, a year later hired a band of the same instrumentation led by violinist Herb Lindsay[19] to accompany her in front of a steamboat drop. But where the Creole Band had been a great success, Elaine and company were, to judge from the reviews, a flop. So coming from New Orleans and having the same instrumentation was no guarantee of acclaim.

Brief Note on Sound Recordings

We live today in a time when every band, every would-be star can make a CD—although distribution is another matter. Why don't we have blues records from the 1890s? Why didn't Buddy Bolden make commercially issued recordings? And so forth.

Actually, we do have field recordings (on cylinder) of Native American music from the 1890s. These were made for purposes of study or archival documentation. Probably the main reason we don't have blues recordings is that American folklorists got interested in Indian music first. But a recording that would sit in a museum collection to be listened to by a select group of musical anthropologists isn't what we're talking about. What we wish had existed are "commercial" recordings pressed in hundreds, even thousands, of copies and distributed all over the United States and potentially purchasable by anyone with 75 cents or a dollar to spare—and a phonograph to play them on. But 75 cents was a major expenditure in an era when a penny or two would buy a newspaper, 15 cents a meal—spartan, but still a meal—and a dime would pay one's way into the gallery of a vaudeville theater.

As to the choice of music to be recorded, the companies were guided then, as now, by popular appeal, but with a heavy emphasis on vocal music and instrumental novelties by instruments that recorded well. There was a small but prestigious segment of the market devoted to recordings by the great operatic stars of the day, with Enrico Caruso being the best remembered.

Recordings used published music for the most part, as turned into sound by reliable professionals—studio musicians in today's parlance. Publishers would permit compositions they owned to be recorded because—after 1909 at least—they'd get a so-called "mechanical royalty" on each selection. Performers, if they were soloists, might come into the recording laboratory (to use another expression of the time) without written music, but when it came to dance music, the studio ensembles read from orchestrations. Oh, there might be a medley or two of "old-time tunes" or an attempt to get onto record an impression of a minstrel show, part of which might be played by ear. And a few recordings of African-American vocal quartets exist—from as early as 1895—but, after all, African-Americans were expected to perform by ear.[20]

Notwithstanding the preponderance of vocal selections, whether traditional songs, hits of the day, or operatic favorites, and instrumental novelties, there was plenty of dance music made available. The earliest catalogue available to me is that of the New Jersey Phonograph Company, from before November 1891. Among the 270 pieces were some 50 dance selections.[21] This is just one company, but one can generalize: for the next twenty-odd years, we find in record company catalogues among the many selections recorded by dance orchestras, none from Chicago, San Francisco, New Orleans, or even Boston. The simplest answer as to why dance orchestras from these or other places didn't appear on record is that all recording was done in New York City. From our vantage point, it's amazing that the record companies didn't realize what a wealth of (to us) original, inventive, and exciting music was out there for the taking. Nor did it apparently occur to them that musicians from far-off places could be brought to New York, as finally happened with Art Hickman's San Francisco ensemble in 1919, or that portable recording equipment could be carried to the boondocks, which eventually happened around 1924.

The couple of instances in 1913–1914 when African-American dance musicians were recorded was most likely because they were the chosen accompanists for fashionable ballroom dancers: Europe's Society Orchestra made it into the Victor studio on the coattails, so to speak, of Vernon and Irene Castle, and Joan Sawyer's Persian Garden orchestra was recorded by Columbia because of her notoriety. Despite the fact that the musicians involved were musically literate, there are passages, especially from Europe's Orchestra, in which the band departs excitingly and uniquely from the written score. So far as I know, these players were either from New York or some other place north of the Mason-Dixon line, and they are playing published hits of the day. The bands also followed fashions of the time in the foregrounding of banjorines (or banjo-mandolins) and the drum set.

When you hear these bands, you can nevertheless understand why the Castles or Joan Sawyer would have loved dancing to their music. The same goes in lesser degree for the thirteen recordings made in wartime London in 1916 by the American band at the high-fashion Ciro's Club (alas, called a "Coon Orchestra," although that might have been a selling point). There were also ten tunes recorded in 1917 by them. So far as I know these were not imported to the United States or issued on U.S. Columbia or a subsidiary.[22]

It is not so surprising, perhaps, that, as soon as the managers of the Victor Talking Machine Company became aware that there was a really unusual band of African-Americans—southerners, as well—playing at the Winter Garden doing a terrific job of accompanying Mabel Elaine's clog dancing as well as playing by themselves, they became interested in the commercial possibilities. And, to believe George Baquet (via Danny Barker), this most important of all U.S. phonograph companies really tried to sign them up.[23]

Then when Victor heard another new band from New Orleans (via Chicago) at Reisenweber's at the end of January 1917 and saw how excited the dancers were, I imagine they thought it worth a try to record them. The try (the first record of the ODJB) did very well indeed. But we can imagine that if the men in the band had gotten disgusted and gone back home, their one record would have been a curiosity, and another group would have had the honor of being the first jazz band.

Eventually, of course, the companies came to understand that (1) there was a wide potential market for up-to-date dance music, especially from bands with a novel performing style and solo players of merit; (2) there was an African-American audience for blues, sermons, and hot dance music performed by African-Americans; (3) there were singers, preachers, and bands that had never left the South that could make records that would sell; and (belatedly) (4) there was a white, rural population that would buy string band music and "country" singing, sacred as well as secular. All of these things made phonograph recordings of the 1920s a more nearly complete documentation of local musics, including those of oral tradition and ethnic minorities.[24]

Perhaps the moral is the truism that things don't happen before their time. And the more unusual the novelty, the more preparation is required. The history of the Creole Band is partly one of changes in U.S. entertainment and dancing that made their acceptance possible, partly the role they played in the eventual taking over of our national musical ears by a once purely local way of making music.

I Dramatis Personae

READERS OF BIOGRAPHIES of the great "classical" composers—Mozart, Beethoven—suspend disbelief willingly enough and grant the relevance of the small details of an artist's life to his or her work. But even in the case of a musician considered to be "ordinary" when compared to the extraordinary Beethoven or Mozart it's nonetheless interesting to be able to cite some event, some fact of the day-to-day existence of the musician that explains something about the work.

With the members of the Creole Band, what we know about their lives is decidedly patchy: There are virtually no letters, no diaries, and few interviews or photographs. Thus it's hard to say how interesting their lives might have been apart from their music—and for most of them, alas, there's little or no surviving written or recorded music. Why bother? For me, the answer is that even if we can say little about them as individuals, we can nonetheless place them in some kind of New Orleans context and make some guesses as to the musical habits or training stemming from their social milieu. And knowing what bands they worked with permits some suggestions as to musical style. But in any event, I've chosen to see the band, its triumphal career and eventual disintegration, as the most significant thing—historically and artistically—in their lives.

Perhaps the most vexing problem for the writer is the unevenness of documentation. A great deal is known about Bill Johnson, a fair amount about Morgan Prince, Palao, and Keppard. Norwood Williams is virtually a cipher, despite Bill Russell's interview with him, as is Eddie Vincent. Falling in between are the three clarinetists, Baquet, Delille, and Noone. To devote a full chapter to each of the musicians strikes me as overkill, although Bill Johnson might well merit one, not only because of the relatively rich source material but also because he was in fact the organizer and manager of the group.

A further decision was made to separate the biographies prior to 1914 from those coming after 1918, not only because it gives a kind of shape to the narrative but because the earlier biographies have to do mostly with New Orleans while the later ones virtually do not at all. The writer realizes that the amount of detail found below will try the patience of readers not enthralled with New Orleans genealogy; I assure them that it could be worse and suggest that skimming will do little harm.

James Palao

James Florestan, or more familiarly Jimmy Palao,[1] was born in Algiers, a short ferry ride across the Mississippi from New Orleans, on February 19, 1879, the son of the newly wed Felix Palao and Clotile (sometimes spelled Clotilde, the standard French form) Rebecca Spriggs.[2] Presumably, Jimmy was born at the Spriggs family home at Homer and Verret Streets.[3]

As one might suspect from their names, his parents represent two quite distinctive themes in the ethnic symphony of New Orleans. It's not clear whether the name Palao is Spanish, Catalan, or Portuguese in origin, and the variety of spellings as found in city directories and legal documents is disconcerting. In any event, while Jimmy was standoffish about learning French, he nonetheless had printed in about 1924 a business card on which he called himself "Creole Jimmy Palao"[4] and his residence in Algiers, a relatively new community escaping the easy French-American dichotomy of New Orleans proper, might disappoint a structuralist.

The Spriggs family can be traced in Algiers as early as 1870, when the household consisted of James, a 36-year-old cook, his wife Clara keeping house, and their four children: Rebecca (11), Henrietta (7), Hannah (3), and Marie Louise (1).[5] It seems likely that James Spriggs was related to another Algiers resident, Berry Spriggs, an illiterate laborer born in Kentucky, recorded by the census in 1880 on Madison Street. James Spriggs passed away on April 4, 1883, but the family continued to live on Verret Street. (Clara lived until 1922.)

After his mother's early death in 1884 (September 28 in Algiers, of epilepsy, according to the death certificate[6]) Jimmy continued to live with his grandmother, and the connection with her family was so strong that he was sometimes called "Jimmy Spriggs" by his contemporaries. Several sources stress that Mrs. Spriggs was an important member of the sodality of the church of the Holy Name of Mary, located at Verret and Alix streets, just a stone's throw away from the family home. One is led to suspect that Clara Spriggs was "creole" by birth, since tradition has it that she insisted — to no avail — that young

1.1 This studio photograph of Felix Palao possibly dates from ca. 1920. [Palao family scrapbook]

Jimmy should learn to speak French. (The 1900 Federal Census has her born in Louisiana of parents born in Virginia.) However, Jimmy's widow, who had grown up speaking both French and Spanish, thought that Mrs. Spriggs's grasp of the language was weak.

Jimmy's father was a handsome man whose features were not particularly African. One might even judge him to have been Cuban, an impression conveyed perhaps by the straw hat and light summer suit of the only photograph known to me. His family background is not entirely clear—what else is new in New Orleans genealogy?—but it seems most likely that he was the son of Edouard Onésiphore Palao (ca. 1830–1897), who for some years kept a cigar store at the corner of Chartres and Hospital (now Governor Nichols) Streets. Be that as it may, he departed from what seems to be the norm for many downtown "Creoles of color" by not having a specialized trade (e.g., plasterer, bricklayer). As nearly as one can tell, he earned his living as a longshoreman.

Edouard and Marie Madeleine Perrault (d. 1911) were married around 1857 and had four or five children: Maximilian (born 1857), Malvina (1859), Felix (1860), Vincent (1862), and Edgar J(oseph) (1864).[7] Edgar interests us because he was a violinist, and he occasionally pops up in New Orleans oral histories, perhaps because despite his early demise in 1914 he had gone to Cuba during the Spanish-American war as a member of the 9th U.S. Volunteer Infantry regimental band, famous for including a number of members of the Onward Brass Band.[8]

After the death of his young wife, Felix continued to live in Algiers, but by 1889 had moved across the river to the Eighth Ward, sharing quarters with his brother Vincent at 209 Spain Street. At some point he fathered two children with Josephine (I don't know her maiden name): Felicia in 1892 and Norman in 1897, both recorded in the Palao family bible. The 1900 Census however, showed Josephine and Felix at separate addresses. A few years later he married Madeleine Ferrand. It would be pointless in this context to attempt to get to the bottom of these decidedly tangled relationships, but one might suggest that the existence in New Orleans of at least two children fathered by Jimmy Palao, but not with Armontine, shows him to be no more punctilious in the observance of the bonds of matrimony than many other New Orleanians of the nineteenth and early twentieth centuries. Certainly Armontine Palao still had bitter memories of Jimmy's extracurricular adventures when I spoke with her in 1978 or 1979.

It seems that Jimmy remained living in Algiers in his maternal grandmother's house at Homer and Verret Streets until 1900 at least, an only child yet surrounded by relatives. According to family tradition Felix took an interest in Jimmy's musical studies and paid his bills for violin instruction so he wouldn't have to do anything but play music.[9] This largesse would no doubt have covered the lessons with the "old professor from the French Opera," as Tom Albert (1877–1968) remembered him. Jimmy would take a lesson, then pass it on to Albert with the assistance of an ABC violin method (see the Milton Martin interview; he suggests Palao also taught Albert solfege).[10] Albert lived in his birthplace, Bellechasse (on the river below Algiers), until 1888, beginning to play guitar rather late when he was about 17 (i.e., 1894), then violin soon after. This provides at least one date that might help to verify the identity of the "old professor," should one wish to do so.

That Palao continued to live in Algiers explains a network of youthful connections, some of which endured for his entire life. First, there was Albert, whose family lived on John Saux Lane, a barely populated and rather desolate street even in 1985. Eddie Vincent, later to be the trombonist of the Creole Band, lived with his father, mother, and sister in the family house also on John Saux Lane. He is further said to have roomed at Albert's house, was taught music by him, and was in one of the first musical groups Albert recalled playing with, a quartet of guitar, violin, trombone, and (probably) string bass. Fred Keppard also would sleep at the Albert house after his nightly stint in the "Dis-

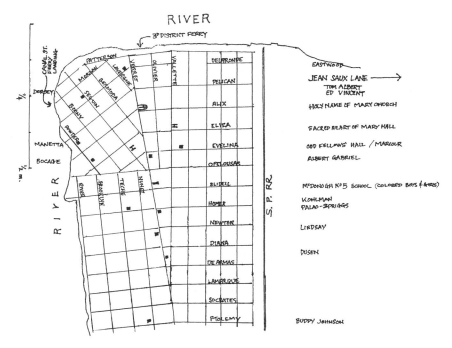

RIVER
3D DISTRICT FERRY

CANAL ST. FERRY LANDING
PATTERSON
MORGAN
BERMUDA
LAVERGNE
VERRET
OLIVIER
VALLETTE
DELARONDE
EASTWOOD
JEAN SAUX LANE ⟶
TOM ALBERT
ED VINCENT
DERBY
SESSON
BERALY
PELICAN
HOLY NAME OF MARY CHURCH
PONTESA
ALIX
SACRED HEART OF MARY HALL
MANETTA
ELIZA
ODD FELLOWS' HALL / MARCOUR
BOCAGE
EVELINA
ALBERT GABRIEL
OPELOUSAS
R I V E R
RIVER
BROOKLYN
TECHE
NUNEZ
SLIDELL
S. P. RR.
McDONOGH Nᵒ 5 SCHOOL (COLORED BOYS & GIRLS)
KOHLMAN
PALAO-SPRIGGS
HOMER
NEWTON
LINDSAY
DIANA
DUSEN
DE ARMAS
LAMARQUE
SOCRATES
PTOLEMY
BUDDY JOHNSON

1.2 Sketch map of central Algiers ca. 1900 with residences of some known jazz or ragtime musicians. The residences indicated are those of the 1900 Federal Census. (There were several Bocage and Manetta family homes; the ones shown are those for the well-known musicians Peter and Emanuel, respectively.)

trict." This would have been at the beginning of Keppard's career, since Albert moved across the river to New Orleans proper after 1907.

Other musical residents of Algiers were trombonist Frank Duson, Buddy Johnson, another trombonist, the Manetta family, particularly Manuel with whom Palao played in the District, and the Bocages. Thus there was no shortage of musical associates in what might seem something of a backwater. Also, Albert recalled at least three halls where dances might have been held and could have served as incubators for unseasoned musicians. It comes as no surprise that the first band that an Algiers native worked with were fellow "Algerians." Thus Peter Bocage began with Eddie Vincent (trombone), Tom Albert (cornet), "Nootzie" Reuben (bass), "Skeeter" (guitar, cf. Tom Albert), the Lindsay family, and Albert Gabriel (clarinet).

Jimmy Palao married (Cecilia) Armontine Carter (b. 1889) in October, 1905, at St. Catherine's church. She remembered meeting Jimmy at the first dance she ever attended, at Violet Hall—presumably in the small community of Violet in St. Bernard Parish, three miles downriver from Chalmette—with music perhaps provided by the Imperial Orchestra, of which Jimmy was a member. He sent someone to teach her to waltz and took her home. They lived only briefly in the Spriggs house in Algiers.

Armontine was a native of Barbados and had emigrated to New Orleans when she was 5 or 6 years old. She remembered her grandmother as being from Haiti, her father from Cuba and Puerto Rico. She bitterly recalled being subjected to the apparently usual hazing of "monkey chasers" from the West Indies. In any event, she worked between 1905 and 1909 for a succession of Mexican consuls in New Orleans. After a first baby who died, their children were Clotilde (or Clotile) (1909), Mary Mabel (1912), both born in New Orleans, Agatha, born in Los Angeles in 1915, and Rita Anita born in Chicago in 1918. Mrs. Carter thought that Jimmy already had one child when they were married. This could have been the Joe Palao recalled by Tom Albert as a long-time employee of Blandin's funeral home. And in 1998, I was introduced to a person born in early 1913 who said she was his daughter.[11]

Eddie Dawson remembered many details of a band that played at Harry Parker's 101 Ranch, ca. 1907 or perhaps a bit later, with Dawson (guitar), Manuel Manetta (piano), Jean Vigne (drums), Willie Humphrey, Sr. (clarinet and saxophone [*sic*]), later replaced by George Baquet, and Palao (violin). One night Fred Keppard was asked by owner Parker to join the band, even though it was forbidden for brass instruments to play in the District.[12] The story goes that Parker requested and received special permission from the mayor for Keppard to join the band. This band or a version of it also played at the nearby Huntz and Nagel's Casino, operated by Eddie Groshell and Hans Nagel, where the girls flocked to hear Keppard because brass instruments were so new in the District.

As might be anticipated, the story is a bit more complicated, if we are to believe Louis Keppard, Fred's older brother. According to him, Fred was the first trumpeter working in the District, with the Lindsay family band, Johnny (bass), Herb (violin), and their father, John Sr., as guitarist. They persuaded Fred to join them in working at Hannan's saloon at Custom House and Liberty Streets, perhaps only hustling on the sidewalk in front.

During his interviews ca. 1960 Dawson ranked the fiddlers of the day: in descending order, Jimmy Palao, Manuel Manetta, Peter Bocage, Valteau, and "Tinette."[13] He further described him as a good reader who could also fake and play the blues. Others didn't agree: to Johnny St. Cyr, Palao, although a good jazz orchestra violinist with a "business style," was not in a class with A. J. Piron and Peter Bocage. St. Cyr's memories may mostly go back to

Chicago between 1918 and 1925, when it seems that Palao was playing banjo and saxophone more than violin. Peter Bocage, eight years younger than Palao, recalled the good violinists of his youth as "old timers" Henry Nickerson, Palao, and Valteau.

Palao's earlier career prior to the important job at the 101 Ranch[14] is difficult if not impossible to reconstruct in any detail. Surely he would have been playing professionally by 1900 if not before; at least he was recorded as "musician" by the 1900 Census. It would seem that the earliest reasonably well-documented group with which Palao played was the Pacific Brass Band, an Algiers-based group led by E-flat cornetist Joe Lezard (or Lizard). Palao would have played alto horn, and indeed there was a small photograph in the Palao family album showing him in a band uniform, holding one.[15] As was apparently rather common, some subset of the Pacific Brass Band also played for dancing. Manuel Manetta (1889–1969) knew of two bands in Algiers, one led by Frank Dusen, the other by trombonist Buddy Johnson, who was connected with Lezard's Pacific Band. As Manetta recalled it, the Johnson band always played at the Sacred Heart of Mary Hall at Vallette and Evelina,[16] a job Mrs. Spriggs, "a Creole lady high in the Sacred Heart Society," got for Jimmy Palao, who, as a violinist, would have been called the leader of Johnson's band. These dances were for polite society, as could be supposed from what we know of Johnson's career. The "ratty" element patronized the Odd Fellows Hall at Seguin and Eliza Streets, where a band led by Frank Dusen usually held forth. In exchange for sweeping the floor, Manetta was allowed into the hall when dances were held, frequently hearing Buddy Bolden there, and on one occasion Alphonse Picou. A reasonable time frame for this period in Manetta's life would be 1900–1905, and sometime during these years Jimmy must have branched out on his own, no longer in need of the assistance of his grandmother.

According to Armontine Palao, Jimmy would go out to the country to give instruction to bands and get them started. This was evidently a common practice for those musicians with some instruction themselves—for example, Frank Clermont in the 1890s and Willie Humphrey, Sr. Again according to Mrs. Palao, one of her husband's individual students was the legendary—to use one of the favorite adjectives of jazz history—Charles "Buddy" Bolden.[17] There were no doubt others.

The social organization of the larger dance orchestras of early twentieth-century New Orleans needs brief explanation since it bears directly on Palao's musical career. Two photographs from R&S can serve as evidence. First, the studio photo of the Superior Orchestra (p. 135) dated 1910 has all seven mem-

1.3 Young Jimmy (ca. 1900 is my estimate) holding what looks like an E-flat alto horn. Unfortunately the badge on his band cap can't be deciphered. [Palao family scrapbook]

bers in uniform *comme il faut*, with "Superior Orchestra" clearly written on their caps. Seated front row center is the youthful violinist Peter Bocage. His cap reads "leader," while that of string bassist Billy Marrero says "mgr.," that is, manager.

A photo of the Imperial Orchestra (p. 164), from the same studio and dated 1905—the date may be several years too early—shows violinist Jimmy Palao with "leader" on his cap, while guitarist Rene Baptiste's cap has embroidered on it "mgr." However, the Imperial Orchestra is frequently designated as cornetist Manuel Perez's band.

The interpretation is simple: the violinist is the leader because he calls the tunes and sets the tempo, easier for him to do than for the wind instrument players. Someone else, rather often the bass or guitar player, is the manager—(i.e., does all the negotiating for engagements). Finally, another player may be the most respected or noteworthy player. The Creole Band was very much in conformity to this practice. Jimmy Palao was violinist, therefore the leader; Bill Johnson was the manager; and as the judgment of history would have it, the band is often called Fred Keppard's, since he was, although the youngest member of the band (save for Jimmie Noone during the last season), the "star."[18] In any event, during the Creole Band's four-year career, the only individuals advertised with the band were Bill Johnson and, for a brief period only, H. Morgan Prince.

Around the turn of the century these seven-piece orchestras were, I believe, exceptional; three and four-piece bands were more common in the saloons and dance halls of the District and perhaps elsewhere in New Orleans.[19] A common instrumentation was mandolin or violin, guitar, and string bass, with one wind instrument; but it seems that an accordion in the place of the solo mandolin or violin was still fashionable, with Henry Payton (or Peyton) being most widely remembered. Noteworthy is the absence of a drum set, as well as piano, the first of these probably becoming gradually essential during the course of the first decade, the second coming to prominence as the cabaret formula took root in New Orleans, and it was necessary for singers to perform the latest hits from sheet music.

A photograph in *New Orleans Jazz: A Family Album* is described as being "Jimmy Palao's Orchestra (about 1900)"; this is almost certainly incorrect, although the date may be reasonably accurate. The original is now part of the New Orleans Jazz Club collection at the Old Mint, part of the far-flung Louisiana State Museum, and is accompanied by two documents. The first of these states that the photo was given to trumpeter Herb Morand by Willie Parker on November 7, 1948, and identifies the musicians more or less as in the *Family Album*—except that the seated guitarist is "Mann Creole," with the person standing next to the bassist being another guitarist, Rene Baptiste, who is also in the Imperial Orchestra photograph mentioned above. Stated to be absent was drummer Joe Martin. The location is given as Douglass and Alabo Streets (today a thinly populated section in the Ninth Ward very close to the parish line), the date as the year of the Spanish-American War. The presence of two violinists and two guitarists makes one wonder if two separate musical organizations came together for the occasion.[20] Willie Parker's (1875–1965) interview—he's the clarinetist standing on the extreme left—on file at HJA would suggest that most of the persons in the photograph belonged to Toby Nuenutt's (Toby NuNu) Magnolia Orchestra.

Another early photograph—it could come from any time during the first decade of the century—is of a large picnic at an unidentified location with a rather formally dressed five–piece band, with the following reasonably identifiable players: Buddy Johnson, trombone; Louis Delille, clarinet; Jimmy Palao, violin; and an unidentified guitarist and string bassist.[21]

The 1910 Federal Census listed Palao as living at 1311 Liberty Street (now Tremé, at about Bayou Road at the very edge of the Faubourg Tremé), describing him as a musician working odd jobs. From this location Palao would have had a comfortable fifteen-minute walk to the chief District dance halls. These included the 101 Ranch mentioned above, and dance halls known by the names of their proprietors or managers: Hans Nagel's and Eddie Groshell's, Rice's, and Abadie's. I theorized above that around the turn of the century most of the music had been provided by four-piece or, at most, five-piece bands. At some point, either by new construction or renovation, some rather large spaces were specifically designed as dance halls. The most famous of these was the Tuxedo, at Franklin Street, the site of a sensational mutually homi-cidal gun battle between rival saloon owners in 1913. A fringe benefit of the fracas was quite detailed descriptions in the *Times-Picayune* of the interior, as well as the general entertainment milieu of the District.

The Tuxedo had space dedicated to dancing of some 3,000 square feet (i.e., 30 x 100), with an orchestra gallery elevated twelve feet above floor level. The system in force involved the purchase of absurdly expensive drinks for the fe-male work force, for each of which the women would receive a check or chit, which they would redeem at the end of the night's work. This resembles the conditions of the Barbary Coast dance halls in San Francisco. The importance is that under this system musicians could at least play entire numbers, although not so long as to interfere with the purchase of drinks during strategically timed intermissions.

Other testimony exists—particularly in Pops Foster's autobiography—in-dicating that the taxi dance hall formula in which only short choruses would be played was also beginning to be known in New Orleans. In either case, a premium would be placed on stamina and professionalism. Further, since the male dancers were tourists, visiting sailors, and the like, one would suspect that up-to-date hits from the Tin Pan Alley publishers and musical comedy would be in order leading to a degree of versatility perhaps unnecessary for the local dancing public. Also to be borne in mind is the vogue for cabaret entertain-ment, beginning in 1911–1912, which would only have reinforced cosmopol-itan musical tastes. The account of the double murder published in the *Times-Picayune* includes a succinct phrase regarding repertory: "Here a negro band holds forth and from about 8 o'clock at night to 4 o'clock in the morning plays varied rags, conspicuous for being the latest in popular music, interspersed with compositions by the musicians themselves" (Tuesday, March 25, 1913).

There were perhaps no more than four to six venues in the District at any given time that called for larger orchestras of six or seven pieces. So far as I can tell, these were always (or almost always) African-American. One wonders why. Certainly the saloon keepers were not indulging in affirmative action, but it's possible that the patrons looked for the "hotter" ragtime that was widely believed to be the purview of black musicians. Additionally, their services may have been substantially less expensive than those of white musicians.[22] At any rate it provided a greater degree of security than freelancing.

Having taken some trouble to suggest that the musicians working in the District had been infected with cosmopolitan habits, it may strike the reader as perverse if I make a case for local style and repertory. My evidence is provided by Oscar Samuels, the New Orleans correspondent of *Variety*, who in 1911 claimed that the new "erotic" (the word is his) dances, allegedly from San Francisco, had actually originated in New Orleans some fifteen years before. These dances included the Turkey Trot, the Grizzly Bear, the Todolo, and the Texas Tommy.

According to Samuels, the locale was "an old Negro dance hall" at the corner of Custom House (now Iberville) and North Franklin Streets. There the music was provided by a "colored band, which has never been duplicated. The band often repeated the same selection but never played it the same way twice."[23] My speculation is that Samuels was referring to the "28," later the 101 Ranch.

Be that as it may, Jimmy Palao, along with Fred Keppard and perhaps George Baquet, was a new breed of musician for New Orleans, where one customarily played music on an amateur or semiprofessional basis while following one of the traditional trades (building, cigar making, shoe making, etc.) of the "colored creole" population. What was novel about the new situation was the steadiness of the work. Armontine Palao recalled his earning $8 a night, considerably more than is mentioned elsewhere as standard pay for playing in the District, but this possibly included tips.

Besides that, working in the District surely offered a musician many opportunities for amorous relaxation. That Jimmy stretched or broke his marriage vows seems hardly surprising. In any event, sometime in the latter half of 1912, Armontine Palao decided to sell the furniture that she'd accumulated, using $17 of the $19 proceeds for a one-way ticket to Los Angeles.[24] The continuation of the story of the Palaos belongs to the beginnings of the "real" Creole Band and will be found in the next chapter.

Despite varying opinions as to his violinistic skill, it's undeniable that Palao was musically literate and associated with some of the best-trained African-American musicians of New Orleans, such as Manuel Perez, George Filhe, and George Baquet. Testimony to the last-named relationship is a lilting composition of 1911, "O You Sweet Rag," which Palao had published and dedicated "To My Friend George F. Baquet."[25] This is one of a very few copyrighted compositions from New Orleans African-American dance musicians

1.35 Considerably later in the decade, perhaps around the date of composition of "O You Sweet Rag." [Palao family scrapbook]

of this era. Some others are A. J. Piron, Gilbert "Babb" Frank, Alphonse Picou, and pianists Clarence Williams and G. W. Thomas.

As to externals, the cover—which given the publisher's reputation might have been a stock item—shows a swell in a loud checked suit, accessorized with a gleaming stickpin, derby hat, cane, and cigar sticking jauntily out of one side of his mouth. He appears mighty pleased with himself, but is being pointed to by three smiling women, in mockery is my guess.

The piece is in three strains scored for violin and piano, with no tempo and dynamic markings, except a solitary crescendo-decrescendo in the first measure of the piano part. The melody catches our attention with the emphasis on the major 7th (marked "a") as well as the recurring submediant harmony (G 7th) ("c"). But the most striking features are the cadential phrase D C B♭ G B♭ C B♭ ("d"), best known perhaps with the text "Baby, let your hair hang down (or down)," as well as the bluesy phrase ("e"), which I know from a 1919 piece by clarinetist Achille Baquet (the younger brother of George).

1.4 (a, b, and c) "O You Sweet Rag" by James Palao, published by song shark H. Kirkus Dugdale of Washington, D.C., in 1911. These copies were made from a faded second-generation electrostatic copy made from the original in the Library of Congress, which, alas, has been mislaid. [Thornton Hagert collection]

(d)

1.4 (a, b, and c) (*continued*)

1.4 (a, b, and c) (*continued*)

The piano accompaniment is awkward and doesn't take advantage of the harmonies implied in the melody. Palao would have done well to enlist the help of a skilled arranger, in my opinion. Nevertheless, the melody is strong and memorable and is successful in small band performance. We are left wondering just what kind of dance might have been done to it; it's certainly no rag of the usual sort calling for a one-step or fast two-step.

George Baquet

Although Palao surely traveled and performed beyond Orleans Parish from time to time, he did not, so far as I know, do any extensive touring in the manner of his friend Baquet, whose early musical life was in some respects rather like Palao's.

George F. (for Florestan) Baquet was born in July 1881, the oldest living son of Theogene Baquet (1854 [perhaps several years earlier]–) and Leocadie Martinez (1856–1921). This is according to the 1900 Federal Census, which found the family living at 1820 Conti Street between Derbigny and Roman Streets, only a block and a half from the St. Louis no. 2 cemetery. Both Theogene and George were listed as cigar makers, although in the 1870s and 1880s Theogene's occupation was usually given as shoemaker. Also living at home were George's younger brother, Achille Joseph (1885–1955), who would eventually also make a career as a clarinetist. The two daughters living at home were Eddia [sic] (1883–) and Alma (1887–).

Théogène V. (for Vidal) Baquet[26] was the son of Myrtel Baquet (1816–), a mulatto shoemaker, and had four or five siblings. Prior to the Civil War there were at least two, perhaps three, households headed by free women of color named Baquet, any of whom might have been Myrtel's ancestor. But tracing these fine points of family history might prove very difficult.

It is worth noting that in the 1880 Federal Census Theogene and his family were enumerated as white. Whether this was by judgment of the census taker or declaration of the head of household is not known.[27] The point of going into this is that one of Theogene's sons, Achille, passed for white in New Orleans—not without providing fodder for gossips—and in his eventual home, the Los Angeles area. Photographs show him to be of dark complexion, suggesting to some observers that he was Mexican in ancestry.

T. V. Baquet was a cornetist by avocation, and from at least the early 1880s leader of one of New Orleans's best-known African-American brass bands, the Excelsior. It is, in any event, no surprise that both of his clarinet-playing sons were musically literate and received formal instruction in the instrument.

In fact, Achille was thought to have allowed such instruction to interfere with his gift for creative improvisation. George claimed to have been taught by clarinetist Louis (or Luis, if you prefer) Tio, who had been making his mark in New Orleans after the Tio family's return to New Orleans from Mexico ca. 1878.

Theogene, however, led a rather complicated family life—if not all that unusual in New Orleans. The 1910 Federal Census found him as a 59-year-old insurance agent living at 1835 Ursulines with his wife of 26 years, Josephine. Still living at home were their seven children (three had died), daughters Bertha Lavigne (24) and Cecile (6), and sons Richard (22), Lawrence (20), Th[eogene] (18), Arsene (14), and Albert (8). This branch of the family produced the vaudeville performer Hal Bakay, who was notoriously (and fatally) shot in a fracas with songwriter Spencer Williams in 1931, as well as Eddie Baquet, Sr. (1922–1993), whose restaurant was to develop a national reputation in the 1980s.

Both Theogene and his son George received mention in the theatrical pages of the *Freeman* at the end of 1898. On the occasion of a visit to New Orleans, members of the Georgia Minstrels were entertained by W. J. Nickerson's "student orchestra," which included T.V. Baquet, as one of three cornetists, and George, as player of the clarinet.[28] Perhaps at the urging or with the assistance of Nickerson or Louis Tio, both of whom had toured with the Georgias in the late 1880s, George joined the combined Gideon's Minstrels and Nashville Students company in Memphis, Tennessee, in 1901. This was a large and pretentious show with a roster loaded with New Orleans musicians, such as Dan Desdunes, Ralph Nicholas, and Alcibiade Jeanjacque. The occasional programs published in the *Indianapolis Freeman* show an eclectic mix of standard overtures (*Poet & Peasant*, *Raymond*, etc.) and light classical pieces along with more up-to-date popular tunes and ragtime. Baquet remained with Gideon's through 1902, moving to Richard & Pringle's Georgia Minstrels band and orchestra for the 1903–1904 season. This group of musicians included some of Baquet's colleagues from Gideon's show along with other New Orleanians, such as Frank Clermont, Alphonse Guiguesse, and Frank Castry (actually from Biloxi).

By the close of 1904, Baquet had been replaced by Henry Fitzgiles with the Georgia Minstrels and was probably back in New Orleans.[29] A brief item in the *Indianapolis Freeman* of June 24, 1905, has him as a member of Prof. George Moret's band, playing concerts at Lincoln Park.[30] It must have been around this time that Baquet had a kind of conversion experience (if not an epiphany!) which he recounted to Frederic Ramsey in 1940. It's worth quoting in extenso, as it details a dilemma which must have faced many of the more formally in-structed musicians born around 1880 or so.

In Ramsey's paraphrase, "Up to this time, Baquet . . . had played nothing but strictly 'read' music. With his careful training Baquet easily obtained employment with Robichaux's Orchestra when he returned from his tour. This orchestra was hired for fashionable social gatherings, and for dances. On such occasions, the men played straight music, as written, consisting of "sets" of different dances. A typical set opened with a one-step, continued with a schottische, a mazurka, rag, waltz, and ended with a quadrille." Ramsey goes on to quote Baquet: "I'd been home two days and was out late celebrating with some of my friends, when we went to a ball at the Oddfellow's Hall, where Buddy Bolden worked. I remember thinking it was a funny place, nobody took their hats off. It was plenty tough. You paid 15 cents and walked in. When we came in, we saw the band, six of them, on a low stand. They had their hats on, too, and were resting, pretty sleepy. We stood behind a column. All of a sudden, Buddy stomps, knocks on the floor with his trumpet to give the beat, and they all sit up straight, wide awake. Buddy held up his cornet, paused to be sure of his embouchure, then they played *Make Me a Pallet on the Floor*. . . . I'd never heard anything like that before. I'd played 'legitimate' stuff. But this—it was somethin' that pulled me! They got me up on the stand that night, and I was playin' with 'em. After that I didn't play legitimate so much."[31]

The nine years between Baquet's coming off the road with the minstrel show bands and his joining the Creole Band in Los Angeles must have been the usual mixture of dance engagements, parades (in which his poignant E-flat clarinet playing particularly impressed listeners), picnics, and employment in the saloons of the District. He mentions having a five-piece band at Billy Philips's cafe (variously, the 101 or the 102 Ranch).

The second installment of Ramsey's essay on Baquet offers a story that on the surface seems to contradict much of what is known about the earliest days of the Creole Band. In it Baquet states that Bill Johnson was his band mate in the Olympia orchestra (of which Freddy Keppard was also a member) and decided to form a group that would hustle all over Dixie, "just like the German bands used to do." As published, there seems to be no gap between this group and the Creole Band proper that played at prize fights in Los Angeles in 1914. The problems are many: the small band that Bill Johnson took to California ca. 1908 didn't have Baquet in it so far as we know; Johnson was already in California prior to that and again in 1909–1910; Johnson is not elsewhere mentioned as a member of the Olympia; and there certainly was no continuity between the band of 1908 and that of 1914. This entire matter will be dealt with below.

Lacking access to Frederic Ramsey's notes, one can only suggest that in the process of converting telegraphic phrases and disconnected names and dates into a coherent and continuous narrative, Ramsey created a plausible fiction. Another possibility might be this: Jelly Roll Morton speaks of a trip that Keppard made to Memphis in 1910 or 1911, so it's conceivable that this was the Olympia—since if anyone is constantly cited as a member of the Olympia, it is Keppard—and that it might have been part of a barnstorming tour.

Louis "Big Eye" Delille was interviewed by Robert Goffin in 1944 and asserted that he was the first choice for the Creole Band when it organized in Los Angeles, but that an affair of the heart kept him from accepting. He suggested George Baquet as a substitute.[32] In an address to the New Orleans Jazz Club shortly before he died, Baquet recalled that three of them—by extrapolation Baquet, Keppard, and Vincent—were sent for on May 7, 1914. This comes between April 5, when the California Eagle ran an ad for the "Creole Orchestra," and June 13, when we find an ad for the "Imperial Band of New Orleans." Perhaps only with the arrival of a "front line" did it seem proper to label the seven-piece group with what, after all, was a quite prestigious name in New Orleans.[33]

To sum up, of all the musicians in the Creole Band, Baquet seems to have had highest social status and the best instruction, not to speak of professional seasoning in his three or four years with the most eminent nationally touring African-American minstrel companies. Of his musical literacy there can be no doubt, and in the concluding biographical section there'll be occasion to mention a number of works Baquet had published (or copyrighted) in the early 1920s. As to his conversion to "ear music," this didn't involve a total abandonment of his "legit" musical past if the recordings he made in 1929 as a member of Jelly Roll Morton's Victor recording orchestra are any indication. Nonetheless, the rather refined and precise technique is combined with a number of hokum tricks, which he could have picked up as early as his stint with Gideon's or Richards & Pringle's.

Baquet in his prime was certainly handsome, if a tad chubby: Ramsey wrote that while he was with the Creole Band he "sported a fine diamond-horseshoe pin stuck carelessly and flauntingly into a graceful, flowing cravat." Ramsey may well have derived his description from the photograph published in *Jazzmen*, which clearly shows the stickpin. Although it came from cornetist Sidney Desvigne, the photo is inscribed in an elegant, careful hand: "With Sincere good wishes to Emanuel Perez, from George F. Baquet, Aug. 20, 1915."[34]

1.5 An appealing photograph of George Baquet made by the Orpheum Studio, South Bend, Indiana. It was inscribed to Emanuel Perez just at the beginning of the band's fall 1915 season, although the photograph may have been taken in January, just prior to their opening at the Grand Theater, Chicago, judging by Baquet's rather heavy suiting and vest. A similar jewel-set horseshoe pin was also worn by Freddie Keppard and "Big Eye" Louis Delille (see illustrations 4.6, 4.7, and 5.2) but I suspect this was a common item of jewelry around the turn of the century without special significance. [Courtesy of Frank Driggs; first published in *Jazzmen* from Sidney Desvigne]

Eddie Vincent

Most of the earlier jazz histories give his name as "Vinson," sometimes "Venson."[35] That this was a normal confusion is evidenced by New Orleans city directories in which we see cross-references from Vincent to Vinson (and vice versa). The "Venson" spelling was also that of the Los Angeles business card loaned by Bill Johnson to Bill Russell and reprinted in *Jazzmen*.

The 1900 Federal Census of Algiers lists a Vincent family, which most likely is the one in which we're interested. On Saux Lane (sometimes written as John Saux or Jean Saux Lane) the family of day laborer Henry Vincent (1849–) and his wife Caroline (1851–) was enumerated.[36] Of her eight children, only three were living. Edward (also a day laborer) was born in July 1878, and Virginia was born in November 1889. Some seventeen dwellings along the lane toward the river was the family of Nellie Albert, including a son, Thomas, born in December 1879. Almost all the residents of this somewhat isolated street were

1.6 This portrait of Eddie Vincent was taken at the Metropolis Photo Studio, 253–255 Tremont Street, Boston. It must have been quite chilly, to judge by the gloves and heavy overcoat, thus probably dates from the band's visit with *Town Topics* in January 1916 rather than April 1917. [Prince scrapbook]

black, with most males listed as day laborers and females as washerwomen. Nevertheless, quite a few of these homes were owned rather than rented.

The twenty-nine-year-old dry-dock worker enumerated on Wagner Street in Algiers in the 1910 census might be the musician in question. Wagner was about six blocks distant from John Saux Lane, and it often seems to be the case that moves are made within the same district or neighborhood. This Vincent had been married for 8 years to Carrie Harris and had two sons, ages 11 and 3.[37]

Cornetist Charlie Love, born in 1885, lived in Algiers between about 1895 and 1901 and met both Tom Albert and Eddie when he was a kid, recalling that they lived in the first house going along "John South" [recte John Saux] lane,

1.7 Two buddies from Algiers: Eddie Vincent and Jimmy Palao, en route to an unknown destination. [Palao family scrapbook]

beginning at the west gate of the Navy Yard. (The Navy Yard was constructed ca. 1900–1901.) They'd practice every day with a bass player named "Ti," and Vincent, at the time playing valve trombone, would drill Love on the cornet. Vincent could read music and Love wished that he could be great like Vincent, who could "take solos and all." Vincent would have his trombone on a chair and every time Love would make a chord on cornet, Vincent would say, "That don't chord. Make this," and demonstrate it on trombone.

Nevertheless, it's really quite striking how rarely his name comes up in the oral histories of the older musicians. Peter Bocage remembered him as a member of the group he first started playing with: Bocage, violin; Tom Albert, cornet; Vincent, trombone, Gabriel (probably Albert), clarinet; "Skeeter," guitar, and "Nootzie" Reuben, string bass. He's cited as a member of the Excelsior Band, which makes sense as his fellow Algiers musician Peter Bocage took over the directorship. He's further mentioned as a member of the Olympia Band, thus an associate of Keppard. Perhaps he was a bit slow in developing;

Charlie Love thought that he learned a lot when he was gone from New Orleans. Certainly in Chicago he played with some first-class orchestras and was much admired by such a skilled musician as percussionist Jimmy Bertrand.

The patronymic "Vincent" (including its alternative spellings) doesn't allow linking Eddie to a lineage of French-speaking free people of color, or for that matter any other group. (Perhaps one should mention the obvious: Vincent and Norwood Williams had the most "African" features of the members of the band.) He could read notes and had some instruction, either solfege or trombone specifically. Later, in Chicago, he played saxophone—one might even say that he owed his demise to that instrument (see below). As to his style, the few (very) recordings from the 1920s that stand some chance of involving him are quite disparate. They'll be discussed below.

Norwood Williams

Even more than with Vincent, there's really little to say about the career, either pre– or post–Creole Band of Norwood James "Gigi" Williams, despite the fact that Bill Russell spoke with him in California in 1940.[38] First off, he was not a native of New Orleans or surrounding parishes but was from Bayou Sara in West Feliciana Parish (some 90 miles northwest of New Orleans as the crow flies), where he was born on August 19, 1884, the son of Charles and Emmaline Williams.[39] At the time of the 1910 census, he was living uptown in the 11th Ward, at 2924 Dryades Street, with the occupation of pullman porter.[40] In 1900, he had been living in the same general neighborhood, at 2233 South Rampart Street.[41] Oddly, considering the hundreds of musicians figuring in the interviews in the New Orleans Jazz Archives, Williams left no trace as an active musician in the Crescent City.

He then moved to Los Angeles where the 1911 city directory listed "Norwood Williams, porter" at 826 S. Central Avenue. In 1912 and 1913, he was found at 422 Ruth Avenue. At some point shortly after moving to California, he married Maude Williams. The couple apparently had no children.

While Bill Russell was in Los Angeles in 1940 studying with Arnold Schoenberg, he nevertheless continued his interest in early jazz. Bud Scott had told him that Williams lived in Watts, and the McNeils (trombonist Zue Robertson's sister and brother-in-law) were able to provide the precise address, a filling station with adjacent lunch room on 116th Street, close to the interurban tracks to Long Beach.[42] Williams provided interesting information regarding the Creole Band, with much of the conversation emphasizing that he was the most responsible person in the group.

The topics of greatest interest to Russell were, naturally, the Creole Band and Buddy Bolden. Williams, in fact, claimed to have played with and even toured with a group called the Bolden Troubadours. He further stated that Bolden began his musical career around 1890, and was much inspired by the spirituals and shouts he heard at the First Baptist Church (nicknamed "the Gymnasium"), and played in Audubon Park. None of these points can be corroborated, and one, the date of 1890, is highly unlikely, Bolden having been born in 1879. Tantalizingly, Williams recalled playing musical bow in a trio with Joe Oliver (who played conch shell!) and a drummer. Williams also recalled some details of playing in a string trio with Bill and Dink Johnson in Los Angeles; there's even a suggestion that he might have played with some of the Johnsons in Biloxi.

There's no way of making a coherent story of these random remarks nor of linking Williams with some of the guitarists present in every New Orleans dance band photograph from the era. Even more regrettably, although Williams showed Russell the very guitar—a small-bodied round-hole instrument—he had played while traveling with the Creole Band, there are no indications of questions or answers regarding matters of style, technique, or equipment.

Fred Keppard

Keppard[43] is at once the youngest member of the Creole Band and the one who figures most prominently in all histories of early jazz. This was surely due to the fact that he can be heard on more than a few notable recordings made in Chicago in the 1920s. While this is also true of Bill Johnson, a cornet soloist is many steps higher in the jazz pecking order. Accordingly, even though he died before any nascent jazz historians were able to speak with him, he figures in a very large number of published articles as well as many oral histories.

The result is perhaps predictable: the Creole Band is almost always assumed to have been Keppard's—that is, organized by or led by him. It's possible that he was the most flamboyant or assertive musical voice—in fact there is at least one strong indication that this was the case—but nothing to show that he had a role in organizing tours, choosing repertory, signing contracts, and so on.

Fred was the last of three living (three had died) children of Louis Keppard and Emily Peterson Keppard,[44] born February 27, 1890, according to his death certificate and Orleans Parish birth records.[45] His sister Mary was born in February 1882, and his brother Louis, in February 1888.[46] In city directory entries their father's occupation is usually given as cook.

1.8 Keppard was, at least in his own eyes, the star of the band. The ornate inscription is presumably in his own hand. The cropping of the photograph no doubt eliminated the name and location of the studio. [Courtesy of Frank Driggs; first published in *Jazzmen* from Sidney Desvigne]

Matters are even more impenetrable when one tries to follow the family tree further back in the nineteenth century. Emily was 50 years of age according to the 1910 Federal Census. That of 1900 gives her birthdate as November, 1846. More to the point, her father is stated to have been born in North Carolina, her mother in Virginia. Thus, she may well have been born a slave—in any event her roots do not go far back in New Orleans. Louis is said to have been born in September 1856. One would like him to have been the son of one John Keppard, a coffee house keeper and brother-in-law of P. S. B. Pinchback, the well-known Reconstruction era politician.[47] This is the more plausible in that John Keppard's turf and the location of his Nightingale Coffee House at Treme and Conti Streets was the Fourth Ward, in proximity to the various addresses of Louis Keppard (Sr.) and his family.

A fair amount of effort hasn't succeeded in establishing a link to John Keppard or any other person of that name—however one might spell it—and consequently Fred can't be identified as "Creole," in the sense of having been

1.9 This rarely published shot of Keppard is from the same Boston studio as Vincent's portrait in figure 1.6. To my eyes, it radiates an uncommon degree of self-assuredness. The cornet is probably a Conn "Perfected Wonder" instrument, a large-bore horn sometimes called the "circus model." [Courtesy of Frank Driggs]

brought up in close contact with French language or culture. Nor is there any solution to this question, despite the fact that Louis Keppard, who lived to an advanced age, spoke about his brother in some detail.

The house in which the family lived in 1900 was on the lake side of North Villere street, no. 427, only a few lots away from St. Louis Street. It was in fact one of the few houses in the area that didn't fall victim to the urban renewal passions that virtually razed the District and its vicinity. It was also here that Louis Keppard, Sr., died of acute nephritis on the May 21, 1901.[48] (Visiting the block today, however, is daunting, since the surrounding "projects" [subsidized, low-income housing] are unwelcoming to strangers.) In 1900, the residents of the block were predominantly black working class, although the next-door neighbors, Alexis Bothman, a jeweler, and his wife, were white. One wonders, incidentally, if Bothman helped young Fred get a job with one of the four or five jewelers who had shops at Royal and Bienville Streets—a job that subsequently passed to Louis once his brother began playing music.

The two brothers worked in the District shining shoes when the cops were looking the other way, but they also began playing music early, Louis on a homemade guitar and Fred on a violin. Both of them were taken to Manny Gabriel's house where they learned "all those old songs." This would probably have been on Marais Street between St. Louis and Toulouse, no more than a block away from the boys' home, or on Miro between St. Louis and Conti.[49] Louis recalled that his brother had some violin lessons with "old man 'Bourboy'"—perhaps the same person sometimes referred to as "Bouboul" Fortuné, with whom the young Alphonse Picou played in the 1890s. At some early point, Fred began playing picnics with Joe Petit's band, but complained to his parents that in this group or perhaps others he couldn't be heard. Accordingly, they bought him a cornet, and he began to study with "old man Adolph Alexander."[50] In addition he just picked up mandolin and accordion, qualifying himself for almost any orchestra job one could think of.[51]

According to Sidney Bechet and Louis Keppard, Fred founded the Olympia Orchestra/Band. The year 1907 or thereabout is a plausible date. Alas, there seem to be no photographs of the orchestra. The ledger of the Société des Jeunes Amis records that an Olympia Orchestra rented their hall for a dance in October 1907. No earlier date is known. According to Sidney Bechet, Billy Marrero was actually the manager, a role he also filled with the Superior Orchestra.[52] One wonders, then, whether Louis's notion that his brother founded the Olympia is correct. Marrero was about fifteen years older and presumably much more experienced in the band business; one can imagine him looking for a young cornet star, however. Be that as it may, Keppard's name is solidly linked with the Olympia, and, apart from his early association with Joe Petit as violinist, we don't find him freelancing and gaining a broad experience with every band in sight.

We need to remember, nevertheless, that Fred hung out with various musicians living in Algiers, especially the Lindsays, Eddie Vincent, and Manuel Manetta. Brother Louis especially stressed the friendship between Manetta and Fred. Their musical association was strong as well, and both of them began playing in the District about the same time.

If indeed it was while with the Olympia that Keppard amazed the music listeners of Memphis with his version of *New Orleans Blues*—the correct one according to Jelly Roll Morton—that would testify to some degree of cosmopolitan touring for the group. In any event, one is tempted to think that the newly founded orchestra came at a crucial time in the history of popular music and dancing—the first mention of a dance called the "turkey trot," soon to become nationally famous—comes from New Orleans in 1907. And although New Orleans bands seem to have kept playing the old menu of polka, mazurka, redowa, quadrille, and so forth, up to World War I, it was high time for a change to the ragtime two-step and eventually, after 1912, to the blues fox-trot. But there's really no more evidence to justify more speculation on this subject.[53]

Young Keppard appears to have been musically literate, even though Willie Humphrey, who played with Keppard from the Stark "Red Back Book" of rags in Chicago, was uncertain as to whether he was reading or had just learned the pieces by ear. And Charlie Gaines, who played with him in Philadelphia in 1920, found that he could read scores that Fred was incapable of deciphering. Manuel Manetta, recalling the days before Keppard left for California in 1914, "played light classical music from the written score in duets of piano and cornet."[54]

One curious item of biography comes from the 1910 census. While on the one hand, band musician Fredie Kepid [*sic*] was located on April 20 at 1813 St. Ann Street with the rest of his family, on April 19 the enumerator found one Fredrick Keppit [*sic*], a musician playing for private parties, as a lodger at 1918 Conti Street with Wallace Bernard, also a musician playing for parties. Wallace and his wife Anna were childless but made up for it by housing eight lodgers. "Keppit" is listed with his eighteen-year-old wife of one year, Cecile.[55]

There's a lot of often contradictory commentary on his playing style strewn here and there in the treasure trove of Tulane interviews, as well as in many other published sources. All comment on his power, but many also say his sweet style was beautiful to hear. Some characterize him as a freak player, using a wide variety of mutes and techniques, such as flutter-tongue and half-valving; others suggest he was a much straighter player than Joe Oliver.[56] Such a careful listener and authoritative commentator on musical matters as Jelly Roll Morton was full of unqualified praise for Keppard; the younger Louis Armstrong used the epithet "fancy" in a not entirely positive sense on several occasions.[57]

Henry Morgan Prince

The odd man in the Creole Band was their star singer and dancer, Henry Morgan Prince. Not only was he not from New Orleans but he'd had a good deal of theatrical experience, even touring in Australia and New Zealand. Not only that, reviews of the band often praised his contribution to the act beyond measure and for a period of time the band was advertised as his. According to Jelly Roll Morton, "Morgan Prince, the comedian with the band, was not a Creole and he took Fred seriously. In one argument he hit Keppard across the head with a cane and that started the breaking up of the band."[58]

Prince was born in Birmingham, Alabama, on March 15, 1885, the son of Roy Prince and Martha Body, both of them from Alabama. He recalled attending Alabama A. & M. College for three years, where the music and mathematics teacher was W. C. Handy.[59] When Handy left his teaching post to rejoin Mahara's Minstrels as bandmaster, Morgan Prince went along, being listed as one of the comedians of the troupe and a few months later as an alto saxophonist, an instrument in which Handy was much interested at the time. For some three years Prince stayed with Mahara's company, listed variously as a baritone singer in the vocal quartet and as a member of the saxophone quartet.

By the fall of 1906, Prince, now married to Emma, also an entertainer, worked with Ferdon's Quaker Medicine Show, which toured widely but especially in the Middle West. By the end of 1908 Ferdon's show was in California, where Prince is listed as a new member of San Francisco's Local 6, American Federation of Musicians, along with other members of Ferdon's band, such as Syd Carter, George Bryant, Fountain B. Woods, and Roy Taborn—more fully, George Leroy Taborn.[60] My best guess is that he spent most of 1909 working at Lew Purcell's So Different Cafe in the Barbary Coast. By the end of 1909, however, he'd joined the Black Patti company with his wife, touring with them during 1910.

By 1911, Prince put down temporary roots in Chicago, opening a theatrical boarding house at 3306 South Wabash Avenue. In May of 1912, he left on a world tour with Hugo's Minstrels, which in addition to Billy Kersands counted among its performers Leonard Scott, who may be identical with the Scott who replaced Prince for the Creole Band's last season. Prince married an at least partly Maori pianist, Ollie Fitzsimmons, in New Zealand, with the pair arriving back in the United States around the beginning of 1914. They worked for a while in San Francisco, then went to Los Angeles.

As Prince recalled in a 1959 interview, he heard the Creole Band in Los Angeles in the street, playing little advertising jobs here and there. On another occasion, he said that he heard them playing on a truck, passing in front of McKee's Cafe (in downtown Los Angeles) where Prince was probably working. He'd never heard anything like their music and tried to get them to come with him back to Australia. He claimed credit for getting permission for them to play in the ring at Doyle's arena, prior to the Leach Cross and Joe Rivers bout. Carl Walker and Ed Fisher of the Los Angeles Pantages Theater were so im-

1.10 Although Henry Morgan Prince traveled with the Creole Band as singer and dancer, it seems clear—both from newspaper items and this superb photograph from Eureka, California ca. 1907–08 of the Great Fer-Don's Medicine Show band of ten pieces—that he could hold his own as an instrumentalist. Prince identified the musicians, going from left to right, as George Taylor, bass drum; Skinny Harris, snare drum; Willie Dyer, cornet; unknown; Fountain Woods, trombone; George Bryant, cornet and leader; Prentice Griffin, tuba; Sid Carter, clarinet; Roy Taborn, baritone horn; H. Morgan Prince, peck horn (or alto horn). At the end of 1908, the band joined the San Francisco musicians' union (Local 6), with Prince going to work at Lew Purcell's So Different Café on the Barbary Coast. [Prince scrapbook]

pressed by their success that they asked them to show up the next morning at 10 a.m., so they rehearsed all night.[61] They also had a number of pictures of the band taken by Bushnell, the theatrical photographer.

At some point, the union with Ollie Fitzsimmons came unstuck, and she struck out on her own, working as Ollie Prince at the Waldorf cabaret in Los Angeles in 1916.[62] Prince then appears to have married a woman named Eunice, also a pianist, but they seem to have been divorced ca. 1921. The many city directory entries for Prince from San Francisco during the 1920s and 1930s list "Madeleine" (in various spellings) as his wife.[63] At the end of his life he was married to a white woman named Edna.

Prince recalled in 1959 that after the band's early January 1917 engagement at the Grand Theater in St. Louis, he took sick and stayed in bed for some

1.11 The Myers studio of San Francisco took this photograph of Prince, perhaps upon his return from the Hugo Brothers Minstrel Company tour of Australia and New Zealand at the end of 1913 or beginning of 1914.

three months, at which point he left to work in a factory. As confirmation, Prince had a certificate dated January 2, 1942 from the Carnegie Steel Corporation's Gary works attesting that he had worked there as a crane man from March 10, 1917 to August 23, 1918. In any event, he would not have made the 1917 trip to New York nor participated in the arguments that led to the band's temporary breakup in Boston. He never rejoined the band on any permanent basis, although he possibly appeared with them from time to time as they toured the greater Chicago area.

William Manuel Johnson

When William Manuel Johnson—we'll refer to him as Bill henceforth—passed away in New Braunfels, Texas, on December 3, 1972, the death certificate declared him to be 100 years of age and a native of Talehega, Alabama. The age was quite possibly wrong, the place a simple misspelling for Talladega. Other documents exist that have him born in 1874 or 1876, even 1879–80; for reasons explained in the notes, I'm inclined to accept 1874.[64] In any event, he was probably the oldest member of the band and the last to pass on. And whatever his date of birth, one can reasonably assume that he became consciously aware of music prior to 1890, before the beginning of the craze for cakewalk and ragtime—or the two step that was danced to it—and even before the widespread dissemination of blues.

Thanks to the careful research of Peter Hanley, Bill's early history has been considerably clarified. Where diligent examination of the 1880 Federal Census for Talladega county proved fruitless, a similar search of the city of Montgomery, Alabama, met with success. On June 15, 1880, the census taker found at 359 Monroe Street the family of Richard and Margaret Johnson: their sons Dick (age 24), James (13), Joseph (10), Dick's wife Hattie (21), and two grandsons—no doubt Hattie's children—Willie White (5) and Robert (2). Race was carefully noted: Hattie and her two sons were mulatto, the rest of the family black. While there's a possibility of misidentification with a name so common as Johnson, the fact that Bill gave his mother's maiden name as Hattie White on his 1939 application for a Social Security account and the reasonably close correspondence in the ages of Bill and his brother Robert between the 1880 and 1900 censuses is strong evidence that we have the right Johnsons. If so, Bill never mentioned a stay in Montgomery in his few interviews. When Hattie and her children left Montgomery is not known, but probably no earlier than 1886, since the 1887 Montgomery city directory records a Richard and a Hattie Johnson at 118 Court Street.[65]

We know that the Johnson family lived in Biloxi, Mississippi, at the turn of the century, yet Bill recalled having lived in New Orleans prior to that time. There isn't any documentation—apart from his death certificate—of an early association with Talladega, Alabama.

The Johnson family history is tangled and obscure and any extended treatment would be both out of place and inconclusive. But a few points seem relatively certain. Hattie Johnson had seven children who survived infancy—not all with the same man. Bill was the oldest, followed by Robert, Bessie, James, Martin, David, and Ollie.[66] At least two of his siblings, Robert and Ollie, became professional musicians, and his sister Bessie was Jelly Roll Morton's consort—a word chosen so as to leave open the matter of legal status: wife, common-law wife, or lover.

Many acquaintances of Bill's were struck by the lightness of his complexion and the "whiteness" of his speech.[67] The former argues for the possibility of his father being white, the latter for a childhood in or close to New Orleans. Jazz historian William Russell claimed that WMJ could and did on occasion "pass for white."

A few scraps of information regarding his early childhood or youth were collected by an interviewer in 1959; these few nonetheless remain the major source for his life prior to the organization of the Creole Band. Bill recalled having delivered groceries to whorehouses in New Orleans for Tony Galeti on Gasquet Street around 1888, give or take two years. Exploration in New Orleans city directories between 1883 and 1899 found no Galeti (or other similar spellings). On the other hand, beginning in 1887 there were a fair number of Coletti or Colletti, sometimes also spelled Collet or even Collette. Some of them were in the grocery business, for example Rosario at 188 Bienville and Samuel at 184 Bienville, possibly the same as the Samuel M. Collet, who in 1891 was in the grocery business at 51 North Basin Street, both addresses in the thick of the sporting district that would become known in a few years as Storyville.

There were other connections with Gasquet Street, a major thoroughfare of the Uptown red-light district: he mentions hanging out in a barber shop at the corner of Gasquet and Liberty and learning to play the guitar and mandolin there. At some time during this period, he recalled having lived at Bayou St. John and Esplanade, "way downtown," then moving with his mother to Biloxi about 1900.[68] He may have returned then to the Gasquet and Liberty neighborhood prior to his first visit to California ca. 1904.

One source asserts that Bill was not only born in New Orleans but attended school there. It also outlines his early musical accomplishments: playing the harmonica at age 11, the guitar at age fifteen (playing in bands three years later). This fits with what Johnson recalled toward the end of his life: his first professional musical experience was playing guitar with William Tuncel, a mandolinist. The duo, or perhaps trio, if the mandolinist Tom Brown joined them, played at Lulu White's sporting house. They were obliged to play facing the wall, presumably because the nudity of the women was reserved to paying customers. Bill recalls being eighteen or twenty at the time; thus the date is around 1895.[69]

Granted that the search in documentary sources for someone named Johnson, much less William Johnson, is more difficult than the proverbial search for a needle in a haystack—at least a powerful magnet can aid in the latter—I nonetheless was on the lookout for any musicians or entertainers named Johnson in the African-American press between ca. 1890 and 1920, especially with given names William, Bill, or Billy. While several persons can be found meeting these criteria, the only one who seems even a remote possibility is the W. M. Johnson who was "musical director" or leader of the orchestra of Puggsley's Tennessee Warblers in 1898. This company was originally formed by the Puggsley brothers of Nashville and has been described as a "jubilee" group of some prestige. It would be a long shot indeed if this W. M. turned out to be William Manuel.[70]

Piecing together information from the 1880 and 1910 Federal Censuses, we can establish that Tuncel—there are a number of spelling variants—was born between 1874 and 1876, thus a contemporary of Bill Johnson, and was probably a native of Mobile, Alabama, where there were living a number of African-Americans of that name in 1880, two of them shingle makers. A 1908 newspaper article states that he moved to Mississippi in 1890 without specifying the city or region. The same article, quite possibly written by Tuncel himself, describes him as "the best mandolin player in the Southern states." In 1908, the guitarist with Tuncel's band was Robert H. Johnson, Bill's younger brother; an offhand remark may confirm the association of Bill and Tuncel: "R. H. Johnson, the guitarist of Biloxi, is an artist, and is getting more like his brother William every day."[71] In any event, the histories of Tuncel's band and the "first" Creole Band are intertwined and will be dealt with in the next chapter.

Bill said that he began playing string bass around 1900,[72] and was playing in a trio with Tom Brown on mandolin in Tom Anderson's Arlington Annex at the corner of Basin and Iberville Streets between 1903 and 1905.[73] Charters tells us that he played occasionally with the Peerless Orchestra or with Frankie Dusen's Eagle Band, and tuba with the Excelsior during Carnival.[74] The source of the notion that he played alto horn is not known; but any reasonably talented musician would probably have been able without difficulty to play alto horn (or "peck horn," after the frequent use of repeated notes in alto horn parts) in its usual accompanying role.[75]

Anderson's rather pretentious saloon was strategically placed to be the first port of call of visitors to Storyville,[76] and playing in the house band can be taken to be substantive proof of Bill's reputation as a performer on his new instrument. It would also, to be sure, make him highly visible. It's to be regretted that most of the musicians interviewed for the Tulane Archives were too young to have any memories of this venue.

Tom Brown is little more than a name: the 1910 census lists him as Thomas P. Brown, born in 1865 or 1866 in Pennsylvania, of parents born in Delaware. He was living at 1429 Gasquet Street with his only slightly older sister Alice Howard.[77] Rose & Souchon designate him the brother-in-law of musicians

"Papa" John and Willie Joseph, so he should have been married at some time to their sister. He's said to have died around 1918.

In 1908 Brown was mandolinist and manager of the Tramps Orchestra, said to have been playing at all the conventions held in New Orleans. There were three others in the group: S. Morant, bass violin; E. A. Jones, trombone; and C. C. Washington, guitar, the last-named with connections to the Tuncel circle of musicians.

Who was the third member of the trio at Tom Anderson's? An obvious and perhaps most likely possibility, if Brown played only the usually melody-bearing mandolin, is a guitarist, for example C. C. Washington, who was later associated with Brown, Johnson, and Tuncel in different musical groups.[78] One can also, although less readily, imagine a violinist or even an accordionist as the third member. It seems evident that Bill found the trio format comfortable. Trombonist Preston Jackson reported to French jazz fans in 1935 that Bill was touring Michigan with the Smizer trio, consisting of Bill, Ed Weir [no doubt Wyer], violin, and Smizer, guitar. In 1947 Johnson told Bill Russell that he wanted to record in a trio with piano and concertina, or perhaps guitar and concertina.[79] This might strike us as a trifle strange, but it appears to be the case that accordion (which we might reasonably assume to include concertina) was in favor in small New Orleans bands in the 1890s. It's worth noting that, according to undocumented report, accordionist Henry Peyton led the string trio that played at the opening of Tom Anderson's.[80]

Bill (or his amanuensis) was emphatic in a New Year's Day 1959 letter that he had first gone to California in 1904 "to visit a cousin and look over the ground." This is supported by the memory of Armontine Carter Palao, who recalled that he was already in California when she and James Palao were married in 1905.[81] He also asserted in his 1959 interview that he had been across the bay in Oakland on the day of the great San Francisco earthquake and fire, April 18, 1906, with a policeman cousin (the same or another?) at a poolroom or saloon on Seventh Street operated by Baxter.

He surely returned to New Orleans not too long after that, since the beginnings of the "pre-Creole Band" can be traced to 1908 at the latest, or perhaps to 1907. The journey to California with the band will be discussed below as part of the history of the band proper.

It was not long, however, before Bill was back in the Golden State. One might have been inclined to take with a grain of salt his statement that he traveled from Oakland to the Johnson-Jeffries prize fight in Reno, Nevada, on July 4, 1910, except that more than a few advertisements in 1909–1910 show him as one of the two proprietors of the Main Event, a pool parlor and cigar store at 1718 Seventh Street in West Oakland.[82] It has to be said that Johnson's memories (he was in his late 80s at the time, attempting to recall events half a century earlier or more!) are often incomplete and not free from contradiction, mostly in chronology. Nonetheless, in this instance his memory receives the documentary support that is mostly (and understandably) lacking.

A few facts help to appreciate the significance of the location of the Main Event. It was only a stone's throw away from the Oakland Mole, an enormous wharf, which until the 1950s was the principal railroad depot for all passenger traffic going across the bay to San Francisco. In fact, the Southern Pacific tracks ran down the middle of Seventh Street on their way to the wharf. In the first decade of the century there were located on the 1700 block of the street six cigar stores, thirteen saloons, and three or four restaurants, in addition to a bath house and a skating rink.

WHETHER JOHNSON WENT back to New Orleans between the summer of 1910 and the end of 1912, when Armontine Carter Palao, the temporarily estranged wife of the soon-to-be violinist of the Creole Band, arrived in Los Angeles[83] and ran into him there, is not known. There is no event, no particular musical association that requires it, unless his repeated claims to have hired the young Fred Keppard refer to this period rather than 1906.[84]

Not only was WMJ something of a rolling stone, but he also liked to move with a fast crowd—of gamblers, for example—and had no compunction at being supported by wealthy women. He seems as well to have been willing and able to try his hand at occupations other than musician. For that we have the firm evidence of the Main Event in Oakland. When Mrs. Palao arrived in Los Angeles two years later, Bill was running a combination cigar stand and barbershop (she took pains to say that he didn't cut hair himself but hired others to do so)—but also pressed her into service to run an ice cream store that would serve as a front for a "Chinese lottery" gambling operation in which he was involved. Much later in Chicago he ran a small restaurant and may also have done so in Los Angeles at the time Joe Oliver played there in 1922. Perhaps restaurants were a kind of family occupation, since Bill's half brother Dink operated one when Alan Lomax spoke with him ca. 1950, and his sister Bessie seemed inordinately proud of the fried chicken at the motel she operated with her husband in the 1930s and 1940s.

Finally: in terms of date of birth, Johnson, Vincent, and Palao, all born in the 1870s, were the oldest, with Johnson and Palao best seen as the core of the band, one as manager, the other as leader. Then come, in order, George Baquet, Norwood Williams, Morgan Prince, with Keppard, the youngest and the self-elected "star." If "creole" is taken to mean, as it was for many Americans around this time, light-skinned (for an African-American) and possibly with some "Caucasian" features, then the term appropriately applies to Johnson (especially), Palao, Baquet, and Keppard. The only band member who seems to have descended from the old New Orleans "creole" group, that is, "colored Creoles," originally composed of "free persons of color," and its relatively French artistic strivings, seems to have been Baquet, who with Palao had a significant degree of formal musical instruction. Baquet probably had some general schooling past grammar school if his address to the New Orleans Jazz Club is an indication.

More important than any of these points is that a majority of the men in the band had played together in New Orleans in various permutations, although never in the precise configuration of the 1914–1918 Creole Band. Four of them also had music as their first and primary trade, although this doesn't rule out their having had recourse to other jobs when necessary. This is a drastic break with the past, when most of the African-American musicians of New Orleans practiced a steadier trade than music; it's reasonable to see the members of the future Creole Band as professionals rather than cigar makers, bricklayers, shoemakers, barbers, who also were avocational amateur musicians. This turn to professionalism was quite possibly a precondition of their being able to compete in the more cosmopolitan musical world outside the South.

2 Before the Beginning

THE FOREGOING BIOGRAPHICAL sketches and the network of links of personal and musical acquaintanceship there displayed might be thought sufficient to account for the eventual Creole Band of 1914–1918. In fact, there was a band led probably by Bill Johnson that traveled from New Orleans to California and back ca. 1908. And to make matters more complicated, Bill Johnson remembered another band from the preceding year that to him at least was part of the story.

But at least a couple of other topics—neither one thoroughly researched—seem to me quite important for the reader to know something about before we launch into the "prehistory" (or, since this is 2003, the "back-story" or even "prequel") of the Creole Band: the makeup of dance bands, and the ways in which New Orleans musicians traveled to other parts of the United States, either by themselves or in orchestras and bands.

Instrumentation

The further back we go before World War I, the less our received ideas of what constitutes a New Orleans jazz band fit the reality. We're hard pressed to locate any bands with the instrumentation of the ODJB (cornet, clarinet, trombone, piano, drum set) for the excellent reasons that (1) pianos were not normally part of a dance band around the turn of the century, and (2) even the drum set only gradually became de rigeur in a hot dance band. Both instruments make an orchestra less portable; it's also been suggested that the usual pianos one would encounter were either mechanically deficient or miserably out of tune. As to the drum set, its presence certainly raises the dynamic level of any ensemble and has the potential of either making rhythmic counterpoint to the melodic instruments or laying down a solid, steady, and exciting beat. This could well have corresponded to a far-reaching change in musical style.

Leafing through the pages of the wonderful *New Orleans Jazz: A Family Album*, we see quite a few bands from 1905 or after with a lineup of violin, cornet, clarinet, trombone, guitar, drums, and string bass, enough of them so that we might well think this was the prototypical New Orleans jazz or ragtime band. There are variations on this theme: Buddy Bolden's orchestra circa 1905 apparently had no violin and two clarinets; John Robichaux's orchestra of about the same date had two cornets. two violins and no guitar, and so forth.[1] In any event, the Creole Band as photographed prior to departing on their vaudeville tour corresponded to the "prototype" suggested above.

There's a fair amount of evidence that such six- or seven-piece bands were not the usual setup for a dance band around the turn of the century, or might normally be encountered only when the hall and the dancing audience were quite large and the affair well financed. Also, in the 1890s and a bit later, we find mentioned on several occasions the accordion as a professional musical instrument in an ensemble.

In the New Orleans lexicon, a three- or four-piece band of, for example, violin or mandolin, guitar, string bass, and one wind instrument, normally clarinet or cornet, would still be a "string band." The exact configuration is not so much the important point as the manner of playing. One can hardly imagine the "Dixieland" style played by such small "string bands." Also, most of the instruments were not capable of playing as agressively as cornet, trombone, and to a lesser extent clarinet. A case in point is the Tio-Doublet Big 4, one of the most noted bands of the late 1880s.[2]

Traveling

The underlying Big Question here is how, before the availability of sound recordings (including film), a music whose essence couldn't be represented by written notation might be transmitted. Obviously music is transmitted when performed and heard, but once is hardly enough to learn or copy a musical style or repertory. So without the help of written music or recordings, the would-be copier either must learn it from the practitioner (as an apprentice from a master), or else by repeated listenings. This is feasible enough when a musician or group of musicians performs repeatedly in the same place or plays occasional engagements throughout a city, or when there's a well-defined local style.

Some lessons, it's true, can be quickly learned. Paul Howard in Los Angeles and Sid LeProtti in San Francisco were mightily impressed by the Creole Band and may well have embodied aspects of its music in their own. (These will be cited in the next chapter.) Likewise, the band played so much in and around Chicago that a musician who was fascinated by their music could hear it repeatedly.[3]

It hadn't been uncommon for New Orleans dance musicians to travel. Certain of them, such as James Humphrey, Frank Clermont, and, apparently, James Palao went out to the adjoining parishes and small towns and plantations along the Mississippi to offer instruction to newly organized brass bands; this was in the 1890s or later. The most highly reputed ensembles would also go from time to time to small towns within easy traveling distance from New Orleans that lacked a band of their own. Some of these engagements were exotic indeed, for example to the small fishing villages in St. Bernard Parish. And a New Orleans band might go as far away as Shreveport or Memphis. Finally, bear in mind that many New Orleans African-American musicians between 1885 and 1905 (these dates are only approximations) played in the three or four leading African-American minstrel companies that toured the entire country. I know of no instance, however, of a New Orleans band touring outside the South for an extended period until the Creole Band.

But back to business. The story begins with a few cryptic sentences from George Baquet as they appeared in the groundbreaking article contributed in 1941 by Frederic Ramsey, Jr., to *Down Beat*. In talking about the Creole Band, Baquet said that, organized by Bill Johnson, it left New Orleans in 1908 and traveled on "'a hustlin' trip all over Dixie,'" making money as they barnstormed, "just like the German bands used to do at that time."[4] This is embedded in the midst of remarks that can only apply to the "real" Creole Band of 1914–1918, and one surmises that in the heat of jotting down notes, then converting them into a magazine story, Ramsey conflated a number of remarks linked only by the role played by Bill Johnson.

The piecing together of the actual story turns out to be rather more difficult than solving a simple jigsaw puzzle: it's as if we had to deal with a collection of pieces from several puzzles all mixed in together and none of them adding up to a complete picture. My first version of the story would have offered the reader excruciating detail concerning the contradictions and obscurities of the various sources and their relationships. On further thought, I've decided to pretend that a reasonable narrative is possible, in full awareness that another writer might put the pieces together differently.

Here are the principal sources for this "prehistory":

1. Bill Russell spoke with Bill Johnson in Chicago in the fall of 1938. While some of this information made it into *Jazzmen*, many of the references to the "pre–Creole Band" remained unpublished, although saved for posterity in Bill's notebook now at the Historic New Orleans Collection. In 1940, Russell also spoke with Mayme Johnson in San Francisco, who recalled important details regarding the 1908 band. These, too, remained unpublished.

2. A useful source is the article based on George Baquet's reminiscences published in DB under Frederic Ramsey, Jr.'s byline (see above).

3. Another piece by Ramsey combines some of what he wrote in 1940–1941 with information that must have come from Bill Russell's 1938 talks with Johnson. With the title "Going Down State Street," this appeared in the would-be periodical *Jazzways*, vol. 1, no. 1 from 1946 (the only issue ever published).

4. Although Bill Russell seems to have been fully aware that Bill Johnson had more to say, Russell wasn't sure where Johnson was after he last saw him in Chicago ca. 1950. Finally in 1959 a young European jazz researcher located Bill in San Antonio, Texas, and over a period of four days spoke with him about the old days. Bill's memories were less detailed and rich than one might have hoped—he was over 80 years of age—but still much of what he had to say about the "pre–Creole Band" repeated what Russell had already collected in 1938 and served as confirmation. Russell was informed that the interviews had been relatively unproductive; otherwise, he might have arranged for his own interviews with Johnson, since the oral history project funded by the Ford Foundation was at that time in full operation.

5. Johnson wrote (or had written for him) a number of preliminary letters to the young researcher, who responded with nearly 100 pages of extracts from all the known sources, a detailed chronology, and some 80 probing and finely focused questions, most of which were never answered. No clear idea of the 1907–1908 band emerged, since all the researcher had to rely on was Ramsey's *Jazzways* article. But in his only truly detailed reply Johnson recounted some details regarding the 1907–1908 band but misleadingly blended them with others that refer to the 1914 band. Johnson also alluded to a fire in Chicago that had destroyed two wardrobe trunks containing a wealth of memorabilia.

6. Bill Johnson did reveal the existence of a novel—or rather a collection of vignettes—by Miriam Monger, published in 1945 under the title *Tales from Toussaint*. Although it was loosely, very loosely, based on the "barnstorming" tour of the 1907–1908 band, it's virtually useless as a historical document. That it exists is certainly noteworthy.

7. By the time my 1988 article "How the Creole Band Came to Be" appeared, the notes of the 1959 interview with Johnson (although none of the correspon-

dence) had come into my possession. In addition, obsessive reading of the theatrical pages of the *Indianapolis Freeman* had revealed links between the 1907–1908 bands and an obscure Mississippi band led by William Tuncel. All of this was supported and expanded by an investigation of city directories and federal census returns.

8. Here and there were scattered other bits that helped confirm the early presence in California of Bill Johnson and his band. An example would be the offhand remark by Benjamin "Reb" Spikes, published in Tom Stoddard's compilation *Jazz on the Barbary Coast*. He's quoted as saying "Will Johnson came here in 1907, playin' bass with his Creole Band. He had Ernest Coycault with him on trumpet."

Tuncel's Big Four String Band

The reader will recall that the Johnson family, including Bill, who seems not to have been in residence, was enumerated in Biloxi by the federal census taker in 1900. Biloxi was the largest of a string of small Gulf Coast towns between New Orleans and Mobile, easily accessible from New Orleans by the Louisville & Nashville railroad. It was a center of fishing and oyster harvesting, as well as shipbuilding and, as Jelly Roll Morton told it in 1938 in his oral biography, supported its share of saloons and sporting houses. Just a few miles to the west was Gulfport, an upstart with a very large and prestigious resort hotel as well as a deepwater pier. It was also the terminus of the Gulf & Ship Island Railway, which led northward to Hattiesburg, some 70 miles distant and the largest and most dynamic town of the region.

In early 1908 there began appearing in the theatrical pages and local correspondence columns of *IF* a number of items publicizing mandolinist William Tuncel of Hattiesburg and his orchestra, the Big Four String Band. The most detailed of these must stem from Tuncel himself, to judge by an unusual amount of biographical detail. Tuncel, a native of Mobile, Alabama, came to Mississippi in 1890, then joined forces with banjoist Charles C. Henderson in 1900.

The first detailed article came from March 21, 1908:

C. C. Henderson, the famous banjoist of the Tuncel Big 4 orchestra has made his departure for his old home, New Orleans. Prof. N. M. Tuncel [*sic*], the leader and general manager and proprietor of the orchestra, regrets to lose his most valuable man on the right side of him. Mr. Henderson and Mr. Tuncel joined hands in music in the fall of 1900 and from then until the spring of 1908 he has been with the orchestra, and Mr. Tuncel is the only old member of the Big Four Orchestra at the present time, and the new members of the band are R. H. Johnson, guitar; T. A. Dickson, cornet; F. H. Brown, clarinet; Emanuel Holly, bass soloist; W. B. Jones, drums; W. M. Tuncel, mandolin. They have signed to play fourteen weeks at the Love Drug Store in Front Street. [Hattiesburg]

A report of the orchestra's appearance at a Fourth of July dance in El-lisville—some 25 miles north of Hattiesburg on the rail line to Meridian—included additional detail.

Mr. Tuncel came to Mississippi in 1890, and began his music career when quite a boy in the city of Mobile. Since then he has traveled through many different states of the Union. He has won the name of being the best mandolin player in the Southern States. Manuel Holly, the bass violinist, is a musical genius. He is of Mobile also, and has spent most of his time on the coast in the grand summer resorts. R. H. Johnson, the guitarist of Biloxi, is an artist, and is getting more like his brother William every day. T. A. Dickerson, the cornetist, is in Jackson. C. C. Henderson, of New Orleans, has won great fame with his banjo. His wife Mrs. Nannie Henderson is a first-sight reader at the piano. The orchestra will go to Gulfport in a few days to entertain in the Great Southern Hotel. This is the best orchestra on the coast. It is required to have a soloist, and Mr. Tuncel has made arrangements with Willie B. Jones to accompany them. Mr. Jones is of Columbus, Ga., and is a nonpareil baritone soloist, and the first one to travel this side of Nashville with Madame Magdalene Spicer, one among the greatest prima donnas of her race. He closed with her when he signed up with the Southern Minstrels at Mobile in 1907.[5]

Although the March item had reported the departure of C. C. Henderson, an intervening mention in the issue of June 20 stated that both he and his wife had returned to Hattiesburg "for permanent residence."

It's not surprising that a regional band like Tuncel's would travel widely in the area, nor that they would play at an important resort like the Great Southern Hotel. The Love drugstore job strikes us as unusual, as does an engagement providing entertainment at the E. C. Neely department store, likewise in Hattiesburg. The latter was reported in the local paper:

CROWDS CONTINUE LARGE AT NEELLY'S. Record breaking crowds continue to visit the "Forced Sale" at Neely's. Yesterday the store was crowded and bargains were had. The string band constantly on the floor makes purchasing very pleasant. The negro members performed many stunts as negro actors and comedians and besides buying the people were entertained through this medium."[6]

After this salvo of publicity, nothing more is heard of Tuncel's band until July 1911. The local notes from Biloxi tell of a chicken and spaghetti supper given by Mrs. Johnson in honor of the "Tunsel orchestra, of which her son is a member." Then two weeks later the Misses Taylor and Johnson of New Orleans and the Trinsel [*sic*] Orchestra were entertained at a delightful dinner offered by Mr. and Mrs. Robert Spears.[7]

A tantalizing hint of further activities of the Tuncel band came from an interview with saxophonist "Captain" John Handy (1900–1971) conducted by Richard B. Allen in 1958. Handy was from Pass Christian, about halfway between New Orleans and Biloxi, and his father had a band that used to play for excursion trolley rides from Biloxi to Pass Christian and vice versa. The fact that his father's band played ragtime led to a digression on that kind of music, in the course of which John Handy recalled a recording that his father had by a man named "Tunsall" or "John Tunstall." It was ragtime music, recorded on a cylinder, which Handy remembered from around 1906 or 1907. His father was quite fond of it and played it for the Sunday rehearsals of his band. But he also let John and his younger brother Sylvester play it. To quote from the transcript of the interview: "I think Tunstall had about the best band at that time. So we just, we just keep playing that one over and over—jumping and dancing and hollering and we'd play it again [on the wind-up phonograph]." As Allen pursued the topic, it developed that in all likelihood the cylinder was no longer extant:

> Well, I [John Handy] didn't know they were worth anything, and I know he [his father] didn't know they was worth anything; he just got tired of them laying around in the way; he just throw them out in the yard and broke them up. Had about twelve, fifteen of that [that] he threw out there—trash. After he belonged—I mean, after he joined the church, he don't worry with that no more. He sit down and look at television; that's his biggest "idle" now; just sit down there, after he come from work, and look at television and sleep. [Handy's father was ca. 78 years old at the time.][8]

Handy recalled arguments between himself and his cousin as to the date of the recording, which apparently was written [printed?] on it. It's possible that they were looking at a patent date: I'm looking as I write at a 4-minute cylinder by Collins and Harlan, on which not only the title and artist but "Pat. July 29 '02" is embossed in white on the end. Would it have been a commercially produced recording? Otherwise put, would a Dictaphone cylinder have stood up to that kind of heavy use?[9]

Tuncel may have moved to New Orleans by 1920. The federal census of that year located a William Tunso, age 49, and his wife, Julia, at 219 North Franklin Street, right in the heart of the former Storyville. The surname was spelled "Tuncel" in the city directory of that year.

Bill Johnson's involvement with the Tuncel band is affirmed by the *Freeman* article (above) comparing Robert Johnson's skill with that of his brother Bill. But prior to the Hattiesburg-Biloxi orchestra, an eighteen- to twenty-year-old Bill played guitar along with Tuncel on the mandolin at Lulu White's bordello.[10] Ship captains would throw elegant—albeit entirely nude—parties at which the musicians were obliged to play facing the wall.[11] In the same context, Bill remembered Tom Brown, who played "negro mandolin."

This receives some confirmation from the brief biography published in *Esquire's 1945 Jazz Book*,[12] almost certainly based on information collected from Johnson by the editor. It states, ". . . started playing in bands as a guitarist at 18. About 1900 he switched to string bass, played in a trio at Tom Anderson's Annex . . ." Other sources recall Tom Brown as leader of a string trio at Tom Anderson's around the turn of the century and for some years thereafter.[13]

This phase of Bill's musical life, entirely typical of the period, came to an end around 1904 when he went to Oakland to visit a cousin named Baxter. Baxter was a policeman and may also have operated a saloon on Seventh Street, the main drag of the black community of West Oakland. Bill may have stayed in Oakland at least until the great 1906 San Francisco earthquake and fire of April 18–19, which he observed from the safety of the other side of the bay.[14]

The Hattiesburg Excursion Band

In the various recountings of the next phase of his career, Bill was quite consistent in dating it in 1907 or 1908. He was playing at Tom Anderson's and was approached by some "Northern newspapermen" or by New Orleans's leading daily, the *Times-Picayune*, to go along on a Louisville & Nashville excursion train to Gulfport, and from there on to Hattiesburg.[15] This band consisted of Bill Johnson, guitar; William Tuncel, mandolin; Alphonse Ferzand, string bass; Charley "Henderson," banjo; John Collins, trumpet. In a 1959 letter, Bill said that they changed trains (presumably from the main line of the L & N) in Gulfport and took a much slower special train of ten Pullman cars to Hattiesburg. Bill said this was a "log road," which might mean that the rail line was primarily devoted to bringing the lumber being harvested in southern Mississippi in the first decade of the twentieth century to Gulfport for further shipment by sea. (Or perhaps the tracks were laid on a bed of logs.) The band played with great acclaim for a week at the Hattiesburg Hotel, making $45 per man plus another $100 in tips—very big money for the time.[16]

The band made enough of an impression that it was offered a contract to play in Chicago and New York, but the men in the band were afraid to risk leaving New Orleans. In explaining their reluctance, Bill described his compatriots as "not very great musicians, but who knew their trade." The roster of musicians makes perfect sense: Tuncel we've encountered before as a long-time associate of Bill's, and banjoist Charley "Henderson" [the quotation marks are from the original interview notes] is possibly identical with C[harles]. C. Washington. Both Alphonse Ferzand and John Collins were Gulf Coast musicians about whom at least a few salient details may be noted.

Alphonse Ferzand is almost certainly the Alphonse Farzan enumerated on Grand Jack Alley in Biloxi in the 1900 census. He was born in September 1874 and was a day laborer. He'd been married for three years to Emma, age 22, who had apparently borne no children. Their next-door neighbors were the Bertrand family, whose young son James became a quite successful and well-known drummer in 1920s Chicago. In his interview on deposit at Tulane Jazz Archives, Bertrand said that his uncle Farzan played a three-string bass and left Biloxi with the Original Creole Band, which had Fred Keppard in it. Keppard, of course, was so far as we know only in the 1914 band, not that of 1908.

John Collins, Jr., was the father of the well-known jazz trumpeter Lee Collins, a sailor by trade but also a cornetist, born in 1874. At the time of the 1900 census, he was living with his father, mother, and four siblings (not to speak of in-laws and four nieces) on Hancock St. in Bay St. Louis. Lee Collins's autobiography suggests that the family may also have lived in Gulfport, where his grandfather ran a saloon and restaurant at the train station. Again according to Lee, "my father was not a jazz (it was called "ragtime" in those days) cornet player. He played legitimate, minstrel shows and such, and if he had stuck to it he would have been the pride of New Orleans. But he always did like to do sideline work."[17]

Charles C. Washington, besides the connection with Tuncel mentioned above, has connections with both New Orleans and California. The California connection emerges in a brief item from *Indianapolis Freeman*, October 17, 1908:

The Tramps orchestra is making good in New Orleans, playing at all conventions that are held at that city. The band consists of four pieces: T. P. Brown, mandolinist; C. C. Washington, guitarist; E. A. Jones, trombonist; and S. Morant, base violin. T. P. Brown, manager.

A related item from two weeks later describes Washington as a "comedian and all-round athlete, formerly of the Creole Orchestra of Oakland."[18] More of this later.

Despite the fact that Bill Russell had collected significant details regarding the Hattiesburg excursion when he spoke with Johnson in the fall of 1938, the story didn't make it into *Jazzmen*, surfacing only in the obscure *Jazzways* article by Frederic Ramsey.[19] It's interesting that Johnson thought of the band hired to play in Hattiesburg as the "Creole Band"—or at least so it was recorded by Russell. So in Johnson's mind at least the beginning of the story was in 1907 (or 1908). Also, it seems that he thought the end of the story came in 1923, when he left Joe Oliver's band.

One might think that such an excursion would have been mentioned either in the Hattiesburg paper—which began publication on May 1, 1907—or in the *Times-Picayune*, but attempts to substantiate it have so far not borne fruit. A news story from the *Hattiesburg Daily News* of May 19, 1908 bore the headline "MANY MISSISSIPPI EDITORS ARE GUESTS OF HAPPY HATTIES- BURG" and gave a few details of the forty-third annual session of the Mississippi Press Association. But this seems too late and in any event there's no mention of the band, or any band.

The matter of a special train of ten Pullman cars brings railroad history into the picture and a few words on the situation seem to be in order. When the no doubt carousing newspapermen (or publicity men) got off the train at the Gulfport station to go to Hattiesburg, they transferred from the main line of the Lousville & Nashville to the Gulf & Ship Island Railroad, a small railroad of important but local consequence. Beginning with a line from Gulfport to Hattiesburg, it had extended its line from Hattiesburg to Jackson, Mississippi, already in 1900, which would permit freight and passengers to take the main line of the Illinois Central northward to Chicago. For that matter, two other small lines served Hattiesburg. The bulk of the business of the G & SI was clearly freight from the steadily expanding port of Gulfport, but once the grandiose Great Southern Hotel had been built, there clearly would have been an interest in attracting tourist trade from the North during the winter months. It's not impossible, consequently, that through sleeper cars began to run, not only from Chicago to New Orleans but also to Gulfport. Although we might hope that such an event would have garnered mention in the railroad columns of the daily press (all of the larger metropolitan dailies appear to have had them at the time) or in the railroad trade periodicals, investigations have so far not met with success.[20]

The Hattiesburg excursion band may strike readers as not quite belonging

to the history of jazz, lacking as it did the "classical" front line of [...]
inet, and trombone. It was in fact a string band of mandolin, guitar, b[...]
string bass with one wind instrument. (The banjo is not at all a typical [...]
ber of such a group in New Orleans — or in U.S. dance orchestras generally [...]
so far as I can tell.) Perhaps we should think of it as a member of a dying
breed, since over the next few years the "standard" jazz band was to become
and remain dominant. There remains the question of whose band it actually
was. Although Bill Johnson appears to claim leadership of the quintet, it may
be another instance of divided responsibilities, with Tuncel giving his name
and actually leading the band and Johnson taking care of finding work.

The California Band

Johnson had already formed the notion during his trip to California in 1904
that a New Orleans band had commercial potential in the Golden State. Now,
perhaps frustrated by the unwillingness of Tuncel et al. to leave New Orleans
(or Hattiesburg and Biloxi) for the untested waters of Chicago and New York,
he decided to act on his idea. How long a period elapsed between the Hattiesburg excursion and the organization of a new band is difficult to say, but most
probably not more than a few months. With himself on mandolin, he enlisted
the services of four other musicians: guitarist C. C. Washington, double bassist
Alphonse Ferzand from Biloxi, valve trombonist Harold Patio, and cornetist
Ernest Coycault.[21] This is still an augmented string band, but with interesting
possibilities of cooperation between the two brass instruments.

They left New Orleans with a ticket taking them as far as Morgan City,
Louisiana, 80 miles west on the Southern Pacific line, paying the conductors
cash bribes for their further progress west. Next came Lafayette still in Louisiana, then the Texas cities of Houston, Dallas, Fort Worth, Hutchins (assuming this is the reality lurking behind "Hudgin"), Waco, and Galveston, followed
by Phoenix, Yuma, and possibly Bisbee in Arizona. More than a few were on
the main line of the Southern Pacific, viz. Morgan City, Lafayette, Yuma, but
others were not, such as Galveston, Dallas, Phoenix, Waco. (These are, however, on branch lines.) Also mentioned is Bisbee, Arizona, although in what
connection is unclear. A parenthetical notation "(Coppermine)," remains mysterious.[22]

How long such a trip might have taken obviously depends on how often the
band left the train to play. At one point, it's stated that nine months elapsed;
at another, that it arrived in California in the summertime. There are two bits
of evidence that, while they confirm the band's arrival in California, only al-

to the time. The first comes from an interview with
conducted by Patricia Willard in May, 1980. (Reb was
) "[Keppard] come here in around 1907 or '08. Fred
brother-in-law, Johnson, bass player . . . they came
|t—they call him Ernest Johnson, too. He came out
:eoles came out of about a year or so apart. They was
·er—went up North—Pappoose or something—
ames. They all came through here '7—1907 or '8, '9,
...., you know."25

The second bit of evidence came from Mayme Johnson, a long-time San
Francisco resident interviewed by Bill Russell in 1940, who claimed to be Bill
Johnson's wife. In fact, when Bill registered for the World War I draft, he listed
her as such.24 And she still had a large-format version of the famous Creole
Band photo from Los Angeles hanging on her wall. She was familiar with the
history of the "pre–Creole Band" and recalled that it came to California in the
year that the Great White Fleet under the command of "Fighting Bob" Evans
visited Los Angeles and San Francisco. This brandishing of U.S. military clout
occurred in 1908 with the fleet arriving in San Diego at the beginning of April
and departing from San Francisco for the Far East in early July. She also rem-
inisced about visiting WMJ in the hospital after he had been shot by a white
girl and beating him up with a gold-handled umbrella.

Once again, Patio had left an impression. Mayme recalled that he had been
the original trombonist of the Creole Band, but had later lost his mind. She
also thought that an early drummer with the band was an otherwise unknown
"Horace Greeley."25 Russell thought she seemed quite familiar with New Orleans names.26

If they legally married, Bill and Mayme might have become so back home
in New Orleans, or he could have met her when he was in Oakland between
1904 and 1906 or 1907. Be that as it may, Mayme was out of the picture by
1920, when Bill was living in Chicago as the husband of Ada. The link to the
extremely notorious and precisely dated presence of "Fighting Bob" Evans's
fleet, however, is for the moment the best bit of evidence we have for dating
the band's stay in California.

Tales from Toussaint and Miriam Monger

Of an entirely different, semifictional if not mythical, order is the bizarre
episodic novel from 1945 by Miriam Monger, *Tales from Toussaint*. No rational
search procedure would ever have uncovered its connection with Bill Johnson

and the "California Band." Knowledge of its existence is entirely due to a 1959 letter from Bill revealing that Miriam Monger, his employer in San Antonio—and quite possibly in Chicago in the mid-1940s—had written a book based on his trip from New Orleans to California.[27]

One can hardly do better by way of introduction than to quote the publisher's blurb from the dust-jacket:

> On different evenings four white men gathered in a Chicago club to listen to tales by Toussaint, celebrated quadroon orchestra leader and composer.
>
> In her third book, the author of *Diana of the North Country* and *Midland Saga* has achieved an extraordinary work. Toussaint's melodious Negro accent and quaint phraseology, throbbing with drama, color, and charm, cast a spell over the reader as he narrates his fascinating adventures in traversing "the lynchin' country" with his musicians some twenty-five years ago . . .
>
> This author writes with a cynical daring which throws into blinding relief the plight of the colored race.

Indeed the front of the jacket depicts a victim of hanging, his strong African features twisted in rage. The club at which these tales were told was called, by the way, the "Creole Club."

We know comparatively little about Miriam Monger. She was born February 21, 1891, in Iowa. The 1900 census found her in the small town of Anamosa with her widowed mother, Catherine, and her siblings: Shubal A., age 24; Myrtle (the dedicatee of the *Tales*), 17; Marjory, 15; Mildred, 12; Charley, 5.

An investigation of Chicago city directories and telephone books helps somewhat in documenting the later history of this family. The 1918 Chicago city directory locates Mrs. K. L. Monger at 6107 Woodlawn Avenue on the South Side. Five years later Katherine L. Monger, designated the widow of Charles H. Monger, had moved to 4720 Dorchester Avenue. By 1928, Katherine, Mildred, Miriam, and Charles H., a salesman, were at 4340 (South) Lake Park Avenue, where they were all enumerated in the 1930 census. Only Charles was listed with an occupation: commercial traveler in wholesale lumber. Perhaps his earnings were enough to support his mother and two unmarried sisters.

Mildred and Miriam were still there in the June 1940 and June 1946 telephone directories, but in June 1954 only Miriam was listed, at 4827 South Lake Park. Her listing disappeared entirely a year later, perhaps at the time she moved to Texas. Putting all of this together: Katherine quite possibly died between 1930 and 1940, with Mildred moving away between 1940 and 1946.

Oddly enough, none of the Mongers were listed with an occupation, except for the listing of Charles in 1928 and 1930. I'd be inclined, barring evidence to the contrary, to think that the family was reasonably well off, leaving Miriam ample scope to exercise her genteel literary talents.

Assuming that the entire family had moved from Iowa to Chicago on or before 1918, Miriam Monger lived there for nearly half her life—1918 through 1954. How and in what connection she became acquainted with Bill Johnson is still a mystery. She was in San Antonio by 1959 and may well have remained there until her death in early 1971. I was unable to locate an obituary, but her death certificate conveys one rather startling point: Bill Johnson signed it as "William Monger." Just what this might show about their relationship I leave to the imagination of the reader.[28]

Monger took exceptional pains to conceal Bill's identity in *Tales from Toussaint*, turning a light-skinned ragtime performer on mandolin, guitar, and string bass into the quadroon Toussaint l'Ouverture Davis, a classically trained pianist. Toussaint began his bandleading career just as he turned 21, working with five other musicians. After beginning in New Orleans, the group developed a following in an imaginary "Cawtersville . . . about a hundred and fifty miles up in Mississippi" so much so that they made it their headquarters. This may well be an echo of Johnson's involvement with Hattiesburg, in fact about 150 miles from New Orleans.[29]

Back in New Orleans after the "Cawtersville" adventure, Toussaint took a trip to Oakland, where a cousin ran a restaurant and saloon. Upon his return he convinced his group of cornet, clarinet, trombone, guitar, and string bass, (with himself on piano or violin) that a lot of money could be made out West. He advanced everyone enough money to take them to the first stop, after which they were going to work their way to California, principally in Texas.

Here Monger allowed her fantasy to run riot in inventing a series of Texas and New Mexico place names that, so far as I can tell, never existed: Battlegap, Roarback, Stagwater, and others.[30] She exercised even more ingenuity in concocting a version of black speech that one might have thought had gone out of fashion many years previously. I offer only one characteristic example:

> Offahed me mo'n you, suh—hundred and fifty—would help pay on a new place. But, Wayne's a bad acto' ef you-all crosses him up—licked a man 'cross the face with his ridin' crop one day last spring—cut iz eye—sicked a gang on him whin he tried tu take it tu law. (p. 219)

If we were to discover draft notes that Monger scribbled when talking to Bill, I don't doubt that many, if not all, of the various incidents recounted had a basis in fact. But to attempt to work backward from the book to historical reconstruction is a losing proposition. One example may prove instructive.

In the notes for the 1959 interviews with Bill we read "In Texas Sheriff was a bad man. He hired them for $20 for a sporting house where bad women 4 hours—scared to leave—drunk—the madam advised them to leave—the Sheriff knocked at the door—everybody left by the back—80$ little town in Texas." Monger uses the basic situation, expanding it to thirty-two pages of her "Episode 4: At Madame Spinoza's" and introduces a complex subplot. Oddly—from the musician's point of view—she omits any mention of the money.

Finally, it's worth mentioning that Monger's protagonist is said to have worked in vaudeville, then been a headliner in a big Shubert production in New York. His Chicago residence is stated to have been "South Parkway" where in fact Bill lived during the 1940s and '50s.

NOTHING IS CERTAIN about the band's stay in California. In one place, seemingly in response to a question, Bill insisted the band never went to San Francisco. If we take this literally, they still might have spent some time in Oakland. Indeed, the Oakland *Sunshine* (an African-American paper) ran an ad on December 21, 1907, for a dance at the West Oakland Skating Rink with music to be provided by the "Creole Orchestra."[31] The reader will recall that in the October 31, 1908, issue of *IF*, C. C. Washington is identified as formerly with "the Creole Orchestra of Oakland, California" (in addition to being a "comedian and an all-round athlete"). Several possibilities present themselves: (1) Bill Johnson's band, already called "the Creole Orchestra," played in Oakland; (2) C. C. Washington stayed on in California after the others went home and either joined an already existing Creole Orchestra or went to Oakland and started his own band, naming it "Creole Orchestra."

Yet another possibility is this: circa 1919–1920 a Creole Café (or Café Creole) was a notorious locale in West Oakland patronized by white slummers where "white and black patrons dine and watch the entertainment." While some musicians interviewed by Stoddard in 1982 said that the café didn't open until 1919 or 1920, pianist Wesley "Fess" Fields remembered it as one of the three places where he had worked with his band around 1910.[32]

Bill mentioned two places where his band played in Los Angeles. One was the Wonder Bar, on Seventh Street near Central Avenue; the other was the Red Feather. The first of these, however, may be part of the history of the 1914 band. The second, although it can't be found in city directories, may be identical with a place that advertised itself in 1915 and 1916 as The Railroad Boys Headquarters, Red Ribbon Buffet, Red Ribbon Beer on draught, 821 East Fifth Street."[33] (This would have been practically at Central Avenue.)

A BRIEF SUMMARY might be helpful at this point. For two of the musicians in the Creole Band that began to tour vaudeville in August 1914, viz., Johnson and Baquet, there had been an earlier Creole Band. The group formed by Johnson involved a number of musicians, including himself, who had previously worked in William Tuncel's Big Four String Band of Hattiesburg and Biloxi. Baquet may well have combined a recollection of this group—one with which he doesn't appear to have been directly connected—with that of other bands which, inspired by the example of the California trip, made increasingly ambitious sorties from their home base, New Orleans.

As for the other members of the group, the trombonist Pattio is quite possibly to be identified with the H. Patio who deposited his transfer card with Local 145 (Vancouver, B.C.) from Seattle sometime prior to February 1920 and was announced as a full member seven months later.[34] Your guess is as good as mine regarding his eventual fate. The same goes for Alphonse Farzende (or Ferzande), the bassist. As we've seen, C. C. Washington seems to have returned to his post with Tuncel in Hattiesburg, at least for a while, then wound up in New Orleans by the end of the year. He was still there for the 1910 census and the 1913 city directory. Coycault appears to have remained in California for the rest of his life.

Bill Johnson was rather insistent that the members of the California band all took the train back to New Orleans with their pockets full of money. If so, he himself couldn't have stayed there for more than a year, since there's documentary evidence that he was back in Oakland by the fall of 1909. In the October issue of a rare weekly boxing and sports newspaper, *The Referee*, we find a small ad for a West Oakland pool parlor and cigar store, "The Main Event." The proprietors are listed as Kid North and Wm. Johnson, with Joe Thompson the manager. At the left and right hand of the text are two small photographs, the one on the left is recognizably our Bill, his fedora cocked rakishly to one side. That his companion is Kid North—an acquaintance of Jelly Roll Morton—and not Thompson is borne out by entries in the 1910 Oakland city directory.[35] This combination of pool hall and cigar store crops up again five years later in Los Angeles, when Bill and Ritch Baker ran a similar establishment at Fourth Street and Central Avenue.

Johnson also recalled attending the prizefight in Reno, Nevada, between

KID. NORTH }
WM. JOHNSON } Props.

JOE THOMPSON
Manager

The Main Event

Pool Parlor

ALL HIGH GRADE CIGARS AND TOBACCO

Phones—Home A 1334—Oakland 2388

1718 Seventh Street   **Oakland, Cal.**

2.1 From the October 1909 issue of *The Referee* (considerably enlarged). Very few African-Americans figure in the pages of this sporting (mostly boxing) paper, either in ads or in the accounts of cabaret life. To be sure, in 1909 there were many thousands of persons named "William Johnson," but I dare say few, if any, who so strongly resembled later photographs of the manager of the Creole Band. The association with Kid North reinforces the identification. [Courtesy of Special Collections, University of California at Los Angeles Library]

Jack Johnson and Jim Jeffries on July 4, 1910. To suggest that such a peripatetic individual as Bill lived continuously in Oakland between the Main Event ad and the Johnson-Jeffries bout, or that he remained there until he moved to Los Angeles in 1912 or 1913, would be hazardous. But his more or less continuous residence in California might go far to explain why he is so little remembered in the oral histories collected by Bill Russell and others between 1957 and 1962. He just wasn't in New Orleans that much during the transitional decade between the older and the newer ragtime. By contrast, the names of Keppard, Palao, Baquet, and Delille, who were all quite active in New Orleans during the first decade, crop up frequently.

After his "Oakland period," Bill moved to Los Angeles. Perhaps this was because his mother had moved there and his sister Bessie, better known to jazz history as "Jelly Roll" Morton's paramour and muse, Anita Gonzales, spent much time there as well. Prior to becoming an Angelena, Bessie had lived in Las Vegas, Nevada, where her younger brother Ollie "Dink" Johnson came from Biloxi or New Orleans to assist in the running of a saloon she managed, the Arcade. This was probably in 1911 or 1912.[36] "Dink," one should recall, was the Creole Band's drummer before they left on their vaudeville tour.[37]

When Armontine Palao arrived in Los Angeles sometime in 1912, she ran into Bill Johnson. He had a combination barber shop and cigar store at First Street, near the railroad depot, hiring others to do the haircutting. Johnson also was involved with a Chinese lottery shop[38] and used Armontine as a screen, putting her in charge of an ice cream store fronting on the street. After a space of time recalled variously as seven or eight months to a year, the estranged couple decided to give marriage another go and Jimmy came to Los Angeles perhaps around the middle of 1913.[39] At first it was difficult to find work, but eventually Palao joined up with his old pal Bill Johnson and probably guitarist Norwood Williams in a string trio.[40] By the end of 1913, then, four of the members of the band were in Los Angeles and were working together: Bill Johnson and his brother Ollie, Norwood Williams, and Palao.

Some accounts would have it that the other members of the group—Baquet, Keppard, and Vincent[41]—were sent for in order to play at the lightweight bout that took place in August, 1914. This seems unlikely in view of George Baquet's characterization of playing at prizefights as a "sideline" for which the band was paid only by passing the hat.[42] Be that as it may, Baquet recalled that the telegram arrived from Los Angeles on May 7, 1914.[43] Assuming it would have taken a few days to pack their bags and find substitutes for jobs they already had in New Orleans, we might conservatively estimate their date of arrival in Los Angeles as between May 15 and 20.

Parenthetically, it's interesting and important that in their oral histories many of the early New Orleans ragtime-jazz musicians mention playing at boxing matches. For example, clarinetist Tony Parenti heard Louis Armstrong, Johnny Dodds, and Kid Ory on advertising wagons, "but most of all I'd see them playing between rounds at prize fights." This would be ca. 1918, if he heard them together.[44] We can't help wondering whether the practice of featuring instrumental ragtime between rounds (or bouts?) was known in other cities. Yet another project for someone!

In filling in the details of this period, a perusal of the African American newspapers published in California proves useful. The *California Eagle* of April 5, 1914, announced music by the Creole Orchestra for the Easter outing of truck drivers that was to take place a week later at Seal Gardens. This could well have been the four-piece combo alluded to above. But the arrival of three new members meant that the small string band was now a pretentious seven-piece group, as so amply illustrated in R&S.

On June 13 the *California Eagle* advertised the "Imperial Band of New Orleans" at the Emancipation Day carnival to be held June 18 and 19 at New Germania Park in Playa del Rey. Finally, the music at the Fourth of July all-night ball held at Dreamland Hall was furnished by an even more grandiosely named "Johnson's Imperial Band of Los Angeles and New Orleans." The name "Imperial Band" may have been common at the time, but its further designation as from Los Angeles and New Orleans links it strongly to one of the leading New Orleans orchestras of the first decade of the century. Following the tendency to assume that the cornetist is the leader of any band, jazz history associates the Imperial Band primarily with the name of cornetist Emanuel Perez. The evidence of a photograph taken ca. 1905 or a few years later (R&S 164) is that James Palao was the leader: his cap bears that legend. My working hypothesis is that calling the group Johnson's Imperial Band is strong testimony to a partnership between Johnson and Palao.[45]

The Creole Band Photograph

This might be a good place to take a breather from our headlong exercise in chronology to examine the very widely distributed photograph of the band, which is, after all, eloquent testimony to the new group brought together by Bill Johnson and Jimmy Palao.

In my article "How the Creole Band Came to Be," I merely alluded to the incorrect dating of the often reproduced—in fact the only—photograph of the band.[46] As an illustration to the article, however, was a tattered but nonetheless original copy of the photograph from the collection of violinist James Palao's daughter, Clotile Palao Wilson. By "original" I mean uncropped (I think) and unaltered by masking of the background or similar changes. I'll call this BMR. [See Frontispiece.]

What light it shed on the career of the band, however, wasn't stated in that publication. So here goes:

The credentials of the best-known version—in *Jazzmen*—would seem to be impeccable: it had been provided to Bill Russell by William Manuel Johnson, the manager of the group. But compared with BMR, it's been cropped as well as having the background whited out, perhaps for use as a halftone newspaper cut. These manipulations produce an odd effect, making the heads of some of the players seem quite a bit larger in JM. Actually, there's more. Other photographs of Bill Johnson show him to be rather tall, but here he seems several inches shorter than Baquet and especially Keppard and Vincent. The versions published in *DB* in 1936 and 1940 appear to be the same; my guess would be that they stemmed from Bill Johnson, who was in Chicago during the '30s and '40s.

Both BMR and JM have legends written on the bass drum head, JM reading "The Original Creole Orchestra" and BMR adding "[ ]ne Main 1405" with the first word being undoubtedly "Phone." A white smudge in JM strongly suggests that the phone number from BMR has been erased. Keepnews & Grauer's well-known collection, *A Pictorial History of Jazz*, prints a version that's less cropped but still with the background whited out, and more strikingly, with "1912" written in place of the phone number. The source is said to be George Hoefer, the long-time *Down Beat* columnist, but where he found it isn't stated. Hoefer was a Chicagoan and I suspect that Bill Johnson was again the source.

But the photograph probably had no inscription at all in its original state. First, the drum set is set up as seen from the player's position, perhaps so as not to block out the lower part of Jimmy Palao's body.[47] In any event, it makes no sense to have an inscription on the inner head—unless, perhaps, the drum did double duty for dancing and marching. Second, the title reads "The Original . . ." which is not the title as given on the business card printed on the bottom half of the *Jazzmen* page. If the purpose of the photograph with the drum head inscription was to advertise the group, then it would make sense to include the local phone number where they could be reached, that of the Central Avenue cigar store operated by Bill Johnson. Once they'd left L.A., the number would have been useless, therefore was erased. Third, the lettering strikes me as neat but unprofessional; it also seems to be unaffected by the irregularities of surface and coloring of the skin head. Finally, when given to someone interested in the Creole Band, such as Bill Russell or Paul Eduard Miller, it would have been reasonable to include the date of "1912"—incorrect though it was—which would not have been useful to include on a more or less current publicity photo.

Another version was published in the Christmas number of *Variety* at the end of 1917. It too is cropped at the bottom but not at the sides, and doesn't eliminate the background. Only enough of the bass drum head is present to show "The Original Creole Orchestra," but on the snare head is written "Compliments / of / Geo. F. Baquet / to my friend / Geo. Landry / Feb. 18, 1915" —incidentally, when the band opened in Saginaw, Michigan.[48] Underneath the snare head we can read the embossed stamp of the photographic studio "Empire / Los Angeles."

What's odd about this version is that Baquet had left the band in mid-1916. Did Johnson write back to George Landry for the photograph?—or perhaps Baquet never sent it. That Bill Johnson didn't have a store of publicity photographs is not a ringing endorsement of his business sense.

To sum up:

1. BMR is the earliest extant state of the photo: no cropping or removal of background, but with an inscription and, most tellingly, with the phone number, something relevant only for Los Angeles publicity purposes. I believe that the name "The Original Creole Orchestra" was added at the same time, possibly by the photographer, since BMR has both inscriptions. There were also large-format versions of the photograph, seen by Bill Russell in 1940 at the homes of Norwood Williams and Mayme Johnson, but it's not known whether they had the inscriptions or not.

2. This photograph was used for newspaper publicity during the band's active touring only four times. The version used in Danville, September 25, 1917, is BMR, complete with orchestra title and Los Angeles telephone number.

3. *Variety* is as described above, but cropped at the bottom so that it's not possible to determine whether it had the phone number or not.

4. By the time jazz researchers began asking Bill for photographs in the later 1930s, he had a version, but not an "undoctored" one. At this point, the no longer relevant telephone number was eliminated.

5. For PHJ, the date "1912" replaced the telephone number. This could have been done by Johnson or by another person, such as Hoefer.

So much for photographic forensics. The oddest thing about the photograph, however, whatever the version, is that all members are in formal evening dress with white tie. A diligent search through the dozens of photographs of bands in Rose and Souchon's far-ranging collection, shows none of the New Orleans bands prior to World War I, black or white, wearing formal evening dress with white tie. During the 1920s of course, tuxedos with black tie, often with a wing collar, are so commonly seen as to be considered a standard uniform for dance musicians. This is true in New York, Chicago, New Orleans, and, I suspect, all over the United States. In any event, to use this photograph for posting outside vaudeville theaters (or in the *Variety* ad) would be a gross misrepresentation of the character of the act, which was of the traditional rube or plantation variety through and through: overalls, straw hats, red bandanas, and the like. Could it be that they couldn't stomach the stereotype? Or did they use a stock drawing for display outside the theaters? In any event, for theatrical purposes any drawing or photograph ought to have included singer and dancer Henry Morgan Prince.

One last point: George Baquet is shown with two clarinets, probably one the normal B flat type, the other in A. This would be appropriate for dance orchestra work, one that used scores calling for the alternation of instruments, but not for a vaudeville act or marching in the streets. Finally, the presence of Dink John-son with a drum kit also tells us this was a dance orchestra, since Dink didn't travel with the band in vaudeville. (It's not impossible that he joined them briefly when they played in Los Angeles, Oakland, San Francisco, or San Diego.)

The seating or standing order of the musicians is not unusual, with the leader who called the tunes and set the tempo—almost always the fiddle player—seated in the center. With one small variation, this order is that of the Superior Orchestra ca. 1910, which shows violinist Peter Bocage with "leader" embroi-dered on his cap, and bassist Billy Marrero with "Mgr" on his. The photograph of the Imperial Orchestra, supposedly ca. 1905 but in my opinion very close in date to the Superior, is similar (and shot in the same studio apparently) al-though no one is seated. Here the leader is violinist James Palao, with guitarist Rene Baptiste labeled as manager.

The order is dictated to some extent by the instruments themselves. The bassist will be standing, and shown to best advantage at the end of the row; the trombonist is best in the rear (standing) rank, to give room for his slide; the drummer should be in front, given the amount of space occupied by the bass drum. (One necessarily wonders whether a collection of band photographs between 1890 and 1920 from, say, Chicago or Seattle would show some of the same characteristics.)

So much for objective analysis. Still, one can hardly eschew reading attitudes into the Creole Band photograph. Dignity and pride are perhaps the adjectives most readily coming to mind, surely in part due to the formal dress. Although many photo sessions of a somewhat later date—the one showing the Clarence Williams—A. J. Piron orchestra that was organized for a 1916 vaudeville tour is a good example—will have (1) a formal photograph such as the one we've just discussed; (2) another with the band playing; and (3) one playing in some kind of joke or "novelty" postures. Perhaps there were other poses that are no longer extant.

A word on the business card: the sentiments of "Let us do your playing" and "Reasonable Prices to Everyone," as well as the indication of versatility ("balls, parties and picnics") are conventional enough. It's worth pointing out that the group is not yet called "The Original . . ." but rather "the famous," but not as part of the title. Oddities which I can't explain are the designation of Norwood J. Williams as W. M. Williams, and Eddie Vincent as Eddie Venson. Perhaps the latter reflects a French-influenced pronunciation? The lengthy quotation from the *Defender* used as a caption for the photograph plus business card by the editors of *Jazzmen* is unfortunately not dated, but in addition to mentioning "Keppard and all there [*sic*]" it cites "Bill Williams," not "Nor-

2.2 The band's Los Angeles business card printed between mid-May and early August 1914. The only known example was loaned by Bill Johnson to the editors of *Jazzmen* in 1939, which is the source of this copy. It's exceedingly odd that Vincent's name is misspelled and Norwood Williams has become an otherwise unknown "W. M. Williams."

wood" or "Gigi" (his nickname). The mention of "jealousy of the Northern brothers" is surely tantalizing and not otherwise known.

Only a brief period separated the organization of the seven-piece Creole Orchestra announced by the business card and depicted in the photograph and the start of their vaudeville career. Undoubtedly, they accepted the entire range of work that their New Orleans background had prepared them for. In addition to the balls, parties, and picnics of the business card, we might add advertising jobs and parades.

This is as good a place as any to acquaint the reader with some features of downtown Los Angeles geography ca. 1910. Central Avenue was soon to be, if not already, the mainstem of African-American business. One of the most important features to be borne in mind is that the Southern Pacific "Arcade Depot" was located on Central between Fourth and Sixth Streets. It will be re-called that the address on the Creole Band business card was 401 Central, just at the northern corner of the depot. A few blocks to the east was the Santa Fe depot—its tracks ran along the Los Angeles river—and opposite it on the other side of the river was the Salt Lake depot—the San Pedro, Los Angeles, & Salt Lake Railroad. The Golden West café, soon to be cited as one of the hottest spots in the city of Los Angeles, was strategically nestled between the Santa Fe and the S.P. depots.

Further down Central Avenue, about a mile south of the cigar store cum pool hall headquarters of the band, was the intersection of Twelfth street, the location both of the hotels run by Norwood Williams after he left the band and the one operated by Anita Gonzales around the same time. This was also the locale of the Spikes brothers' music store. Less than half a mile further

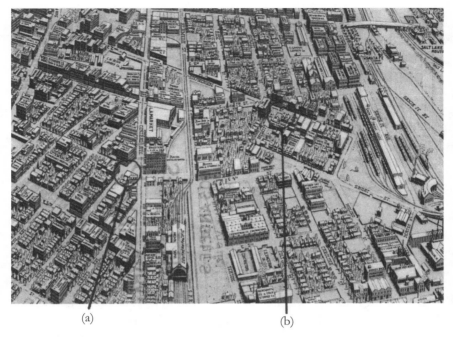

(a)   (b)

2.3 (a) The Central Avenue neighborhood, with Bill Johnson's cigar store and
barbershop at 401 South Central Avenue, and (b) the Golden West hotel and saloon
at 716 Stevenson Street. The proximity of no fewer than three major railroad
stations is noteworthy. [Panoramic Map collection, Map division, Library of
Congress, drawn by Worthington Gates ca. 1909]

south was the intersection of Washington Boulevard (in the place of Nineteenth Street) and Central Avenue, the location of Lee Larkins's home mentioned in the next paragraph. Fifth and Central was, let it be said, only a short
stroll from Broadway and Main Street, important arteries of downtown L.A.

We're fortunate to have the memories of Paul Howard, a skilled musician,
about the beginnings of the band prior to their vaudeville career. "They practiced and practiced there [at the Clark Hotel] every day," and, in a foreshad-
owing of the legend concerning Keppard's rejection of the Victor recording
offer, "they didn't want me to stay around there. I would play any tune that
they had." Howard was also impressed that the band didn't play loud.[49] A bit
further on in the same interview Howard recalled rehearsals in the home of
Lee Larkins at Washington & Central Avenue. Larkins was a friend to musicians, to the point of providing a keg of beer at the rehearsals. On an earlier
occasion, Howard told William Russell that the band played a dance at the

2.4 The old conventions for depicting African-Americans died hard as this cartoon accompanying Danger's account of the fast life at the "Golden West" amply illustrates [L.A. Record, July 3, 1914]. What a shame that the artist didn't depict the band, which I believe must have been the Creole Band.

Central Labor Council Hall on Maple, between Fifth and Sixth Streets, and there he heard their first piece, "The Egyptian." It was the first time he ever liked the clarinet in the low register. When Russell asked what their way of playing was called, Howard replied, "Swinging syncopation. They don't syncopate music nowadays."[50]

There are a couple of reports that may possibly refer to the Creole Band prior to the arrival of Keppard, Vincent, and Baquet. The first is frustratingly vague; nevertheless, it shouldn't be ignored. The writer, one C. L. Bagley, produced a very detailed retrospective "History of the Band and Orchestra Business in Los Angeles" that appeared in successive monthly numbers of the Local 47 (Los Angeles) magazine, *The Overture*, in 1931. For January 5, 1914, we read "ball of colored folks in Blanchard Hall," then a bit further along, "During some of this period a colored orchestra appeared at dances in the Hotel Alexandria, but I cannot give the personnel." On April 3, "Mrs. Harry C. Mayer entertained at Merritt Jones Hotel, Ocean Park. A colored orchestra played."[51]

Far more tantalizing are a series of sensational accounts from the pen of "Johnny Danger" that began appearing in the June 25 issue of the *Los Angeles Record*. The *Record* was a trashy, slangy daily that sold for one cent—thank heavens for yellow journalism! Danger's first article involved a visit to such well-known night spots as the Ship Cafe and Nat Goodwin's; the second, an expedition to Baron Long's Vernon Country Club. A separate article detailed the efforts of Santa Monica authorities to suppress rag dancing.

Finally, on Friday, July 3, Danger reported on the goings on at the Golden

West, "a resort at 716 Stephenson Avenue, where women and men of all colors go to blow off steam."[52] The music is described in Danger's usual lurid terms:

ENTICING MUSIC

In a corner of the cafe a strange orchestra was producing melody which would have caused an Apache redskin to emit a blood-curdling yell and go on the warpath. The music had a weird minor strain and a rhythm so enticing that the temptation to dance was almost overwhelming . . .

IMPROMPTU DANCING

Dancing was in progress in one end of the long room. Holding their dusky dolls in amorous embrace, the negroes hitched about the restricted space in time to the syncopated strains of the latest rag. Strange as it may seem, the "Golden West" is the only place in the city where public dancing has been openly conducted in a room where booze is sold.

All the dancers were not black. Snuggled in the entwining arms of sable sports, white girls slipped and wriggled over the concrete floor in dreamy bliss. Their flashy gowns looked to be somewhat faded and their complexions smacked of the rouge-pot, but they were seemingly highly prized by their Ethiopian escorts . . .

Finally,

Last Sunday night there was no dancing, contrary to custom. But the place was crowded and the orchestra was very much on the job. Three white men entered and took seats at a table near the orchestra. At the next table a young colored girl winked at them with boozy coquetry. Then she finished up her tall glass of liquor and sprawled over the dishes—drunk . . . [two tiresome paragraphs about a crap game omitted]

The orchestra began operations. The musicians worked hard. The fiddler rolled his eyes ceilingward and jigged madly without leaving his seat. The cornetist bent to the floor and then leaned backward until it seemed as if he would go over, chair and all, while he blew uncanny sounds from his horn, interspersing through the music imitations of yelping dogs, crowing roosters, locomotive whistles and terrible groans. In a corner the bass-fiddler shuffled about, hitching his shoulders and guffawing in joy. From time to time he spun his instrument around like a top.

There are many additional picturesque details about this establishment: efforts by the police to close it down, the sale of 20-cent lettuce sandwiches to circumvent regulations requiring the consumption of food with liquor, the connection of the back of the Golden West with a saloon on Hewitt St. Finally

2.5 Mexican Joe Rivers vs. Joe Mandot at the Vernon Arena, Thanksgiving Day 1912, as photographed by the Dingman Studios [courtesy of www.antekprizering.com]. Perhaps someone snapped the Creole Band playing in the ring at Vernon in 1914, but until a copy is found, this ringside shot will do in conveying the atmosphere.

"Verily, verily, the 'Golden West' is one of the cutest as well as wildest little night-life joints in town. Just where the house gets its pull is unknown. It is said that the proprietor has great influence with the negro voters. Perhaps that makes a difference." Strikingly enough, the proprietor of the place was one George Brown, who was Jelly Roll Morton's nemesis during his Los Angeles stay between 1917 and 1922.[53]

Alas, no names, either of the band or its members. But if this group is not the Creole Band (or Johnson's Imperial Band of New Orleans and Los Angeles) I can scarcely imagine what it might be. There were black musicians living and working in Los Angeles even at this early date, but what we know about them inclines us to believe them quite staid. Additionally, Keppard was known to produce freak sounds on his cornet, such as a horse's whinny, and Bill Johnson for shouting out in the middle of a tune as well as spinning his bass.[54] Most important of all is that Norwood Williams was able to give the name of "John Danger" and his newspaper to Bill Russell when Russell interviewed him in 1940.[55]

The same problem of anonymity afflicts the interpretation of other items. In my reading of the *Record*, which began with April 27, 1914, I saw quite a few ads for boxing at McCarey's Vernon Arena; finally there begin to be reports at Jack Doyle's training camp, in the same location. The one for Saturday, July 11 read, "a great throng of boxing enthusiasts witnessed a good card at Jack Doyle's training camp in last night's contests. A negro orchestra kept the spectators on edge with a number of lively airs." Some two weeks later, we read: "BEST FIGHT CLUB IN CALIFORNIA IS JACK DOYLE'S by Tom Lewis . . . I don't believe it has ever been my pleasure to witness a better boxing card anywhere in the United States than that which was run off by Matchmaker Earl Mohan, Friday night . . . The ragtime band was one of the best features of Doyle's show and the music this band rendered was well worth the price of admission . . ."[56] Finally, in his account of the Cross-Rivers bout, the paper's reporter gives the band a name: "The New Orleans Creole band enlivened proceedings by rendering a number of ripping good ragtime selections."[57]

DOYLE'S TRAINING CAMP—apparently known as McCarey's Arena on the two occasions each month when McCarey put on fights (Doyle's were every Friday night)—was at Thirty-eighth Street and Santa Fe Avenue in Vernon, approximately 3 miles as the crow flies from downtown Los Angeles and right on the no. 19 streetcar line. Vernon was and is one of many enclaves in and around the metropolis and since apparently the restrictions on hours and types of entertainment as applied in somewhat puritanical Los Angeles did not apply, it was a natural place for sporting life in its many varieties to flourish—as were also Venice, Santa Monica, Watts (still outside the city limits) and other surrounding communities. Vernon figures in the early history of jazz chiefly for Baron Long's Vernon Country Club (so-called), only two-thirds of a mile south of Doyle's, at Forty-ninth and Santa Fe. It functioned from 1912 until its destruction by fire in 1929. Many of the hottest musicians in Southern California appeared there, such as clarinetist Gus Mueller, saxophone virtuoso Rudy Wiedoeft, the Abe Lyman band. Jim Heimann's *Out with the Stars* gives further details, as well as a handsome photo of the club.

The *Los Angeles Times* reported on the first of these evenings of boxing at Doyle's at which music helped entertain the audience. The issue of Saturday, July 11, 1914, tells us under the headline "Music and Bouts at Doyle's" that "a big crowd enjoyed the fight fest at Jack Doyle's last night, with a colored band thrown in for good measure."[58] Another event of a similar character was cited by the same paper on August 1 in an account of the fights at Doyle's: "There was a full house and during the intermission the crowd was entertained by Battling Brant and a colored boy with some good dancing." One can justifiably assume the presence of a band for accompanying Brant's act, as well as that of the "colored boy"—who, to be sure, might have been a full-grown man, perhaps even Morgan Prince.

That the band had played at Doyle's more than once is clearly indicated in the review of their first appearance at Pantages, published on August 18: "This orchestra has been performing at the famous "Honest Jack" Doyle's Friday night boxing shows, where the boxing fans accorded them a warm welcome." The interracial contest between lightweights Leach Cross and Joe Rivers was not just another bout, and excited great interest in the local sporting community and the country at large.[59] In fact, it had already been revealed at the beginning of the year that promoter Tom McCarey "thinks that the right order of things [in contrast to a bout between Ad Wolgast and Rivers] would be to inflict Leach Cross and Joe Rivers on the Southern fans again and then send the winner against Wolgast. Of course, Rivers will beat Cross, as he already has done three times . . ."[60] Such a bout was originally scheduled for July 28, but moved forward to August 11. Both men weighed in at a maximum 135 pounds, and were scheduled to go a grueling twenty rounds.

George Baquet recalled for Frederic Ramsey the routine the band used for the tune "In Mandalay":

> They played between bouts. Fred Keppard, the cornetist, climbed up on a bench, put his derby over the cornet, and the crowd began to sway as he opened with *In Mandalay*. "Get up in the ring and play, get up in the ring," an appreciative audience howled, and the Creole orchestra took over the arena. The incident was written up in the Los Angeles *Times*, where a cartoon of Baquet playing his clarinet was published.[61]

Baquet contributed a somewhat more detailed account a few years later when he spoke to the New Orleans Jazz Club:

> And when we played the then popular number In Mandalay, Fred Keppard our cornetist stood up with his egg mute and an old Derby Hat on the bell of the instrument. The crowd stood up as one man and shouted for us to get in the ring, and screamed and screamed. When we got down, Mr. Carl Walker, Mr. Alec Pantages' manager, stepped up asking for our card, and asked if Mr. Pantages would send for us, would we come to the theater. A few days later we went to the theater there and played a few numbers for he and his family, including the famous Oklahoma Bob Albright, the noted cowboy singer. So Mr. Pantages jumped up on the stage and asked us to form an act, he did not care what, so long as he had that music. So, go-

ing into a huddle we formed a plantation act with a comedian, the character of Old Man Mose (with some corrections from Baquet's autograph notes and some punctuation added).[62]

It was tempting to follow up the leads provided by Baquet, especially in the first of Ramsey's two *Down Beat* articles,[63] and Bill Russell spent some time looking in vain through the files of the *Los Angeles Times* for the cartoon. In fact, the account of the incident in the *Times* was hardly complimentary:

DISGUSTING EXHIBITION MARRED THE FIGHT
by Harry Carr

What otherwise would have been a brilliant fight was marred last night by an exhibition of vulgar bad taste on the part of the management, and by a preliminary so tame that it would be a compliment to both "fighters" to suspect them of a frame-up . . . While waiting for Rivers and Cross, some one connected with the management had an unhappy inspiration to allow a company of negroes, perpetrating a vile imitation of music, to enter the ring and insult the audience by very obviously begging for coins. To complete a thoroughly disgusting, low and vulgar exhibition, Battling Brant, a tramp fighter, crawled into the ring and was permitted to give a low imitation of a muscle dance.[64]

[A muscle dance is a version of a belly dance, or the hoochie-kooch.]

From the standpoint of 2002, when boxing itself has been demoted, many would say, to the status of a "disgusting, low and vulgar exhibition" these words seem excessive. Nevertheless, it's good to be reminded that New Orleans ragtime/jazz, these days a potent and revered cultural icon, could excite such intemperate reactions.

Inadvertently misled by Baquet, Russell was looking in the wrong newspaper. Both a laudatory story and a cartoon—presumably the one Baquet remembered—were found in the somewhat less classy but more widely read *Examiner*:

After promoting boxing in Los Angeles for some twelve years, Promoter McCarey pulled a new one on the populace by installing the Creole Orchestra at the ringside, and what those colored boys didn't hammer out of "seven pieces" wasn't worth calling for. The "Road to Mandalay" was traveled in a way that would have brought spasms of joy from old Al Jolson. Without knowing the ace of spades from the ace of clubs we are willing to bet a few iron men that the cornetist and slick trombone juggler came from that dear old New Orleans. . . . Johnny Arrozay and Patsy Riley essayed to box ten rounds between "This is the Life" and "Mississippi Dreams." Thirty minutes of fast tangoing without a slip to a "draw" decision.[65]

By Hal Stephen

2.6 Cartoonist Hal Stephen of the Los Angeles *Examiner* was at the Rivers-Cross fight and found the Creole Band interesting enough to draw—but not to name. George Baquet remembered this cartoon, but not the correct newspaper. [L.A. *Examiner*, August 13, 1914]

These days, of course, we must protest "colored boys" and perhaps even "ace of spades," but Walker is light years ahead of the *Times* reporter in his willingness to grant artistry to the musicians. He thought enough of them to give their name, give an accurate count of the number of players, to refer to two of them, to hazard an informed guess as to their hometown, and even cite some of the tunes they played.

Irving Berlin's "This Is the Life" was copyrighted in two versions in January and February 1914 and was surely in circulation. Also, its popularity is attested to by the existence of eleven recordings from 1914–1915, as many as "Alexander's Ragtime Band." Oley Speaks's setting of Rudyard Kipling's "On the Road to Mandalay" comes from 1907 and was already something of a standard piece. As to "Mississippi Dreams," there certainly ought to be a piece with that title but I've never seen or heard one. Possibly it was Al Piantadosi's "Mississippi Days"?

There are several contenders for a "Mandalay" song, however, besides the pompous setting of the Kipling poem. One likely candidate is "I'm on My Way to Mandalay" by Fred Fisher and Albert Bryan, published by Leo Feist in 1913; another is "In Far Off Mandalay" written by Al Johns and Alex Rogers for the Bert Williams vehicle *Mr. Lode of Koal* and published by Will Rossiter in 1909. The two are quite different in character, the first rather raggy, the second exotic, with a kind of moody drumming accompaniment at the start. Perhaps "In Far Off Mandalay" would lend itself better to performance with egg (or pear) mute and derby, but our vote has to go to the Fisher-Bryan song, for a reason to be mentioned in the next chapter.

The cartoon by Hal Stephen was published the following day. Most of it is devoted to the fisticuffs but in the upper right-hand corner is depicted Battling Brandt (referred to in the *Times* report) dancing to the music of three caricatured black musicians. The middle player is indeed a clarinetist, flanked by a cornetist and a string bassist. It is hard to imagine the musically well-schooled Baquet, handsome and light in complexion, taking much pleasure in the cartoon, as much publicity value as it may have had for the band.

The two other Los Angeles dailies that I was able to consult commented briefly on the music. The reporter for the *Record* wrote:

> The New Orleans Creole band enlivened proceedings by rendering a number of ripping good ragtime selections. The crowd seemed to enjoy the music, but there was far too much delay between the time the preliminary boys vacated the ring and the first appearance of the main event principals,

and the *Tribune* reported laconically:

> The "Creole Orchestra" ably aided by Battling Brant, whiled away the "watchful waiting" periods.[66]

The *Tribune*, which had generally good theatrical coverage, confirmed the story of discovery by Pantages, with the omission of the middle man remembered by Baquet, Carl Walker.

> Last week at Vernon, during the progress of the Cross-Rivers engagement, Alex Pantages discovered a new vaudeville attraction, a colored ragtime band with a style of comedy-music all their own. The vaudeville magnate believes he has secured a unique attraction, and to try the public opinion of the act before sending it over the circuit will present the band here as an added attraction with the week's show.[67]

Perhaps if the preliminary bout was as uninspired as Harry Carr of the *Times* thought, the band came as welcome relief, one the audience was happy to keep in the ring while waiting for a fight the outcome of which *The Announcer* had suggested was predetermined. (In fact, the prediction was incorrect: Leach Cross won by decision in the full twenty rounds.)

This is a pretty and a credible story, but Mrs. Armontine Palao, James Palao's widow, recalled an incident when the woman for whom she worked, a Mrs. Kimball, whose husband managed the Moreland truck factory, had a picnic and hired her husband's band in order to give them some public exposure.[68] Nothing came of this, apparently, so Mrs. Kimball arranged then for them to appear in the ring at a boxing match and invited all the newspapermen to come and hear them. The next day, she said, "all the papers had open eyes to musicians, they'd never heard music like this before." How this account relates to the "received version" as it came from Baquet is hard to say. Which boxing match was it, and when? Did Pantages hear the band more than once, and so forth? Did he perhaps hear the quartet prior to the arrival of the additional players from New Orleans? Mrs. Palao was under the impression that one boxer was Gene Tunney, a fighter "who didn't fight no colored boys." Tunney, who was born in 1898, would hardly have been fighting heavyweight bouts in 1914; but it's conceivable that Leach Cross had such a restrictive policy in his choice of opponents.

At this point the vaudeville history of the group begins and will be found in the next four chapters. It might be useful to step back and summarize this "pre-history."

The main points that emerge are that there was an important sortie made from New Orleans to Gulfport and Hattiesburg, most likely in 1907. After a brief interval, Bill Johnson organized another band involving some of the same musicians; this began a relatively lengthy barnstorming tour to California, playing in the intervening states of Texas, New Mexico, and Arizona. This extended in all probability into 1908. It seems likely, lacking evidence to the contrary, that these earlier groups provided dance and entertainment music but were not a theatrical act with the proviso that African-American musicians were, in my opinion, expected to offer singing, dancing, and comic interplay along with their dance music. One need only remember the newspaper report of the Tuncel band's appearance at the Neely department store in Hattiesburg. There is also nothing to indicate that the groups of Afro-American musicians mentioned here — Tuncel's Big Four String Band, the Imperial orchestra, and the string band at Tom Anderson's — were the only ones to begin to spread the New Orleans manner of playing ragtime. I'm inclined to think, however, that they didn't go outside the South.

It seems clear that there was never any concerted decision to form a large group and attempt to crack big-time vaudeville. The nucleus of the band — the Johnsons, Norwood Williams, and James Palao — went to California at different times and for different reasons, only some of them, perhaps, musical ones. The best-trained and most versatile musician, Palao, joined forces with Bill Johnson, a gregarious and resourceful manager with considerable musical experience (he was forty years old already), and invited Keppard, Baquet, and Vincent to join them in the spring of 1914.

Most indications are that the chief drawing card of the group, at the beginning and for the duration of their vaudeville career, was ragtime music played in a recognizable New Orleans style. Nonetheless, they were to present themselves as a traditional plantation darky act. Armontine Palao, the wife of the leader of the band, said that she only saw the band in action once, when they were at the start of their career. She was distressed by the fact that they were dressed like field hands, overalls, straw hats, and red bandannas. As good as they were, she said, they shouldn't have had to dress that way. If we are to believe Baquet, this was their own choice. But the "choice" was hardly completely free; one doubts that they could have succeeded in any other way than by embracing the plantation formula.

In retrospect, this choice was momentous so far as their place in history is concerned. The reputation of the Original Dixieland Jazz Band was based on its brand of hot dance music, not on the performers' abilities as all-around vaudeville entertainers. Otherwise put, the product of the ODJB, enhanced by the superlative recording technique of the Victor engineers, could be disseminated in a matter of months to millions of dancers. The Creole Band on the other hand, beginning as a New Orleans dance orchestra transplanted to California, attained national fame as a vaudeville act, which, although seen and heard by many thousands of persons, was perceived in a quite different way. Most important of all, its music couldn't be played over and over again on the wind-up phonograph, and even studied by slowing it down.

3 The First Season

THE REACTION OF Alexander Pantages to the band's audition at his Pantages Theater is surely the stuff of showbiz legend. One imagines him exclaiming in a Greek-accented English: "You boys are terrific. I don't care what kind of act you make up, I've got to have that music"[1]—only a slight dramatization of Baquet's story as given in the preceding chapter. But we have yet to hear from a major witness to the band's career, Henry Morgan Prince, who as "Old Joe" (or "Old Black Joe") was the much-appreciated singer and dancer with the group. What follows, although composed as an objective account, summarizes a 1959 interview with Prince.

Morgan and Ollie Prince returned to the United States in late 1913 after their lengthy tour with Hugo's Minstrels and began singing at the Lester Social Club in San Francisco,[2] then moved to Los Angeles and a gig at McKee's Cafe on Main Street. McKee's was a quite fashionable cabaret, and around the same time the Princes were performing there young Ferde Grofé made what must be one of his earliest appearances in an important venue.

Prince heard Bill Johnson's band playing an advertising job in the street—possibly on a truck—for a dollar a man: he had never heard anything like their music before. He thought they would make a good act together and might return to Australia; accordingly, he gave them lessons in singing, presumably in four-part harmony, and in general stage appearance.

When the bout between Joe Rivers and Leach Cross was announced for the Vernon arena, Prince requested permission from Jack Doyle for the band to appear in the ring. Permission granted, the band performed to wild applause and more than $200 in tips thrown into the ring. By a lucky accident, Ed Fisher and Carl Walker, both assistant managers for the vaudeville tycoon Alexander Pantages, were there and so impressed by the band that they invited them to come to Pantages' office at 10 the next morning.

3.1 Henry Morgan Prince instructing the chicken that might be considered the eighth member of the troupe. For those skeptics who wonder just how one goes about the task, let me suggest Marian Breland and Robert E. Bailey, "How to Train a Chicken," http://vein.library.usyd.edu.au/links/Trainingchicken.pdf. [Prince scrapbook]

They rehearsed all night long in preparation for their 10 a.m. appointment. (Instead of Oklahoma Bob Albright in the office, as in the Baquet version, it was the famous—and outrageous—Eva Tanguay.) Pantages offered them a contract as a solo act, although for a moment there was some question that they might play behind Tanguay for her tour.

The management bought them "decent" costumes and the "following Monday"—which would have been August 17—they went to the Bushnell photo studio, where six different poses were taken, one of them with a rooster that was to figure in the act. These photographs did not include the one of the band in evening clothes, which has been published many times over and discussed at length in the previous chapter, since it was obviously intended as publicity for a dance band: white tie and tails, and the phone number where they could be reached on the drum head. Besides, it was taken by the Empire studio in Los Angeles.[3]

It seems probable that the Bushnell studio photographed the band in its "de-

Back Again By Request of Hundreds of Lyric Patrons
The Original New Orleans

CREOLE BAND

That Unchallenged Aggregation of Colored Singers, Dancers, Comedians and Instrumentalists, the "Daddy" of all Jazz Musical Organizations, in the Unique and Delightful Comedy Skit, "Uncle Eph's Birthday."

Oh-h-h Man! How They Do Rag!!

3.2 Three depictions of the Creole Band: (a) is found only in the Rocky Ford, Colorado, *Gazette* for December 1, 1916; (b) was masked and cropped for an ad in the *Indianapolis Sunday Star* for May 30, 1915; (c), a drawing made from (a), was used a number of times, with this version, again from the *Indianapolis Sunday Star*, December 2, 1917.

cent costumes," either in the studio or possibly on stage at the Pantages Theater, given the presence of the log cabin. This shot was subsequently utilized in several ways. In the source photograph my eyes detected the ghost image of a guitarist between the bassist and the old man—this is, however, not evident in the reproduction here, and I can't imagine why he would have been removed.

Bill Johnson's less copious remarks about the band's discovery supported both Baquet and Prince. He remembered that Carl Walker—correctly designating him as manager of the Pantages theater—"got a fellow to teach the Creole band to sing in a quartet for two months," that both Walker and Pantages were at the fight, and that it was the latter who sent a note addressed to Johnson, as "Manager of the Band," requesting that he come to Pantages's office the next morning at 10:30. The proposal made was satisfactory to Johnson—although not the salary initially offered—but he felt that he needed to consult the other musicians.

We must wonder if the fellow who taught them to sing was Morgan Prince. It is quite remarkable that neither Johnson nor Baquet refer to him even if only to deny him a role in the organization or stage training of the band—something for which Johnson claimed entire credit. That he was acting as manager for the band is undeniable, given the evidence of the business card describing him as "manager and bass violinist," and giving the address and phone number of his cigar store.

The most drastic conflict is between the romanticized "lucky break" story (more or less serendipitous discovery and ad hoc construction of an act by putting their heads together) and the other, in which Carl Walker enlisted the help of Morgan Prince in grooming the band for stage work, perhaps also introducing them at the minor four-round bouts put on weekly by Doyle. In point of fact, this is the version supported by the review of their maiden appearance in the *Record*, which is cited below.

It may be that Alex Pantages was more directly involved than Prince or Johnson asserts. He had arrived in Los Angeles on Friday, July 24, at 8 p.m. while on an automobile tour and proceeded without delay to catch the show at his Los Angeles theater.[4] He could well have been at any fights between then and August 11. In any event, more than one press release credited him with the discovery of this exciting new act.

Interested as he may have been, Pantages was not naive enough to book the untried group around the circuit without some trial. Accordingly, they were placed beginning Monday, August 17[5] as an "added attraction" at the Los Angeles Pantages Theater on Broadway, along with the acts already scheduled and "the usual comedy motion pictures," possibly a Keystone two-reeler. The ads billed them as "The Original New Orleans Orchestra and Rag-Time Band"; reviewers used permutations of these words, sometimes adding "Creole" to the mix, such as "the New Orleans Creole Rag-time Band." Such variation in nomenclature was the norm throughout their career.

The *Tribune* takes the prize for printing freshly minted copy straight from the Pantages publicity writers, beginning on Monday with the following:

> Last week at Vernon, during the progress of the Cross-Rivers engagement, Alex Pantages discovered a new vaudeville attraction, a colored ragtime band with a style of comedy-music all their own. The vaudeville magnate believes he has secured a unique attraction, and to try the public opinion of the act before sending it over the circuit, will present the band here as an added attraction with this week's show.[6]

But two days later, there appeared in its columns a blurb more stupefying in its hyperbole and overheated adjectives than the band was ever again to receive. It's difficult to imagine that the paper, as well as the *Oakland Enquirer*, which printed exactly the same copy three weeks later, was willing to devote so much space to this milestone of verbosity without a monetary quid pro quo from the Pantages office. The reader will, I hope, pardon my including the bulk of the text below:

COLORED OCTET AT BROADWAY HOUSE MAKES HIT OF SEASON WITH STUNTS

> . . . you will hear music made to be laughed at: weird nerve-tickling harmonies dispensed by a colored octet. The serious musician who has not been long time dead will writhe beneath his monumental marble should these uncultured strains penetrate so far, but the live ones who patronize vaudeville shows will cling desperately to life while it holds such attractions as the New Orleans Ragtime Band. The colored players despise anything else than ragtime, and their interpretation is so suited to the spirit of that musical excrescence that when they play Mandalay one really believes "Mandalay to be an island far away," and almost hears the Mandalasiatic tomcats carolling on the cornices of the pagodas.
>
> This band is an institution, distinct, different, indescribable. In operation its thermal variations wander from the lilting love song of the midnight coyote to the crooning of the new-born calf in the alfalfa patch. The very instruments assume new personalities. The staid and dignified bass viol does a tee-to-tum, flaps its wings and clarions a challenge to every feathered chanticleer in the corral. The cornet forgets its ancient and honorable origin and meanders madly through the melody, falsetto, throat and chest register, squeaking like a clarinet with laryngitis, jabbering like an intoxicated baboon, and blaring like an elephant amuck.
>
> The clarinet squeaks, squawks and squirms, and the trombone, whose business is clawing, becomes a howling musical maniac. The colored octet furnishes these specialties concurrently, and, consequently, da capo, and del signo, forte, sixty, and

mirabile dictu. They are the hit of the Pantages show. There are plenty of musicians in the world, but if anybody else is furnishing this unclassified brand of delirium, the vaudeville scouts have not discovered the fact.

There are seven other numbers on the Pantages stage this week, but the best remembered will be the New Orleans Ragtime Band.[7]

Much as one may be inclined to dismiss this, except as an object lesson in rhetorical excess, there are at least several details that may actually describe what the band did. First, the publicist wrote, "when they play Mandalay one really believes "Mandalay to be an island far away." In fact, the chorus of Fred Fisher's song "I'm On My Way to Mandalay" has the immortal couplet "Oh, let me live and love for aye, / On that Island far away;" (The exotic land of the Johns and Rogers song "In Far Off Mandalay" is no island and uses no such language.) Second, it's by no means unlikely that Bill Johnson—he would have been pleased to have been mentioned first—twirled his bass, and that Keppard exhibited the extended range that is often mentioned by those who heard him at a later date.

The other papers were laconic yet descriptive. On Wednesday, the *Examiner* said:

> these are the real Creole musicians from New Orleans, and one has to hear them to appreciate what rag-time really is. Their combination of bass viol, guitar, violin, clarinet, cornet and trombone is the right one for the lively rag-time and it was impossible for one to sit quiet while they were playing. They also sing "Old Black Joe" and "Old Kentucky Home."

None of the other papers—except one—stress the instruments or ragtime, although the *Evening Herald* mentions the two Stephen Foster melodies. The *Graphic* reviewer was impressed by the "rapid fire of noise and action" of a unique act.[8]

The *Los Angeles Record* review of August 18 not only lends strong support to the band's having played at Doyle's a number of times prior to the Cross-Rivers bout, but it singles out Fred Keppard in a manner never again encountered in their entire vaudeville career. The excerpt here presented begins at the very start of the review:

> The cornet player with the famous Creole band, appearing this week at Pantages', scored a dictinct [*sic*] hit with the theater-goers last night and the New Orleans orchestra responded to several encores.
>
> This orchestra has been performing at the famous "Honest Jack" Doyle's Friday night boxing shows, where the boxing fans accorded them a warm welcome, and

it is probable that they will make a tour of the Pantages circuit, following their success at the local theater. All members of the company were well received, but the cornet player in particular came in for a rousing round of applause.

Steve Corola has a worth-while band in this outfit.[9]

Armontine Palao went to hear the band for the first and only time during their maiden engagement; they were in shirt sleeves, with red bandanas around their necks. (Later, they were to go the whole way, wearing overalls, straw hats, and so forth.) According to her daughter, she was disgusted with the way they had to dress. She felt that "as good as they were, they should have been more dignified."[10]

The week of August 24 is a blank.[11] Possibly the band was sent to Pasadena, Fresno, or Sacramento. Bill Johnson recalled being scheduled to take one of the two ships, "Harvard" or "Yale," that made the regular run between Los Angeles and San Francisco; but, he said, Keppard missed the boat, so they were obliged to take a freighter once they found him.[12]

The band—advertised as New Orleans Ragtime Band—opened at the San Francisco Pantages on Sunday, August 30, with Charles J. Carter, "Man of Mystery"; Bob Albright, "the Male Melba"; Nadje, "the Vassar Girl"; Ross & Sunnen; and Ed Howard & Company in "Those Were Happy Days." Curiously, perhaps, both Bill Johnson and Morgan Prince remembered working beside Bob Albright, also known as "the Oklahoma Cowboy." I've not succeeded in finding anything but the briefest of mentions in the press: the *Examiner*'s attention was devoted at some length to the show at the Orpheum, saying about the show at the Pantages merely "A Creole band is a feature."

The next week at the Oakland Pantages at Twelfth and Broadway, the band fared somewhat better. The *Enquirer* published the maniacal blurb already given *in extenso* above. The advance copy in the *Tribune* was more temperate, to say the least, reiterating Pantages' personal role in their discovery:

> Manager Pantages is personally responsible for the discovery of the big scream of the bill. It is that of the original New Orleans Creole Orchestra, an octet of ragtime near musicians and colored comedians who are said to evoke strains of melody that would make a real musician return from the land of shades, however they make people laugh and so accomplish the result aimed at.

As in the more fulsome review, music is emphasized, despite the hardly complimentary "near musicians." That the orchestra is said to be an octet may simply mean that in this maiden outing Bill's young half brother, Ollie "Dink" Johnson, was still playing drums with them. It is said that Pantages was in the long run reluctant to pay for an extra man—a view that must strike us as rather odd, given the central importance of the drum set to jazz as it was to develop. The *Tribune's* reaction on Monday was laconic, although complimentary: ". . . one of the biggest hits Manager Pantages has ever produced." The great adventure was about to begin.

An exceptionally interesting memory of Bill Johnson and his band was collected during the 1950s from pianist Sid LeProtti. He had begun his career as a musician ca. 1903, working in Oakland, Purisima (perhaps the famous mission near Lompoc), Angel's Camp, and Salinas. After the earthquake, he began working in San Francisco at Lew Purcell's So Different Cafe on the Barbary Coast. The following passage comes from a tape-recorded interview rather than the transcription published by Tom Stoddard in *Jazz on the Barbary Coast*:

> *Interviewer*: Sid, about what year was it that you switched over to the New Orleans type of instrumentation?
>
> *LaProtti*: It was 'long about nineteen hundred and [long pause] twelve.
>
> *Interviewer*: Had Will Johnson's band been up there at that time?
>
> *LaP*: Yeah, he'd been here and then later on come King Oliver's band. I think Will Johnson . . . like in here says that . . . name some of the first New Orleans jazz bands, but Will Johnson was the first one that I ever heard of when he went east and come out here. Quite a character, he was real light. I don't ever remember seeing a cigar lit, chewin' it and he played the bass fiddle with a glove on it, see, and we out here West was kinda 'mazed to see a man pick a bass. We know that in symphony orchestras and theater orchestras the pickin' was generally what they call pizzicatta on the bass, see, and to see him pick it like that and that's where I got the idea. I listened and I says to the fellas "You know that old [illustrates at the piano with a standard "oom-pah" accompaniment] I said, "you know we got to get it [plays r.h. quarter-note chords over the same bass, but now also in quarter-notes]" Four beat! bum bum bum bum bum bum bum. See, I can hear that rhythm. I can hear the difference in the rhythm which was changin' them days, see. Now they play the two beat and they play it , errr, well, I think a little more solid than we did in them days.[13]

The critical move in this change of musical style was getting rid of drummer Pete Stanley, who had come up through minstrel bands before the turn of the century, replacing him with George Huddleson, a much younger four-beat drummer. There was also a change of instrumentation from the orchestra at Lew Purcell's in 1914, which had Stanley on drums, Adam Mitchell (clarinet), Gerald Wells (flute), Roy Taborn (euphonium), and LeProtti, a decidedly idiosyncratic combination of instruments, to the band that he took into the

Portola-Louvre after the Barbary Coast closed down ca. July, 1915. The Creole Band was in Oakland and San Francisco in September and December 1914; and again in October 1916. I'm inclined to believe that Sid heard Bill Johnson in 1914, rather than later.[14]

A word about the Greek immigrant Alexander Pantages (1871–1936) and his theaters. He was an interesting character—many of the vaudeville magnates were, to be sure—a living embodiment of the rags-to-riches American dream, whose fortune began as a waiter in a Klondike honky-tonk. As the Gold Rush simmered down, he settled in Seattle as the proprietor of a shoe-shine parlor cum fruit stand, next to the Sullivan & Considine Theater. In short order, he had created the first links in a chain of theaters that was eventually to cover the West Coast, then into western Canada and as far east as Kansas City.[15]

He had a reputation for bypassing agents and booking acts directly. The contracts he negotiated were not always completely on the up and up, however. *Variety* in 1915 reported "the Pantages office usually routes an act for 12 or 14 weeks stipulating in the contract from one to four towns will be played at two-thirds of the regular salary. [T]he 'cut' weeks generally depend upon the business sagacity of the contracting parties."[16]

Be that as it may, it is interesting that the *Freeman* had reported the following in 1910:

Alex Pantages has opened up a new house here and promises the people of Los Angeles a good legitimate show and also promises to book all of the colored acts that he can get so all the good colored performers that want some western time can find Mr. Pantages in Seattle as he has a good string of houses in nearly every city in California and some eastern cities.[17]

In this connection, it's worth pointing out that he was willing to book Roscoe "Fatty" Arbuckle after the murder trial that made him box-office poison. One could say that however questionable some of his business machinations may have been, Pantages had a laudable sympathy for the underdog.

The "Pantages time" was not considered big-time vaudeville, as defined by the Keith and Orpheum circuits; he had no theaters in the large Eastern cities and consequently his acts would not automatically get career-advancing reviews in *Variety* or the *Clipper*. Still, although locked in an ongoing struggle with the Sullivan & Considine chain in the Western United States, he was a major force and some success on the Pantages circuit might well serve as a stepping stone to more prestigious chains. All this is relative of course: what might seem small-time to a Caucasian act could reasonably be regarded by black performers as having arrived.

Looking at the dates when his lavish new theaters were constructed, it seems that Pantages had by 1910 entered into a phase of major expansion. By the end of 1914, his empire reached from Manitoba to the Pacific coast and back again to Salt Lake City, with theaters in Winnipeg, Edmonton, Calgary, Victoria and Vancouver in Canada; then Spokane, Seattle, Tacoma, Portland, San Francisco, Oakland, San Diego, and Salt Lake City.

There may have been other theaters under Pantages control at this time, Fresno and Sacramento for example. And a map in the special Christmas edition of the *Missouri Breeze* in 1913 indicates by stars on a large map of the United States the following cities in addition to those already named: Pasadena, Colorado Springs, Pueblo, St. Joseph, Kansas City and Joplin, and possibly Minneapolis, Racine and Beloit, and Dixon, Ill. Finally, Cincinnati and New York City are shown; perhaps there were booking offices in those cities.[18]

Some of the Pantages theaters were large and elaborate. For example, the Oakland Pantages, built in 1912 at a cost of $250,000, held 2,000 seats. The San Francisco Pantages, completed at the end of 1911, was only slightly smaller, with 1,700 seats. Next came the houses in Portland and Edmonton at 1,400, with the smallest perhaps being the Calgary Pantages with a mere 900 seats, close, one would think, to the lower limit for profitability.

Most Pantages houses played three a day: afternoon, early evening and night show. Together with a film, five or six acts would easily fill two hours. The ticket prices were not onerous. The afternoon show cost a mere 10 or 15 cents; in the evening admission was 15 or 25 cents. The top price in both afternoon and evening would sometimes be higher, but at any rate always affordable in the less expensive seats.

No doubt due to the particular difficulties of rail transport and the long distances to be traversed, Pantages generally made a practice of putting together road shows, or bundles of acts, that traveled as a unit around the circuit. Thus the Creole Band found itself in the company of a relatively elaborate juvenile act titled "Yesterdays," headed by Frances Clare and Guy Rawson, accompanied by six chorus girls;[19] Arthur Whitlaw, an Irish monologist; Roy and Anna Harrah, dancing on roller skates; and McConnell & Niemeyer in a song-and-dance act with a strong baseball number at the end. While five acts are not generous by the normal standards of the time, I suppose that Clare, Rawson & Co. made up for the brevity by holding the stage for half an hour or more.

From Oakland, it took the five acts a week to get to Winnipeg, where they opened on Sunday, September 20, with the band as "a special closing feature." Winnipeg was at that time a city of around 135,000, but far more important than its actual population would indicate. It was one of the leading grain markets of North America and the site of the Western offices of most of Canada's manufacturing, commercial, and financial organizations.[20] Bill Johnson recalled that they paraded up and down the streets in a wagon.

On Monday, the leading newspaper, the *Manitoba Free Press*, had little to say: "the oddity of the bill is the New Orleans Creole Musicians, a collection of colored performers on various instruments who temper with a pretty touch of pathos the singing of the old time darky songs." A close second in the circulation race, the *Winnipeg Telegram* was more verbose: "Some real old time southern melody, offered by the New Orleans Creole musicians, is a most welcome diversion from the usual run of ragtime and present day songs . . . most acceptable to the patrons. These people have a style all their own and their music is most pleasing in that it is just a little different from the customary offering." The theme of "just a little different" surfaces in the brief comment by the reviewer of the *Tribune*: ". . . the New Orleans Creole Musicians play some weird instruments in a wonderful way." Finally the weekly *Saturday Post* commented: "The Creole Musicians from New Orleans display a nice sense of lilting rhythm in their variegated selection of old time melodies for voice and old-fashioned instruments. This is quite an interesting turn."

To these might be added the reactions reported in the *Missouri Breeze*, a Chicago show business weekly intended for professionals. Characteristically for such papers, the mentions are terse in the extreme. First we read "New Orleans Creole Musicians; style all their own; comedian very good," then elsewhere a comment from W. B. Lawrence, the manager of the Pantages: "best all-round show for some time."[21]

Evidently these reviewers didn't quite know what to make of such exotic musicians. No doubt they had seen their share of "plantation acts" devoted to the recycling of "old time darky songs" and long-whiskered minstrel show routines. This was something more, obviously, but exactly what was not easy for them to say.

The traditional part of the band's act can be described in some detail, thanks to accounts by both H. Morgan Prince and Bill Johnson. Although small details may have changed over the band's four-year career, the evidence of countless reviews points to its remaining the same in essentials. According to Johnson, the act began with the playing of "the Gypsy," Bill's name for Abe Olman's intermezzo "Egyptia" (see above) before or while the moon rose and the stars shone. This was a solo feature for the clarinet, and as such was remembered many years later by Sidney Bechet and his friend John Reid, as "Egyptian Fantasy." A steamboat's arrival was announced, a whistle was sounded in the wings, they unloaded the boat, humming the tune "Swanee

River" (i.e., "Old Folks at Home"). An old man in blackface—Uncle Joe—came out of his cabin; it was his birthday and the band serenaded him. This warmed his old bones to the point that he danced a vigorous buck and wing. There was a chicken involved in the act, which sometimes escaped into the audience.

More detail is provided by Morgan Prince, who, to be sure, considered the act to be his creation. It was a typical "plantation scene," with a cotton field, a cornfield, and a river depicted. On stage left were a log cabin and a church; there was a gourd of moonshine hanging on the cabin. As the curtain rose slowly, the band arrived in an old car, playing "some tune from New Orleans." Then the moon rose, thanks to a "moon box," stars appeared in the sky, and a boat passed on the river.

Bill Johnson would ask loudly for "Uncle Joe." After much commotion, old Uncle Joe came out of the log cabin and said, "Why all this noise?" Bill Johnson answered that the band was looking for Uncle Joe so that they could serenade him on his birthday. Then they sang and played "Old Black Joe." The old man, wearing a Prince Albert coat—no doubt somewhat tattered—wept with emotion, and the rooster crowed. At this point, Morgan Prince would dance to a wild band rendition of "Ballin' the Jack." Prince remembered that the trombone player—not recalling his name, apparently—moved the slide with his foot.

During this first trip around the Pantages circuit, however, the band seems not to have had the "special scenery" that Prince said was made in Kansas City for them, and which so often receives admiring mention in later reviews. However, the basic plantation setting and the conceit of playing music so exciting that even decrepit Uncle Joe finds that he can cut a buck and wing like a youngster can easily be imagined without the elaborate set pieces that they were to have constructed.

To determine how far back "old man" impersonations go would be a project in itself. Suffice it to say that the theme of the "old darky" was enshrined in the famous songs of Stephen Foster: "Old Uncle Ned" (1848)—deceased but fondly remembered, as the text of the song makes clear—but, first and foremost, "Old Black Joe" (1860)—not yet dead but moribund. We marvel today at the collective delusion that not only did slaves live a long life, they also looked back through rose-colored glasses to their days serving "old massa." (Cf. Foster's "Massa's in the Cold, Cold Ground" from 1852.) But the nostalgic melancholy of Foster's songs is only one facet of the "old man's" personality. It also suited the purposes of the minstrel stage to show that there could be life in the old geezer yet.

The *Indianapolis Freeman* of September 23, 1916, published a death notice of the famous comedian Billy (William Francis) Johnson, 58 years of age (thus born in 1858), whose first show business appearance was with Hyatt's Minstrels in 1881, with "his own song The Trumpet in the Cornfield Blows, an old man speciality and stick dance of which he was the originator." Presumably, this other Johnson had one noteworthy version of this stereotypical role; repeated references in the press make it clear that the old man role was extremely common.

The show moved on to Edmonton for the week of September 27. There the *Daily Bulletin* saw fit to mention a nearly correct instrumentation—citing mandolin instead of Norwood Williams's guitar—while labeling the musicians in the time-honored and patronizing fashion as "half a dozen culle'd gentlemen." Once again "Old Black Joe" is cited as one of the songs, along with "My Old Kentucky Home." When the same paper reminded its readers of the Pantages show on Thursday, it had a lapse of memory: "The curtain rises on a barn yard scene in Virginia with five dusky lads from the south playing a 'rag' on their various instruments." In any event, the applause was described as "prolonged and sincere."

The *Journal* sent a pseudonymous (one hopes) "Marmaduke" to cover the show in his column "In the Footlight Glow." His lead paragraph read:

> The favorite at the opening performance of the week at Pantages did not have much to travel on, but so long as they pleased the crowd they can hardly be expected to worry. The Creole Band, which was given tumultuous applause, made a lot of noise, but that was all it was. The ordinary admirer of band music would much prefer the Newsboys' organization. The old colored gentleman who sang "Massa's in the Cold, Cold Ground" and "My Old Kentucky Home" had a passable voice, but the songs themselves carried him along.

This, at least, does not come either directly from the Pantages publicity office or small-town paraphrasers. But however much Marmaduke's delicate ears may have been insulted by their "noise," the public loved it—and so, presumably, did Alex Pantages.[22]

The next week's review in Calgary's *Morning Albertan* introduced a new point of view:

> The New Orleans Creole Musicians have combined odds and ends of talent with unusual personality. This band of ragtime musicians is composed of mulattos and quadroons of distinctive types. Their numbers include the popular rags and a few old plantation melodies in oddly assorted variety. They are both amusing and entertaining.

Although not entirely accurate—Prince and Vincent were rather dark-skinned —the observation is interesting as an indication that the band did not "black up," or at least not always. Prince, however, in his role of "Old Uncle Joe" would presumably have done so. It's also worth attention that the reviewer found that they had "unusual personality" and were "distinctive types" in a kind of entertainment that emphasized personality to the nth degree.

SHORT ESSAY ON READING REVIEWS

Hours of immersion in the jargon of vaudeville publicists—as well as the local scriveners who imitated them—induce a profound malaise which, oddly perhaps, becomes one of the touchstones for identifying reviews that are actually by a real person and about something real that happened on the stage. On reading them, one wakes from a stupor as if jolted by an electric shock. Such reviews are not always complimentary; they may in fact be quite churlish, but all the better for the historian.

Bookers and agents were, I am sure, not unappreciative of good reviews that also say something specific and useful to *us* in reconstructing the career of the band. Nonetheless, given the mysterious springs of public approval and theatrical magic alike, it was really enough that the act "got over," who cared how. Thus, it is amazing how brief the notices of the Creole Band were at times, sometimes a single word will do, that is, "pleased," as in the shortest notices of the *Missouri Breeze*.

A general practice of bribery is assumed to pervade the reviewing of theatrical attractions, particularly perhaps in the world of vaudeville. Money could change hands, of course, or perhaps expensive dinners or a new suit might do the job. Further, for the urban dailies, some part of their income flowed from the theatrical ads, often quite tiny for most of the week, to be somewhat compensated by quite sizeable display ads on Saturdays or Sundays. It would not do to displease the local manager or the home office. And on occasion one notes the absence of ads for a particular theater, quite likely the result of some negative publicity.

Another factor needs to be mentioned, accounting for the brevity or noncommital character of some vaudeville notices. If a performer played split weeks, as was quite common in areas where quick and reliable transportation existed, and especially if he played in the first half of the week, opening on Monday (sometimes Sunday), it would be almost pointless to bother printing much of anything about the act. By the time the Tuesday evening paper hit the stands, there might be only one day more of performances.

Additionally, the fact that the Creole Band was not only a recycling of traditional plantation routines but a contemporary and creative musical expression offers a problem to reviewers. The description of music is a difficult task in any event, requiring either a technical vocabulary that would be Greek to the average reader, or metaphors or descriptive language that, although it might mean something to a broad public, are difficult for the trained musician to attach to any specific musical techniques or devices. In any event, none of our reviews even begin to use the first approach, and rarely bother with the second. The appeal of the band's ragtime was powerful and direct . . . which of course is what mattered.

One other aspect of the publicity machinery can be mentioned here. It was obviously a common practice for the booking offices to provide halftone cuts for publication. These would appear unpredictably and singly from Monday to Friday, sometimes it seems merely to fill space. On weekend theatrical pages, however, there would often be quite elaborate collages of photographs of performers of the coming week. I know of only four instances in which the Creole Band had its photograph printed in a local newspaper. Given the hundreds of performances and the popularity of the act this can hardly be ascribed to chance. To make a long story short: I assume that many readers would have been displeased to have their daily rag besmirched by photographs of Negroes—uncomplimentary caricatures, as in the *Los Angeles Tribune*, of course, would be chuckled at.

The presence of African-Americans on the vaudeville stage often seems to have unleashed a flood of clichés, clichés going back several generations at least. First and foremost is the notion that the interest of a colored act lies in being "characteristic" in the nineteenth-century sense: that is, in its success at conveying qualities—characteristics—assumed to be true of African-Americans as they had been defined by antebellum servitude. Although the modern Negro, as molded by urban life, with his sharp dress, his razors, and his propensity for gambling, was well known in the lyrics and covers of the coon songs of the 1890s, this was fodder for vaudeville only to the extent that it could be made comic.

For the "Negro," slave or contemporary American, was above all comic. Think, after all, of the early cylinder recordings of George Johnson—African-American in fact—or Billy Golden, one of the best-known "negro delineators," to borrow a term from the dawn of blackface minstrelsy. They laugh uproariously, hysterically. Second, he was melodious, songful. The acceptance of the Fisk Jubilee Singers, the Hyer sisters, Black Patti, and eventually more high-toned singers like Harry Burleigh, is symptomatic of the notion that "the Negro" is adept at song because he or she is a child of nature whose natural feelings have not been corrupted, repressed, by civilization. Third, he is rhythmic by nature; when you hear his music, your feet just can't stay still.

What he is *not* in this way of thinking is truly creative. He can imitate, "ape," to use an opprobrious word, the actions of his betters with amazing quickness and skill, but he cannot innovate, cannot invent. Thus while a black musician may perform with great facility, you couldn't expect him to *compose*. That much of this network of prejudices is self-serving, functioning to maintain the social status of the dominant majority, is sadly obvious. Of course, these matters have been discussed time and time again; I offer this quick summary in order that we be mindful of some home truths in reading the reviews of the remarkable "colored act" that was the Creole Band.

These early reviews have been quoted at such considerable length for a purpose, at first to set the stage by passing in review the usual clichés stimulated by the band's appearance, a mishmash of phrases culled from the advance publicity, of conventional stereotypes, and from time to time a remark that tells us something about their actual behavior. As we trace their progress around the country, only reviews that add something to our knowledge, or provide evidence for a point in doubt, will henceforth be cited *in extenso*.

The week of October 11 was spent in transit between Calgary and Spokane. There were several choices for traversing the Continental Divide. The northernmost was the Great Northern line passing though the Blackfoot reservation and Glacier Park at Maria's Pass. To the south, one could take the Northern Pacific going through Helena and crossing the Rockies at McDonald Pass, more than a mile high. The former of these offered the more direct route to Spokane. Can one imagine the thrill for these neophyte vaudevillians, born and bred in New Orleans, where 20 feet above sea level is a significant elevation?

Spokane was a booming city—the only one of consequence in eastern Washington—about the size of Winnipeg, with a Pantages theater seating 1,200. On Sunday, when the troupe opened, there were four shows; for the rest of the week, three a day. The reviewer for the *Spokesman-Review* found their manner of doing plantation melodies a "change from the ordinary run of band and orchestral music." As often was the case, H. Morgan Prince was singled out for praise, as usual without mentioning his name.

Seattle was another matter, with a bylined review (J. Willis Sayre) that even mentioned the band in the subheadline: "Audiences Enjoy Merit of Clare & Rawson and Give Enthusiastic Recalls to Seven Negro Melodists." Pantages must have been even more delighted to read the text in the body of the article:

The New Orleans Creole Musicians took the house by storm, and won encore after encore. They are seven negroes. Six of them are instrumentalists, playing the slide trombone, cornet, clarinet, violin, guitar and bass viol respectively. Their quaint symphony orchestra struck the Pantages taste with a bang, and so did the singing and dancing of the principal, in an old man character. The ensembles singing also had the melody that only negroes can put into the simple ditties they have grown up on.

Grown up on, indeed!—as if these idealized songs of plantation life had anything to do with New Orleans. The players' heads must have swelled on reading these words, only to be brought down by learning that Morgan Prince was "the principal." I am sure this has something to do with the minimal importance of Prince in the later recollections of the others.

Of the reviews in the *Post-Intelligencer*, the first also mentions Morgan Prince, albeit in a subordinate position:

> The Creoles comprise a ragtime orchestra, the equal of which has seldom if ever appeared at this house. The organization is composed of six men, who coax really infectious ragtimey music from a bass fiddle, guitar, violin, clarinet, cornet and slide trombone. It also boasts, in addition, an old darkey whose singing and dancing is a decided comedy asset. The orchestra made a tremendous hit at the opening matinee.

In the Thursday review, the ostensible lead act (Frances Clare in "Yesterdays") had become an "also ran." The words on the band, while they repeat Monday's review to some degree, ignored Prince and include a quite remarkable and rarely encountered perception of the way the band played:

> In the New Orleans Creole Musicians and their ragtime orchestra, the extra added feature of the current bill at Pantages, the management of that theater claims to have an attraction that is not only a winner in every respect, but is unique as well.
>
> This orchestra, composed of a bass fiddle, guitar, violin, clarinet, cornet and slide trombone, plays ragtime music that no one ever heard before, but they play it in such a manner that they have the audience marking time from its beginning to end. No one of the members appears to play the same piece, but, as a whole, they turn out something that makes it hard to compel the feet to behave.

The *Star* was brief but made an explicit point that we did not doubt but nevertheless are happy to have confirmed: "A Creole Band of seven men score second, with Southern melodies and some catchy music that is not written down in books."[23]

Their next week's venue was Vancouver, British Columbia. There's not much to note about their reception with the exception of the notice in *The Daily Province*, the Vancouver daily with the largest circulation. It seems rather more musically perceptive than what we've seen so far:

> The New Orleans Creole Musicians scored the biggest kind of a hit yesterday with their characteristic playing of present day ragtime and old plantation ballads. They

constitute a remarkable orchestra and prove to be masters of syncopation. Their solo and chorus singing, however, is even more to be commended.[24]

The next stop—to the provincial capitol, Victoria—required a brief sea voyage, during which Bill Johnson recalled the band played for the entertainment of the passengers. My guess would be that the band played on many similar occasions for which there is no record, quite likely passing the hat for a little extra money. The Victoria press took no particular note of them, with the exception of the usual kudos for "the uncommonly good tenor voice" of the "old darky," that is, Morgan Prince once more. Playing during the same week at the Royal Victoria was Bill "Bojangles" Robinson, however, and that show attracted more publicity.

At Tacoma, beginning on the Monday matinee, November 16, the band's ragtime music set "the house shuffling," according to the *Daily News*. The reporter for the *Daily Ledger* made the same observation but had a bit more to say:

> The Seven "Creole" musicians were a riot. As a matter of fact, they appear to be colored men and not creoles, but their music hits the bullseye and they are masters of "barber shop" harmonies in their singing . . . the instrumental numbers have a lilt that would make a stone man want to shake his feet.[25]

One assumes that the writer of these lines thought of creoles in the sense promulgated by reactionary writers like Grace King, for whom the idea of "creoles" of mixed race was repugnant. To them, creoles were Caucasian descendants of original European settlers, usually French.

In Portland, where they opened on Monday, November 23 they were as big a hit as ever. Here, their coming was announced with copy that sounded an original, even unique, note:

> Direct from extraordinary triumphs at their native city, the New Orleans Creole musicians . . . special added attraction . . . the quaint dances of the old French stronghold also are truly depicted in a way that is certain to please, the act having historical value as well as being banner entertainment.[26]

Not only that, the display ad called them "America's Foremost Musicians." The Pantages office was working overtime, one has to think.

The Tuesday review in the *Evening Telegram* is more than a rehash of the Pantages publicity:

> The audience couldn't get enough from the Creole Band, composed of colored instrumentalists. This aggregation of colored chaps offer one selection after another

in rapid succession, giving new and old tunes, and they landed the biggest kind of a hit with the Pantages' patrons.[27]

A remarkable story from the *Oregon Daily Journal* shows that the "colored chaps" were happy to play at greater length than the twenty to thirty minutes they would have in a vaudeville performance. The headlines read "Fun Rages Rampant for Four Hours at Portland Press Club / Superb Program Keeps Audience at Highest Pitch of Enjoyment All Time / Creole Band Makes Hit. The account goes:

> Four solid hours of entertainment given in the rooms of the Portland Press Club . . . The occasion was the Thanksgiving jinks for the newspapermen and their friends, and it brought out a large number of prominent men, including both city and county officials . . . One of the biggest surprises of the evening was the appearance of the Orleans [*sic*] Creole band from the Pantages theatre. After hearing the band once, the audience would not let it go until the members had played every number they knew.
>
> They began with ragtime and finished with ragtime, though the selections that made the biggest hits were old southern melodies. Arthur Whitlaw, from the same theatre, told a number of funny stories before the Creole band was introduced.[28]

The trip from Portland to San Francisco was made by ocean vessel, apparently taking long enough that the week of November 29 is a blank. Neither the San Francisco engagement, beginning Sunday, December 6, nor the Oakland one, a week later, attracted much notice, despite four dailies in the former city and two in the latter.[29] It was recognized that it was a return engagement, the Oakland *Enquirer* even stating that it was "a return engagment . . . in a new number." One can hardly be certain, but it's plausible that playing the same locales at an interval of three months, the band would have revised the act somewhat.

Apparently some members of the band stayed in Oakland for this two-week period. James Palao sent a picture postcard to his wife, as from 1777 Tenth Street, Oakland—although the illustration on the front is "A Corner in the Hazelwood, Portland, Ore." The text reads:

> Dear Wife: This is the Hotel we where stoping at in Portland. I is now in Oakland and will open in Frisco Sunday. [If] you need any money, let me know as soon as you get this. Love from this husband. J. Palao

From the same address, Palao sent another picture postcard (of the state capitol in Sacramento):

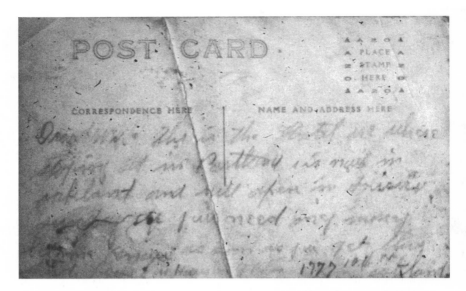

3.3 The descendants of Jimmy Palao have kept some two dozen of the postcards he wrote while on the road with the band. This depicts "a corner in the Hazelwood, Portland, Oregon." The message reads: "Dear Wife This is the Hotel we where stoping at in Portland i is now in oakland and will open in Frisco Sunday [if] you need any money let me know as soon as you get this Love from this husband J Palo 1777 Tenth Street Oakland." The date would be either the first week of December 1914 or the first week of October 1916.

3.4 The band as it was depicted in a spread for the Pantages theater in the Los Angeles *Record* for December 21, 1914.

Dear Cloddle [for Clotile, his eldest daughter]: Papa is on his way home, will have you on his lap soon, will be home on the 21th of this week.

And, indeed, the band opened the Los Angeles Pantages on Monday, December 21, just three months after their first tryout appearance. One suspects that here, too, the act was somewhat changed, since two of the local papers stress the amount of noise they produced. The *Times* was not exactly complimentary:

The New Orleans Ragtime Band is an outfit of brunette musicians who make up in volume for what they lack in finesse. They have a darky jig dancer who is really good, and their act is entertaining as well as commendably brief.

But the *Tribune* reviewer seemed not to mind:

Judging from the volume of applause that greeted it, the New Orleans Ragtime Band came under the wire first. That it made the biggest noise on the program will not be disputed . . .

The *Examiner*'s language particularly stressed the instrumental music, and for once did not single out Morgan Prince. The *Record* was terse but no less telling: "The New Orleans Ragtime band is one of the best things ever seen on the Pantages stage." Of no small importance was that *Variety* for the first time took notice of them: "Pantages . . . New Orleans Ragtime Band, entertaining."[30]

It must have been a happy Christmas at the homes of the band members;

they had obviously made it in show business, something one imagines they had never planned or expected. The money was more than respectable, $50 a week per man, according to Bill Johnson's recollection, when they would have to really struggle to make $20 a week in New Orleans. And just by comparison, the union scale weekly salary for a pit musician in a New York theater was around $35. Of course, with the deduction of living expenses on the road—I believe rail fare would have been taken care of by the Pantages office—and other charges, there was not all that much to send home.

There was more of the Pantages circuit to come, of course, but one suspects that some arrangements were underway for further touring in the East or Middle West. That they had special scenery made for them in Kansas City suggests that there was an agent on the scene who would bankroll the construction charges.

The week of December 28 was spent in San Diego, which at a population of 49,000 was one-tenth the size of Los Angeles, and far from the metropolis it has become. No reports are available for this engagement. Pantages shows at their next stop, Salt Lake City, ran from Wednesday to Tuesday, owing to the length of the jump from San Diego, thus January 6 through January 12. Multiple encores were again the order of the day.

The band proceeded to the Orpheum, Ogden, Utah, for Thursday and Friday only. The theater was designated in the ad as "Marcus Loew's Orpheum," and the other acts were totally different from the assemblage that had gone over the Pantages circuit from Winnipeg to Salt Lake City. There was a brief but telling note in the local paper:

> The original Creole band made a big hit in an appropriate stage setting. The aggregation consists of six instrumentals [sic], with something out of the ordinary in their selections and manner of playing, and expert buck and wing dancer.[31]

Since other evidence indicates that their special scenery was made in Kansas City, their next stop, I assume that the Ogden house had some kind of generic plantation drop. But possibly Pantages had provided them with an earlier version of the set for which they were later noted.

In 1959, Bill Johnson recalled having met Victoria Johnson in Ogden; she was a chambermaid in a hotel, some thirty years of age. He then married her ten months later in Ogden. So far as we can judge from the Creole Band's itinerary, Bill was in Ogden in January 1915, then again in November 1916. The interval between these two visits was substantially more than ten months. On the other hand, Bill probably spent some time in Salt Lake City after the Boston breakup in April 1917 and its resurrection in October, which corresponds with an interval of ten months. Inquiries to the Weber County office concerned—Ogden is the county seat—were unsuccessful in locating a marriage license in Bill's name, including the many possible variations. In any case, Bill's 1918 draft registration card designated Mayme Johnson (see above) as his wife, so the entire incident remains a mystery.

The jump to their next engagement in Kansas City was on the order of 1,400 miles and surely must have taken several days. At any event, they were advertised as opening at the Monday matinee, January 18, 1915, at the Hippodrome with six other acts. Kansas City boasted of at least four vaudeville theaters, with an Orpheum playing seven acts and the Orpheum travel weekly; Marcus Loew's Empress, with a similar program and the Globe with six acts and pictures, playing split weeks. The first two of these were clearly more prestigious than the Hippodrome. (During the same week, Bill "Bojangles" Robinson was at the Empress.)

According to an article written by Onah L. Spencer and published in 1941 under the melodramatic title "Trumpeter Freddie Keppard Walked Out on Al Capone!" Keppard received a telegram informing him of his mother's demise while in Salt Lake City in 1914. To quote Spencer:

> His reaction was normal—he got drunk. He went to sleep at an open train window and froze the entire left side of his face. His ear was as big as a baseball.
>
> But that didn't stop the show. Freddie went on with a poulticed and bandaged face. Next day, more drunk than ever, he fell down a flight of stairs, gashing his lower lip deeply. Yet, he played better and louder than ever that night.[32]

My suspicion is that Keppard's face indeed suffered frostbite but was incorrectly associated with his mother's death, which actually took place in 1916 (see chap. 5). This, combined with taking a header down the stairs might well have been behind the review in the *Ogden Standard*:

> Johnson's Creole Band must have been in a hurry last night to get somewhere, as its act was rather abbreviated. This created some dissatisfaction, the audience being in a mood to appreciate several more song and dance numbers. The band has plenty of talent and its short program made a big hit.[33]

This is the only time a newspaper report complained about the brevity of their act, something readily understandable if the star cornetist had his face bandaged. One can only surmise what the reaction would have been to the next night's show with Keppard playing with a wounded lip.

A poignant clue to their possible whereabouts after Kansas City is offered by a picture postcard of "Lincoln Highway by Night, Mishawaka, Ind." sent by Palao to his wife in Los Angeles. It reads:

> Dear Pap, It taken what I made last week to [illegible] but will [send?] you some this week. Let me know how you and the children geting along. This is only a little town, not much in it. [Still waiting (or wanting?)] to hear from you.
> Anser this wright away to the Grand Theatre 31th State St. Chicago Ill. Will be there on Sunday for one week.

Mishawaka is, in effect, a suburb of South Bend, some four miles to the east, with a population of about 15,000 at the time Palao wrote the postcard.[34]

In Chicago

The management of the Grand Theatre, at 3110–12 South State Street, had contracted to bring the Creole Band to Chicago as their Pantages tour was drawing to a close. Tony Langston, the theatrical editor of the *Defender*, reported in its issue of January 9 that a contract had been closed. Confusingly, he also said that they were "direct from the Hippodrome Theater, Sidney [*sic*], Australia." It would be closer to the truth to say they were "direct from the Hippodrome Theater, Kansas City, Missouri!"

There were at one time five theaters in Chicago with the name "Grand." This one was at 3110 South State Street; it was newly built and opened on March 19, 1911, by George Smith and perhaps others. It was not a large house, with a rated seating capacity of 800 or a trifle more, only 50 feet wide and with a smallish stage measuring 32 feet from the back wall to the curtain line, plus an apron of eight feet. This left at most sixty feet for seating space on the first floor; there was one balcony only—thus a rather intimate theater with a five-piece orchestra, the smallest Chicago house in which the Creole Band played.

The *Breeze* commented at the end of 1913: "To find an empty seat at the first show is something unusual. The theater is in the heart of the colored district and the show starts late. The second show at night seldom gets under way before ten o'clock. Smith, Braman and Ingalls own the house. Their aim is to have one colored act on every bill, but good numbers are not always available."[35]

It's interesting that at this time, the Grand—sometimes called the New Grand to differentiate it from the "Old Grand" at 3106 South State (eventually the Phoenix movie theater)—was not considered a "colored house." Clearly, however, as the black population of the South Side increased, it became so, with most of the acts being "colored" as well.[36]

BILLY KING & CO.

10TH WEEK. WAITING FOR THIRD SHOW.

3.5 Even in its barely legible condition, this halftone cut from the *Defender* of July 8, 1915, of the crowd in front of the Grand Theater, Chicago, waiting for the late show, conveys something of the atmosphere that must have greeted the Creole Band six months before.

In 1915, the theater was booked by Lew Cantor through the Matthews office. Since the agency of J. C. Matthews was the Chicago booker for Pantages, it could well be that the band was chosen to make its first Chicago appearance at the Grand by Cantor.

The next week's issue said that they were one of three acts that would be appearing in the near future: the other two were the two Toms, Lemonier and Cross, and Andrew Tribble, "in a tableau called Possum Hollow University." Two weeks later came the announcement that they would be opening on Monday, February 1. The ad billed them as "Original Creole Band / featuring H. M. Prince / An Organization Composed of Past Master / Musicians with Screaming Comedy."

On Monday, Tuesday, and Wednesday they appeared with the Loos Brothers, vocalists; Hal Davis and Jane Ware in a tabloid called "The Unexpected"; Jerome & Lewis, a song and dance act, with Lewis a female impersonator; and a rather odd act called The Golden Horse & Lady, in plastic poses.

For the first time they received reviews from African-American reviewers, Tony Langston in the *Defender* and Sylvester Russell in the *Freeman*. Langston, in general an indulgent reviewer, was pleased:

> The Creole Band, an aggregation of comedy musicians, opened a week's engagement here on Monday night. The members of the band know how to extract the most weird effects from their various instruments, and are assisted by a character comedian of good voice. The act was a novel one and went well.

Sylvester Russell, often known to offer rather acerbic critiques and no friend to old-time hokum, found it less novel:

> The Creole Band is here at last, in ragtime and Southern pastimes that were quaint in ancient days and so anew they please us now. There was a violinist, harmonist and a dancer, who ventured out into sentiment.[37]

One can hardly gain a clear idea of what the act was like from this — not the number of performers, their instruments, or the role enacted by H. Morgan Prince. It should be added that Russell was on record as decrying the reliance of black performers on the hoary routines of blackface minstrelsy. He thought that they should break out of such stereotypes and be regarded according to the same criteria as mainstream performers.

The Grand normally played split weeks but made an exception with the band, who continued through to Saturday. They were joined by four new acts: the tabloid "The Red Bottle"; Kennedy & Bart; John A. West & Co.; and Baader La Velle Co.

Both appearances received typically succinct mention in the Missouri *Breeze*, which had generally comprehensive, if inconsistent, coverage of local Chicago theaters. The first half review said that they were "very good," together with the Loos Brothers, and again in the second half review:

> The Red Bottle: the bottle is all right, but the man's pants needed pressing. John A. West & Co.: good. Creole Band: very good. Kennedy & Burt: good. Baader-LaVelle trio: very good.[38]

Fifteen years later, Dave Peyton, in 1915 the leader of the Grand Theater orchestra, remembered the event:

> It was way back in 1910 [*sic*] when the original Creole jazz band hit Chicago. They played their first engagement at the Grand theater. On this engagement they were such a hit that word hit the Loop booking agents. They came out to 31st St. to hear this sensational seven-piece band, whereupon they were bidded for by every the-atrical agency in the city. They accepted one of the offers and were immediately routed over one of the big circuits. Freddie Keppard, famous cornetist, now in Chicago; Bill Johnson, eccentric bass player, also now in Chicago; Fred Barkay, clar-inetist, now in Philadelphia and brother of the popular jazz director of the Regal theater, Hal, were with this Creole Jazz Band.
>
> When they hit Broadway they were a great sensation and would be on the road today were it not for dissatisfaction among themselves and the loss of several of their members by death.[39]

While they were not the only "colored act" to have appeared on Pantages time, that was nonetheless a distinction. Bear in mind also that they had been greeted with exceptionally enthusiastic applause.

In 1938, Jelly Roll Morton recalled being at the Grand and nagging Bill Johnson from a box. He also remembered them opening with "The Egyptian," his version of the title of Abe Olman's intermezzo, "Egyptia." Would that he had described his reactions in more detail![40]

While an appearance at the Grand would count for a lot in black show business, and some in the larger world of mainstream vaudeville—it seems that at least a few white bookers and agents went to shows there—an act would still need to be tested in front of an audience that wouldn't be predisposed to applaud. Beyond the theaters that will soon be mentioned, H. Morgan Prince remembered three theaters in Chicago: McVickers—where they did not go over (also in Bill Johnson's recollection)—the Great Northern (or more fully, Great Northern Hippodrome), and the Haymarket, none of them in the first rank. The Haymarket played burlesque, and the other two were "popular priced" vaudeville houses, a term of mild derogation. Neither advertisements nor reviews have been found to confirm their presence at these theaters.[41]

The week of February 14 was more momentous. For the first half of the week they showed at the Colonial in the Loop. The *Breeze* was reasonably detailed and complimentary:

Colonial—Three of the big features of the Colonial bill for the early part of the week were just off the Pantages tour . . . the Creole Band, which has been seen at the Grand since it got to Chicago and Maurice Samuels & Co. in "a Day at Ellis Island," which recently concluded its second successful tour of the Pantages time. All three acts scored big. Palfrey, Barton & Brown have a classy, smart and up-to-date revue based on dancing and bicycling and cleverly constructed. The Creole Band has seven colored musicians, special scenery, playing cornet, slide [*sic*], violin, guitar, clarionet & bass viol; these six musicians serenade an old colored man who sings & dances. "A Day at Ellis Island" is a good act. Maurice Samuels is a clever actor and has competent support. The boy violinist is particularly good.

This surely would have helped to cancel out the poor impression they had made at McVickers. And the contact with Samuels obviously counted for something. In the same issue of the *Breeze* we find: "Maurice Samuels Buys Band. Maurice Samuels has bought the Creole Band act seen at the Colonial early in the week and sent it to Saginaw Thursday, with Butterfield time booked."[42]

I confess ignorance of what it meant to "buy" an act. One imagines that the purchaser would take over booking and would also earn a percentage of their salaries, in return, for a lump-sum payment, but perhaps not. If so, Samuels would be a relatively unusual case of a performer who not only trod the boards but could handle the business end of things. But what was the advantage to the band? Were they temporarily at loose ends, having come to Chicago but somehow failing to impress the Chicago representatives of the big Eastern booking agencies?

Off to Saginaw they went, appearing the second half of the week at the Jeffers Theater, "6 big classy acts. All matinee seats 10¢. Nights 10/15/20/25¢." Obviously, this was a precipitous placement, since on the preceding Saturday only one of the acts that eventually appeared was advertised. Further details appeared in the Wednesday evening paper, February 17, which informed readers that the show to begin at the Jeffers was the one that had played in Bay City the first half of the week, but improved by two changes and one addition. It went on: "the booking office at Chicago was able to secure at the last moment the headliner, the famous original New Orleans Creole Band [which] carries its special setting." Disappointingly, we find neither review nor photographs.[43]

We can, however, cite the temporary theatrical colleagues of the band— billed in first place as "A Rag-Time Riot"—viz, America's Greatest Dancing Experts: Max & Mabel Ford; A Thrilling Dramatic Playlet: The Night Hawks; Acrobatic Funsters: Reed Brothers; Fascinating Novelty Piano Act: Arnold & June; the Musical Rube: Fitch Cooper. All of this was pretty standard fare for small-time vaude, except, to be sure, a hot ragtime band from New Orleans.

W. S. Butterfield was a big fish in a small pond, owning and operating, as the Michigan Vaudeville Circuit, theaters in the larger cities of Michigan, with one—somewhat incredibly—in Cobalt, Ontario. He himself does not seem to have acted as a booking agency. In the Christmas 1914 *Variety* it's stated that his houses were booked by and affiliated with the WVMA (Western Vaudeville Managers' Association) and the U.B.O. (United Booking Office, i.e., the syndicate formed by Keith-Albee and Orpheum). While not show-business Siberia, Butterfield time was nevertheless a provincial stopgap for the band.

After Saginaw, the band proceeded to Detroit, where it spent the entire week at the Miles Theater, a smallish theater of 1,000 seats playing three a day and a two-hour picture show thrown in before the matinee. Oddly, the Miles seems to have been embroiled in a booking dispute. A note at the end of their Sunday display ad in the *Free Press* stated that "the Miles-Detroit Theatre Co. has cancelled all relations with Marcus Loew. Past 2 weeks shows furnished by Affiliated Booking Co."

There were apparently some changes in the band's advance publicity, since they were now billed as the "Creole Orchestra"—in some reviews also called "Seven Creole Orchestra." Furthermore, in the *Free Press* the act was called "A Southern Reverie." But it must have been substantially the same, to judge by the four reviews it garnered. These perhaps were less detailed than they might have been, since also appearing on the same bill was boxer Willie Ritchie with his sister in an act titled "From Ballroom to Gymnasium." As the recently dethroned lightweight champion from 1912 to 1914, he naturally would have attracted a great deal of attention.

For the most part, despite the changes in nomenclature, all is as before: "Old Black Joe"—so called—sang and danced, a "special scenic equipment showing a southern plantation" was noted, but the *Journal* deserves to be quoted:

> [after much on Ritchie] There's quite a contest for second honors. The Seven Creole Orchestra had the crowd going Monday evening. The applause continued well into the next act and only an encore appeased the "Oliver Twist" feeling. The orchestra is composed of seven accomplished musicians and they play everything from "Old Kentucky" to "Ballin' the Jack."[44]

There must have been some experimentation with the order of the acts, perhaps because of the overly long applause. According to the *Detroit Times*, the Creole Orchestra brought "the show to a riotous close."

Once again, the band appeared in a predominantly popular venue, the Miles. The Orpheum was on a higher rung of the ladder—and, interestingly enough, their "owner," Maurice Samuel, was booked there with his "A Day at Ellis Island" for the following week. On the other hand, at the Gayety, a burlesque house on a lower rung, it would be fair to say, there appeared concurrently with the Creole Band an upcoming star, Toots Paka, the excellent Hawaiian performer.

The Creole Band disappears for the week of February 29. There were Michigan cities with Butterfield-owned theaters in which none of the show business weeklies recorded their presence; but a survey of local newspapers hasn't pinned them down. One tantalizing possibility: Bill Johnson recalled an incident in Hancock, Michigan in which Keppard was so drunk that he passed the entire night [. . . (illegible word) . . .] with his legs hanging under a bridge. The next day he was brought back to the theater on the milk train.

Why on earth would they have been in Hancock, a copper mining town of some 11,000 on the Upper Peninsula of Michigan, some 350 miles from Detroit as the crow flies? Be that as it may, the pages of the *Evening Copper Jour-*

nal were carefully read from January 7 to May 10, with negative result. The two principal theaters were the Kerredge, which offered either movies or legit shows, not vaudeville, and the Orpheum, which was a combination house, presenting movies with an act or two of vaudeville. As evidence that, small as it was, Hancock could nonetheless attract a major artist, the violinist Fritz Kreisler appeared at the Kerredge on May 17.

Conceivably, they might have appeared in this out-of-the-way place during their second sortie into Michigan, at the beginning of 1918. But they seem not to have been there at that time either. Hancock is rather close to Duluth, Minnesota, where they did play at the end of the week of February 17, 1918, but there is no time unaccounted for several weeks on either side of the Duluth engagement.

All falls into place for the following week. The band opened, advertised as "Seven Star Syncopators from New Orleans," at the Bijou theater, Battle Creek. One gathers from the one extant review in the *Evening News*, as well as the notices in subsequent Butterfield appearances, that Morgan Prince was given less to do: the emphasis is on instrumental music making and ensemble singing.

> The best pleased balcony audience this year, said a patron of the Bijou . . . Chief interest lies in Princess Ka . . . A novelty, too, is the Cerole [*sic*] band. Made up of seven dusky musicians, singers and dancers, with an elaborate scene setting depicting an old plantation, the Creole Band offers the essence of syncopation in melody. Such ragtime as they play has never even been approached in the Bijou before. Weird, fascinating minors run through the music, and give it an extraordinary charm. The harmony singing, especially in "Old Black Joe," was really fine, and was liberally applauded.[45]

For their last week on the Butterfield time, the band first went to Jackson, then to Ann Arbor. At Ann Arbor, the home of the University of Michigan, the vaudeville performers had to share honors with a comic photoplay, "Fanny's Melodrama," starring James Lacky. Once again their reception was exceptional, with the audience calling them back five times.[46]

We once again lose sight of our musicians. No listings in the professional weeklies, no reviews, no good clues in the reminiscences of Bill Johnson and Morgan Prince allow us to place them until May 9 . . . unless this is the period when they played at the North American Restaurant in Chicago. The source for this notion is Paul Eduard Miller, who, along with John Steiner and George Hoefer, made pioneering contributions to our knowledge of the early jazz scene in Chicago. Miller would probably have had his information from Bill Johnson, the only member of the band to whom he had access in Chicago.

We read, for example, in *Esquire's 1946 Jazz Book*: "That same year [1913] the Original Creoles played an engagement at a Loop theatre, the Colonial, while the following year they took up a four month's stand at the North American Restaurant, at the northwest corner of State and Monroe."[47] Bill Johnson's chronology was often shaky—he maintained that their start in vaudeville was 1912—and 1914 seems to be impossible. The period of March, April, and May 1915 seems most likely. One problem, however: there aren't four free months. Bill Johnson, however, in addition to having a shaky memory for dates, also on occasion seriously overestimated the time that the band spent on a particular engagement.

A long-term engagement at the North American would be of special interest for a number of reasons. First, because they would have stayed put long enough for musicians and fans who were attracted to their music to hear them repeatedly and figure out how it was done. In vaudeville, by the time the word got around that there was a really interesting musical act at the local theatre, they'd be gone. Second, the North American could hardly have been more central, the corner of State and Monroe being one of the busiest corners in the United States, if not the world. Third, Brown's Band, one of the other pioneers in bringing New Orleans ragtime-jazz to the North, was to arrive just at the end of the Creole Band's hypothetical residency at the North American, on May 13.

The idea of having a restaurant in an office building is surely not novel, but the restaurant in the North American Building was remarkable in functioning as a cabaret, or as a kind of hybrid cabaret, which also presented vaudeville, as many as seven acts in addition to dining and dancing. We know who booked the acts—Morris Silvers, who also edited a weekly entertainment guide, the *Loophound* (no copies appear to have survived), and who led the ten-piece orchestra—Jimmie Henshel—and we have either act lists or reviews during the period that seems most likely for the band to have been there. Strange, then, that we find no trace of the Creole Band at the North American in the spring of 1915 (nor any other time, for that matter!).[48]

It strikes me that if the North American operated as other cabarets did at the time, there would have been in residence a couple of exhibition ballroom dancers, both to drum up trade for the dance floor and to offer instruction. Throughout 1914 and 1915, such couples began to use African-American orchestras to back them up for both cabaret and vaudeville appearances, most notably Vernon and Irene Castle and Joan Sawyer and her rapidly changing partners. In and around Chicago Mr. and Mrs. Carl Heisen used an orchestra led by violinist Charles Elgar, originally from New Orleans. That an engagement in a subsidiary position, accompanying ballroom dancers, was not mentioned by Baquet, Johnson, or Prince may merely reflect a degree of chagrin at having to play second fiddle for some weeks.[49]

Somewhere during this period, Maurice Samuels stepped out of the picture, never again to be heard from in connection with the band. The new agent—nothing this time about "ownership"—was the Simon Agency, which inserted a notice in the May 14 issue of the *Breeze*: "The Creole Band is playing the Kedzie and Wilson Theater this week." To play these seemingly unimportant neighborhood houses may seem something of a comedown for the band; but many rather well-known acts were placed at them, especially, one guesses, when they were being tried out or groomed for tours by the WVMA. One unfortunate fact attended performing at such theaters: only the indefatigable *Breeze*, of all the theatrical weeklies, made a regular effort to cover the neighborhood houses—and we have already seen how terse their comments were. *Variety* would sometimes take cognizance of acts at these theatres, but in the Chicago column, in very fine print amid the advertising pages toward the back of the paper. Also, of course, the Chicago daily papers would not bother with them, and for the most part, they carried no ads from such humble venues.

When John B. Simon died at his home in Hollywood on September 1, 1934, he had been an agent for over thirty years, first for vaudeville, then for the movies. He began as an usher in Louisville, Kentucky, then worked as an agent for the Gus Sun theaters in Birmingham, Alabama, and for the Jake Wells circuit back in Louisville. When he came to Chicago in 1910 he worked in Jake Sternad's office, then established his own in late 1912 or early 1913. Soon after, he had over 100 acts working.

Two items of interest appeared in the *Breeze* of January 16, 1914. He was in trouble with the WVMA for accepting commissions from the outside agents, forced in fact to dissolve his corporation. The paper reported no hard feelings, however, since the Simon Agency "might be granted the permission to operate on the Association floor in the same manner as other agents, in the next few weeks."

In a "Who's Who" item, Simon was described as a "dapper young fellow" who "visited New York oftener than any other Chicago vaudeville man." He brought his brothers, Irving and Freddie, into the business and they remained with him until the thirties.

He had married Irene Warfield of Louisville, an actress and Essenay film star, in 1911, but she sued for divorce in 1915. At some subsequent date, he married another film actress, Edith Allen, who survived him.

Of greatest import to the band was, undoubtedly, his connection with Harry Weber, one of the most important vaudeville agents of New York. This went back to 1915 at least and continued until the Weber and Simon agencies merged in 1931.

The Wilson Avenue Theater was at 1050 Wilson Avenue, some six miles north of the Loop, at the intersection of Wilson with Broadway. But it was not at all difficult to reach, with a major branch and a station of the north side elevated at that very corner. It was a lively neighborhood. To quote *Variety* in November 1916:

> The Wilson Avenue was at one time the best paying "pop" vaudeville house in the country, located in the heart of Chicago's busiest neighborhood section and apparently immune from opposition because of the lack of ground.[50]

It was apparently lively in other ways. Two years earlier, a West Coast sporting paper had seen fit to print a lengthy extract from the Chicago *Saturday Evening Telegraph* concerning prostitution in the Wilson Avenue district.[51]

The Kedzie, at 3202 West Madison, corner of Kedzie Avenue, was closer in—some four miles from State & Madison—and directly accessible by trolley and elevated; it was also considered a profitable venue. It had serious competition from the Imperial, at Madison and Western, and especially from the recently built and quite large New American, at Madison and Ashland—only a stone's throw away, by the way, from Mike Fritzel's Arsonia cabaret at which some of Chicago's earliest New Orleans immigrant bands played in 1916–1917.

It was considered noteworthy to the *Clipper* that there were three outlying vaudeville theaters within the space of three miles on West Madison Street, all of them attracting the attention of the vaudeville colony.[52] (These are to be distinguished from the cluster of somewhat disreputable theaters much closer to the Loop on West Madison and Halsted, the Empire, the Virginia, and two burlesque houses: the Star & Garter and the Haymarket.)

Of these two venues, the Wilson Avenue Theater was the more interesting in connection with the Creole Band. Its manager was Mitchell Licalzi, who, with the aid of a bequest from his recently deceased father, Anthony Licalzi, had bought a controlling interest in the theatre. He was obviously willing to spend money, apparently on occasion from $1,000 to $1,500, to attract top acts that would put his new toy on the vaudeville map. Licalzi was a native of New

Orleans, and in fact was responsible for signing Lawrence Duhé's band in 1917 after hearing them at Pete Lala's cabaret, to come to Chicago to accompany tap dancer Mabel Elaine.[53] Mabel Elaine, of course, had toured with the Creole Band for five months at the beginning of 1916.[54]

The only record of these engagements is the brief reviewlet in the *Breeze*: "The Creole Band closed the program nicely, scoring in the late position."[55] The show had opened with Rozella & Rozella, harpist and comedian; followed by Lewis & White, a female singing pair; George Richards & Co. in a comedy sketch; and in fourth position Larry Comer. The elegantly dressed Comer opened with an Irish character song, then sang "When Sunday Comes to Town," and finished with a dramatic recitation, "The Quitter." He was the hit of the program, and on the front page was also dubbed one of the seven hits of the week. He also appeared during the second half of the week at the Kedzie. While the band did well—presumably also at the Kedzie—it seems as though they functioned as a rousing send-off, not as the focus of the bill.

Nonetheless, the Simon Agency had important plans for the Creole Band announcing that they had been given a contract "running far into 1916," one of some thirty acts, ranging from Princess Kalama to the Ching Wha Four.[56] This news was important enough to be picked up by the *New York Star*, which informed its readers that the band was booked through May 17, 1916, after a season opening at the Columbia theater in Davenport, Iowa, on August 16, 1915.[57]

Indeed, in pre-air-conditioned America the 1914–1915 season was drawing to a close for many theaters; vaudeville theaters often ceased operation around Decoration (Memorial) Day—May 30—to open again around the beginning of September. There were still a few weeks for booking, however, and the band appeared in Champaign, Illinois, at the newly constructed Orpheum theater on North Walnut Street, for the first half of the week of May 16.

They made a favorable impression:

> Last time this evening of the Creole Ragtime Band. This act is composed of seven men, all real colored musicians, and the verdict of the vaudeville goers the past few days is that this band plays "some rag." There are several other acts [four, in fact], combining comedy, melody, and acrobatics, on this show which by many has been proclaimed the best vaudeville show of the year.[58]

The Simon Agency was apparently sending its notices far and wide, not just to New York papers but also to the *Freeman* in Indianapolis, which printed a relatively lengthy item, with what I assume to be supplementary information added by the paper's theatrical editor, since it gives the names of the members of the troupe, something notably absent in the publicity printed in mainstream papers:

The Creole Band, under the management of Will Johnson, featuring J.[*sic*] Morgan Prince, is booked solid to May, 1916, on the Western Vaudeville Association time. Other members are Geo. Boquet, Fred Keppard, Ed Vincent, Norwood Williams, Jas. Palao. They have gone to Champlain [*sic*] and will be seen next week at the Empress Theater, St. Louis.[59]

Replete with typographical errors as it is—J. Morgan for H. Morgan; Boquet for Baquet, Champlain for Champaign—this passage makes the relative positions of Johnson and Prince clear, and also adds an otherwise unknown engagement in St. Louis to their itinerary.[60]

Morgan Prince recalled that the band played in St. Louis six times, including some appearances at the Anheuser-Busch brewery. Exactly when this was is impossible to establish. St. Louis, for all that it was an important hub for East-West trade as well as river traffic, receives very little coverage in the show-biz professional weeklies, and the daily newspapers have surprisingly little theatrical news, given that it was the fourth largest city in the United States in 1910.

We do know that the band was sent to Indianapolis as the headline act for the entire week of May 30 at English's Theater. The advance puff in the Sunday *Star* was more detailed than usual and was even accompanied by a photograph, which, if it actually depicts the band, is the only one showing the band in costumes like those they actually played in. Surprisingly enough, the *Times* also printed a photo, but it was the well-known one in formal attire from the Empire Studios in Los Angeles. The *Star* described the band's act thus:

old time plantation act . . . special scenic production . . . showing the South before the war, with the cotton fields in full bloom, the negro quarters and the "big house" where the master resides, who has the band present their plantation pastimes after their chores were done.[61]

Incidentally, it was on this day that Ralph de Palma won the Indy 500 at a blinding 90 miles per hour.

The *Star*'s review two days later said that the band "kept the audience in good humour for almost half an hour . . . a big hit and was forced to respond to a dozen encores." The *Times* was no less favorable, describing them as the best act seen "in many a moon." Not only did it appreciate the singing and the comedy but also the "accomplished musicians." In another review the next day, the singer of "Old Black Joe" was said to have been greeted with tremendous applause, being "forced to respond to encores at every performance." This was surely Morgan Prince.[62]

We draw a blank for the next two weeks, before the Creole Band resurfaces at Mannion's Park in St. Louis for the week of June 20. Mannion's, at 8600 South Broadway, was a summer entertainment park, one of the hundreds that entertained our ancestors in the early part of the century. Rather more modest than today's theme parks, they nonetheless offered to the sweltering masses a varied menu of eating and drinking places, band concerts, dancing, the usual carnival games of "skill," and, in larger cities, important theatrical attractions.

The *Globe-Democrat* announced on Sunday in a notice devoted to the current week's attractions at Mannion's that the band consisted of "8 negro entertainers," making us wonder whether the band had added a temporary member. On Monday the *Star* included one sentence in a brief review of the acts playing at the Park.[63]

For the first half of the next week, they moved to the Empress Theatre, at 3616 Olive Street at some distance from the city center. The local press paid no mind to their appearance at this relatively insignificant venue. Remarkably, however, the *Argus*, an African-American weekly, tells us not only that they were at the Empress but that "they entertained at the Keystone Cafe Tuesday night."[64] This confirms what was remembered by Bill Johnson: that wherever they were, they played other engagements besides those at the vaudeville theater. More important, the Keystone was operated by and for the African American population of St. Louis, a matter of some interest, since virtually all of the band's theatrical appearances were before "mainstream" audiences.[65]

For the close of the week, they crossed the Mississippi to the Alton, Illinois, *Airdome*, where they were one of two acts that accompanied two movies; the other act was "Rose Garden and her trusty piano." A concert was advertised for 7:15 p.m., with vaudeville beginning at 7:45 and a second show at 9:15. Admission to this undoubtedly modest open-air movie theater, ancestor of the drive-ins so beloved in later years, was minimal at 10 cents for adults and a nickel for children. One wonders how the proprietor could have afforded the band. Be that as it may, the local *Evening Telegraph* found them worth attention: "a real novelty in a real ragtime band, playing ragtime airs and singing them in a novel manner [on] many different instruments . . . pleasing immensely."[66]

The band moved back to St. Louis for the entire week of July 4—surely they also would have been hired by someone to help make Independence Day festive for a picnic, parade, or dance—at the Hamilton Theater, also an "airdome" or "skydome," at 5900 Easton Avenue. We have no record of any reaction.

Once again they vanish, this time for four weeks, until the opening in Davenport on August 16. Morgan Prince said that at one time they played the Gus Sun time in Dayton and all through Ohio and this would be a possible time for such a tour. If so, we should commiserate, since the Sun circuit exemplified "small-time" at its grimmest. Any appearances under such auspices could only be for the purpose of continuing to work, come what may—which seems to have been the band's attitude throughout its career.

Borrowing freely from Joe Laurie, Jr.'s classic work on vaude, I cannot resist a few words depicting the eccentricity of the founder and guiding spirit of the chain. Born as Gus Klotz in Toledo, Ohio, he started as a juggler and "equilibrist," then became a circus manager and owner. The first link in the chain of what eventually numbered hundreds of theaters was forged in Springfield, Ohio, shortly after the turn of the century.

He is said to have been the first to introduce split weeks; the cancelation clause in contracts, permitting the theater manager to close an act after the first performance; and subtracting one-seventh of the week's salary when shows could not play on Sundays; and he was notorious for communicating with his acts by telegram—collect. It was not difficult to be booked on Sun time, and despite ludicrous pay, many acts were happy to accept it, hoping after such experience to advance to bookings of higher status and salary. Laurie includes many other details in his affectionate account.[67]

They say that in life "timing is everything." During their first season in vaudeville the Creole Band hardly showed themselves to be masters of timing in managing their career, although they were working steadily (with a few gaps). That they began well with the Pantages tour is undeniable, but thereafter there's no clear pattern: a few Chicago engagements, including one in a major Loop theatre, followed by comparative exile to the Butterfield circuit and five following weeks when they vanish from our obsessed view. The problem may well have been with their purchase by Maurice Samuels and a fairly rapid subsequent parting of the ways. By the time this happened and the Simon Agency picked them up, the season was drawing to a close and there really wasn't much to do but fill in here and there and go back and forth between Chicago (and perhaps smaller Iowa and Illinois towns) and St. Louis.

4 The Second Season

THE CREOLE BAND that Bill Johnson had brought together in Los Angeles in the spring of 1914 almost certainly didn't have a show business career in mind at the outset; they were still a dance band. Once Henry Morgan Prince linked up with them, however, it's possible, even likely, that vaudeville became one of their options—indeed, that may have been the reason for the association in the first place. Considering the enthusiastic applause that greeted them at virtually every stop on the Pantages tour, it must have become obvious that they might have a future in vaudeville.

Despite their success on the Pantages time, however, it seems to me that their career stumbled after their appearance at the Grand Theater in February and their "purchase" by Maurice Samuels. It was, after all, a matter of timing. All longer-term bookings and contracts would have been made by the time they came off the Pantages circuit, and being sent to Michigan to tour the Butterfield theaters could hardly be regarded as anything more than a stopgap. By the time John Simon, with his New York connections, especially with Harry Weber, stepped into the picture, there was really nothing to do but wait for fall and the beginning of a full season going the rounds of the Midwestern theaters under the auspices of the WVMA.

From the standpoint of the history of the development of jazz, the engagement at the North American restaurant-cabaret—still shadowy in its details—becomes very important, not just because they stayed put for a reasonably long time and could be heard repeatedly but because at the beginning of 1915 one may say the Chicago scene was ready for hot New Orleans ragtime. Two figures who are considered of no real consequence by orthodox jazz history figured in this preparatory phase. One was Bert Kelly, the banjoist from San Francisco, who opened at the College Inn of the Hotel Sherman in January 1915 with a band he later insisted was a jazz band—at least according to his understanding (it was not actually called such). Also, the tenor saxophonist Paul Biese was appearing at the Hotel LaSalle in a group called "El Quintette Real." As everywhere, the vogue for "modern dancing" was still vigorous, and "modern dancing" required syncopated music.

In my imaginings, the Creole Band may have been heard in Chicago by Joe Gorham at or after their debut at the Grand, giving him the idea to go to New Orleans to sign another hot ragtime band for the Lambs' Cafe, a basement club in the heart of the Loop and something of a show business hangout.[1] In the event, it was Brown's Band he put under contract, but, however successful it may have been, it didn't make the kind of hit that the Original Dixieland Band did a year later.

Excursus on Brown's Band

Brown's Band came from New Orleans to play at Smiley Corbett's Lambs' Cafe, a big reverberant space in the basement of the Olympic Theater building at Clark and Randolph Streets. They started around May 17 and continued without a break until August 28, when Corbett closed the place for expansion. Corbett wanted them to continue after Lambs' reopened, and released them only under condition that they not play in another cafe. Who exactly had the idea of filling in by playing in some WVMA theaters is not known, but they had photographs made, along with dancer Joe Frisco, who was also working at Lambs'. Cornetist Ray Lopez recalled playing three split weeks, including one gig at the Palace in Hammond, Indiana. Despite a mutual agreement with Frisco that neither party would accept work without the other, Frisco supposedly went to New York to work with the Ted Lewis's band at Rector's. (I write "supposedly" since this is many months earlier than Lewis is known to have been at the famous Broadway "lobster palace," whether under his own name or Earl Fuller's.) This must have been after the one engagement reported by the *Breeze*, which reported on the group, with "an eccentric dancer"—no doubt Frisco—at Chicago's American Theater between September 16 and 18. The *Breeze* believed that this was their first appearance in vaudeville.

Harry Fitzgerald, a New York–based agent, saw Brown's band and persuaded them to come to New York, allegedly to appear in *Dancing Around*, a show starring Al Jolson. *Variety*, however, stated that they had arrived in New York on Monday, September 27, to be placed in some unnamed Broadway restaurant. Unfortunately for them, the show never opened, due to disagreements between Jolson and the Shubert brothers. Fitzgerald then placed them in *Town Topics*; Lopez is careful to point out that they didn't appear in the show itself but played for dancing in the "foyer" before and after. This sounds much like the job that Will Vodery's sixteen-piece Ragphony Orchestra had. Again according to Lopez, the show closed in a couple of weeks, and they weren't paid.

Another agent, Jack Goldberg, managed to book them for about ten weeks on the Loew's time. While most of these jobs were probably in smaller theaters around New York City, such as Hoboken, New Jersey, they did appear in two major houses in Christmas week, 1915: the American Roof from the 27th to the 29th, and the Seventh Avenue Theater for the last half.

What you've just read is a summary of the recollections of Ray Lopez, as told to Richard Holbrook. To verify everything in detail would be a relatively major project by itself, and at least one detail seems only partly correct. According to the *Clipper* of September 25, 1915, under "Shubert Plans": "Al Jolson, in 'Dancing Around' will continue his tour of the West until after the first of the year, when he will be brought to New York City to be featured in a new Winter Garden production." This is verified until October 23, when the show is listed as playing Cincinnati in the "Routes Ahead" of *Billboard*. It then disappears.

Nevertheless, the outline is both credible and startling in the manner in which, for the most part, it barely misses meeting the trajectory of the Creole Band. It seems that just as Brown's Band was beginning the job at the Lambs', the Creole Band was at the end of a split week at the Kedzie. Then, as Brown and company held forth in the Loop, the Creole Band was playing in downstate Illinois and St. Louis. At just about the time Brown began to appear in Chicago vaudeville, the Creole Band came back to town for a week, then left for a month. During this time, Brown's Band departed for New York, eventually to play for dancing in the mezzanine dancing space at the Century Theater during the run of *Town Topics*; and they were surely in and around the city when the Creole Band finally arrived at the beginning of December. One wonders, of course, whether they were aware of each other's presence in and around Chicago and New York. Be that as it may, it's evident that both cities were on the brink of accepting New Orleans ragtime by 1915.[2]

The refurbished Columbia Theater in Davenport, Iowa, opened for the season as scheduled on Sunday, August 15. Strangely, the Sunday listing of acts for both halves of the week in the *Democrat & Leader* failed to mention the Creole Band. Nevertheless, they were there as the headliners and were admired as a "collection of colored minstrel men with dancing, singing, comedy, and negro folklore."[3] The *Daily Times* did rather better in its Monday review:

Featuring the show are the seven Creole ragtime entertainers who are acquainted with every angle of syncopated music and are able to play it with a queer accent that last night made everyone's feet move to the time. Special scenery is carried in this act and there is a pretentious effort toward comedy which is successfully done.[4]

They were announced in *Variety* for the Hippodrome Theatre in Terre Haute, Indiana, for the week of the 22nd. A full week would have been quite unusual in such small-town theaters, and in fact they appeared only for Thursday, Friday, and Saturday, August 26–28. In a bylined review of the show at the Hippodrome, W. R. Simmons wrote:

After wading through several acts at the Hippodrome the spectator finally comes to the Creole Band, the feature act of the week-end bill. After hearing the dusky performers, it is hard to leave the theater. The old southern melodies and dances strike a responsive chord with the audience. Yesterday round after round of applause greeted every effort of the entertainers. Once in a while the vaudeville follower finds an act that draws them back for the second time. The Creole Band is that kind.[5]

The competing newspaper, the *Tribune*, was perhaps even more effusive in a bylined piece by Mique [*sic*] O'Brien:

There are at least two acts on the bill that will be discussed in the lobby of the Terre Haute house, over demi-tasse at the Deming, and during breaks in programs at the picture houses. The Creole Band which closes the show presents a hum-dinger of an act. The music is of the wheezy sort, to be expected of an organization made up of "Creoles" who play for amusement. Plantation tunes incite the old darky who is being serenaded, to dance. And a very clever, eccentric dancer is the leader of this band. Yesterday's audience kept the Creoles fiddling and tooting away long past the time usually taken up by a feature act.[6]

Following this decidedly promising start, they appeared to have toured in a normal and fairly predictable way the theaters under the management of Finn & Heiman and booked by the WVMA. The F & H chain was relatively extensive, consisting of three houses in Chicago: the American, the Lincoln, and the Bryn Mawr; nine theaters named "Orpheum" in Rockford and Champaign, Illinois; Gary, South Bend, and Michigan City in the Hoosier state; Green Bay and Madison, Wisconsin; and Des Moines and Sioux City, Iowa. Added to this were the Fuller Opera House in Madison, the Empress in Decatur, Illinois, the Columbia and American in Davenport, the Majestic in Waterloo, Iowa, and

Springfield, Illinois, and the New Grand in Evansville, Indiana, for a total of twenty theaters, enough for ten split weeks.[7]

With the engagement of September 2 to 4 at the Majestic in Springfield, the band began a more or less continuous stretch of travelling that would last some two and a half months. The *News-Record* found them to be "excellent black face comedians [who] were tendered a good 'hand' and repeated encores." The *Illinois State Register* in its advance publicity could not get the size of the act straight. On Wednesday, the eve of their appearance, they were "six talented musicians . . . greatest exponents of syncopated melody," but on Thursday they were a "double quintet of colored boys." As in their season debut at Davenport, the act appears titled as "Plantation Days," a billing that continued throughout the fall of 1915.

Labor Day fell on September 6 in 1915, and the band could hardly have found itself in a locale more sympathetic to the labor movement than Decatur. According to the *Herald*, the celebration was the "biggest . . . in the history of Decatur or Central Illinois." It involved 1,600 workers and stretched some twenty-seven blocks. George Fenberg, the manager of the Empress and a veteran in the vaudeville game, saw to it that the theater had a horse-drawn float bringing up the rear of the parade, carrying all of the week's actors, including the Creole Band. As reported in the *Herald*, "The Capital City band, the Mueller and Goodman bands, with the addition of the Empress musicians [context makes it clear that the Creole Band is meant], furnished plenty of music during the circuit of the business section."[8] The *Breeze* reported that they were a hit in the theater, and also that Fenberg had them play the "latest rag selections" on the Labor Day float.

On Thursday, they opened again in Chicago, at the American. The *New York Clipper*'s attention was drawn not only to the American but also to the West Madison Street scene (see above). Their reporter more than liked the show:

> The American had a splendid show the last half of last week, a bill which agents say it is impossible to get right along. All five acts were comedy: Halkings, comedy shadowgrapher; William Morros & Co., "Happy's Millions," sketch with Esther Joy; the Creole Band, a regular colored plantation act, scored big in third place; Smith, Cook & Brandon; Romeo the Great, Alfred Drowiskey's monkey . . . American doing tremendous business—good publicity by Ned Alvord, Finn & Heiman management.[9]

The *Breeze* was also taken with their routine, although not missing the chance to point out that it was not exactly novel: "Next came the Creole Band, a colored act, introducing the familiar 'Uncle' and 'the boys' which has been a part of colored shows and touring minstrels for years, but it got the audience."[10]

Also on the front page, enclosed in a box, was the following "advice to ambitious act" from Sam Kahl, the booker of the American:

> Of course the language is not that of the cultured, dignified Sam Kahl, booking representative of the Finn & Heiman interests [sarcasm?] But it is the language of an actor who talked to him. Telling the advice of the vaudeville authority, quoting Mr. Kahl, the actor put it: "Put in a little more jaz, Bo'; there is enough of this dress suit stuff." Sam Kahl is the booker of the American, managed by Finn & Heiman and the publicity agent is Ned Alvord . . . The "classy" stuff is pretty to talk about, it furnishes inspiration for the dramatic writer, but it is the hocum, the jazbo, what vaudeville styles "comedy acts," which please an audience.[11]

It's most interesting that this early citation comes from a man who had undoubtedly seen the Creole Band. We know that the term "jaz" was endemic in show business circles around this time—and for how many years previously? What was novel was to apply it to music in Chicago. After all, Brown's Band at the Lambs' Cafe in May had been given the bowdlerized billing of "Jad Band."[12]

[Thereby hangs a tale, recounted by Ray Lopez to Richard Holbrook. It was the third week of Brown's Band tenure at the Lambs'; they had just finished a "beautiful" number, *Hawaiian Butterfly*, when a South Side grifter named Darby Kelly shouted, "Jazz it up, Ray" and the band played the up-tempo "Banana Peel Rag." Two "big wheels" from Lyon & Healy—the most important music store in Chicago—were intrigued by the music and the word "jazz." Smiley Corbett, the owner of Lambs', had his waiter bring over a dictionary from the hotel across the street he also owned. Corbett and the two men from Lyon & Healy tried in vain to find the word "jazz" in the dictionary, but found what seemed to them close: "jade, a wild and vicious woman." The remembered date is too late since the famous advertisement with the term "jad" was printed on Saturday at the end of their first week.]

For the first half of the next week, the group moved to the Windsor Theatre at Clark and Division Streets on the near North Side. The *Breeze* reviewed this show as though they had never heard of or seen the band before:

> The Creole Band is a very good act of the Southern plantation style, although orchestra is probably a better word than band, as the instruments used are cornet, trombone, clarinet, bass, violin, and guitar. A colored comedian of the darkey preacher sort lends comedy to the offering and the special setting, including a log

cabin, is very appropriate. Their different rag selections are delivered in strict keeping with the surroundings."[13]

This was not the first time—nor would it be the last—that a reporter could not decide whether the act was a bit of superannuated blackface minstrelsy or a modern musical act. It is, nonetheless, useful to have confirmation that the instrumentation of the band remained unchanged. It is curious that in this very week, following in the footsteps of the Creole Band, Brown's Band appeared at the American in one of its first—if not the first—appearances on the vaudeville stage.

Although the band was scheduled to go to the Orpheum in Racine, Wisconsin, for September 16 through 18, the *Breeze* reported that the Welsh Quartette went instead. Where the band was is unknown. But for the first half of the week of September 19 they gave their answer to the age-old question, "Will it play in Peoria?" as they appeared in that city, which, at 70,000 inhabitants was the second largest city in the state, albeit one-thirtieth the size of the metropolis.[14] Here, although the reviewer failed to notice the presence of George Baquet—perhaps he was in fact absent—he gave them one of their longest reviews, one which additionally focused on the music to an unusual degree:

Humor is one of the rarest things to be met with in music—a fact which lends additional value and interest to the act of the Creole Ragtime Band . . . The five men of the band have a peculiar way of muting their instruments which gives them an alien tone and suggests the squealing of strange Oriental instruments rather than the familiar fiddle and guitar, cornet and trombone of the average band. That it is not inharmonious in spite of the wild wailings the darkies draw from their instruments is no small triumph for the players.

The music of the band quite as much as the fun making of the act shows the southern plantation darky as he really is in his sportive hours and the act is interesting as well as picturesque and amusing. The men sing exceptionally well, and the song numbers are highly enjoyable also, making the attractions [*sic*] one of the big hits of the show.[15]

The second half of the week found them at the Majestic in Bloomington, Illinois. The assemblage of acts piqued the imagination of both the publicist and the reviewer. The ads designated the act as "African"; the review explained that the show comprised five acts by different nationalities, Australian, Irish, Japanese—Sumiko, among other things, sang ragtime—Americans and The Creole Ragtime Band (Africans) who "play and sing harmony in a wonderful way and also introduce some comedy and pathetic numbers."[16]

For the first half of the week of September 26th the band played the Lyric in Danville. Two features of the publicity were quite astonishing. First, on Saturday the usual photo taken in Los Angeles was used. Second, something of a shocker: the theater ad billed them as "Mr. and Mrs. Vernon Castle's Creole Band in Plantation Days." The advance blurb went into greater detail: "The Creole Band, the original Mr. and Mrs. Vernon Castle Creole band which first put across the music for the Castle Walk and other dances, will close the bill." The review on Tuesday repeated this link to the Castles:

> The closing act is a scream in negro harmony, the original Creole band, the same who came into prominence with Mr. and Mrs. Vernon Castle. Vocal and instrumental harmony is there, from the wierd [sic] plantation tunes to the most modern and rhythmic ragtime.[17]

In fact, it was James Reese Europe's orchestra that had accompanied the Castles on their famous "whirlwind tour" in the spring of 1914. (Before them the Castles employed another African-American band, led by Tony Tuck.) Perhaps all African-American musicians looked alike to the copywriter in Chicago. There's no such easy explanation for the mention of the Castles, and Vernon's trip to Quincy, Illinois, to entice them to join him and Irene in vaudeville was mentioned only in the October 15 number of the *Breeze* (see below) as having taken place the week before.

For the last half, they went once again to the Empress Theater in St. Louis. While no published comment has survived, the *Breeze* served up in their elaborate fall issue an evaluation that is enlightening regarding the range of attitudes toward their music—as distinguished from their traditional minstrel show routine. It appeared under the rubric "Music."

> The Creole Band, now on Association time, could not be mentioned as a musical act, although it is a band; the music is among the worst heard in years. The offering makes good because it is hocum served up correctly.[18]

This flies in the face of the advice given by Sam Kahl, the booker for the American theater in Chicago (see above) when he said: "it is the hocum, the jazbo, what vaudeville styles 'comedy acts', which please an audience." The conjunction of "jazbo" and "hocum" is apparently new in 1915 and of more than passing interest.

[The Oxford English Dictionary designates "hokum"—the usual spelling today—as U.S. theatrical slang and offers as first historical witness an excerpt from the *New York Sun* of August 5, 1917, which read: "'Jasbo' is a form of the word common in the varieties, meaning the same as 'hokum', or low comedy verging on vulgarity." I've managed to collect a number of similar uses of the two terms from two years earlier. For example, Walter J. Kingsley—the author of the passage from the *Sun* and the press agent for the Palace theater in New York, wrote the following in the *Dramatic Mirror*: "Vaudeville finds the public tired of the old things. 'Hokum', 'jasbo', and 'gravy', as slap-stick comedy is termed in the argot of the two-a-day, have palled upon the palates of the variety fan. Ragtime and dancing, acrobatics and animal turns, staccato personalities, with inhuman courage in thrusting bold humor across the footlights, are wearing on the public." To be sure, Kingsley seems to be following the standard Keith push for clean, respectable family vaudeville.

But closer to the center of the Creole Band's activity in 1915, the *Breeze* uses the term on a number of occasions. On March 26, it proffered the "wail of the small-time manager," viz. "Class may come and class may go, but HOCUM goes on forever." In the same issue as the derogatory valuation of the Band found above, a Johnny Dooley is quoted as saying:

> I lay claim to being one of vaudeville's hokum artists . . . if slapstick humor and hokum comedy are presented in a clean, classy manner, minus any comedy makeup whatever, or any tinge of vulgarity . . . the people absolutely prefer this to the exclusion of almost every style of entertainment found in the usual vaudeville bills.

This seems in light of other remarks a futile attempt to reconcile the irreconcilable: class is class, hokum is hokum, and to speak of classy hokum is surely oxymoronic.

Again in the pages of the *Breeze*, at the close of the selfsame year, we find Murray K. Hill inserting an ad reading, "Just to Jaz 'Em Up / SIMP HOKUM / New - Murray K. Hill - New." Murry K. Hill was an old-timer, born in 1865, and a noted purveyor of comic monologues as well as a singer. He had about four dozen recordings to his credit—for Victor, Edison, and U.S. Everlasting for the most part—and is described in the 1917 Victor catalogue as a vaudeville favorite who "always keeps his hearers in roars of laughter by his droll delivery of a very witty store of jokes, parodies and nonsense in general." A year later the *Breeze* equates "hocum" to "nut material," which is going a bit far, in my opinion, but there you have it.

Finally, and very interestingly, *Variety*, in its November 24, 1916, issue states, "Now that "Jazz" bands are getting popular the boys will have to start writing Hokum Music." The network of connotations of "hokum" and "jazzbo" or "jazz" is clearly a very complicated one, but the connection to the new (to northerners) music from New Orleans is clear. One notes that Brown's Band, when it entered vaudeville in 1915, became "Five Ragtime Rubes" and that the Creole Band, had they been white, would have been called a "rube act." But a black act wearing overalls and indulging in slapstick humor in a rural setting was a "plantation act," a pretext for entertainment obviously unavailable to white vaudevillians.

A further connection to jazz lies in what I call musical hokum, that is, the use of corny, slapstick devices that make a direct—one could say vulgar—appeal to audiences. These are particularly evident in certain clarinet tricks, glisses, cackles, slaptongue, and flutter tongue, which as practiced by vaudevillians were designed to amuse. When we hear such devices integrated into a context that has what we call a "more musical" interest, we interpret them in a different fashion. But all the early New Orleans or Dixieland clarinet players could use these tricks: Larry Shields, Achille and George Baquet, Johnny Dodds, to name only a few. That the line between expressive ragtime-jazz performance and good old vaudeville or minstrel show hokum was a subtle one can be heard in such a player as Wilbur Sweatman. And then there is the conventionally derided Ted Lewis, certainly a skilled and much-admired exponent of hokum and accepted as a jazz artist in his early recording career.

Presumably, the rationale for the use of corn-fed hokum, rube costumes, eccentric performance techniques, and the like by early ragtime or jazz bands was, first, that musical acts generally need some kind of gimmick to be interesting to notably impatient vaudeville audiences; second, that while their more "musical" pioneering innovations might have been unacceptable to audiences, they were made palatable by a sugar-coating (as it were) of hokum.

In the river town of Quincy, Illinois, for the first half of the week of October 3, the band was plainly a hit. The advance puff had prepared Quincyites for a "complete scenic production" by "the laughing hit of the big time theaters." The review on Tuesday ignored all of the plantation routine, although it did still suggest that African genes and syncopation went hand in hand:

> The Creole Band closed the show and closed it with a bang. Where do these colored gents get their sense of syncopation? It must be born in the bone. Such ragtime never was heard; it was inspiring. The Creole Band is an act worth sitting through Mr. Dean's gaspings to hear.[19]

During this engagement they were offered an opportunity that might well have turned their career in another direction. A small item in the ever-productive *Breeze*—so tiny that it escaped my notice the first two times through—reported under the headline "Surprising Offer" that

Vernon Castle travelled to Quincy, Illinois, last week to see the Creole Band, and is said to have offered the act $400 per week to go with him. The band could not accept, as it is booked on Association time.[20]

It's odd that such an offer was not recalled by Baquet, Prince, Johnson, Williams, or Palao's widow. Perhaps they felt that $400 a week was not that good an offer, since they were probably making close to that amount already; possibly they were chagrined at not grasping the chance to appear with a major star of the day, even if they would have been in an accompanying role.

The Castles were around this time in Chicago, in the touring company of *Watch Your Step*, an important musical with music and lyrics by Irving Berlin; they were also dancing at Rector's cabaret. Vernon and Irene Castle are well known for having made their whirlwind tour of major Eastern and Midwestern cities the year before, with music provided by a band organized and led by James Reese Europe. Prior to their association with Europe they had employed other African-American musicians to give their dancing a syncopated flair. Since Castle had never had a chance to hear the Creole Band so far as is known, he must have received convincing recommendations indeed to make the trip to Quincy. One imagines that he would have been startled at their New Orleans warmth and swing compared to the New York bands he'd known; to use such musicians would have been a new departure for the couple.

The Castles had approached another band during their stay in Chicago: a four-piece outfit led by San Francisco banjoist Bert Kelly. As Kelly tells the story in his unpublished autobiography, the management of the Hotel Sherman's College Inn, where Kelly's band was a regular feature, told him that Vernon Castle had been offered a contract to dance at Ravinia Park during the summer but would only do so if Kelly's band would play for him. Whether or not this actually came to pass, Vernon Castle also wrote to Margaret Hawkesworth in New York, stating, "If you want to get the finest dance music in America, get Bert Kelly and his Jazz-Band, who are playing at the College Inn, here in Chicago." A few days later Kelly was approached by Basil Durant, Hawkesworth's dancing partner, with a handsome offer to play in New York, Saratoga, Havana, and Palm Beach. Kelly did not take up the offer as he was earning more money in Chicago.[21]

We know of no attempts by the Castles to find another band. Castle left *Watch Your Step* at the beginning of December, amid rumors of an impending separation from Irene. One journal even stated that he would go into vaudeville as a single. He neither separated nor went into vaudeville, going off instead to pilot training to do his bit in the war then raging in Europe.

Announced appearances in Galesburg, Illinois,[22] Joliet (possibly), and Chicago's Lincoln theater, carried the band through to the week of October 17, when they made a relatively long jump to La Crosse, Wisconsin, playing on Sunday, Tuesday, and Wednesday, with the Monday show wiped out by a traveling musical comedy. They then went to Rock Island, Illinois, where they received one of those reviews that makes slogging through the local papers worth it:

> The Creole Band of seven made the feet of every auditor at the Empire Theater—and there was a big house last night—move in time to the swinging, syncopated tunes which they ground out on an original instrumental arrangement. These colored boys are expert musicians but have acquired the queer knack of playing ragtime with an original twist. It is such odd times they get that the audience last night sat for some time trying to straighten the thing out. When they finally did catch the wild syncopation, they broke into applause for better rag playing has never been heard here. There is also good singing and a lot of comedy in the act.[23]

This is an inversion of the usual reviews—which I take to be based on the publicity sent in advance of the show—that emphasize the plantation songs and comedy but rarely give much space to the music.

An appearance in Cedar Rapids, Iowa, from October 25 through 27, was rescheduled; they performed instead at the Majestic in Dubuque from Sunday, October 24, through Wednesday, October 27. The advance publicity described them as "one of the most pretentious offerings Manager [Jake] Rosenthal has ever brought to Dubuque." The brief Monday review nevertheless pulled out all the stops:

> one of the biggest novelties of recent seasons—the Creole Band.
>
> The organization numbers seven, and when it comes to syncopated melodies, they're marvels—that's all. Their music is weird and fascinating, and as its setting it has a scenic surrounding which is romantic in its picturesqueness and appealing in its charm. Wholesome, natural comedy runs smoothly through the spectacle and adds to its enjoyment throughout.[24]

Waterloo, Iowa, heard them for the last half of the week October 28 through 30, and the local newspaper observed that their ragtime and negro melodies turned "the audience from laughter to tears, winding up by sending the crowd away smiling."[25]

The following performance, at the Orpheum in Sioux City, Iowa, gave rise to the most detailed review yet published:

Plantation Songs at Orpheum. The mask of minstrelsy is torn off and plantation days of the old southern darky are portrayed in native settings by Creoles at the Orpheum theater this week. A change in bills was made yesterday, with the Creole band offering the headline attraction [of 5 acts] in an all-comedy program.

Several Creole musicians appear. An old darky sings tunes of the antebellum days. The strum of the bass fiddle puts vigor into the old man's rheumatic knees. The cluck of a chicken awakens a memory. He vanishes and reappears with the fowl clutched in his fists. The Creoles responded to three encores.[26]

Since the band was on its way to Omaha, it would have made sense for them to have played the Lincoln Theater in Des Moines at the end of the week. Be that as it may, they opened at the Empress Theater, Omaha, on Sunday, November 7, with three other acts and a three-reel Essanay production, "Despair." The puff described the "seven raggy artists" as having been the only act that was ever held over for a full week at the Hippodrome Theatre, Chicago. This is quite likely the Great Northern Hippodrome at 26 West Jackson Boulevard (between State and Dearborn Sts.), since Morgan Prince remembered playing at the Great Northern in 1915. It may be possible to verify this, as the Great Northern Hippodrome was important and central enough to advertise in the daily papers, at least some of the time.[27]

The actual review was very brief, stating that the seven colored musicians had "the house in a continuous applause from the rise to the fall of the curtain." We observe, however, that in this newspaper all reviews of all theaters are generally fulsome in their praise. This was certainly not the case at their next stop—on the way back to Chicago—at the Majestic in Cedar Rapids, Iowa. Cedar Rapids was notorious for the vitriolic pen of W. J. Slattery, the manager of the Majestic, who, contrary to the usual practice in vaudeville reviewing, was often extremely harsh. Neither was the Creole Band spared.

The advance publicity was as usual, with the extra detail that several members (of eight) had gone to Australia with the Hugo Minstrels. In fact, only Morgan Prince had made this trip. The review published on Friday evening took off the gloves, no doubt about it:

> When the "big act" in a vaudeville performance fails to come up to the expectations of the audience, a considerable portion of the audience is likely to forget they enjoyed other features of the bill. Also, nine out of every ten patrons of vaudeville imagine they could run the affair in a manner that would suit the general public much better than the chap who is handling the theater is doing it. If the writer of this pinnacle of veracity were in charge of the show at the Majestic for the last half

4.1 Cedar Rapids (Iowa) *Evening Gazette*, November 12, 1915. The artist gets no points for originality, since this is the same drawing seen above in 3.2c.

of the week, the Creole Band, billed as the headline feature, would open the show instead of closing it, and the act would be cut to about seven minutes. Judging from the applause with which the Creole Band was received, the audience expected something it didn't get. It is expected that there would be some real "coon singing." There was not. The "Ragtime Band" music was commonplace, and so was the comedy.

Ouch! We have to wonder whether members of the band were so ill or so hung over that they were unable to thrill the crowd in their usual fashion; and we also question the qualifications of the reviewer to know that the rag music was commonplace. He wouldn't have been the first reviewer with a tin ear. Still, if the principle that a long review is a good review holds, the band might not have been entirely displeased. Not only that, the same paper printed a not uncomplimentary cartoon fifteen pages later.[28]

The band returned to Chicago and the Wilson Avenue for the first half of the week of November 14. The *Saturday Evening Telegraph*, an ultrascarce weekly devoted to show business and sports, published a pen sketch by Z. A. Hendrick that speaks volumes: it shows the moon and a log cabin in the background. In the center foreground is a bent-over Morgan Prince in a frock coat with a battered hat and cane, singing—or rather, shown as singing—"Old Black Joe." Bill Johnson is using his bow on a diminutive bass, from which emanates "My Old Kentucky Home." He might almost be playing to a figure in blackface makeup sticking his head out of a window and asking, "Whar's Nancy?" A cornetist playing with the bell of his horn facing directly at the audience is drawn in the right foreground. Miscellaneous properties are a jug labeled "Gin" and a scrawny chicken. This forms part of a panel, which shows the four other acts on the bill, with the largest figure being Lou Anger, "The Neutral Soldier" with two of his presumed quips in balloons. Finally, in the upper left corner, W. H. Buhl, the business manager, says: "We've been doing wonderful business lately."[29]

According to the *Breeze*: "Lou Anger gets big money and should out do the Creole Band, which closes the show, but somehow he didn't." Elsewhere, the band is listed as one of the six hits of Chicago vaudeville in that week.[30] While it would have been natural for them to move to the American for the last half, they were not one of the five acts reviewed by the *Breeze*. The most startling news of the week, however, appeared in *Variety*, where we find an ad reading, "7 Original Creole Ragtime Band 7, opening at Bushwick, Brooklyn, week Nov. 29th Eastern rep. Harry Weber, Western rep. Simon Agy." We have seen that Weber and Simon were personal acquaintances; but this is the first evi-

4.2 For all that the Wilson Avenue Theater was many miles north of the Loop, it had ambition and bills good enough to merit this excellent composite drawing by Hendrick.

4.3 The ground was prepared for their first appearance in New York City by this small ad in *Variety*, November 19, 1915. Nevertheless, *Variety*'s "Bills Next Week" for November 29 doesn't list the band at the Bushwick. It's true that their initial appearances in the metropole were a bit improvisatory. [By permission of Variety, Inc.] [Chicago Historical Society]

dence that (1) the band was slated to go East, and (2) that it was under the auspices of the powerful Weber.[31] This marks a major change in the course earlier mapped out for them by the Simon Agency, which had them on WVMA time until well into 1916. The band had evidently shown to Simon's and Weber's satisfaction that they were ready for New York, if not the most prestigious Manhattan venues at first, at least for downtown Brooklyn.

In 1947 the somewhat disreputable but often knowledgeable Harrison Smith contributed an article to the English jazz magazine *Jazz Forum* that mentions, among other things, the Creole Band, Harry Weber, and the Winter Garden Theater. Like much of what he wrote, it's a disconcerting mix of fact and fiction, but the facts are often things mentioned in no other source. The stimulus of the article was the release of the movie *New Orleans*, which was apparently being shown at the Winter Garden, "recalling 1918 [*sic*] when the Original Creole Band got it's [*sic*] 'Big time' start there. The building was originally

Studebaker's Wagon factory and Horse Market and I can recall the time, around 1910, when the building with the original walls still intact was transformed into a beautiful and spacious theatre . . . Each Sunday night, the management presented ten vaudeville attractions and the spot became the most important showcase for artists who desired to show their acts to the booking managers of various circuits covering the U.S.A. from Coast to Coast . . . The late Harry Weber, foremost manager of the era, who managed Shelton Brooks, Miller & Lyles, The Tennessee Ten . . . got one of these dates for the Creole Band, who came, played and conquered. A repeat date sewed up an Orpheum Circuit tour for the unit at $800 per week which was a lot of money for a band in those days . . . [follows a lengthy list of cities coast-to-coast where they played]. Upon its return to New York City, Weber placed the band with Ned Wayburn's revue *Town Topics* . . . The revue played on the roof of the nations first million dollar theatre, the Century Theatre. . . ."[32]

It ought to be possible to track their progress East between November 18 and their surfacing in New York on December 5, but the only sighting is at the Lyric Theater in Indianapolis, beginning on Thanksgiving Day, November 25. They were obviously a smash hit to judge from the reviews in three separate papers. The *Times* found them a "real novelty and a worthy headline feature." To the *News* "much of the music [was] the typical negro 'rag' time and was greatly appreciated at the opening performances." It gives a small detail of the act besides: "A bit of comedy is worked into the act when the old colored man is unable to resist the influence of the music and breaks into a shuffling dance that is very amusing." The *Star*, which had on Sunday pronounced them one of the year's vaudeville sensations, also referring to their success at English's the week of May 30, was longer and more eloquent. The band produced "syncopated music that sets the feet a tappin' and the body swaying"—it was their chief stock in trade. They were the headline feature and "delighted immense crowds yesterday." Finally, "Whoever staged the act of the Creole Band has the right idea of what vaudeville patrons want, and the members of this aggregation certainly 'put it over.'" This would surely have been music to any agent's or booker's ears, and would go far to erasing any doubts raised by the negative report from Cedar Rapids.[33]

The *Breeze* of December 10 reported that they had been placed for a New York showing, after a midwest tour, and that they had immediately secured a big-time route; it also stated that the band was at the Grand in Pittsburgh during the current week (December 5). In fact, they were at the New Davis, not the Grand, and if they actually had secured a big-time route, this was soon to change. It is conceivable, although not possible to prove, that this was the point at which the band had a falling out with Harry Weber, and he told them that they would not work in New York.

Bracketing the Pittsburgh engagement were two Sunday "concerts" in New York City, the first at the Columbia burlesque house in Times Square, the second at the prestigious Winter Garden. These Sunday concerts were a way of presenting vaudeville on Sundays, when New York City's blue laws did not permit the usual theatrical performances. They also provided a convenient showcase for bookers, agents, and other vaudevillians to see new acts. The *Clipper*, fortunately, made a practice of going to these shows, and gave the band a quite favorable review:

> That Creole Band of six pieces, cornet, trombone, guitar, clarinet, fiddle and bass viol played a rather ragged selection for a starter, the clarinet particularly being strong for the comedy effect.
>
> The old darkey whom they were serenading responded by singing "Old Black Joe" and the band chimed in with fine harmony both instrumentally and vocally. The playing of some ragtime melodies worked the old darkey to dancing pitch, and he did pound those boards until the kinks in his knees reminded him of his age. Lots of bows, an encore, more bows and another encore stamped this offering O.K.[34]

The *Evening Journal* and the *Herald* both announced that they would play Proctor's Fifth Avenue Monday through Wednesday, along with seven other acts, most of them new; they even received a bogus review in the Monday edition of the *World*, when in fact the band had gone to Pittsburgh.[35] It can't be said that they did well there. First of all, the bill at the Davis featured a flashy novelty, a fashion show on stage with "20 Beautiful Girl Models." Second, the Smart Set Co.—owned, operated, and staffed by African-Americans—was at the Lyceum doing excellent business; one reviewer mentioned that the audience was not exclusively African-American. Finally, the band was for the first time facing a Keith Vaudeville audience, with the admission pegged at a hefty 25¢ to 50¢ for matinees, 25¢ to $1 in the evening. B. F. Keith and the booking agency he founded obsessively pursued the cause of clean, polite, and respectable vaudeville, and the cost of admission would certainly produce a higher-class clientele than that characteristic of the Chicago neighborhood houses, or for that matter the Pantages circuit.

This is, I suggest, the reason why several reviewers single out hard work or loud playing by the band. For example, the *Post* said: "A catastrophe in strings and brasses clattered the seven Creole serenaders into view, switching to the pathos of "I Hear Dem Voices Calling"—a slightly inexact quotation from the words to "Old Black Joe." The *Press*—which was the paper with by far the largest circulation—was quite harsh:

> The Seven Creole Serenaders would be better if, into their syncopation they introduced a little better time and more tune. One member of the company is a good comedian. The old-time songs are splendidly given. But the "rags" are so "blarey" they almost are devoid of rhythm.

The *Gazette Times*, while less acerbic, still found the act noisy:

> Seven musical colored people, including an excellent character actor, give an act in which a wind and string orchestra makes lots of noise and serves as an accompaniment of a well-rendered old-timer, "Old Black Joe." The act is amusing and the musicians work hard.

And possibly part of the problem was the changed billing: "7 Creole Serenaders, Ragtimers in Plantation Pastimes." One thinks of a serenade as rather more restful, even genteel, than the hot ragtime that formed part of their offering. One can imagine, in any event, that Weber—assuming that he was still in the picture—would have had some strong advice for the band upon reading these reactions. While I imagine that the band would have had no trouble in playing softer, it might not have been so easy to modify the carefully honed comic style that had worked so successfully for them for over a year.[36]

The band was back in New York for the December 12 Sunday night concert at the Winter Garden, no longer "serenaders" but a "band" once again. This strongly suggests some kind of link with the Shuberts, as the house was theirs and served on Sunday nights as a showcase for attractions in their stable. They were announced as appearing at Keith's in Jersey City for the last half of that week, a large and important house, but newspaper ads fail to confirm this.[37]

They appeared yet again at a Winter Garden Sunday concert on December 19. The ad for the Winter Garden in the *Herald* used the same basic format as the week before, but with the band significantly higher in the cohort of vaudeville stars. I have yet to find a review of this performance; perhaps there was nothing new to say.[38]

The Bushwick Theater in downtown Brooklyn keeps entering the picture of this somewhat confusing month in the band's career. The *Dramatic Mirror* for December 11 prophesied their appearance there for the week of December 20 through 25 and did so again a week later. *Variety* for the 17 thought they'd be there during that week. Then the *Mirror*'s Christmas issue indicated that they were currently there, although the brief review of the show only

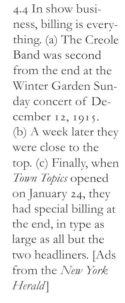

4.4 In show business, billing is everything. (a) The Creole Band was second from the end at the Winter Garden Sunday concert of December 12, 1915. (b) A week later they were close to the top. (c) Finally, when *Town Topics* opened on January 24, they had special billing at the end, in type as large as all but the two headliners. [Ads from the *New York Herald*]

mentioned Emma Carus as topping the bill, and *Variety* had no reviews that week.

Just before the New Year, the band played at Loew's American Roof Theatre, from Monday, December 27 through 29. The review in the *Morning Telegraph* was reasonably encouraging, though hardly musically expert:

> The Creole Band consists of six husky chocolate-colored men, three of whom play upon stringed instruments. One is a cornetist, another a trombonist, while the sixth plays a clarionet. A little darky covered with black grease paint and gray whiskers supplies most of the fun with eccentric dancing, following his singing of "Old Black Joe." Cultured students of music might refer to the chords of the Creole Band as discords, but nevertheless they are tuneful and catchy.

Variety was unkind (or simply objective):

> The Creole Band did a number of syncopated melodies not fully appreciated. The dancer appeared to draw the applause, for up to his appearance it looked as though things were not going to break for them. The closing needs reframing.[39]

This minor setback mattered little, as the band was about to join the resurrected revue *Town Topics*, which began a five-month tour of major cities from Boston to Chicago under the management of the Shubert Brothers.

Exactly how the band and the Shuberts linked up is not clear. Their placement with the lavish but flawed revue *Town Topics* was announced in the press on Christmas Eve: "Frank Bohm's Creole Band Opens with Town Topics" and is absolutely confirmed by interoffice memos from the Shubert Archives. A memo from Gertrude Bock to I. Helstein, dated December 24, reads: "Herewith contract between the Creole Band and 'Town Topics.' Kindly acknowledge receipt."[40] Unfortunately, the contract does not survive. It does seem that the Simon Agency was still in the picture, for a full-page ad on the back cover of the December 17 issue of *Variety* finds the Creole Band listed as one of 108 acts.

Nevertheless, it could well have been around this time that Harry Weber and the band had a falling out, and when, some two years later, they write of his threat that they would not play New York, possibly it was a matter of not playing New York—or anywhere else—on the really big time, that is, Keith or Orpheum vaudeville. And for that reason, they never would have "played the Palace," the Olympus of vaudeville, despite Jelly Roll Morton's assertion that they did.[41]

Curiously, it was not Weber but another agent who was recalled with displeasure by Morgan Prince in 1959. There was an offer in 1915 from a Times

VARIETY

AN ARTIST EXPECTS
"RESULTS"
FROM HIS AGENT
AND
"RESULTS"
ARE OBTAINED BY

The SIMON AGENCY Inc.

THESE STANDARD ACTS WILL TELL YOU THAT IS WHAT
WE GAVE THEM
WE CAN DO THE SAME FOR YOU

Bell and Fredo	Bison City Four	Kartelli	Coakley, Hanvey and Dunlevy
Benny and Woods	The Volunteers	Lua and Analeka	Creole Band
Barry Girls	Creighton Bros.	Lunette Sisters	Clark and Verdi
Bobbe and Nelson	Fay, Two Coleys and Fay	McGoods and Tate's Co.	Corelli and Gilette
Harrison Brockbank and Co.	Guerro and Carmen	Neil McKinley	Cook and Lorenz
Burns and Kissen	Richards and Kyle	E. Merian's Swiss Canines	Tom Davies and Co.
The Dohertys	De Leon and Davies	Medlin, Watts and Townes	Joe De Koe Troupe
Earle and Edwards	Karl Emmy's Pets	Dainty Marie	Melnotte-Lanole Company
Ergotti and Lilliputians	Evans and Sister	Monarch Comedy Four	Hufford and Chain
Frear, Baggot and Frear	Fanton's Athletes	Miss Leitzel	Howard and Fields
Geo. M. Fisher and Co.	Dancing Kennedys	Newhoff and Phelps	Mrs. Louis James
Girl in the Moon	Friend and Downing	Tom Nawn and Co.	Kenny and Hollis
Musical Geralds	Freeman and Dunham	Pearl Bros. and Burns	Hugo B. Koch and Co.
Robbie Gordone	Al. Fields and Co.	Shirley Sisters	Thos. F. Swift and Co.
Claude Golden	Those French Girls	Art Browning, Mgr. "Svengali"	Maizie King
Hanlon and Clifton	The Gaudschmidts	Thalero's Circus	Keno and Greene
Imboff, Conn and Corinne	Royal Gascoignes	Townsend's "Waterlilies"	Bert Kenny
Imperial Troupe	Hanlon Bros.	Warren and Dietrich	Four Le Grohs
Princess Kalama	Hardeen	Willing, Bentley and Willing	Vera Mesereau
Kerville Family	Chas. F. Semon	Neal Abel	Senator Francis Murphy
Bixley and Lerner	Steindel Bros.	Lou Anger	Mystic Bird
B. D. Berg Productions	Ed. and Jack Smith	Busch Bros.	Inez McCauley and Co.
Toots Paka	Frank Stafford and Co.	Dorothy Brenner	Owen McGiveney
Boudini Bros.	Trovato	Van and Belle	The Rials
Primrose Four	Travilla Bros. and Seal	Ching Ling Hee Troupe	Rawson and Clare
	Harry Van Fossen	Clark and McCullough	Little Lord Roberts
	Wood Choppers	Carl McCullough	Santos and Hayes

Every detail incidental to our business is executed by a member of the firm, Irvin C. Simon, B. W. Cortelyou, John B. Simon, and **your business,** entrusted to us, **is in competent hands.**	**John B. Simon is now in New York,** care Gene Hughes and Jo. Paige Smith, Palace Theatre Building, and it is suggested to artists contemplating playing in the Middle West that they get in touch with him.

The SIMON AGENCY, Inc.   1405-1406 Majestic Theatre Bldg. CHICAGO

Booking Only With
Western Vaudeville Mgrs.' Assn.   -   U. B. O. (Chicago)   -   Interstate   -   Orpheum Circuit

4.5 In breaking into big-time show business, the Creole Band was in the classic position of a small frog in a very big pond. (You can find them listed second from the top of column four.) [*Variety*, July 21, 1916, back cover]

Square theatrical agent, Lee Muckenfuss, for the band to go to England to play in a London music hall, then on the Continent, for $80 per person per week. But everyone in the band except Prince was afraid to cross the Atlantic because of the German U-boat attacks. (The *Lusitania* had been sunk on May 7, 1915.) The incredibly named Muckenfuss—perhaps from the German Mueckenfuss, meaning gnat foot—replied: "All right, get out and don't ever

The Second Season : 155

come back." He also threatened that the band would never work again, in the entire United States.

Bill Johnson's recollection was only slightly different. In 1916, he said, a booker named McNeil—or something like that—with offices in the Singer Building, offered them a contract in France, England, and Italy for $500 a week.

[Lee P. Muckenfuss was indeed a real person, with headquarters at the end of 1914 in the Palace Building, but in July 1916, in the Putnam Building (1493 Broadway), along with a number of other agents and the Marcus Loew Agency. Coincidentally, Frank Bohm had his office there, although on a different floor. In another source around the same time, his address is given as 1564 Broadway, the same as the agency of Albee, Weber, and Evans. He is listed as representing 25 acts—a rather small number and none of them "names."[42]

As to the Singer Building, while there is such a building in Manhattan, it was miles away from the theater district, in the southern tip at Broadway and Liberty. No theatrical booker or agent that I can find in the 1916 city directory or the Billboard directory has offices there.

Much more likely is the Singer Building in Chicago, at 120 South State Street, between Monroe and Adams Streets. While the Billboard 1915 directory lists no booker or artists' agent at that address—and none is named McNeil or some variant—the Jones, Linick & Shaefer Circuit had offices at 110 South State.]

The Creole Band was thereby entering show business territory utterly unlike any they had experienced. With the band at this crucial juncture, we might well spend a few pages on three subjects: two of them, the dancer Mabel Elaine and the revue *Town Topics*, of direct relevance to their future, the third, Brown's Band, of indirect relevance in the broader context of the history of the dissemination of New Orleans ragtime is treated elsewhere.

The history of *Town Topics* and its original producer, Ned Wayburn, is also part of the history of a remarkable (and huge) theater building. Originally called the New Theater, at Central Park West and Sixty-second St., it was built according to plans submitted to a national contest sponsored by some of the wealthiest men in New York City. It was deliberately located away from Times Square, and was thought of by some as a kind of "national theater," following the lines of grand European theaters or opera houses. Opened in November 1909, it was technically advanced but acoustically unsatisfactory. Renovation did not make it more tempting to audiences, so its original wealthy patrons attempted to realize their project of a national playhouse in the Times Square area.

The name of the house was changed to the Century, sometimes called an opera house, sometimes a music hall. It was, in any event, a remarkable building. In addition to a sizeable theater seating more than 2,000, it had in 1915 an English Tap room for the gentlemen, and, on the mezzanine floor, an English Ladies' Bar and Restaurant in which dancing was permitted during intermissions and after the performance. On the roof was a large space that served for rehearsals, a full-fledged variety theater, a children's theater, and eventually a variously named cabaret, notably the Coconut Grove.[43] Such an elaborate theater called for pretentious spectacles.

Ned Wayburn, an ambitious and imaginative old-timer in show business, was clearly up to the task, conceiving an exceptionally elaborate revue, *Town Topics* (actually entitled *Ned Wayburn's Town Topics* in the program for the premiere), sometime in the first half of 1915. Perhaps his most noteworthy achievement was to corral very significant financial backing for the show—$150,000 coming from Joseph M. Eccles of Salt Lake City. The program credits both the book (?)—the question mark is as in the program—and the lyrics to Harry B. Smith (1860–1936), a librettist for Reginald DeKoven and Victor Herbert; Thomas J. Gray (1888–1924); and Robert B. Smith. The music was the work of the veteran Harold Orlob (1883–1982), a charter member of AS-CAP, whose only enduring song is "I Wonder Who's Kissing Her Now."

There were twenty-one scenes in two acts, with twenty (!) separate sets, some of them clearly transformations using the Century's large revolving stage. There were 30 principals, some 65 chorus girls, and 26 male singers and dancers. As a revue, it required no plot to speak of, and it had none; but even among revues, it was considered by some reviewers an absurdity, more fashion show than theatrical presentation.

There was no shortage of stars: Bert Leslie, Will Rogers, Lew Hearn, and, among the women, Trixie Friganza, Blossom Seeley, Marie Lavarre. Strangely enough, the cast counted two famous dancing couples—Adelaide and Hughes and Cross and Josephine—in addition to Clifton Webb (as David Dansant, "who trips the light fantastic") and Eileen Molyneux. This army of entertainers was deployed in scenes as varied as a baseball stadium—the Polo Grounds, inside and out, a subway car, a theater lobby and backstage, and a fashion shop, "Madame Flair's Emporium of Chic." These urban locales were to some extent balanced by a prairie scene, featuring Trixie Friganza as an "Indian Suffragette," and a quartet of "Tone Pictures": Summer, Autumn, Winter, and Spring, with Orlob conducting the orchestra. Most remarkably, a Mississippi levee with steamboat, transforming into a cotton plantation, were added to the potpourri close to the end of the second act.[44]

One more than suspects that in a spectacle of this nature, it wasn't a matter of finding players to fit the book but fashioning the book according to the abilities of the players. Thus we find a Lariat Dance, featuring Will Rogers and Miss Josephine. (Rope twirling was, of course, Rogers's first claim to theatrical fame.)

Enter Mabel Elaine (1893–1955), a young blackface dancer, born in Louisville, Kentucky, but brought up in Chicago and trained in the neighborhood theaters and cabarets of that city. She then joined the nationally touring company of a hardy perennial, *The Ham Tree*, featuring old-time minstrels McIntyre and Heath. Perhaps the title of the show says all we need to know about it; but in any event Elaine could hardly have failed to learn some of the age-old routines of blackface minstrelsy in a vehicle featuring McIntyre and Heath. Simultaneously, in their issues of July 9, *Variety* and the *Breeze* announced that Elaine had been signed by Ned Wayburn for *Town Topics*. The latter source stated also that she had been signed for three years by Wayburn. Rehearsals began on July 19, with the original opening scheduled for six weeks later, in early September. It actually opened a bit later, on September 23.

Elaine was a soubrette type and comedian as well as a clog (in modern terms, "tap") dancer and appeared in act one, scene six (a backstage set) as Gertie Gorgonzola, a "small timer" singing "I Want Some One Who's Lonesome." Her second appearance was in the Mississippi levee scene, singing and dancing in blackface, with the chorus, "Cotton Blossom Time." When the set transformed into a cotton plantation, Blossom Seeley appeared, singing "Wake Up, It's Cake-Walk Day." In its review published October 1, Sime [Silverman], the leading writer for *Variety*, was reasonably well impressed and singled out in the backstage scene "a little girl named Mabel Elaine," also mentioning her appearance in the levee scene. Not only that; he also included her in the company of such as Will Rogers and Trixie Friganza as "'the ones who impress mostly." This favorable professional judgment repeated what had already been said in the dailies. The *Journal*, for instance, described her as "little dainty Mabel Elaine. As Gertie Gorgonzola she was delightful and her blackface rendition of "Cotton Blossom Time" brought down big applause."[45]

Did the levee scene also involve a band on stage, in addition to the 31-piece pit orchestra? An examination of the only photographic evidence—in the White Studios "key books"—shows Elaine in blackface in the foreground with a 16 girl chorus, 8 of them dressed as men, and in the background 7 men who *could* be musicians, perched on cotton bales and the like.[46]

If so, it seems likely that they were drawn from "Vodery's Ragphony Orchestra," which, in addition to appearing in the Polo Ground scene, provided dance music on the mezzanine or on the roof. *Variety* observed: "A colored band furnishes dance music upstairs before, during and after the show, but so far no one goes up there afterward to hear it." Nevertheless, mention of the Ragphony orchestra disappeared from the Polo Grounds Scene in a program for the October 4 performance.[47]

PREDICTABLY, *TOWN TOPICS* ran into money trouble. Despite a brief item in the November 12 *Variety*, to the effect that the average weekly gross of between $17,500 and $19,000 was making it possible for the Wayburn management to realize a profit, the sad truth emerged a week later, when it was announced that the Shubert Brothers had taken over the show and would close it after an unimpressive total of 68 performances with the Saturday night performance, November 20. It now appeared that the show was averaging a mere $16,000 a week, with expenses running higher than that. Furthermore, wrote *Variety*, the Shuberts "were anxious to get the production out of the Century, where it had hurt their Winter Garden business, and to control it as well on the road, to prevent further opposition there." Also, the backers were unhappy about a touring company under the auspices of Klaw & Erlanger. As final testimony to their business acumen, we learn that the Shuberts had managed to convince all the principals, with the exception of Will Rogers, who smelled a rat (my words), to accept half pay for the final week.[48]

There was apparently a bankruptcy sale, at which the Shuberts purchased all of the revue's properties (they had already bought Wayburn's production company) for $6,250. There ensued a series of announcements of a reopening, at first in New York, then in Philadelphia on December 19, then on Christmas Eve, either in Montreal or New Haven, then again a week later in Hartford. In fact, there was a New Year's Eve performance in Hartford and both matinee and evening performances on January 1.[49] The show was slated to open in Boston's Shubert Theater on January 3, but *Variety* reported that it would be a day later due to "road delay." The dress rehearsal was reportedly conducted on Monday night, January 3, by J. J. Shubert himself, and the first performance took place on the following evening. *Town Topics* remained in Boston for nearly three weeks.[50]

Neither the blurb, display ads, nor review appearing in the *Boston Globe* make mention of the Creole Band. The review described the show as "a big, glittering and speedy girl show" but did like Mabel Elaine: "In the scenes in the

South Mabel Elaine scores her biggest hit in typical dances, in which she is assisted by a 'heap' of clever steppers." Wouldn't such a novel feature as a genuine colored ragtime band have attracted some notice? This certainly permits the surmise that they were not yet with the show.[51]

Town Topics closed Boston with two shows on Saturday, January 22, and left for their Monday opening at the Winter Garden, between Broadway and Seventh Avenues and Forty-ninth and Fiftieth Streets at the north end of Times Square.[52] The theatrical section of the *Morning Telegraph* for Sunday ran an ad that read:

7 - ORIGINAL CREOLE RAGTIME BAND - 7

A Feature with "Town Topics." W. M. Johnson, Manager. Open Winter Garden, November [*sic*] 24th.

Another ad from the *Telegraph* of January 30 reiterates that Johnson is manager and declares that the band was a "big success."

As far as more general papers are concerned an oversize display ad in the *Herald* omits Mabel Elaine from the dozen members of the cast mentioned. But, notably, "The Creole Band" is listed on the last line, in type of the same size as Cross & Josephine, and Lew Hearn & Bonita. For all that, the short review on Tuesday breathes not a word of Elaine or the band. The same is true of the *Tribune*, which found the second edition smoother, liked the comedy in general, and new cast member Bonita in particular.[53]

Other papers had something to say. The *American* reported that the Creole Band "scored a great hit" and "was by far the most uproarious incident in the performance." Elaine, with her "so-called 'Creole' dances," was thought to come in second. It was the *Telegram* that pulled out all the stops:

Of the newcomers, the feature that aroused the audience to the utmost enthusiasm was the Creole Ragtime Band, a group of colored musicians who played their in-

4.6 (a, b, and c) The group photo shows, from left to right, Keppard, Bill Johnson, and Norwood Williams. Morgan Prince, in whose scrapbook it was preserved, identified the locale as the stage entrance to the Chicago Theater and himself as the photographer. The band's only appearance at that theater was with *Town Topics*, so the date must be between March 6 and April 9, 1916. Why they're in band uniform is another question. Shots b and c of Keppard are clearly in the same locale, although unless he was a quick-change artist they must have been taken at different times. How amazing that these three snapshots have survived! Were there others? [b and c were taken from the Smithsonian Collection LP, "The Legendary Freddie Keppard," to which they had been contributed by Frank Driggs.]

struments as if they were trying to express Richard Strauss in his most extravagant moods. Miss Mabel Elaine, who danced to their wild music, performed with such frenzy that she appeared to have swallowed a corkscrew or a spring mattress.[54]

The show was to remain three weeks in New York City, leaving to play its first road show engagement in Detroit during the week of February 13. There followed single weeks in Cincinnati and St. Louis, then five weeks in Chicago at the Chicago Theater—the refurbished American Music Hall at Wabash and Peck Court, a reasonably large house at 1,500 seats but with a smallish stage and poorly located at the southern extremity of the downtown area.[55] The next stop was Indianapolis, apparently for Tuesday through Thursday only, April 11–13, with the first performance sold out to the Shriners. Bill Johnson remembered that the band provided dance music for the company as it traveled from place to place in private rail cars.

Remarkably, three snapshots showing members of the band in front of a stage door, thought to be that of the Chicago Theater, have survived.[56]

After considerable shilly-shallying, it was decided that the show would lay off for Holy Week, except that the Creole Band was given special permission to work then.[57] J. J. Shubert had requested the road manager, J. A. Reed, to canvass the company to see whether they would accept half-pay for the week. All agreed to do so except Trixie Friganza and Bert Leslie. On April 3, J. J. decided to lay off for the week anyway, writing: "I am not going to give in to any of those 'hams,' under any circumstances. If they want to play for the half salary I must know immediately upon receipt of this letter, otherwise we will just jump them right out of Chicago into the town we are going to play." Claiming a lame knee, Friganza gave two weeks notice (until April 16) on the same day. The road manager suspected that she had possibly signed a contract with Oliver Morosco, and would not be surprised if she were going to play vaudeville during Holy Week.

Reed included in this letter an anecdote that may give an idea of Friganza's personality:

She went to early Mass the other morning and in returning she had to pass the theater, it was eight thirty a.m. the night watchman was still in charge. She did not see her picture in front of the theater and she put up a terriable [sic] howl—the language she used will not do to repeat. She threatened to kick the man in the ba——s and a few more choice expressions.[58]

The company played Indianapolis for the first half of the week of April 10—Trixie was still with the show—where the *News* believed Mabel to be from Indiana: "Mabel Elaine, erstwhile Hoosier, is the most original grotesque in months, particularly in her Topsy guise . . . not to forget the lusty negroisms of the Creole Band."[59]

The show appears to have laid off on Thursday, April 13. But it played Columbus on Friday and Saturday. Here Mabel seems to have been even more of a hit than usual. The review in the *Evening Dispatch* was overall very favorable. Regarding Mabel and the band, it stated: "It's the vaudeville type of musical show . . . Through the show there runs a touch of "Down South" which is concentrated in the cotton plantation scene, in which Mabel Elaine, blackfaced and to the strains of the Creole Ragtime Band, brings down the house. This little dancer, with comedy in her muscles, figures in other scenes . . . "[60]

At this point, Friganza finally took her leave to be, rather surprisingly, replaced by Sophie Tucker[61]—for $300 a week, half of Friganza's salary. Tucker and the company proceeded to Pittsburgh during the Holy Week layoff for rehearsals, opening with second billing (after Bert Leslie) the week after. Some changes were necessary: notably the "Indian Suffragette" number was dropped. Otherwise, with the exception of the first number, which she was to do as her predecessor had done it, she was free to introduce her own specialties.[62]

After the week in Pittsburgh, the show was originally scheduled to leave on a Western tour. This did not come to pass—possibly due to Trixie's defection[63]—and the troupe went on to play in Cleveland, then in Buffalo, each time for one week only. The last stand, in Philadelphia, was two weeks, from May 15 through Saturday, May 27. *Variety* reported a decidedly unhealthy take of $10,000 for the entire fortnight, despite fine weather. Reed wrote that many felt the show lacked "class."

Since *Town Topics* was a big Shubert show, there were many reviews during the tour; many of them are perfunctory and do not even mention the band or Mabel Elaine. And some reviews that mentioned her, practically always with favor, refer generically to "colored musicians." One mention, from the Philadelphia *Record*, will have to illustrate all such offhand remarks: "Mabel Elaine . . . in the old-fashioned minstrel manner . . . But the excitement was fed by the shuffling tunes of a dance hall orchestra composed of genuine colored musicians of the plantation type." The curse of anonymity for the band persisted in another Philadelphia newspaper, in which the anonymous reviewer wrote: "By far the best part of the show was the dancing, and there was plenty of it. Mabel Elaine tried some old-fashioned negro shake-downs, and did them so well with the aid of several colored musicians, that she scored the hit of the evening." It certainly appears that, despite the separate billing (which may well have been a clause in their contract), in the public eye the Creole Band took a back seat to Mabel Elaine. After all, it was she that did a solo clog (or tap) number, merely accompanied by the band. Their reappearance in the finale doesn't seem to have changed the situation.

Some of Elaine's reviews were exceptionally complimentary, considering that she was a nearly unknown quantity on the Broadway stage. Perhaps that was why she declared at the end of March that—as Reed reported it in his report to J. J.—"[she] will not accept less than one hundred dollars a week, beginning with Easter, up to on or about Sept., 1st. For next season she insists on $125.00 per week." This produced a predictable response from J. J., who wrote back on April 3: "In reference to Mabel Elaine, she has a contract and I am going to hold her to it. If she thinks she can get out let her try it. I am not going to be bothered with these people." Having failed in this, Mabel declared her desire to sing a song that was considered Al Jolson's property, more or less, "Where Did Robinson Crusoe Go with Friday on Saturday Night?"

The most passionate evaluation came from the very well-known and powerful Amy Leslie, writing for the *Chicago Daily News* under the headline "Blaze of Color and Big Travesty Romp":

> . . . that small bundle of chain lightning, Mabel Elaine . . . Somebody who knows ought to be able to tell a whole lot about the work of Mabel Elaine, but to me she jumped into a hit straight out of the clear sky. I know she has had the best school of pantomime and negro essence dancing, but this is the first time she streaked across my horoscope, and I fell very hard for Mabel. She does regulation old time essence and double pat jig and buck and wing. Her "Cotton Blossom Time" was a classic and the colored band was the funniest thing in the show. A man did a dance in the tag of this song and did it splendidly, but his name was not on the bill.[64]

Even in this highly laudatory review, the band labored under the traditional curse of anonymity, even though they were now receiving billing as "The Wonderful Creole Band." I take it also that the man who joined her at the end was a member of the band, probably Morgan Prince.

Another famous member of the Chicago reviewing clan, Ashton Stevens, uniquely recognized the symbiosis between Elaine and the band:

> . . . And close to their trail [Bert Leslie and Trixie Friganza] are Mabel Elaine and the Creole Ragtime Band, to whose every syncope she dances a mad Darktown dance that is all pepper, razors and [illegible]. But this Creole Ragtime Band is not to be dismissed between courses. It's nothing short of a paragraph, this combo [*sic* ??] of cornet, clarinet, fiddle, guitar, trombone and double bass. To me, it is much

more fun than Brown's 6 Saxes in "Chin Chin," but perhaps that is because there is less of it. The Creoles do not try to Sousa the whole performance.[65]

The length of the notices from Leslie and Stephens is quite surprising. Remember that this was a show with "really big" stars, a lot of pretty girls in colorful fashions, and ingenious sets. For Mabel and the band to attract such attention must mean that their turn was quite extraordinary.

Lacking script, set drawings, or photos, we have to piece together what the scene was like. Also the version of the Century Theater performance may not have been the one that went on the road. In one case, the "Tone Pictures" of the four seasons were completely cut, since they were designed for the rotating stage of the Century. In the first production, Elaine's blackface scene was act 2, scene 7: "Newport transformed to the Sunny South." This comprised two songs, "Cotton Blossom Time" with Elaine and chorus, followed by "The Musical Mokes," Flanagan and Edwards. The set represented a Mississippi Levee, with big steamboats drawn up to the landing stage. "Another boat drew up and out of it emerged dozens of pretty girls and well-groomed men."

This set transformed into a cotton plantation in which Blossom Seeley sang "Wake Up, It's Cake-walk Day." Once Seeley left the show, alterations were required, perhaps several, but a complete set of programs would be needed to establish what those were. There is extant from the conductor's score folder for the show a list of scenes, cast, and musical numbers, which dates prior to Trixie Friganza's departure. This shows that scenes six and six and one-half, the levee with Full Stage Fly and Prairie Drop, and the plantation (full stage) have been moved from act 2 to act 1.[66] "Wake Up, It's Cake-walk Day" seems to be sung only just prior to the act 2 finale, by Marie Lavarre & Chorus. Musical number 11 is still "Cotton Blossom Time"—Elaine & Chorus, Colored Band Ends Scene—but 11-½ has been penciled in as "Balling the Jack."

A piano-vocal score for number 11, "Levee Scene," survives, which segues into "Cotton Blossom Serenade." There follow 16 penciled solo measures, the last half of which is "Old Folks at Home" in D minor. Finally, a penciled note: "Encore 'Ragtime'" (or possibly 'Rag tune'). The professionally copied first violin part to "Cotton Blossom Serenade" follows the piano-vocal score—although a whole step higher. Sixteen measures are cut at the end, with the penciled note: "2-½ minutes wait," then an arrow to "Cho. 'Balling the Jack' = #12, B♭." Scratched out at the bottom are "Beautiful Baby, Key of C" and "Ginger Cho. B♭.'" The next page consists of a hastily penciled melody to "Ballin' the Jack" in G, and the chorus to "All Full of Ginger" in B♭.'

In fact, the conductor's tune list mentioned above has a penciled addition

"12. Beautiful Baby, *segue* 12-½ Ginger." In the original show, "All Full of Ginger" was sung by Marie Lavarre, but in the conductor's list as well as in a review from the *Buffalo Commercial* it's clear that the song was reassigned to Mabel Elaine, bringing her total of numbers to three. There's no reason to believe, however, that the Creole Band played in any scene other than the Levee Scene.

Reviews, however, make it clear that there were often encores. One possibility for an encore might be Shelton Brooks's 1916 hit "Walkin' the Dog," since a press release from the publisher, Will Rossiter, very shortly before the show closed, states:

> Cross and Josephine are singing and dancing "Walkin' the Dog," and Mabel Elaine is dancing to it, and the Creole Band is playing it—all in the same show, "Town Topics." Some hit, eh?[67]

In this connection it's interesting that at the end of the first violin, 2nd stand, parts, there's a first violin part from the published orchestration of "Walkin' the Dog." Written at the top are two directions in different hands: "MAYBE (?)"; and "After Announcement." Both the verse and trio are cut, with markings indicating that after the four-measure introduction, the chorus was played three times. It seems entirely reasonable to add this strutting melody to the repertory of the Creole Band.

What happened after *Town Topics* closed is not entirely clear. A letter from Clifford Fischer, who handled vaudeville bookings for the Shuberts but also managed various of their properties, including the Winter Garden Theater and the Sunday Concerts therein, to J. J. reads: "Mabel Elaine asked me to be kind enough and ask you whether you want her for any show, so kindly let me know, and oblige." The penciled note from J. J. reads "send Elaine to see me." This exchange was necessitated by the clause in Elaine's original contract of December 15, 1915, for the run of *Town Topics*. If it ran more than 15 weeks—which it did—the Shuberts had an option on her services for the season of 1916–1917, starting October 1. Although she was enjoined to appear and perform in public or private without prior written consent, there's nothing that speaks to the period between the closing of the show and the beginning of the new season. Perhaps she was just hoping she might find something that would tide her over.

With respect to the Creole Band, there can be found in the Shubert Archives six brief communications between Fischer, J. J., and Lee Shubert, beginning with Fischer to J. J. on June 6: "In reference to The Creole Band please let me know what you want to do in this matter, and oblige." The only substantive letter is from Fischer to Bill Johnson at 115 West 133rd Street, Manhattan, stating: "Mr. Lee Shubert begs to inform you that you are at liberty to play from this day until the end of September wherever you want to play." It seems likely that they had a contract something like Elaine's, giving the Shuberts an option on their services for 1916–1917. A telegram sent to J. J. Shubert from Philadelphia by Jack Reed, the road manager of *Town Topics*, expresses concern that the band had not yet been signed to a long-term contract: "If you have not already signed up the Creole Band, I advise you do Sunday when they come over to play Winter Garden. Several vaudeville agents are after them."[68] However, J. J.'s response of May 20 to Reed states: "We placed the Creole Band under contract when we took the show over." If this is literally true, then the contractual relation between the band and the Shuberts would date back to the beginning of December. Unfortunately, no contract has been located in the otherwise amazingly inclusive archive of the Shubert enterprises.

HAVING JUST FINISHED working together to impassioned applause for some five months, Elaine and the Band might well have thought they could hit the vaudeville trail together with essentially the same act. That they may have been making common cause just before the close of *Town Topics* is suggested by a note from J. J. Shubert to Jack Reed dated Thursday, May 25, 1916, confirming the close of the show on Saturday night:

> Do not deduct anything from the actors on account of the Indianapolis week, in fact I would not deduct anything from the principals and I would pay them on Saturday night. Since talking to you on the telephone I have decided to do this, with the exception of Elaine and the niggers. They held us up in New York for $125.00, which must be deducted from their salary.[69]

In any event, it's no surprise to find a tiny item under the "New Acts" rubric in *Variety*: "Mabel Elaine and the Creole Band (Harry Fitzgerald)." Attentive readers will recall Fitzgerald as the agent who bamboozled Brown's Band into coming to New York nine months earlier.[70]

By this time, George Baquet had left the band, exactly where or when is unclear, and a telegram had gone off to New Orleans, asking Louis "Big Eye" Delille to join them. Actually, from a few scattered remarks it's clear that the colorless "left the band" is inadequate to whatever happened. Frederic Ramsey put it this way in his 1941 *Down Beat* article:

CHICK KEEPS HIM IN N.Y.

When the Creole Orchestra returned to Chicago, Baquet stayed in New York to play in an act posted as *Irresistible Rag*. In it, Baquet was a sort of Pied Piper who charmed all those who threatened him in a series of pantomime adventures with his clarinet, and won them to his side. There was a girl in the act and some of his friends say that's why he stayed in the east, and gave up a good job with the Creole orchestra. Baquet just smiles when you ask him about that.

Morgan Prince had a considerably less romantic recollection; he thought that Baquet had left the band in Pittsburgh to get married. Perhaps Prince confused Pittsburgh with Philadelphia; or perhaps—since that's where Sophie Tucker replaced Trixie Friganza—Friganza was the lady in question. This was the belief of Clotile Palao and Norwood Williams.

This synthetic account probably collapses the proximate cause of Baquet's departure with his marriage and formation of a vaudeville act with Oma [often spelled "Orma"] Crosby, née Browne (or Brown). According to the indispensable *Freeman* of September 30, 1916, "Oma Crosby Baquet (not of Indiana) a bulwark of the Broadway players, married not long ago to a Mr. Baquet of New York City, a genial young clubsman and also well known to the state." The remark regarding Broadway players is made clear in the *New York Age*, which lists her as a cast member of the repertory company of the Lafayette Theater, one of the most famous venues for black theatrical entertainment. She was clearly a seasoned performer, being mentioned for the first time in the *Indianapolis Freeman*, December 15, 1900, which identified her as a former member of Isham's *Octoroons*. Shortly thereafter, she appears to have been married to Harry "the Squirrel" Crosby, a well-known ragtime pianist. This union seems to have been brief. A few years later, she was married to an actor, Will H. Browne.[71]

The first mention of an act, however, comes from February 10, 1917, when the *Freeman* found George and Oma playing successfully in Perth Amboy and Plainfield, New Jersey. A month later, the same source reviewed the show at Gibson's New Standard Theater. We read, "The Barquettes, or Ragtime Sam and his clarinette, flirts with soubrettes . . . Mr. Barquette as Ragtime Sam in blackface, is a good musician." [a surfeit of "-ettes," surely] How long the act lasted is not known.

Bill Johnson remembered replacing Baquet temporarily with the trumpeter [cornetist, no doubt] Tobe Brown of Detroit. Brown was a seasoned musician, first surfacing around 1908 in Louisville, where he is said to have had his own band for a number of years; but he had moved to Chicago by 1911, when he was found in the orchestra pit of the "Old" Grand Theater. His departure for Detroit is noted in the *Defender*, June 5, 1915.[72] A continuing connection with Detroit is evidenced by his presence in Ben Shook's large orchestra at the end of the decade. In any event, his stint with the band was very brief, and obviously something of a makeshift.

To some, the single most dramatic event in the history of the Creole Band is in actuality a "non-event"; that is, the failure of the band to seize the chance to make a record for the Victor Talking Machine Company. Not only was this fateful for their career at the time, it meant that ever after jazz history—enormously dependent on the solid foundation of recorded sound—would consider them something of a tangential curiosity.

This is the view from the white side of the fence. Danny Barker in leading up to his 1948 interview with George Baquet (to be discussed at greater length below) introduces a more impassioned note: "There were many old jazzmen who were mad at Fred Keppard for not recording with the Creole Band when they were approached by the Victor Recording Company,"[73] perhaps because recordings from the Creole Band would take from the Original Dixieland Band its position as pioneers of recorded jazz.

The first form of the story to reach a broad public was that printed in the initial chapter of *Jazzmen*, written by Steven Smith and William Russell and based largely on research by the latter:

> Early in 1916 the Victor Phonograph Company approached the Original Creoles with an offer to record. Keppard thought it over, and said:
>
> "Nothin' doin', boys. We won't put our stuff on records for everybody to steal."
>
> He persuaded the other fellows to turn down the recording offer. A few months later, Victor signed Nick La Rocca's group, which under the name of the Original Dixieland Jazz Band went on to fame and fortune.[74]

While it's possible that this anecdote was already in wide circulation, especially among black musicians, the most plausible source for it would be Bill Johnson, whom Russell had interviewed in Chicago only a few months earlier. Speaking against this idea are notes of conversations with Johnson found in the little black notebook in which Russell wrote down many of his Chicago interviews from 1938. Not only do they say nothing about Keppard, they also add a salient and very specific detail that did not find its way into *Jazzmen*. The passage is very brief: "offer Vic Rec. 1916 / Will Vodery ——> Handy Music Co. 1783."

George Baquet in an interview by Fred Ramsey, Jr., published in *Down Beat* of January 1, 1941, offers a clearly related account, which adds another extremely important detail:

> The Victor Phonograph Company wanted to make records. Keppard broke that up, because he didn't want to put the music down so everyone else could steal it.

"Nothin' doin,' boys," was his verdict.

He was further annoyed, Baquet says, because the company wasn't sure that Johnson's string bass would record (it was the talking machine, then, and not RCA-Victor with half-a-dozen microphones in each studio), and wanted the band to come over and make special tests. Keppard couldn't understand "playing a date"—for the tests—and not being paid for it:

"We've been kicked around so much we don't want to record. We'll do it if you give us money, money right away!"[75]

Given the close similarity of the first part of this version with that of *Jazzmen* —organized and edited by Ramsey some two years earlier—it seems not far-fetched to suggest that he combined the earlier version with what Baquet actually said, as revealed, perhaps, by the placement of the words "Baquet says."

There are a number of ways of understanding the asserted unwillingness of Keppard to let his "stuff" be stolen. First, a preternatural sense of the importance which this music was shortly to assume in the national picture; second, a vaudevillian's understanding that his highly polished act was in a very concrete sense his bread and butter; third—as Baquet seems to add at the end of the passage—a generalized resentment at not being paid a just wage for his talent; and fourth, something like the kind of fear reported (apocryphally?) among tribal peoples who believe that a photograph can in a sense steal their identity, even their souls. While the idea of the vaudevillian wanting to prevent competitors from copying his material is attractive, it was, after all, an ensemble performance that seems to have accounted for the band's success, not just solo turns by their cornet star. Also, many of Keppard's effects would have been achieved by combinations of lipping, partial valving, and perhaps muting that wouldn't be given away by the recording alone.

But surely, neither Russell, Smith, nor Ramsey would have invented this reaction of Keppard's. Where might it have come from? Of all the musicians given credit in the Introduction to *Jazzmen*, one name stands out: Sidney Bechet. Bechet was constantly in and around New York City during the period of conception and assembling of *Jazzmen*, and he was surely interviewed by one or another of Ramsey or the two Smiths, Stephen or Charles Edward. Bechet knew Keppard from New Orleans and had played beside him in Chicago in 1918; more important, it's clear that he felt enormous admiration and sympathy for Fred—which we may be pardoned for reading into the well-known photograph of the two musicians taken in Chicago.

Unfortunately, the account given by Bechet in his autobiography, for all its detail and subtlety, lends little support to this hypothesis. It begins:

4.7 Keppard and Sidney Bechet. It's clear from the latter's autobiography that he felt uncommonly close to Keppard, despite being eight years his junior. Although Bechet had passed through Chicago at the end of 1917, he didn't begin working there until the spring of 1918, staying about a year. To judge by the straw hats, this photograph comes from the summer of 1918. [Courtesy of Frank Driggs]

Three or four times while he was up there [touring vaudeville] his [Keppard's] band was engaged to make records. The directors from the recording company, they come to them, wanting to engage them. But they never made those records. There was all kinds of reasons given. These writers since then who have been writing books about Jazz, they all had a reason to give; they was all sure they had an idea why Freddie never made those records. But all that writing, it was just writing from hearsay. There was only one real reason: Fred just didn't care to, that was all.

After a beginning like that, there doesn't seem to be much more to say, but fortunately Bechet went on, first to reject the idea that Freddie was trying to hide something, a notion reinforced by the legend that he liked to play with a handkerchief concealing his valve hand. Bechet seems to believe that it was a joke —and anyway, just looking wouldn't be enough to permit copying.

Bechet offers another reason, clearly identifying it as his own notion:

Freddie never said it just that way, but many times we've spoken of that recording session business, and from his answer it's the only conclusion I've come to: that these people who was coming to make records, they was going to turn it into a regular business, and after that it wouldn't be pleasure music. That's the way Freddie was.

The plot thickens, as Bechet launches into a more general discussion of Keppard's attitudes toward music:

Freddie really understood music; he had a feeling for it. He wouldn't give away any part of the music, and he wouldn't stand for it being played wrong . . . And he had a feeling about that recording thing; he had a feeling that every Tom, Dick, or Harry who could ever blow a note would be making records soon. It would get so the music wasn't where it belonged. It was going to be taken away.

This leads, understandably, to a lengthy analysis of the role and meaning of the Original Dixieland Jazz Band, indicted not just for having stolen numbers originated by black musicians in New Orleans but also for playing them uncreatively: "It was all arranged and you played it the way it was written and that was all."

Obviously, lacking access to the original interviews used in constructing the autobiography, we can't stretch Bechet's words on the rack of scholarship in order to extract the last drop of possible meaning. Certainly, everything quoted is consonant with Bechet's own musical philosophy, which insisted that the music be both intensely personal yet true to the deep collective sentiments of African-Americans. The tangled history of the several stages and authors through which Bechet's words and tape recordings passed on their way to publication has been definitively related by John Chilton, who also presents a strong case for Bechet's propensity to make up stories *ad libitum*.[76] It is still possible, in my opinion, that Sidney was behind the *Jazzmen* version, so often repeated that it has on occasion been termed a legend.

When might Keppard and Bechet have had such intense conversations? They were together for about half a year in 1918, then quite possibly again in 1931, when the Noble Sissle band played briefly in Chicago. Conversations in the latter half of 1918 about the whole business of recording or not recording—and the Original Dixieland Band's role—certainly seems plausible. The ODJB's five Victor records (ten tunes) recorded in March, June, and July 1918 would have been in the stores, no doubt vigorously advertised as well.[77] I have no trouble in regarding some of what might have been said as rationalization, even sour grapes.

Leaving behind the heady and typically impassioned atmosphere of Bechet's complex account, it's something of a relief to present Johnson's story as told in 1959. He said that Victor asked them to record but found they couldn't record the bass because the bass broke the grooves. Bill also maintained that the bass had too much volume, but he added two important details: first, that they made three or four tests, and, in response to a question from his interviewer, that Keppard wanted to record. (He said nothing about the date the tests were made.)

Morgan Prince consistently declared that the band had recorded two numbers for Victor in New York in 1916, one of which was "On the Road to Mandalay."[78]

It seems to me incontrovertible that tests were actually made—perhaps they were informal—to ascertain whether the bass could possibly be recorded. One assumes that the recording engineers were already well aware of the problem that might arise but were willing to at least make the attempt. There seems to be no surviving record of such a test, perhaps because the master was so obviously flawed that there was no point in even assigning a matrix number or making an entry in the laboratory log.

SINCE SOME READERS of these lines may know little or nothing about recording technology prior to the compact disc and magnetic cassette tape, a few words on the technological constraints of the mechanical (usually called "acoustic") recording process are in order. On typical mechanical recordings of the early 1920s the lowest measurable frequencies are on the order of 200 Hz—similar to the lower limit of a cheap AM radio—the highest 3000 Hz or so. The lowest string of the double bass vibrates at about 41 Hz and the top string at 98. Despite this, the ear is tricked into "hearing" these low fundamental tones if the characteristic upper harmonics are present. My impression of Bill Johnson's sound as electrically recorded in 1929 is that the fundamental is very strong with relatively weak harmonics. It's conceivable that a strong bass pitch between 50 and 100 Hz would have overloaded the disc-cutting apparatus. It could also be that the strong initial pluck of pizzicato double bass would present the same problem. Whatever the theory, in practice recording engineers of the day reinforced or replaced the double bass with tuba, bass saxophone, or sarrusophone.

Norwood Williams's guitar, a rather small, round-hole flat-top instrument in the only known photograph, would have presented another set of problems. It's true that solo guitar recordings exist from the 'teens (the name of Octaviano Yañes comes to mind), but the volume achievable with guitar is far less than that of the banjo, very well represented in recordings even of the earliest period. That the weak volume of the guitar accompanying four melody instruments would have been a problem in stage performance is also true, and one certainly wishes that the sole known interviewer of Williams (Bill Russell) had asked him about this.

Finally, there's the matter of the violin, also rather weak when compared with cornet and trombone. One solution was to place it close to the recording horn, with the brass instruments at some distance. Another well-known recording expedient was to equip the violin with a resonator and horn (so-called Stroh violin), to the detriment of tonal beauty and nuance but helpful to the volume.

Be these matters as they may, it's not difficult to understand that the Victor engineers would have found recording the Creole Band a challenge and that they'd have wanted to make more than the usual number of tests.

Additional light on this complex of questions is provided by another interview with George Baquet, by Danny Barker sometime after Baquet's return to New Orleans, most likely in 1948. The place was a dimly lit barroom at the corner of South Rampart and Erato streets that had been bought by Baquet, although managed by an old friend, drummer Ernest "Nenesse" Trepagnier. Barker quotes Baquet *in extenso*—one supposes that Barker has fleshed out his rather more telegraphic notes:

> The main reason that Keppard did not record during the Creole Band's engagement in New York City at the Winter Garden in 1916 was because of the manner in which he was approached by the officials of the Victor company. Freddie and the other members of the band read the current trade

magazines and weeklies. They read *Billboard Advertising* [*sic*] and *Variety*. They knew all about salaries, contracts, the drawing power of various attractions. They knew how many records Caruso sold and what he was paid for those records.

During intermission one night, the Victor official approached Keppard for the fifth time and handed him a contract to sign. The contract specified that Freddie would receive $25.00 and the sidemen would be paid $15.00 to record four songs. Freddie yelled at the official: "Take this piece of paper and stick it up your rear. Do I look like a goddam fool? Why, I buy that much whisky a day."

The faces of the officials turned scarlet and they scooted out the door. In their haste, they left a copy of the contract, which I read. The members of the band angrily shouted as I read out all the long legal clauses that were all in favor of Victor. "Victor shall have the right to do this. Victor shall have the right to do that."

Like many other accounts, this one appears to assume tacitly that Keppard was the manager of the band. But there's no evidence that this was ever so, something Baquet would have been well aware of. Be that as it may, we find confirmation that the band's refusal to record was in part a matter of money. We have to assume that the mention of Caruso, a true superstar, is symbolic, not literal, since the amounts he pocketed from Victor were staggeringly large and no vaudeville performer in his right mind would think he could lay claim to even a small fraction of the tenor's royalties. Keppard and the others might, however, have felt justifiably insulted by a truly insignificant payment for four records, perhaps without a royalty payment per record sold. A couple of years later, the ODJB's Victor contract paid the band $100 per satisfactory take plus a share of the standard "mechanical royalties" of two cents per title recorded, a far cry from the $100 offered to the Creole Band for four records. One thing I have no difficulty in understanding is the anger of the band at hearing the legalese in the contract, all to Victor's advantage. The language of such documents is typically very much in favor of the folks holding the purse strings.

Of great importance is the mention of the Winter Garden as the place of the showdown between Victor and Keppard. This would be quite reasonable, given the band's appearance there in January and February. After a one-night opening in Hartford and some three weeks in Boston—during which it's not clear that the band had joined the show—*Town Topics* opened a three-week run at the Shubert-owned Winter Garden on Monday, January 24.

It was apparently a common practice for the Shuberts to feature the stars of whichever show was playing the Winter Garden in the so-called concerts given on Sunday—a violation of the spirit if not the letter of the city ordinances that prohibited shows on the Sabbath. Thus, on Sunday, January 30, Trixie Friganza, Mabel Elaine, and the Creole Band were advertised—along with other cast members—at the "concert." The same was true on Sunday, February 6. On February 13, however, the show no doubt was on the train for Detroit, where it opened for a one-week run on Monday, February 14.

Although the band also appeared at a Winter Garden Sunday concert on May 21 during *Town Topic*'s two-week swan song in Philadelphia, for the Victor representatives to attempt to get the band's agreement to a contract on five occasions would have required the relatively extended period when *Town Topics* occupied the Winter Garden, between January 24 and February 5. Another sticking point is that by the show's appearance in Philadelphia in May Baquet may have already taken his leave and was therefore not in a position to give first-hand details about it.

An offer to record during the period when the band was again in New York City, in March and April 1917, is ruled out by the fact that both Baquet and Morgan Prince had left the band by that time. Also, the significance of a Victor offer was not the same in 1917 as in 1916. In 1917, the ODJB had already made their first records, and the Creole Band could be regarded as imitators; but in 1916 *they* would have been the pioneers in recording New Orleans instrumental ragtime, perhaps alerting Victor to the commercial possibilities of this new and different music. (Morgan Prince had taken seriously ill in January of 1917 and never rejoined the act, opting instead for employment in a Gary, Indiana steel mill.)[79]

It remains to be seen what the connection of Will Vodery with the Victor Company may have been. It could hardly have been as a middle man between the company and negro performers, given their virtual absence from the Victor catalogue, notable exceptions being James Reese Europe's orchestra from 1913 to 1914 and Ford Dabney, under the *nom de disque* of "Signor Grinderino" (released late in 1915).

Many careful readers of Brian Rust's jazz discographies have been intrigued by the listing of an unnumbered Victor test from December 2, 1918, of the tune "Tack 'Em Down." Rust fleshes out the listing, adding in parentheses, "Possibly Bill Johnson's Creole Jazz Band including Johnson himself on sb." To explain Bill Johnson's presence, and the continued existence of the band after it had broken up, Rust invoked an advertisement for the band in the December 28 number of *Variety* but misremembered the year as 1918, not 1917.[80]

More telling, perhaps, the instrumentation as listed in the studio ledger was cornet, trombone, clarinet, alto saxophone, piano, mandolin, string bass, and drums—quite unlike the Creole Band.

As the band itself observed in a letter to the *Defender* of March 16, 1918, there were many bands riding on their coattails by using the name "Creole," so the name of the unit in a 1918 Victor ledger has no evidentiary value whatever with respect to the 1916 offer.[81]

THE CLOSE OF their second season in mainstream show business found the Creole Band in a quite favorable position with, one can easily imagine, the brightest of prospects for the future. They had been a hit with a Shubert revue and had been approached by the most powerful recording company in the country, if not the world. This would have been remarkable enough for a group of Caucasian performers, but for a bunch of New Orleans black (more or less) ragtime musicians . . . !

The summer months were an awkward time for vaudeville. On the other hand, the Creole Band seemed to want to keep working—I'm tempted to say "at all costs"—contrary to loafing through the summer as vaudevillians who could afford it often did. This could involve playing at an outdoor venue, such as one of the hundreds of parks that diverted Americans up to about mid-century, or a summer hotel. But Pantages theaters evidently saw no need to close despite the fact that part of the circuit traversed the Canadian grain belt (Manitoba, Saskatchewan, and Alberta), and the band's successful first tour made them an attractive prospect for a second. Still, Pantages was not really the big time for which the band seemed qualified; it seems a shame that the plan to form an act with Mabel Elaine didn't bear fruit.

5 The Third Season

THE START OF THE third season of the Creole Band was documented by a comically inexact item from Sylvester Russell's Chicago column in the *Freeman* of July 15, 1916:

> The Creole Band passed through the city last Monday evening to fill three months on the Pantages circuit, after which they will return to the city to be a feature in a big white musical comedy production. The band includes Morgan Prince, comedian; James Palas, violinist, leader; Fred Keppard, cornet; Ed Vincent, trombone; W. H. Williams, guitar; Louis Deline, clarinet, and Fred Johnson, bass violin and business manager.

"Last Monday" would have been July 10; the band opened in Winnipeg on Monday, July 18. These dates are firm, but they call into question the date of the telegram that called Louis Delille[1] ("Big Eye" Louis Delille Nelson) to join the act.

At the end of 1940 there appeared in the pages of a record collectors' magazine of small circulation an interview with Big Eye by Orin Blackstone, a New Orleans resident, important early discographer, writer, and publisher. The story goes that

> There was some difficulty between Baquet and Keppard and on June 8, 1916, Keppard telegraphed Big Eye to come to Chicago to replace Baquet. Finally in the big time, playing coast to coast on the vaudeville stage and earning $75 to one hundred dollars a week, Big Eye was looking forward to a life of security . . .[2]

Another version was collected by the Belgian poet and jazz historian Robert Goffin, who was in New Orleans for two months in 1944. Totally characteristic for Goffin, it offers a mélange of truth and fiction, which may perhaps be traced to a certain latitude in filling in the gaps of hastily written interview notes, if not to an overactive imagination. It asserts that Baquet was homesick and tired of the cold and snowy North. Then,

> Freddy Keppard sent a telegram right away to local 28 [the 28 saloon on Franklin St. is meant] for Big Eye Louis to come and replace Baquet. The telegram had been sent from Detroit and told him to meet the band in Chicago. Louis accepted the offer he had turned down four years before.[3]

A corresponding note from Bill Russell's research notes now at the Historic New Orleans Collection both confirms and confuses: "Noone met in Detroit after Geo was locked in room in New York." Since "Geo" is obviously Baquet, then the clarinetist who met in Detroit—or more likely was wired from Detroit—had to have been Big Eye since Noone did not join the band until the end of 1917.[4]

It seems possible that the date of the telegram was actually July 8, while the band was in Detroit with Tobe Brown (see above) substituting for Baquet. In any event, there is a gap of six weeks between the date of leaving *Town Topics* and the date the band breezed through Chicago. It strikes me as likely that it was during this period that the band appeared a number of times at Coney Island. For example, Bill Johnson told an interviewer that they played at dinner (or for their dinner) at Coney Island on Sundays, in a large dance hall or restaurant on a pier. This fits neatly with an anecdote told by Big Eye to Rudi Blesh:

> The Original Creole Band was playing at Coney Island in 1915 or 1916. Keppard was losing his cafe crowds every Sunday, when an Italian cornet virtuoso played outside with his brass band. This triple tonguing virtuoso held everyone spellbound by blowing opera airs in the florid style of a coloratura soprano.
>
> "Keppard was King—New Orleans, anywhere," Nelson said. "He didn't like this. So one day he stood at the edge of the crowd and waited for him to finish. Then put his cornet up and played every note the guy had played, clearer, and sweeter, and twice as loud. I'll never forget the tune: it was "Carnival of Venice.""[5]

The only reasonable time for this to have occurred is the period between *Town Topics* and the Detroit engagement, since the other period in which the Creole Band with Delille as their clarinetist was in New York City was in March and the first week of April 1917, hardly the season for playing out of doors at Coney Island. Up to America's entry into World War I, there were five pier structures: Steeplechase Pier, Dreamland Pier, Dreamland Chutes (very short), New Iron Pier (originally the wharf for the boat from Manhattan), and the Leap Frog Railroad, a specialized entertainment ride. The first of these is the only likely candidate, since Dreamland had been wiped out in a spectacular blaze in 1911.

If they played at Coney Island only on Sundays, they were probably relieving another group. Since their entire philosphy appears to have been to keep working no matter what, they surely were working elsewhere in New York City during the week, perhaps occasional gigs.

Perhaps the solution is that the telegram indeed dated from June 8, and, rather than requesting Big Eye to meet the band in Detroit or Chicago, asked him to join them in New York. That would leave time for playing at Coney Island. It's interesting that Bill Russell had seen in Bill Johnson's possession a photograph of Big Eye and Keppard in front of a crowd; one likes to imagine this was at Coney Island.[6]

ONE WONDERS WHY they accepted another trip around the Pantages time, which would have to be considered something of a comedown. This would have lasted, in fact, some four months, not three, although the Shuberts could very likely have snatched them away from Pantages at any time. If the *Freeman* is correct in stating that they would be slated to travel with a "big white musical comedy production," they would have something appropriate to the level they'd reached to look forward to. It certainly would have been a logical placement for them given their success with *Town Topics*. And it would necessarily have been a Shubert show, since they were under contract to the brothers at least until April 1917; that is, unless they were loaned to another producer.[7]

The big Winter Garden (i.e., Shubert) production of the fall of 1916 was *The Show of Wonders*, which ran for nearly six months.[8] Mabel Elaine, along with her erstwhile mentors in blackface, McIntyre and Heath, was originally scheduled to be in the show but may have left (or been requested to do so) prior to the show's opening at the end of October. A pairing of Elaine and the band might well have occurred to the producers, since it had been a hit in *Town Topics*. On the other hand, their number was a big production, with the levee set transforming into the plantation, and perhaps would have been difficult to transplant or even revise. Also, it was getting late in the day for this kind of "southern" entertainment. Another possibility would have been to place the band in *So Long, Letty*, which also opened in October at the Shubert Theatre before embarking on tour. The show was thoroughly modern in setting and spirit, and one can imagine the introduction of an up-to-date dancing number.

In any event, the second tour on the Pantages time mirrored the first, starting at Winnipeg and working west. Pantages management put together a package of five acts, with the most elaborate being Jesse Lasky's "Society Buds," the headliner with ten people, mostly women in fancy gowns; it was billed as presenting "classy musical numbers." The others were Welch, Mealy & Montrose, a song and dance act; Claudia Coleman, character comedian and impersonator; and Kartelli, slack wire artist.

During the tour the band was sometimes called the "Creole Band," without the telltale word "ragtime"; but often it appears in both advertisements and reviews as "Johnson's Creole Band." These novelties appear to hold only for the Pantages tour. Once they returned to the Middle West, Bill's name is gone and "ragtime" reappears. That Johnson is prominent in a way he had never been before may simply point to a change in billing specified in the contract; there's no doubt that as long as the band lasted he was always the manager. It did lead to misunderstanding, however. For example the *Manitoba Free Press* said that "Johnson's dancing and southern singing and acting is very appreciable." Morgan Prince could hardly have been pleased.[9]

On the other hand, reviewers often singled out Prince's solo singing—usually "Old Black Joe." The quartet singing also seems to have been soft-pedaled: "My Old Kentucky Home" is never mentioned by name. While the music may not have changed appreciably, surely the advance copy produced in the Pantages office had. Review after review speaks of the "wild and untamed" music displayed by the band. By the time the troupe reached San Francisco, the ante had been raised. We read of "futuristic rag music," "super-ragtime," and "syncopated and macerated music."[10]

The week in Winnipeg was adjudged a "real hit" by the *Breeze*.[11] Two reviewers depart from the rhetoric of the Pantages publicity office, while following a similar line. A very brief mention in the *Telegram* found their music "unusual," while the *Manitoba Free Press* wrote that "the music is weird, reminding one of an old circus band."[12]

Edmonton also proved receptive. The Tuesday review in the *Morning Bulletin* dwelled mostly on the "Society Buds" but found the band "very entertaining." But the next day saw them publish a remarkably lengthy article, which, to my mind, must mirror the extravagant glory of the advance publicity. Most unusually, however, Morgan Prince is singled out at the end for praise, not just generally ("old-time darky") but by his real name.

CREOLE BAND IS BIG HIT

The Original Creole Band, a company of seven musicians from the southland, are one of the big comedy hits at the Pantages theatre this week. About two years ago, this organization toured the Pantages circuit; since that visit the Creole Band has played the largest vaudeville houses of the east and, in addition, has been featured in many of the largest eastern musical productions. They have everywhere been accorded with the most extravagant praise from the press and public; their "Wild and Untamed Music" on such instruments as the cornet, trombone, clarinet, violin, guitar and double bass seeming to strike a responsive chord in the popular fancy. This same organization was, for an entire season, the prominent attraction of "Town Topics," a very successful eastern musical revue. Special scenery which represents a plantation scene along one of the southern rivers is especially picturesque. Morgan Prince, in the role of a delapidated, but active and energetic southern darkey, is the comedian, and adds to the general merriment of the offering by the presentation of several songs and unique dancing steps.

An advance puff from Tacoma a few weeks later also mentions Morgan Prince's name, so it is possible that its appearance here is only testimony to careful reading of advertising matter, not an unwonted degree of personal respect for a black performer. Marmaduke, the reviewer of the Edmonton *Journal* was rather less enthusiastic: "The old darkey's singing of 'Old Black Joe' didn't pretend to be anything of a vocal effort but the crowd liked it."[13]

Calgary followed, with a review in the *Albertan*, under the rubric "First Night at Theatres, by Albertan Dramatic Critic." The brief paragraph devoted to the band may reveal a detail for which there is blessed little evidence.

A noisy Creole band gives a ragtime repertoire, interspersed with fun and jokes. The bandmen are Creoles, but there is a very funny, burnt-cork comedian at the head of the troupe who hits off the hoary traditions of nigger-land amusingly.[14]

My reading of this rests on the single word "but" contrasting the light-skinned Creoles—therefore not blacked-up—with Prince in burnt-cork.

Goffin's semifactual account—deserving of attention since derived from Big Eye—adds piquant detail to the Calgary engagement. Like virtually all that has been written about the band, Keppard is at the focus.

At the end of the engagement [in Winnipeg], the circus went to Calgary. [Goffin confused "Pantages Circuit" with a non-existent "Pantages Circus."] One morning, Freddy Keppard met his buddies. He was sad and gloomy.

"What's the matter, Freddy?"

"God, I had a terrible nightmare!"

"Did you dream you had to go an entire day without gin?"

"No, I saw myself back in New Orleans. I was playing at Billy Phillips and they had just told me that my mother had died." The manager had heard the conversation and staggered.

"What's the trouble, Joe?"

"Nothing, nothing."

The orchestra went on stage, played its usual program and came off with the intention of going for a drink. Freddy was in front of the manager who held out a telegram. Freddy opened it and began to cry. It announced the death of his mother.

"The strangest thing," said the manager as Freddy went to console himself with a bottle, "is that I'd already received the telegram when Freddy told me his dream this morning. I waited for the end of the show so that he wouldn't be upset!"[15]

The death of Emily Keppard is recorded as having occurred on August 6, 1916.[16] In fact, the band played Calgary between July 31 and August 6, so the fateful telegram might well have arrived early on the 6, leaving the often-derided Goffin as an accurate reporter of what he'd heard from Big Eye.

Goffin goes on to mention the other cities on the itinerary: Edmonton, Ledbridge, Montana, Seattle, Spokane, Vancouver. Leaving aside for the moment the improbable town of "Montana," we should stop and consider "Ledbridge"—which can be no other city than "Lethbridge," at 10,000 inhabitants the third-largest city in Alberta, far behind Edmonton and Calgary, but large enough to sport a 1,000 seat theater, the Majestic, as well as the Empress and Orpheum mentioned below.[17] It was on the Canadian Pacific line south, reaching the border at Coutts, the most direct route to Great Falls, their first stop in Montana.[18] In fact, the band played there for one night only, Monday, August 7, at the Orpheum; it advertised "unequalled Pantages vaudeville." The *Lethbridge Telegram*, a weekly published on Thursday, offered a blurb that shamelessly copied the *Calgary Albertan*.[19]

Pantages had just moved into Montana in 1916, no doubt to bridge the non-income-producing gap between Calgary and Spokane. A number of different arrangements were tried out, the first being to play at Great Falls on Tuesday and Wednesday, proceed to Anaconda on Thursday, then play Butte from Friday to Thursday, at which time the acts would jump to Spokane. A one-night stand in Missoula was introduced into the route between Great Falls and Anaconda, simply pushing forward the following dates. The *Breeze* of June 23, 1916, laid out the scheme in fullest detail: nine days were played out of two weeks, for which pro rata full salary was paid, first, two shows at the Grand Opera House in Great Falls on Tuesday and Wednesday, followed by two shows at Missoula on Thursday night. The Margaret Theater in Anaconda—rather large at 1,250 seats—presented the acts for two shows on Friday night; finally the quite sizeable (2,223 seats) Broadway Theatre in Butte would have the acts from Saturday to the subsequent Wednesday.[20]

In fact, the band played only one or two nights in Great Falls (Wednesday, August 9), six days in Anaconda (August 11–16), and one night in Missoula (August 17). So much for the accuracy of information from an ostensibly well-informed theatrical weekly. This left three open days to get to Spokane, on one of which there might have been a performance in Butte.

Their two showings in Great Falls on Wednesday, August 9, elicited considerable enthusiasm the next day:

CREOLE BAND IS THE BIG NUMBER

[Two capacity audiences] . . . and there was one act that was worth the price of admission from anybody. That was the Creole Band. There were other good acts but this was the act par excellence. It was a band of colored musicians of good ability that played the tunes with an appeal to them. One of the seven members of the company rendered a couple of vocal solos, the opening one being "Old Black Joe." This was received with enthusiastic, general and continued applause by the audience.

The headline act, Society Buds, is built around a good idea but it lacks girls who can sing. None of the company merit high favor because of singing ability and the act without voices loses its chief intent . . .[21]

Spokane and Seattle performances occupied the weeks of August 20 and 27. Vancouver followed, with four special Labor Day performances. The four reviews available are all complimentary with, once again, a shift in emphasis from the plantation bits to modern ragtime. The *Daily Province* wrote:

Johnson's Creole Band dispenses a ragtime programme in a way that makes syncopated music seem something to be joyously approved of. The dancing of the aged darky reminds those who see him of the days when negro minstrelsy was at its best.

More or less the same view was repeated in the *News-Advertiser*, although they preferred Claudia Coleman:

Johnson's Creole Band is sufficiently "wild and untamed" to suit the wildest, and there is some of the old standard comedy in the work of the "cork artist."[22]

The unsung member of the cast also received a rare mention in the *World*: "A little good comedy caused by the capture of an unapprehensive fowl, is well appreciated."[23]

The reviewer in Victoria tipped the scales even further in favor of the instrumental music, further commenting on the "wild and untamed" advance blurb:

Johnson's Creole Band was billed to play wild, untamed music, and did not fail. To begin with, the musicians have a combination of instruments possibly without precedent in the musical world. Nobody but six negro eccentric players could shatter so many of the rules of a well-regulated band and make it so enticing to an audience. The cornet, clarinet, violin, guitar and double bass are played by individuals with seemingly absolute indifference to what the other man was doing, but they always managed to arrive at appointed places in full accord. An old darky comic adds an entertaining touch to the offering.[24]

The language employed is remarkably like that used to describe the music of the Original Dixieland Jazz Band a year later; it sounded chaotic but it wasn't. One wonders whether the band was using all of its custom-made set at all engagements, despite the frequent mention of "special scenery and lighting effects" in the advance publicity.

Weeks in Tacoma and Portland finished off the Pacific Northwest, and during the week of October 1 the band traveled to San Francisco for their third appearance there under Pantages auspices. As before, the notices from San Francisco are decidedly minimal, due no doubt to the competition for space from the more prestigious national circuits. Morgan Prince said that it was here he broke his walking stick over Fred Keppard's back, because Fred didn't want to leave a prostitute. This story meshes with one recounted by Jelly Roll Morton:

> They were always in an argument on account of Freddie's big talk. He would arrive at rehearsal an hour late and say, "Let them wait for me. The band can't play till I get there." Morgan Prince, the comedian with the band, was not a Creole and he took Freddie seriously. In one argument he hit Keppard across the head with a cane and that started the breaking up of the band. I don't know when it happened but I understand that was the beginning of the end.[25]

Jelly Roll could have heard this story from a number of sources, direct and indirect, so it's impossible to decide whether the detail of "the beginning of the end" is his own imaginative script-writing. As matters turned out, Prince left the band due to illness three months or so later, at the beginning of 1917.[26]

The band crossed the bay to Oakland and, as before, the papers were able to devote more space to them, especially the comparatively large-circulation *Tribune*, which, like other papers on this tour, was struck by the instrumental performance:

> A hearty act carrying much enthusiasm and a wild desire to express melody through the media of band instruments is Johnson's Creole Band. For a moment after the

rise of the curtain one isn't sure whether he is listening to music or just a mere steamhammer. After a while, when the ears become attuned, one is assured that it is music.[27]

The Los Angeles reviews for the week of October 22 are almost as parsimonious as those from San Francisco. The *Examiner*, however, adds a precious detail to our knowledge of repertory. Under the heading "Johnson's Creole Band Renders Latest Song Hits," the reviewer mentions that "'Walkin' the Dawg' was never walked so fast in syncopation before." Readers will recall publisher Will Rossiter's assertion from May that the band was using the tune in *Town Topics*.[28]

The *California Eagle* for November 4 reported that in San Diego, Bill Johnson had visited the music studio of Will Nash and acquired copies of two compositions: Nash's own "Snakey Blues" and William King Phillips' "Florida Blues" (p. 6). Perhaps these should be added — at least as possibilities — to the Creole Band's repertory.

After the week of October 29 in San Diego and two days transit time eastward, the band played Salt Lake City from Wednesday, November 8 through the following Tuesday, November 14, evidently reverting to their standard act — unless it was a matter of a reviewer less attuned to modern music:

Johnson's Creole Band present "wild and tamed [*sic*]" music by mixed orchestra and add to their southern melodies dancing and eccentric comedy. The stage setting is a southern plantation and the members of the band are characteristically dressed as typical plantation darkies.[29]

The performances in Ogden from November 15 or 16 to 18 elicited singularly negative reviews. The comment from the *Standard* that the band "must have been in a hurry . . . to get somewhere" has already been mentioned. The *Examiner*, although less brusque, was devastating in a review headlined "CRACKERJACK BILL AT THE ORPHEUM. Two Acts Are Screams and the Rest of Them Tag Along Well in Amusement":

If the Creole Band would play one or two more of the old tunes and give a chance for the audience to judge whether they could do ensemble singing, they would make more of a hit. Their selections sound first like a free-for-all musical catch-as-catch-can and in one instance is a bit too long continued. Then the one song is played and sung too low for the audience to get the full benefit of it. The aggregation is entertaining in a way, but could make itself a better card.[30]

Whereas we can quite often ascribe a favorable review to parroting the advance publicity, this is obviously an authentic reaction to what went on on

Thursday night in Ogden. Keppard must indeed have been in poor form. I wonder also whether the band had bothered to unpack its (relatively) elaborate special scenery for so short an engagement.

This messy performance was close to the end of their second Pantages tour. But exactly where it ended is not obvious. The *Breeze* has a brief discussion of Pantages practice about this time: "Pantages now booking the Empress at Denver, using Pantages shows intact which close at Ogden Saturday night and open at Denver Monday. The first Pantages show is at Denver this week."[31] But the band played the Tabor Grand Opera House in Denver and not the Empress.

The rule, one supposes, is that alliances in vaudeville management were volatile. Certainly this is borne out by the ad for the Tabor, which in a display ad on the Sunday preceding the Creole Band's opening in Denver was described as booking "Pantages International Vaudeville." Despite the fact that the acts were the same as those with which the band had begun the tour in Winnipeg—with the addition of Nan Gray—they were listed as an "added attraction."

Although the Tuesday review was brief—curiously designating the members of the band as mulattoes—a staff cartoonist captured an unnamed Morgan Prince in action, along with the other attractions in the show. It shows a figure in black with battered hat and cane, shaking all over in a grotesque pose. Two accompanying musicians are sketchily depicted in broad-brimmed straw hats, one with a fiddle and the other with either a cornet or a clarinet.[32]

The reviewer for the *Times* was able to hear "all the vile bellowing of a bass horn" [could Bill Johnson conceivably have been doubling?]. Otherwise he was impressed by "the latest creations in pajamas." One suspects a deemphasis of the "macerated syncopation" much in evidence on the West Coast.[33]

Should one be surprised that the *Denver Star*, an Afro-American weekly with a miniscule circulation of 1,500, breathes not a word of the band? This was more often the case than not; perhaps there was a feeling that black acts playing in mainstream vaudeville would be adequately covered elsewhere. But the paper carried ads for the Y.M.C.A. band, led by R. A. Spencer and the Queen City Band, headed by Addison O'Neal, as well as for the Keystone Social Club and Cafe, and the 5 Points Cafe. Also present in ads and news items was George Morrison's orchestra, known from one Columbia recording of 1920 and a lengthy interview with Gunther Schuller published as an appendix to *Early Jazz*. Alas, he said nothing about the Creole Band.[34]

The band played Colorado Springs on Monday and Tuesday of the next week (November 27 and 28), Pueblo on November 29, and Rocky Ford on

Perfect Scream is Mr. Welch
+ +   + +   + +   + +   + +
# See Him in New Pantages Show

5.1 Excellent depiction of Morgan Prince shaking a leg. Did the band really wear those large-rimmed hats? [Denver, *Rocky Mountain News*, November 21, 1916.]

Thanksgiving Day, November 30. For the week of December 3 they appeared at the Empress in Kansas City, where the notices were perfunctory, although the brief sentence in the *Thespian*, a Kansas City–based theatrical weekly, captures our attention since it was directed at a professional readership: "Johnson's Creole Ragtime Band is the real headline act of the bill and were a riot."[35]

5.2 According to Big Eye, these were taken in Kansas City, consequently during the week of December 4, 1916. Much care was taken to have shoes shined to a fare-thee-well. It's been suggested that Keppard's slide trumpet was a toy, on what evidence I couldn't say. In the second photo, Big Eye just couldn't keep his alto sax still. [(a) Frank Driggs; (b) Hogan Jazz Archives]

5.3 Published in *Jazz Forum* 3 (January 1947) from a copy contributed by Charles Payne Rogers. Where Rogers got it is anyone's guess. In any event, diligent search has failed to turn up Rogers's print. It's possible that it was taken back home in the Crescent City after the Creole Band's breakup in April 1917. One account would have it that Big Eye sold the sax as soon as he returned, an idea cherished by those who unaccountably thought the saxophone was not an instrument of the true New Orleans jazz.

For the next month or so, the Creole Band worked its way back to Chicago, playing mostly in WVMA theaters, some of them named "Orpheum" although not part of the Orpheum circuit, and the mention of Johnson in the billing vanishes. The route was decidedly peculiar, even improvisatory, going from Kansas City north to Sioux City, Iowa, then returning south to St. Joseph, Missouri, only to go north again to Omaha, Nebraska. Finally, they started east again, to Cedar Rapids and Peoria and Bloomington, Illinois.

This also marked a return to split-week performances with Sunday through Wednesday spent at the Orpheum in Sioux City, booked through the WVMA, and Thursday through Saturday at the Crystal in St. Joseph, which presented "Orpheum-Interstate Big Time Vaudeville." "Big Time" was stretching a point perhaps, since the Interstate time, now apparently part of the far-flung Orpheum empire, was decidedly not. In Sioux City, the band was one of five acts.

The review reported an exceptionally warm welcome in this smallish house (1,200 seats). Once again Morgan Prince's chicken was noticed:

Orpheum audiences yesterday gave unusually vociferous applause to two of the feature numbers . . . the Creole Ragtime Band and Medlin, Watts, and Towns. The gallery whistled. The entertainment offered in the third "spot" by the darky musicians ranged from the most "raggy" kind of orchestral playing to a dance by an old negro, a sentimental song of the plantation type, and a sure enough chicken that ostensibly strayed too near the colored convocation—and the fire. The act has been featured in the larger Orpheum houses, and is obviously entitled to the distinction.[36]

The Crystal in St. Joseph cannot be found in theatrical guides of the time. It played three a day, with a 10 cent matinee. It was large enough to take six acts of vaudeville (plus a motion picture) for the last half of the week of December 10. The advertising on Thursday, December 14 listed "Creele's Ragtime Band of 7 people"; Voyesteke Trio, equilibrists; Reiche & Burt, two harmony girls; Francisco & Vernon, team of pretty girls; Lew Wells, the irresistible Saxophone Monologist; Nada Kesers, singer; and the film "Betty at the Wedding."

The Friday morning review got their name right and showed that they had lost nothing in their ability to close the show with a spectacular finish:

[The Creole Band] proved a near riot at last night's performance. The act is composed entirely of colored singers, dancers, musicians, and comedians, with special "old plantation" scenery. Every member of the band was dressed in the conspicuous regalia of the old plantation darky and the instruments consisted of a big bass fiddle, guitar, violin, clarinet, cornet and trombone, which responded to the touch of these ragtime demons like gasoline on a fire. They fairly took everyone by storm from the first rising of the curtain, and before they had finished, everyone was swaying in rhythm to the fascinating strains of a ragtime "blues." Excellent singing and dancing, with clever comedy prevailed throughout, and despite the fact that they closed the bill, everyone remained seated until the finish.[37]

This is the first time that the word "blues" appeared in any of the many reviews surveyed. Of course, it may not mean a change in or addition to the repertory; only that the St. Joseph reviewer was hipper to contemporary music than most.

The Creole Band opened in Omaha on the same day that the Ballets Russes of Sergei Diaghilev were performing at the Auditorium. One likes to imagine . . . In any event the contrast between performance conditions at the WVMA-booked Empress, where the band appeared, and the big-time Orpheum is worth describing. The Orpheum had only two shows a day at 2:15 and 8:15, with a top price in the evenings of 75 cents. The Empress declared that it presented "Popular Vaudeville" with continuous vaudeville and movies from 11 a.m. to 11 p.m. and a top price of 20 cents. A brief mention under the "At the Theaters" rubric reveals that this meant four shows daily. One easily understands why there were constant complaints in the theatrical weeklies about the exploitation of performers by the continuous "pop" vaudeville format.[38]

There were apparently only four acts offered under this regime at the Empress, with the band billed as a "musical novelty," along with Walters & Walters, world's greatest Ventriloquists; Gilbert Losee, triple-voiced eccentric comedian; Fred and Mae Wadell, odds and ends of vaudeville—about as noncomittal as you can get—along with the lengthy movie "Deep Purple" starring Clara Kimball Young. What's interesting is that the reviewer of the Sunday performances heard only that "All of the numbers rendered are the latest ragtime selections." It could be, of course, that the set didn't get from St. Joseph to Omaha in time. If I'd been in the band, I'd certainly have welcomed a rest from the plantation routines.

A second half appearance at Cedar Rapids fits logically between Omaha and Peoria, and the *Thespian* listed them at the Majestic in that city.[39] The problem is that the act announced in the advance publicity is an otherwise unknown Alabama "Jaz" Band [the quotes are as printed] in headline position. The egregious William J. Slattery—manager of the Majestic—offered "The Manager's Comment on Current Program" in the Majestic's Friday ad in these terms:

> The "Jaz" Band. A real plantation orchestra. This troupe of darkies can play the "blues" to perfection. The original style of interpretation, a combination of wailing and groaning, but always harmonizing, pleased immensely.

Slattery's remark is interesting enough, perhaps suggesting that the term "blues" was included in advance publicity from the WVMA home office, but the actual review a few pages later in the same issue of the *Gazette* is one of the most remarkable ever gleaned by the Creole Band in its four-year career. The astute reader will ask two questions: Why on earth would they have been billed as the Alabama "Jaz" band? and What leads me to believe that the two groups are one and the same? The reasons are four: first, the *Thespian* locates the Creole Band in Cedar Rapids; second, no Alabama Jaz Band appears in vaudeville (or elsewhere) at this time; third, Cedar Rapids is between Omaha and Peoria; and four, the Creole Band had failed miserably with the Cedar Rapids reviewer a year earlier. I take it that they would not have been recognized: mainstream

America had difficulty in distinguishing one African-American from another. Besides, this time they emphasized music rather than plantation tradition.

Under the circumstances, the reader will, one hopes, not object to a lengthy quotation:

AT THE MAJESTIC

The elements took a hand in the presentation of the new Majestic bill yesterday with the result that the matinee was drawn out well past 5 o'clock, owing to the non-arrival of the Alabama Jazz [*sic*] band, the headliners. This negro troupe was delayed eight hours in the jump from Omaha, and it was necessary to "stall" the performance with pictures until the musicians could be driven from the station and grouped on the stage without costumes, setting or rehearsal.

By their performance a new branch of music was laid open to Cedar Rapids listeners. Jazz music has been attempted previously but it has been confined for the most part to trombone moanings and the customary raggy tempo. This is a part of jazz—but it is not jazz. There is included the squeak of a clarinet and the thrumming of a bass viol, all grouped together in some sort of African time which was evidently the basis of ragtime music.

This must have been real jazz, for a group of performers who had finished their work and come to the front of the house to sit across the aisle, writhed in appreciation and shouted approval. Their eastern perception will be accepted. [*sic*]

Among them was Coleman Goet [*recte* Goetz], prodigy of Irving Berlin, who is said to be the youngest song writer in the world. He especially seemed to appreciate this wierd music, although a half an hour before he had sung his "God Gave Me More Than My Share," as though his heart and soul were wrapped up in ballad composition . . .[40]

In contrast, the reviewer's remarks are really quite pointed, even harsh, with respect to some of the other performers on the bill. To wrap up their journalistic triumph, the band was included in the usual cartoon of the current show of the Majestic.

By December 1916, it was unmistakably evident—at least in Chicago—that something new in popular dance music was afoot. At the end of 1915, the Creole Band and Brown's Band had seemed to be in a race to see who would make an impression on New York City first—although it has to be said that the "race" may be only in our hindsight rather than a matter of conscious competition. Now, at the end of 1916 the race was between the Creole Band and the Original Dixieland Jazz Band, to an important degree instigated by Broadway show business.

5.4 Yet another variation on the sketch of 3.2c and 4.1. [Again Cedar Rapids *Gazette*, Dec. 22, 1916]

The Creole Band opened at the Orpheum Theatre in Peoria on Christmas Eve, 1916, bringing out of retirement the act title "Plantation Days," and reverting to one of their earlier *noms d'affiche*: Original New Orleans Creole Ragtime Band. The reviewer found them to be "as fearful and wonderful as anything in the musical line you ever saw."

The second half of the week was spent at the Majestic in Bloomington, Illinois. The Friday review in the *Daily Bulletin* is noteworthy:

> The old-fashioned "jiggers," singers and dancers and the always popular Creole Band which renders tons of harmony and "darkey" songs are here. These colored musicians put their whole heart into the game. The way the old boy on the end saws music out of the old base "vile" is a caution.[41]

What a shame that Bill Johnson couldn't have been given his rightful name. Of course, he was in his early 40s and hardly an "old boy."

Their route turned westward for the next ten days, to Erber's Theater in East St. Louis, the Empress, and the Grand Theaters in St. Louis, all booked by the WVMA.[42] Although the "Routes Ahead" in *Variety* located them at the Lincoln Theater, Chicago, for the week of January 8, other evidence incontrovertibly places them still in St. Louis. A very brief mention in the St. Louis *Star* of Tuesday, January 9, 1917, reads, "The New Orleans Creole Band, with popular 'rags' and southern melodies, scored."

Of incomparably greater interest is the report in the St. Louis *Argus*, an Afro-American weekly:

> The private dance hall of Mr. Sam Shepard's place, 3634 Pine Street, was beautifully decorated for the big banquet which was given in honor of the Creole Band by Mr. Geo. P. Dore, Tecumseh Bradshaw, Robert Anderson, Alonzo Thomas, and Sam Shepard. Fifty guests were present and had the time of their lives with plenty of everything to eat and drink. The band played the sweetest music that was ever heard in St. Louis and the guests enjoyed themselves until 3 a.m. when everyone left feeling very happy.[43]

This is one of the very few indications of the connection of the band to the black community. (There must have been others!) The warmth and sympathy of the passage evince a pride in the accomplishment of the band that speaks volumes.

The listings in *Variety* around this time, when matched against verified performances, prove to be exceptionally unreliable, perhaps demonstrating the same kind of vacillation as that surrounding the McVicker's Theater engagement (see below). It could also be that the illness of Morgan Prince played a role. Be that as it may, the first column shows their location according to Routes Ahead of *Variety*, the second, as substantiated in local ads or reviews, or other sources.

Week of		
January 8	Lincoln, Chicago	Grand, St. Louis
January 15	Palace, Danville IL	Lincoln, Chicago
		Empress, Decatur
January 22	Majestic, Springfield	Lyric, Indianapolis (s.o.)
January 29	Columbia, Davenport	Kedzie, Chicago
February 5		McVicker's, Chicago

When interviewed, Morgan Prince remembered that he took sick on the road from St. Louis to Indianapolis. When they arrived at McVicker's in Chicago, a friend of Prince, one "Scotty Blue," took his place. But Bill Johnson wanted to use another dancer, whom he had met in a club in St. Louis. After the McVicker's engagement, they had one in Cleveland, so, instead of taking Scotty Blue to Cleveland, they took the dancer from St. Louis. They had to cancel the Cleveland date because the new dancer didn't know how to sing and they had to rehearse him. In vain, apparently, since everywhere they appeared the new dancer was a flop and they had to lower the curtain. Bill telegraphed "Scotty Blue" to join them, but he didn't want to anymore. Meanwhile, Prince stayed in bed three months, then went to work in a factory.

It's an interesting story, especially because the singer/dancer with the band for their last tour in 1917–1918 was Leonard Scott. That Prince's "Scotty Blue" and Leonard Scott are one and the same is adequately shown by two reports, one from 1919: "Andy Bryant and Leonard 'Blue' Scott have joined hands, soon to be seen on State Street," and the other from 1926:

> Ruth B. Scott, wife of Leonard (Blue) Scott, of the Four Pepper Shakers, entertained at dinner 15 guests Thanksgiving Day. She will join Blue next month, who now is in the West with the well known act.[44]

The Prince account is clearly confused: for example, Prince had in his possession a certificate given to him in 1942 attesting to his employment at the Gary works of the Carnegie Illinois Steel Corporation as a craneman from March 10, 1917, to August 23, 1918. This means that Prince could not have been bedridden for three months, but only (approximately) half that time. Worse is the fact that extant reviews do not evidence any flops; the period of uncertainty couldn't have lasted more than a couple of weeks.[45]

Two Indianapolis newspapers demonstrate that the band was as much a hit as ever, despite Morgan Prince's illness. On Saturday, January 20, the *Times* ad offered one of the few appearances (in silhouette) of the band in the costumes actually used in the act, and the caption, "Do They Play Ragtime? Oh-h-h-h Man!" Astoundingly, the well-known Los Angeles photograph of the band in dress suits appears, together with copy once again emphasizing their instrumental performance:

> The skit "Uncle Joe's Birthday" provides these clever colored entertainers with a suitable vehicle, but they "shine" especially in their instrumental numbers, their music having that weird and peculiar darkey harmony that is unlike any other music. The band is popular in Indianapolis . . .

That "Uncle Joe's Birthday" puts in its first appearance as the title of the act so soon after the adoption of "Plantation Days" requires eventual explanation no doubt. The *Star* also mentions for the first time in any review one of Uncle Joe's props, a jug of gin, known previously only from the cartoon printed in the *Saturday Evening Telegraph* in November 1915.

The reviews on Tuesday and Thursday are brief but favorable: "Here's an organization that will bring joy to the lover of syncopated melody . . . To say they bring down the house is putting it mildly," and "The Creole Band is as big a hit as it was during its previous visits." Those previous visits are specified in both the *News* and the *Star* as having been at the Lyric, English's, and the Murat (with "Town Topics").[46]

The *Star* found in its expansive Tuesday review that the band gave promise of becoming a vaudeville institution as a

> . . . happy combination of mirth, music and dancing that is inborn in the American negro when his naturally sunny disposition is given an opportunity to vent itself. The ragtime instrumental numbers are, of course, the predominating feature of the act. Only negro musicians of the type to be found along the levees of the Mississippi river and its southern tributaries could dispense such weird, minor harmonies as these players extract . . .

On Friday, the paper fabricated a bit of pseudohistory but also makes a sweeping statement of great significance, whether it originated in Indianapolis or the WVMA office:

> [They] all hail from New Orleans and were working on the levee there when they were picked up by a cafe owner, who engaged them to play in his restaurant . . . an instantaneous hit . . . soon drafted into vaudeville where their present act "Uncle Joe's Birthday" was arranged for them. They are the undisputed originators of the "Jazz Band" craze now sweeping the country.[47]

They returned to Chicago the next week, playing the Lincoln and the Kedzie.[48] Finally the band appeared for the first time in two years in a major Chicago Loop venue for the week of February 4, McVicker's Theater. At 1800 seats it was one of the largest Chicago vaudeville houses, although as a bastion of pop vaudeville—three shows a day and lower ticket prices—not the classiest. It was also one of the oldest theatres in the city, in name if not in the actual premises. Above all, it was in the middle of the Loop, not in one of the outlying neighborhoods.

McVicker's was one of a number of Chicago theatres owned or managed by Jones, Linick, & Shaefer. More important, it was involved in a booking deal between Marcus Loew and Pantages as reported in *Variety* in July 1916 under the headline "Loew's Circuit's 50 Weeks Bookings for Next Season / Addition of Pantages Circuit to Loew Booking Office Makes Big Total, 28 or 30 Full Weeks West, to be Placed by Walter F. Keefe. About 40 Houses in East Kept Supplied by Jos. M. Schenck." Keefe had in mind a route as follows: Toronto, Loew's; Cleveland, Miles; Detroit, Miles; Chicago, McVicker's; Chicago, Crown and Victoria (split week; all Chicago houses booked by Mr. Keefe are Jones, Linick & Shaffer theatres, affiliated with Loew); Milwaukee, New Miller, Saxe; Minneapolis, Pantages; Winnipeg, Pantages and then around the Pantages circuit; after Kansas City (Pantages), Chicago, Colonial and Rialto (under construction); ending at Buffalo, Lyric Theatre.[49]

The deal was stated to have been secured by Keefe the previous week. An addition to the main article datedlined Chicago, July 5 suggested that there might be trouble when Loew-Pantages moved into Minneapolis and Kansas City. Perhaps; but it should be remembered that there were important bonds between Pantages and the WVMA, such that the *Dramatic Mirror* published in the same week as the *Variety* article a description of Jones, Linick & Shaffer theaters in the context of the WVMA–Pantages combine.

Further detail was added in the July 21 issue to clarify misunderstandings that had arisen as to how the new relationship would work:

> Mr. Keefe said, and was concurred in by Jos. M. Schenck, the Loew Circuit general booking manager, that acts engaged in New York for the Pantages time would be given Pantages contracts in New York, to take them over that circuit in connection with their Loew bookings. Acts accepted tentatively for the Pantages Circuit would receive Loew Circuit contracts, carrying an option on their services at a stated salary for the Pantages time, if it should be decided before the act closed on the Loew engagement that it was suitable for the far western route.

This strongly suggests that the band's second trip around the Pantages chain could have been arranged in the Loew office in New York in combination with other Loew bookings, rather than by the Shuberts as suggested above. This would make sense of a decision that otherwise appears incomprehensible, considering the lesser prestige of Pantages time in the big picture. Future events were to show that the Shubert Brothers and Marcus Loew were linked.

Interestingly enough, the McVicker's advertising copy printed in (at least) the *Chicago Herald, Post,* and *News,* listed the band as "Original Jaz Band" or as more fully presented in the *Herald*:

> The original New Orleans Jaz Band, the father and mother of all the jaz bands in the world, is also at McVicker's this week and shows you what a real jaz band is.[50]

The *Breeze* doesn't speak to this point but rather to the shilly-shallying involved in routing the band on its circuitous return to New York City.

> "The Creole Band" is the big feature at McVickers' this week and its coming was a matter of doubt for a time last week, as every advice from New York gave the matter a different bearing. It was a case of "on and off" for several days. One message would proclaim the act "booked," another would declare the engagement "off," the next would authorize the billing of the act, and the following telegram would state that the matter was "cold."[51]

Oddly perhaps, the same house had been host during the previous week to another jazz band, or to use the spelling of the *Breeze*, "jaz" band, described as being from the cabarets, accompanying the Five Bennets.[52] Not only that, but some five months earlier McVicker's had heard yet another jazz band that was soon to become famous, when Johnny Fogarty presented an act accompanied by the Original Dixieland Jazz Band:

> FOGARTY'S DANCING REVUE. "Jimmy Fogarty's Dancing Revue and Jass Band" is a new act which is seen at McVicker's this week. Johnny Fogarty, who has been prominent as a dancer for many years, has seen the popularity of "The Jass Band" and turned it into vaudeville. He has three couples for dancing, and the band not only accompanies most of these exhibitions but it has a number to itself. The band is composed of five white men—piano, drums, slide, cornet and clarinet. There are three dancing couples. Johnny Fogarty and his partner made especially good in a Hawaiian number. the other dancers do well in modern steps. Johnny Fogarty and another chap do some excellent buck dancing. the act closes with some cakewalking. The combination should be a big hit in vaudeville. The band took big applause Monday at the first show. (17 minutes, full stage)[53]

Despite so favorable a notice, the alliance between Fogarty and the ODJB seems to have been only temporary; no tour resulted.[54]

The Creole Band's location for the subsequent week, filling in between Chicago and Cleveland—although not necessarily in a direct line!—remains unknown. At the Miles Theater in Cleveland for the week of February 18, the band, billed in one ad as "A Musical Absurdity with an Irresistible Tickle," made comparatively little impression. The longest notices, in the *Plain Dealer*, thought the act "splendid and unusually attractive" as well as "almost a sure cure for the very worst case of 'blues.'" A bigger splash, however, was made by the tear-jerking film "Patria" starring Irene Castle.[55]

At the Orpheum in Detroit for the week of February 25, the band received one patronizing notice and another that goes over the top with praise. The former comes from the *Times*:

> The Creole Band consists of six players and a singer and comedian in a setting to represent the Mississippi levee district. [Has the set changed?] It is nothing but a collection of popular hits and old melodies with the darky's idea of music, but there is a lot of action and a lot of harmony and the audience took to it immensely.

The *Free Press* with double the circulation of the *Times* at 76,000—although half that of the *News*—ratifies the identification of the band with the latest fashion in music:

> These clever negro entertainers have come to be known in vaudeville circles as the "Jas" band, "jas" being a vaudeville word denoting the putting of speed, ginger or pep into an act.
>
> And the "Jas" band well deserves the name for the act is full of music, fun and speed every moment the musicians are on the stage. Ragtime is played as it never was before. That last sentence is a true [*sic*] but you will have to hear the band yourself to realize how true it is.[56]

The two weeks, March 4 through 17, found them in Times Square, at Doraldina's Montmartre, a restaurant and cabaret owned by Shubert interests, on the northeast corner of Fiftieth Street and Broadway. It was, not incidentally, a mere ten minutes' walk south of Reisenweber's, where the Original Dixieland Jazz Band had been holding forth since the end of January.

The Montmartre was in fact an appendage of the Winter Garden Theatre, 1634 Broadway, between Fiftieth and Fifty-first Streets, which the Shuberts had constructed in 1910–1911 on the site of a livery stable and horse exchange. Henderson comments: "for many years, critics believed that they could still smell the aroma of the stable when they were describing a not particularly engaging revue current on its boards."[57]

Specifically intended for musicals, the Winter Garden was home to twelve successive editions of *The Passing Show*, the weekly Sunday "concerts" occasioned by New York City blue laws, and many shows built around Al Jolson. Closer to our own day, it was the home of the record-setting *Cats* for eighteen years and 7,485 performances, closing in September 2000.

The restaurant and cabaret operation dates from (at least) May 1913, the date of the organization of Dance Palace Co. (president, Emanuel M. Klein) with a five-year lease from the Shuberts. At the beginning of 1917, the Dance Palace Co. in turn leased the premises to Clifford C. Fischer, Inc., who was in charge of the club at the time the Creole Band appeared there.[58]

The restaurant was on the second floor and communicated with the theatre balcony; the dancing cabaret was on the floor above. The cabaret had a rather interesting, if tangled, history. An extensive news item from the Cabaret column of *Variety*, April 25, 1913, gives ample detail:

> The Palais de Danse (Winter Garden Cabaret) started off somewhat slowly but commenced to draw regular business in its second week. Cabaret (restaurant, and dancing floor above) works both ways for the Garden, which also helps the restaurant. The combination makes the Winter Garden more closely resemble a Continental hall of entertainment than anything New York has had as a permanent institution. The title Palais de Danse, is after Berlin's famous Restaurant. The diners in the Cabaret are permitted to wander into the Winter Garden, while the audience watching the show easily finds its way upstairs. The dancing cabaret is kept exclusive through the "evening dress" rule and is attracting the elite set. The ballroom is prettily finished off in a Persian effect, and has the largest dancing floor of any Cabaret in the city. It seats 250 people. Small booths opening on the floor decorate one side. An orchestra of ten colored musicians supply dance music. There is also dancing on the restaurant floor.[59]

On January 26, 1914, an agreement was concluded between Dance Palace Company and dancer Joan Sawyer, who would then manage on a percentage basis only the third floor Persian Ballroom. In the fall of 1914 the downstairs restaurant (The Parisian Room) became the home of Maurice Mouvet and Florence Walton, and was renamed "Chez Maurice." (A piquant detail: Sawyer had been Maurice's partner in 1911 at Louis Martin's cabaret.)[60] This new arrangement apparently cut into the business of the Persian Garden and Joan Sawyer canceled her agreement at the end of the year.[61]

At the end of 1915, Clifford Fischer took over the management of the locale, along with a substantial financial interest, and announced his plans to convert the upper floor to an all-night club, and the floor below to a dancing cabaret. Joan Sawyer again came into the picture, and the new club was named after her, replacing the "Persian Garden."[62] Sometime before the summer of 1916, both floors were renamed the "Montmartre."[63] Toward the end of the year, the Shuberts petitioned for receivership, an action that Fischer fought with an injunction. The matter was finally resolved only at the beginning of 1917, when Fischer sold out his interest for $35,000 and the Schuberts persuaded Doraldina (a dancer with a number of exotic specialties, including the "hula") to take over the management.

Doraldina, said variously to come from Barcelona, Hawaii, or San Francisco, made her first major appearance in New York City in January 1916 with oriental dances, soon thereafter with her version of the Hawaiian Hula complete with Hawaiian orchestra and backup dancers.[64] After her debut at Reisenweber's, where apparently a room was about to be named after her, she moved to the Montmartre around the middle of the year. In August 1916, both she and Joe Frisco were featured attractions.

Lee Shubert was evidently in charge of the arrangements for the Montmartre. On Wednesday, February 28, 1917, he wrote a memo to the incredibly named A. Toxen Worm,[65] who handled much of the Shuberts' publicity:

> I wish you would get up an invitation that we can get out announcing the opening of the Montmartre next Monday evening with new artists.
>
> Also will you get up a dummy that I can insert in the different theatre programs along following lines:
> "After the theatre visit the Montmartre—
> See Doraldina, Jaz Band, Yvonne Gourad and Lloyd—also our other specialties.
> Night place of New York
> No charge for admission."

Another memo on the next day from Shubert to Worm read: "Please get as much publicity about Clifton Webb & Gloria Goodwin and the Jaz Band appearing at the Montmartre nightly from 11 o'clock on. Also Miss Marbury giving a party to LOVE O' MIKE to give Webb & Goodwin a send off on the opening night of the Montmartre."[66]

The "jaz band" in question was, of course, the Creole Band, and the first ad appeared in the *New York Times* (and other papers) on Monday evening, March 5, giving principal billing to "the Original Creole Ragtime Band from New Orleans in 'Jazz' Music." The Wednesday publicity was larger and featured Doraldina, "Greatest Hawaiian Dancer," in first place. Newspaper publicity for them continued through Thursday, March 15.

By the time they received brief notices in the *New York Review*, a weekly bankrolled by the Shuberts, they were on the way out. Still, it's important to

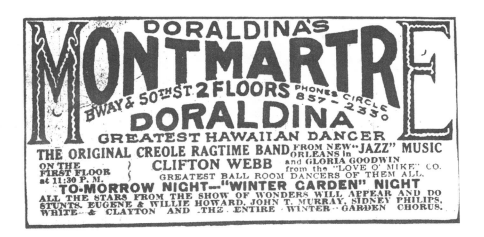

5.5 In March 1917, New York City knew an embarrassment of riches. Reisenweber's was a quite different place than Doraldina's Montmartre. Memos in the Shubert Archive show that the Shuberts deliberately set out to attract a late-night showbiz crowd. [Montmartre: *New York Herald*, March 7, 1917; Reisenweber's: *New York Times*, March 11, 1917. The copies somewhat exaggerate the size of the Montmartre ad.]

note their identification as a jazz band: "the Creole Band, a group of instrumentalists direct from New Orleans, plays "jazz" music of such irresistibility that it would make the dead come to life."[67] In any event, it's inconceivable that they would have continued with their plantation act in this sophisticated, if not high-class, setting. They must have been playing for dancing—which doesn't preclude some specialty or solo numbers. Bill Johnson had little or nothing to say about the engagement, recalling only that the Montmartre was uptown, and that Big Eye had a big bottle with him at the Winter Garden.

One would like to think that our musicians scored a hit of such proportions at the Montmartre that they were kept on for many weeks, just as had happened with the Original Dixieland Jazz Band at Reisenweber's. Such was not the case: on March 19 the dailies carried the Montmartre ad as before, except that the Creole Band had been replaced with "The Original California "Jazz" Band from Frisco in "Jazz" Music." They were to remain at the Montmartre through the end of May, for a run of eleven weeks.

A columnist for the *New York Globe & Commercial Advertiser*, S. Jay Kaufman had a wonderful opportunity but—from our point of view—dropped the ball. He wrote:

> Because you wanted to know what a Jass Band is we went to the Winter Garden on Sunday night and last night at Reisenweber's. At the Winter Garden the band is called the Creole Band, and at Reisenweber's they call it the Original Dixieland Jass Band. What is a Jass Band? Edward [*sic*] B. Edwards, who gave us his engraved card which read "Trombonist" and who is the leader of the originals, said: "A Jass Band is composed of oboes, clarinets, cornets, trombones, banjos and always a drum . . . But the music is a matter of the ear and not of technique. None of us knows music. One carries the melody and the others do what they please. Some play counter melodies, some play freak noises, and some just play. I can't tell you how. You "got to feel" Jass. The time is syncopated. Jass I think means a jumble. We came from New Orleans by way of Chicago . . . To us it seemed a lot of weird effects intended to make one dance with every part of one's body but the feet. And later the dancer did a Jass dance that would have made a jelly fish wonder why it was so named.[68]

Why did the Creole Band leave Doraldina's Montmartre after a mere two weeks? Two decades later, Nick LaRocca was to insist that they had flopped; but there is no contemporary commentary to that effect (see below). A more reasonable hypothesis, in my opinion, is that the Shuberts simply loaned the act to Marcus Loew to help him out at a rather difficult time. There is evidence supporting this idea in the advance publicity printed in the Portland, Maine, *Daily Eastern Argus* on April 26, 1917, the day they were to open in that city at the New Portland Theatre.

The display ad read, "Here's the Big Shubert Management Act that has made New York sit up / The Creole Band / Sometimes Called the Jazz Band . . ." but the significant detail is in the text of the publicity puff:

. . . so good that they are under the management of the Shuberts and are obtained from them by Marcus Loew for a limited number of engagements at some of the best Loew houses.[69]

The Loew vaudeville interests would have had a very good reason to call on the Shuberts — or anyone else — for assistance. On March 8 the vaudeville actors union with the picturesque name of the White Rats had called a strike against all the Loew theatres, to be followed a few days later by one against the Poli chain of New England. To combat the strike, a managers' organization called the VMNA (Vaudeville Managers' National Association), and another performers' union, the National Variety Artists (NVA) were activated. Both the degree of participation in the strike and the amount of disruption to the operation of the Loew's circuit are difficult to gauge, not least because of the opposition of *Variety* to the Rats and their strike.[70]

Be that as it may, there were pickets in front of Loew's theatres, and many performers either walked out or found an excuse not to perform as scheduled. Even more symptomatic of difficulty, Loew's suspended publication of their bills ahead in *Variety* from March 16 through April 13 (for the weeks of March 19 through April 16).[71]

Although this suspension obviously creates difficulty in tracing all the movements of the band during this period, we find them playing, as usual, at the Winter Garden Sunday concerts but, more important, at four Loew's houses. It seems reasonable to assume that the blanks can be filled in by other appearances on the Loew's circuit.

As attested by documents in the papers now at HJA, Nick LaRocca, the cornetist of the Original Dixieland Jazz Band, had a quite different and self-serving explanation for the Creole Band's departure from the Montmartre. Whether Nick LaRocca read the papers closely enough to see the Montmartre ads during March 1917 is not certain. Perhaps he did; but he surely would have been startled to read an interview with pianist and publisher Clarence Williams published in the October 1936 issue of *Orchestra World* in which Williams claimed,

the first hot band to leave from the South and introduce swing music was the Creole Jazz Band . . . Following was the Dixieland Jazz Band which recorded Livery Stable Blues and Tiger Rag which swept the country. The Creole Band was colored and the Dixieland Band was white and they used to play across the street from each other and used to sit in for each other during rest periods.[72]

The same issue contained an interview with Nick LaRocca, which was full of mistakes of fact, for example, that the ODJB was organized in 1908 and played for two years on the riverboats.

The next month, *Orchestra World* published a letter from Williams, backing off from his October claim that "Tiger Rag" was an original Negro tune, stating, "it was not my intention to discredit Mr. Nick LaRocca as the composer of 'Tiger Rag.'" One assumes that LaRocca had brandished his copyright—and if Clarence Williams understood anything, it was copyright. The photocopy of these articles in the LaRocca papers at HJA has the following note from LaRocca:

> This is more Negro Lies Clarence Williams Early Life was in Plaquemine LA where he lived with his grandmother in an alley worked as a shoeshine boy in Ferdinand Herbert's Barber Shop Came to N.O. in his Late Teens and Did Not hear Bolden play.

Williams's claim regarding the Creole Band was apparently enough to make a researcher of LaRocca. His archive contains a sheet of typed excerpts from *Variety* regarding early jazz groups,[73] and a photostat of an article from the same paper from March 16, 1917 on the popularity of jazz bands with New York dancers. On it is written the remark:

> This appeared while the supposed great Creol band was playing at Monmarte (Dolodrina Club). They were unsuccessful 2 weeks—went into vaudeville Pantages time—never was again heard of.[74]

On the back of the photostat, LaRocca continues to rave:

> This appeared in Variety while the supposed Great "Creol Band" was playing (Dolodrina's Ragtime Club) Monmarte a top Wintergarden 50th Broadway Played for Clifford Web and Gloria Goodwin also for patrons to dance to look up NYC papers for verification Mch 6 & 7 1917 Thes negroes were a failure 2 weeks stay.[75]

Although these remarks are certainly in line with LaRocca's resentment at the single-minded insistence of writers on jazz to credit African-Americans for its discovery, it also mirrors his belief—not entirely unjustified—that other Southern musicians who came to New York following the ODJB failed to make their mark and returned home, sometimes with loans from LaRocca.

The Creole Band was replaced by another jazz combination, at first announced as "The Original California 'JAZZ' Band from Frisco" in the leading dailies. Eventually, the billing changed to "The Original Frisco 'Jazz' Band" and was expanded to include "Fanchon and Marco." Fanchon and Marco

Wolff were brother and sister and became extremely well known as producers in the 1920s and 1930s. In 1917 they were in the first stages of their career, with Marco playing violin in the band and dancing at the same time. They continued at the Montmartre through the end of May.

The personnel of the band is mostly known: E. Arnold Johnson (1893–1975), piano; Marco Wolff, violin; Rudy Wiedoeft, saxophone and clarinet; T. E. "Buster" Johnson, trombone. The drummer and banjo player are unidentified.

Wiedoeft was a member of a musical family that had moved from Detroit to Los Angeles and had been a professional musician in the latter city since the early 'teens. He came to New York with the Oliver Morosco show "Canary Cottage" which opened there—its premiere was actually in California—on February 5, 1917, and ran for some four months. In a brief biographical sketch published in *Down Beat* in 1940 we learn:

> In about 1917 Wiedoeft was appearing in the pit at the Morosco Theater in New York with the orchestra of a musical show called "Canary Cottage." Wiedoeft's obligatos from the pit on the musical's hit song were so thrilling that he took more bows from the pit than the singer did from the stage.[76]

Did other members of the band come with "Canary Cottage" as well? Various entries in the reports from locals in the *International Musician* suggest that Buster Johnson (as T. E. Johnson) came along with the show from California. E. Arnold Johnson, although he performed both in San Francisco and Los Angeles, appears to have come to New York from Chicago.[77]

This preliminary attempt to establish the Frisco Jazz Band's West Coast credentials is motivated by the fact that between May and October 1917, they made no fewer than nine issued recordings for the Edison company, in addition to two tests made for Columbia. I, at any rate, find these records of considerable interest and consider it approaching the scandalous that they have not been available *in toto* to the student of early jazz.[78]

The Creole Band's whereabouts for the week of March 19 is unknown. According to a brief notice in the *New York Age*, they were busy at least on Sunday, March 25, playing the "concerts" at both the Lexington Opera House and the Columbia. For the last half of the following week, March 29 through 31, they appeared at Loew's Orpheum, receiving a negative review from the *Clipper*:

> The Creole Band found it easy going, making a noise that some persons called "music." The "band" consists of a violin, bass, guitar, trombone, cornet, and flute, each vying with the other in an effort to produce discord.[79]

That this reception was far from characteristic is underlined by reviews of their appearance at the American and American Roof from Monday, April 2 through Wednesday, April 4. *Variety* had an extensive review of the nine-act program—which they found overloaded with turns dealing with the inner workings of the business—and found the Creole Band a "surefire hit" in closing the first half of the show. The reviewer thought that each time they played at the American, their popularity increased.[80] An ad in the *Journal* located them for the last half of the week at Loew's Boulevard Theatre, far to the north in the Bronx, at South Boulevard and Westchester Avenue.

According to the *Age*, whose news items regarding the band had been reasonably if not entirely accurate, they were at Gordon's Olympia Theatre (booked by Loew) in Boston for the week of April 9. There were in fact two theatres by that name, one on Washington Street, the other in Scollay Square. Neither theater lists the band in any of the seven Boston daily newspapers consulted.[81]

For the week of April 16 one might expect to find them somewhere in the region, say at other Loew's-booked venues in Boston, the Bowdoin Square, St. James, or Orpheum, or in a nearby town, such as Lynn, Haverhill, or Dorchester. Be that as it may, they appeared at the Plaza in Springfield, Massachusetts, for the first half of the week of April 23. Very strangely indeed—because Prince had traded vaudeville glamour for the steel mill several months before—the advance publicity on Saturday billed them as "Morgan Prince and his Creole Band," also mentioning the "special scenery." The local reviews were favorable but anodyne, with that in the *Union* the briefest:

> The Creole Band heads the vaudeville part of the program and they play a number of pieces in a comical manner. Their methods of playing certain instruments are unique to say the least.[82]

The plan was for them to go on to the New Portland Theater, Portland, Maine, for the last half of the week, as we have already seen above. Two exceptionally long items from the *Portland Evening Express and Advertiser* tell a lot:

> The feature is the Creole Band. This is better known in the big time houses as The Jazz Band and it has set New York and other big cities wild this past winter. It is a company of Creoles who are so good that they are under the management of the Shuberts and are obtained from them by Marcus Loew for a limited number of engagements at some of the best of the Loew houses. Portland is the only place in Maine that gets a look at this wonderful band of instrumentalists, vocalists, dancers and all around Creole entertainers. There is an elaborate special drop curtain and a

lot of special stage settings that make a veritable Southern plantation picture as the curtain rises.

The next day it was a different story:

Notwithstanding the fact that the feature act booked for the New Portland failed to show up yesterday with the change of bill, illustrated songs and additional pictures enough were put on to make an excellent performance and today everything will be on schedule again. The Creole Band got as far as Boston when word was received of the death of an immediate and dear relative of one of the principals. He was obliged to return South at once and as the act could not be given without him it had to be canceled. Manager Hutchinson immediately telephoned New York and a fine miniature musical comedy feature was started yesterday afternoon for Portland and will be the headliner for today and tomorrow. It is Miss Match Miss. [7 pretty girls, 2 funny comedians with special scenery and electrical effects][83]

The real story of this first breakup, or one of the real stories, would have made more interesting reading. There's one detailed story from Big Eye—in two versions—and two extremely sketchy ones from Bill Johnson and Norwood Williams.

Big Eye told his story first to Orin Blackstone, who published it in 1940. Four years later he recounted it to Robert Goffin, who dressed it up in his usual romantic fashion.

The Blackstone version begins soberly enough:

Easy money was giving Keppard the "swell head" he says. The Creole Band broke up in Boston one night in May, 1917, leaving Big Eye "sittin' in the depot." The Creoles had finished a date in Springfield and were on their way to Portland. With only an hour or so between trains in Boston, Keppard wandered away and others left to look for him until finally Big Eye was the only one left in the station. The Band never came back. Big Eye went to New York.

The first person he saw that he knew, in New York, was Keppard . . . standing at the corner of 132nd and Lenox Ave. and looking very important. Big Eye says he tried to find out what happened and all he could get out of the supremely self-confident Keppard was the statement that he didn't know, just couldn't keep the boys together. Big Eye's career in the big time was over.[84]

The Goffin version is not greatly different from Blackstone's:

Finally, the band left for Boston. The musicians looked for a hotel in vain, and had to stay in Mrs. Wood's boarding house in Mezzrow [sic] St. After a week, the group was hired to play in Portland, Maine.

They all set a time to meet at North Station. The baggage was checked, with Freddy Keppard holding the receipts. Everybody was on time, except Freddy, who on leaving Mrs. Woods' boarding house, thought it advisable to stop in a bar for refreshments. As he usually did, he had the gin bottle set up on the counter and drank much too much.

When he arrived at North Station, the train had left and the others insulted him. A terrible argument ensued. What could they do? The band couldn't get to Portland on time. They didn't have a job. The furious men reclaimed their baggage and sent it to New York, to the boarding house run by Lottie Joplin.[85]

This fits the band's having gone to Boston to play at Gordon's during the week of April 9, staying at Mrs. Wood's place.[86] They might have stayed on another week, then gone off on a side trip to Springfield for the first half of the week of April 23, perhaps leaving the better part of their effects with Mrs. Wood. Their train from Springfield back to Boston would have arrived in South Station—probably via the Boston & Albany—early on Thursday. (It would have been difficult to play the Wednesday evening show and catch a night train to Boston.) They then would have stopped by the boarding house and proceeded to North Station, whence left the Boston & Maine trains for the short trip to Portland (between two and three hours).

Bill remembered only the bare outlines in 1959, when he was in his eighties and often not able to respond to the interviewer's questions in much detail. He said simply that in Boston—it was summer—Keppard and Big Eye missed the train. This made Bill angry, so he took the scenery and broke up the band, returning to Chicago. Then he went on to Salt Lake City where he spent six months. The band took on another bass player two hours after the train incident and continued to play for a bit. In at least one detail, his account fit Big Eye's perfectly: they stayed with Woods.

Some light is cast on Johnson's activities by an interview conducted in 1958 with clarinetist, Clem Raymond (1894–1962 according to Bill Russell). Born in New Orleans, Raymond claimed musical tutelage with Luis (Papa) Tio and Willie E. Humphrey. At age sixteen he began working the United Fruit Company boats between New Orleans and New York. It was the Johnson brothers from New Orleans who encouraged him to work in music. As he recalled it, the Johnsons were working with the Tennessee Ten, one as a guitarist, the other as a bassist. He further recalled that U.S. "Slow Kid" Thompson had the band, which would close the show on the Orpheum circuit. Raymond joined the band, which took him to California, where he stayed for the rest of his life.

The Tennessee Ten had been organized by impresario Ralph Dunbar in early 1916—and soon thereafter was handled by Harry Weber. The great feature of the act was its seven- or eight-piece "jazz band," which received repeated and enthusiastic notice in the theatrical weeklies. It seems also to have done its share to perpetuate plantation stereotypes: a 1921 photograph shows them in front of a log cabin drop with at extreme stage right a member of the company in "old man" getup, just as Morgan Prince might have worn. The company included at least two women, of whom the most famous was Florence Mills. The roster of musicians—all of whom no doubt doubled in comedy, song, and dance—was quite variable over the years. In 1921, the guitarist with the group was Robert Johnson, who may well have been Bill Johnson's brother.

In late April 1917, just as the Creole Band crashed and burned in Boston, the Tennessee Ten was in New York City and eventually worked its way to Chicago, arriving for the week of July 9. They covered much of the same WVMA territory familiar to the Creole Band for the next three months and then headed for the West Coast on the Orpheum Circuit. New Orleanian bassist Ed Garland is listed in a roster of October 6, 1917. Quite hypothetically, let's assume that Bill and Robert Johnson and Clem Raymond joined the Tennessee Ten in New York; that Bill left the act in Chicago, wanting to proceed to Salt Lake City to be near his wife, Victoria; that Raymond stayed on and traveled to California.

The story collected from Norwood Williams by Bill Russell, ca. 1940, is even sketchier. Although Johnson's name was on the band's business card as manager, Williams claimed to be—as the only one who didn't drink a lot—the de facto manager. As such, he finally got tired of keeping the others in line. Once, when Keppard and most, or some, of the others failed to show up, perhaps at a train station in Boston, Williams got disgusted, came back to Los Angeles and opened a filling station with the money he had saved while on the road with the band. Finally, he recalled leaving the band in Portland, Maine, or in Boston, early in 1917.[87]

What is certain is that on Thursday, April 26, 1917, the train to Portland from Boston's North Station was missed, possibly due to the carelessness of Keppard, quite possibly abetted by others. The absence of one, or even two of the men wouldn't necessarily have stopped the others from going on to Portland and performing as scheduled on Thursday night. But one can easily understand that Johnson and Williams were disgusted enough to call it quits after nearly three years of incessant travel. One wonders whether the members of the band realized that their connection with the Shuberts had done them in, even deprived them of the chance to make an impression on New York like that of the ODJB—and that that realization played a role in their willingness to give up after so many months of effortful (and not enormously profitable) pleasure.[88]

Either Goffin or Big Eye added piquant details to the story which, because false in some important respects, might lead us to reject it entirely. This would be a mistake, in my opinion. In my translation:

Look, here's a souvenir from 1917. I used to stay at Lottie Joplin's boarding house in Harlem. And Louis took out of his wallet a little business card:

Mrs. Lottie Joplin
Neatly Furnished Rooms
by Day or Week
163 West 131

And Louis, overcome by the power of his memories, added these details:

"After I had left Freddy Keppard in Boston, that famous day when the Creole Band broke up, I went to stay at Joplin's, I was eager to see my old friend again, whose ragtime pieces were so moving. Some years earlier he'd finished a operetta that he had great hopes for but turned out to be a fiasco. Alas! when I arrived at 131st street, I learned that poor Joplin had just passed away. Lottie was crushed. I even recall that they were going to bury him on the Wednesday before Easter. A delegation of pious individuals from the neighborhood came to plead that the services not be held on that holy day. That's why the date was put ahead 48 hours and that's how Scott Joplin, the famous author, was buried on Good Friday. I can still see in my mind the funeral procession. On each of the vehicles in the ceremony, they had written the name of one of the works of the great author. Naturally, "Maple Leaf Rag" was at the head.[89]

Easter in 1917 was April 8, however, and Joplin had died a week earlier, on Sunday, April 1, with the date of burial in St. Michael's cemetery recorded on the death certificate as Thursday, April 5. So this could not have happened after the band broke up on April 26. Still, since the band was playing in New York City during the week of April 2, it's not impossible that Big Eye was present at a funeral service. The detail regarding the names of his pieces being displayed on the vehicles in a funeral procession seems quite incredible; and such an event would surely, one thinks, have attracted some attention, at least in New York's African-American weeklies. It did not.[90]

It's surely worth pointing out that the original date of burial shown on his death certificate—reproduced in Berlin 1994—was entered as April 4, which was crossed out in favor of April 5. Perhaps we should conclude, charitably, that Big Eye indeed was staying at Lottie Joplin's, that he could have directly witnessed Joplin's death and burial—with some distortion. Also, despite all the problems with the anecdote, it would be a grave mistake to overlook the fact that Big Eye, like many another African-American musician of the "ragtime era," greatly revered Joplin.

Finally, the rest of Big Eye's memory is rather much in agreement with the recollections of Johnson and Williams.

They got back together again two or three days later in Harlem. Bill Johnson and Williams quickly received an offer for California and left with the band's set, which they sold! . . . One day, Freddy Keppard, who had drunk up his last nickel, ran into "Big Eye" Louis Nelson and Jimmy Palao, at the Cuba Club, at Lennox.

They finished the night in arguing like stevedores. When the band was getting ready to leave, fate smiled on the Creole Band for one last time, in the person of Irving Miller, who came to talk to the group.

"I've got something for you in Philadelphia!"

"Where?" asked Freddy, whose business sense was always on the lookout.

"At the Gibson Theatre."

"When?"

"In three days."

"How much?"

"I'm offering $75 a man."

Good luck had come back. Freddy Keppard didn't have a red cent and managed to borrow $100 from Louis Nelson, then ordered a good bottle!

"In order to drink a good gin," said Freddy Keppard, "I need two things . . . the bottle and me!"

The next day they talked the deal over with Eddie Venson [*sic*]. How could they organize a band without a bass and a guitar? Irving Miller leapt into the breach. Freddy Keppard hired the actor, Morgan Prince, who would sing and be Bill Johnson's replacement. Finally, several hours before leaving for Philadelphia, the band still didn't have a guitar. They hired Jim Slader, a dancer of the *Cuba Club*, who was supposed to show up and pretend to play an old ukulele.

In Philadelphia, it was a triumphal success; for two weeks people were lined up for two blocks. But at the end of the job, Freddie Keppard had drunk up all his pay and refused to pay back Big Eye Louis Nelson.[91]

The story continues for another page in Goffin, giving totally unverifiable details concerning the departure of Nelson, Vincent, and Keppard for New Orleans.

But that part of the story regarding a Philadelphia engagement has a basis in fact. The *Age* announced on Thursday, May 10, that James Slater was appearing with the Creole Band in Philadelphia, and the Philadelphia *Tribune*, an African-American weekly, printed a report of their appearance by C. E. Wells in its issue of Saturday, May 12. It verged on the snide:

> Mr. Gibson presents an unusual novelty this week, in the Creole Band—the original Jass Band. The players have the distinction of having played the Winter Garden, New York, for a long run. It is an act that shows very clearly what the white theatre patrons like the colored performer to do. Everybody who is interested should see them.

Elsewhere, the paper gave the roster of the band: Bob and Jim Slater, Harry and Fred Prampin, Henry Sapiro (correctly "Saparo"), Ralph Nicholas, and Ecaud and Tureaud.

Once again, a curious melange of truth and fiction: there was a C.V.B.A. club—for Colored Vaudeville Benevolent Association—founded apparently in 1909; also, it was located at 438 Lenox Avenue, between 131st and 132nd Streets.[92] More important, dancer and producer Robert Slater (New Orleans, 1869–New York, June 20, 1930) was either a charter member or even the founder. Jim Slater—probably his brother—is recorded in New York in 1917 in a two-act with Bob.

Harry Prampin was a cornetist born in New Orleans as well, and is mentioned in association with Fred Prampin in conjunction with the Creole Band as well as appearing in a C.V.B.A. benefit in June 1917. Henry Saparo, the best known of the group, was also from New Orleans, and so was violinist Ralph Nicholas (Nicolas?), a veteran of the touring minstrel companies ca. 1900. Finally Ecaud and Tureaud were also natives of the Crescent City. One source has George Ecaud working in vaudeville as a xylophonist. Another calls him "the little actor and pugilist."

All of them are mentioned in a story from the *Indianapolis Freeman* of Saturday, May 5, 1917, the week before the Philadelphia appearance:

> The famous Creole Band has made another stop over in the big city. It reminds one of the good old dishes of "Gumbo" that they served down in New Orleans, when we see this band with Bob and Jim Slater, Harry and Fred Prampin, Henry Sapiro, Ralph Nicholas, Ecand and Tureaud and more of their fellow countrymen gather around the big "round" table in the club rooms of the C.U.B.A. for a general pow-wow.

Finally, Irvin(g) C. Miller is extremely well known as a theatrical producer, from ca. 1912 through the 1930s. While it's not known whether he was from

New Orleans, he was married at one time to Esther Bigeou, a beauteous singer from that city.

So far, so good. Many points of Big Eye's (and Goffin's) narrative make sense—Slater, the C.V.B.A. club; what doesn't is his idea that original members of the band participated in the engagement at Gibson's Standard Theatre. One possibility is that Goffin, in reconstructing notes that he took when speaking with Big Eye in 1944, made the assumption that they would somehow have been involved. The only newspaper that published reviews of the shows at Gibson's Standard, which was owned and operated by an African-American, was the distinguished African-American weekly, the Philadelphia *Tribune*.

Gibson's Standard had nothing to do with Loew's, or any other mainstream vaudeville circuit, therefore it seems quite unlikely that the engagement had been arranged much in advance. One can easily imagine matters proceeding much as Big Eye + Goffin recounted, that is, promotion by Miller for a good price—the usual Creole Band weekly salary while on tour. Also, many of the participants were New Orleanians—and the others quite possibly—and were involved with the C.V.B.A. This was a one-shot deal, taking advantage of the undoubted renown of the Band; to be a black act that had succeeded in white vaudeville was no small thing. The reviewer appears to be responding—negatively, to be sure—to this achievement.

Hiatus

In effect, the band no longer existed after the inadvertent, if not farcical, breakup in Boston. Still, one would like to account for their various activities between April 26 and the Logan Square Theater tryout of October 1917 remembered by Jimmie Noone. Palao stayed in New York City with his family, and the evidence indicates that Big Eye went back to New Orleans and Norwood Williams to California. Johnson wound up for a while in Salt Lake City, possibly traveling there via Chicago. Goffin had Big Eye and Vincent taking the train together to New Orleans, leaving Keppard on the platform with a two-dollar bottle of gin. Vincent was in New Orleans just a few weeks later to be married, so perhaps we can in this instance trust Goffin.

ACCORDING TO MY understanding of the always tenuous situation of African-American performers in white mainstream vaudeville, missing the performance in Portland was showbiz suicide, only ratified by the band scattering to the four winds. If they'd still been represented by Harry Weber, he could perhaps have covered for them as well as given them a piece of his mind. As it was, they may well have been regarded—in New York at least—as a bunch of talented but unruly niggers who could easily be replaced.

6 The Final Season

THE UNPLANNED AND decidedly messy break-up of the Creole Band in Boston wouldn't have endeared them to Marcus Loew or the Shuberts. Who brought them back together for what might in retrospect be called a lame-duck season? And why?

By the fall of 1917, the "jazz" craze was in full bloom, with the word cropping up with increasing frequency on record labels, sheet music and orchestration covers, newspaper and magazine articles. Not only that; it was widely believed that the music had originated in New Orleans. Very likely it would have occurred to Bill Johnson and to his former bandmates that, despite its problems, the Creole Band could rightfully cash in on the steadily growing popularity for jazz music, even if many Americans were not very clear as to what it was.

Getting back together again was easier to think about than accomplish, since some of the musicians had gone back to New Orleans, some stayed in New York, and at least two went to the West Coast. H. Morgan Prince had, of course, left the band because of illness in January 1917. When he recovered, rather than rejoin the band he went to work in a steel mill in Gary, Indiana, beginning March 10, 1917. He continued in this job for the next twenty months. One can only speculate why he didn't rejoin the band. Possibly he was tired of the vaudeville grind; or perhaps the band didn't want him back, given the friction with Keppard recalled by Jelly Roll Morton. Whatever the case, as in the previous season, Leonard Scott was back again with the band as singer and dancer in Prince's place.[1] If we believe Goffin's account, Eddie Vincent and Big Eye had gone back to New Orleans together; where Keppard was is anybody's guess. Possibly he remained in New York, as had Palao.

Norwood Williams, to be sure, was alive and well when Bill Russell was in Los Angeles to study musical composition with Arnold Schoenberg in 1940.

Bill had learned from Bud Scott that Williams was operating a filling station on 116th Street in Watts. This is where an interview was conducted, apparently in the presence of Mrs. Williams. Williams claimed to have been the de facto business manager because he was the most reliable and sensible member of the band—as well as the only one who didn't drink a lot or spend all his money on "diamonds, women, and booze." Finally, however, he got sick of trying to keep the others in line and in disgust returned to Los Angeles, where he opened a filling station with the money he'd saved while on the road.

Williams's impatience with his fellow musicians was quite possibly misplaced when it came to Jimmy Palao, who was the only serious family man in the group, with a wife and three daughters to support. Clotile Palao Wilson recalled that the Palao family had lived in New York City for two years, before returning to Chicago in January 1918. If we understand "two years" literally, this meant that they would have moved while the band was on tour with "Town Topics," or even before. This is confirmed by a postcard sent by Palao to his family from Buffalo, May 9, 1916—which is when "Town Topics" was playing there—addressed to 223 West 133rd Street, New York.

Additionally, James Palao, musician, is listed at 35 West 112th Street in Trow's New York City directories for 1917 and 1918. And Mrs. Wilson recalled living on that street, "right near the Jewish synagogue." The family also preserved a snapshot of Palao with his saxophone on what could very well be a Manhattan rooftop. In any event, it appears quite likely that Palao stayed in New York City until the band re-formed in October 1917.

This leaves only Bill Johnson to be accounted for. When interviewed in 1959, Bill stated that after Keppard and Big Eye missed the train in Boston, he took the scenery and went back to Chicago, going on to Salt Lake City, where he stayed some six months. This fully accounts for the time between the breakup and reassembling of the group, if not for the choice of location. My guess is that he may have wanted to spend some time with his mysterious bride, Victoria, whom he had met in Ogden during one of the band's tours on Pantages time.

Some reference to Bill's activities during the hiatus can be found in the muddled reminiscences of Clem Raymond, born in New Orleans in 1894 but from about 1918 on resident in California. Raymond had been working on the United Fruit Company ships between New Orleans and New York. He recalled having been encouraged to leave the boats to concentrate on music by the Johnson brothers from New Orleans—one played guitar, the other string bass. Although they were from New Orleans, to Raymond they were not heavily Southern in their speech and might have come from Missouri.

6.1 This photo was snapped on a New York City rooftop, probably after the band's temporary breakup in April 1917. The little girl would be Palao's third daughter, Agatha, born in January 1915.

The Johnson brothers were with the Tennessee Ten Company, led by "Slow Kid" Thompson, and Raymond substituted for the clarinetist,[2] who either got another job or simply didn't want to come with them to tour the Orpheum circuit. According to the itineraries in the theatrical weeklies, the Tennessee Ten was playing the Colonial, New York, during the week of April 23, just a few days prior to the Creole Band's disintegration in Boston. By July, the Tennessee Ten was in Chicago, then spent the next three months touring the WVMA circuit in close proximity to the Windy City. Finally at the end of October they began heading West on the Orpheum time.

The potentially most valuable witness to the band's last season was Jimmie Noone, not only because he was very well known to jazz fans and record collectors but also because he was always readily available in Chicago or, at the end of his life, Los Angeles. It's something of a mystery that more of an attempt to

6.2 Two of Jimmy Palao's business cards, the first dating from 1916 or 1917, no doubt prior to establishing a permanent address in New York City and from the time when "jaz" was all the rage. It's of course interesting that he had already acquired doubling skill on the saxophone, like many violinists at this time. The second card comes from ca. 1924 after the Palao family moved back to Chicago from Milwaukee. The uncentered "Creole" looks like it might have been an afterthought. In any event, Palao seems to have been bent on maximizing his business opportunities, although specifying both C melody and tenor sax strikes us as overkill. [Hogan Jazz Archive, gift of Al Rose; Palao family scrapbook]

explore his memories was not made. Fortunately, there was one interview, conducted by Wesley M. Neff around 1940, that gleaned some substantive detail. Noone recalled that Keppard sent for him from Chicago in 1917, and that, as soon as he arrived, they tried out for a new contract at the Logan Square Theatre. They were found ready to go out again and were assigned to the "Junior Orpheum" circuit, touring until the spring of 1918, at which time Noone returned to New Orleans.[3] Noone's dates—though approximate—are correct, and indeed the old Michigan circuit of W. S. Butterfield theatres was by then affiliated with the Orpheum chain and quite likely known, along with some other Midwestern small-town venues, as the "junior Orpheum."

The choice of Noone was, to say the least, interesting, not only because he would be the youngest member of the group but also because, of all the band members, he was the only one to make a graceful and quite successful transition to the jazz world of the late 1920s and early 1930s. As such, he also left a very sizeable body of recordings; these are varied enough in date, tempo, and type that one feels on firm ground in assessing his overall sound and style.[4]

According to the information garnered by Neff, Noone had begun playing clarinet when he was about sixteen, shortly before moving with his family to New Orleans in 1910. He received "priceless instruction" from the precocious 13-year-old genius Sidney Bechet. Maurice Durand, who lived close to Noone when they were young, said that it was Fred Keppard who suggested that Noone play clarinet. Subsequently, Noone studied with Paul Chaligny,[5] who was one of a handful of African-American musicians in New Orleans with a reputation for teaching, along with William Nickerson and James Humphrey (to cite the best known). One presumes that if the instruction lasted any length of time, Noone would have become acquainted with at least the rudiments of written music.

Again according to Noone, his first paying job was only in 1913 and came about by accident. He had brought a clarinet to a gig to loan to Bechet, who then failed to show up. Noone played well enough as a substitute that he continued to play (for about a year probably) with Keppard. When Keppard left town, a Young Olympia Band was formed, and for the next two years or so, Noone worked with them, at the side of Buddy Petit, Arnold DePass, Simon and John Marrero, and Zue Robertson. He also remembered working in a trio or quartet under his own leadership on the Roof Garden of the Pythian Temple during the summers of 1916 and 1917. Although he seems to have moved in some challenging company, he was far from being the seasoned player that Baquet and Delille had been.

In an interview given in 1960, Emile Barnes stated that he was "supposed to leave here [New Orleans] in Jimbo's place" and later that "he should have left with the first bunch but he just didn't believe in going anywhere." To judge from the recordings made by Barnes when he was in his 60s, his contribution to the Creole Band would have been very different from Baquet, Delille *or* Noone; but he stressed that when he was younger he was more versatile and able to fit into many different kinds of bands.[6]

We can also speculate on some other possible choices for the slot vacated by Big Eye. The twenty-year-old Sidney Bechet would have been unavailable, having just left town with the Bruce & Bruce vaudeville company; Johnny Dodds was comfortably ensconced in the Oliver-Ory band; Lorenzo Tio, Jr., was presumably equally well established in the A. J. Piron orchestra.

THE LOGAN SQUARE THEATRE was not among the important neighborhood vaudeville or combination houses in Chicago, although it was conveniently located at the terminus of a branch of the elevated railway system, at Milwaukee and Kedzie avenues on the near northwest side. *Variety* remarked in October 1917—probably just about the time that the Creole Band appeared there— that, although the theater had been "for years a consistent bottomless pit of losses with stock, vaudeville, or pictures," this season "it has been turned into a money-maker through the talents of Walter Meskin, who can 'buy' acts economically, and Sam Lederer, who can 'sell' 'em efficiently."[7]

Fifteen months later, Jack Lait uncapped his bottle of purple ink and described the theater in *Variety*'s Chicago column:

> the home of ambition on Wednesday night, tryout night. Here far from the glitter of the downtown houses where set and routed acts skim the cream, the two types that have given to tryouts their comedy and tragedy show themselves, the old-timers who have slipped and the youngsters who are hammering at the doors of opportunity . . .[8]

Indeed, the band had skimmed the cream of the Loop theaters in previous years, but appearing at the Logan Square—whose offerings were not reported in the theatrical or general press—is a telling index of how nervous the bookers were about them after the Boston debacle. An act that had successfully played from coast to coast for some three years was reduced to playing an audition in an obscure Chicago house! Perhaps the true story behind their breakup in Boston had gone the rounds of all the booking offices; perhaps also the substitutions of personnel, especially that of Leonard Scott for H. Morgan Prince, made agents want to see and hear the new configuration before signing them to a new contract. At any rate, it was hardly favorable for their prospects that they were looking for bookings when the fall season was well under way. Most acts would have been signed by the end of the previous spring season or at least during the summer.

Worse yet, for purposes of tracking their progress, such a late start would more or less guarantee that their bookings would be often a last-minute affair, as substitutes or to fill in an empty slot in the week's bill. Where in previous years their appearances had been rather comprehensively reported in one or another of the theatrical weeklies, the band now disappears from view for weeks on end.

Be that as it may, the band's first appearance for the 1917–1918 season was reported in *Billboard*'s advance bookings for the week of October 22, as one of a five-act bill at the Palace Theatre, Moline, Illinois, a house served by the WVMA.[9] From October 25 through 27, they played the Palace in Fort Wayne, Indiana, "a jazz organization," according to the brief review. Next came Detroit's Colonial Theatre, for the week of October 29.

The Colonial was a brand new house somewhat north of the downtown section that had opened on Monday, October 8. It began by running six acts of continuous vaudeville interspersed with motion pictures. *Variety* noted a novelty: the proprietors, the Hoffman brothers, had no affiliation with a booking office, preferring to book their acts directly. By the end of the month, a new policy of two-a-day was instituted, with reserved seats. It was also reported that an effort was being made to attract "big-time names" as necessary to ensure the new theatre's success.[10]

The act title from previous seasons, "Uncle Joe's Birthday," was retained, and the reviews from the *News* and the *Free Press* repeated the usual clichés with a few special details. The former listed the band in its Sunday edition as "The New Orleans Jazz Band" and said that each of the twenty [!] musicians would play a solo novelty. On Tuesday they were once again "the original Creole ragtime band" but spiced their "splendid program of southern music" with "a touch of jazz." The *Free Press* emphasized that they were "real New Orleans musicians."

They played the first half of the week of November 12 at the Orpheum in Peoria, a house presenting five acts of vaudeville with movies and a newsreel for three shows a day. News items from both Monday and Tuesday singled out "the aged 'Uncle's' chicken chase—a real chicken," along with the usual praise for the comedy and the "plaintive" singing.

A week later they were in Decatur at the Empress Theatre, where they had appeared in the fall of 1915 and possibly also at the beginning of 1917. Like the Orpheum in Peoria, the Empress offered a mixed program, three shows a day, of varied vaudeville—four acts only—with motion pictures, all at the modest ticket price of 10, 20, or 30 cents. Some details of the advertisements were novel, beginning with the act title "On the Old Plantation." More significant surely is their designation as "Colored Kings of 'Jazz' Music . . . Syncopated Melody Makers Extraordinary." For unknown reasons, neither of the town's daily newspapers offered a review.

Billed appearances at two WVMA houses in Chicago, the American and the Lincoln, remain unverified and unreviewed in any of the usual sources. On Thanksgiving Day, November 29, they were "received enthusiastically by three capacity houses" at the Orpheum in South Bend, Indiana, a small house of about a thousand seats. Their advertising advance blurb called them the "positive creators of jazz music."[11] The *Defender* for a change noted their appearance at this theatre, adding, "The act is working so steadily that the horns have blisters on them."[12]

The band's next stop may have been the Lyric Theatre, Indianapolis, for the week of December 3. But there are a number of puzzles: the act's title was given in ads and advance blurbs as "Uncle Eph's Birthday," and the title role was said to have been filled by H. Morgan Prince. Finally, the instrumentation was given as piccolo, banjo, bass viol, violin, cornet, and slide trombone. Notably, their offering of "jazz music" was underlined, with one paper stating that "the Creole Band is said to be the 'daddy' of all jazz organizations—a heavy responsibility."[13] One wonders, especially from the novel act title, whether Morgan Prince assembled a group of musicians on his own for a one-time appearance at the Lyric. Or perhaps he merely substituted briefly for Leonard Scott; after all, he was working in Gary, an easy 140 miles from the state capital. The designation of "piccolo" may have been occasioned by another substitution—that of Gilbert "Babb" Frank, known to have been in Chicago around this time—for Jimmie Noone. Surely, even the densest newspaper reporter could tell the difference between a clarinet and a piccolo? [Prudence suggests we answer "no."]

For the first part of the following week of December 10, the band found itself as the chief attraction at a small (500 seats) house in Lafayette, Indiana, the Family Theatre. The *Journal* offered what seems to be a real review, headlined "A Clever Bill At Family Theatre. Creole Ragtime Band Enthuses Audience." The instruments specified this time were violin, bass viol, guitar, banjo, cornet, trombone, and clarinet, exactly right if we suppose that Morgan Prince (or Scotty Blue) might double on banjo as well as sing and dance The daily student paper of Purdue University copied—with a few alterations hardly sufficient to escape a charge of plagiarism—the review from the *Journal*, but added a number of rare and precious details regarding the production. "The scene depicts an old southern plantation. In the background is seen many little darkie huts, while in the foreground is seen Uncle Joe's Little Cabin. The act begins with a dawn serenade by the darkies in front of Uncle Joe's hut in remembrance of his birthday. They play several numbers which brings Joe out and the comedy of the act is here started, and is good, clean, wholesome and enjoyable. The boys are all garbed in costumes of the typical southern darkies."[14]

They moved for the second half to Muskegon, Michigan, where Earnestine Gunn, Jr., thought their music "rather circusesque jazz" and the act in general entertaining, although "a many times done idea." Although neither the Lafayette nor the Muskegon venues appear in the usual lists of theaters owned or controlled by W. S. Butterfield, a list of places booked by the W.U.B.O. printed in the *Clipper* of February 7, 1917, adds four towns in Indiana (Fort Wayne, Indianapolis, Lafayette, Logansport), two in Michigan (Muskegon, Pontiac), and one in Illinois (Danville) to the usual list of seven or eight Butterfield theaters. It seems likely that for some of the missing half weeks in their schedule, the Creole Band could be found, say, in Fort Wayne or Pontiac.

The appearances on this circuit that have been verified in local newspapers are as follows:

Dec. 10	Lafayette
13	Muskegon
17	Kalamazoo
20	Battle Creek
24	Jackson
27	Lansing
31	Flint
Jan. 3	Saginaw
6	Bay City (Sunday only)
17	Danville, Illinois

Most of the advance publicity as well as the reviews stress that the band played jazz music. In Kalamazoo, the blurb printed on Sunday (their first day in the city) read: "There has been much contention as to which has been the original 'Jazz' band, but there is not very much room for argument when one sees the original New Orleans band which headlines the bill."[15]

Under the rubric "What the Press Agent Says" the *Bay City Times-Tribune* noted that the Creole Band was the first to introduce the jazz band in vaudeville, "and jazz stands preeminent as the ragtime of now."[16] The one small cloud in the otherwise completely blue sky of press notices was proffered in Saginaw, where the reviewer wrote:

> The success and appeal of the Creole Ragtime Band in presenting "Uncle Joe's Birthday" as the headliner on the current vaudeville bill may be attributed not so much to the performance of the cast as to their coinciding in action with what the audience thinks the darkies of the southland do. There is song, dance, and jazz music in a pleasing combination that gets a big hand.[17]

This echoes a sentiment expressed on previous occasions, particularly in the African-American press.

An important document appeared at the very end of the year in the Twelfth Anniversary number of *Variety*; it may cast some light on the band's fortunes. W. M. Johnson is still the manager, with the "Western Representative" listed as Simmons Agency. The same issue of *Variety* has a large ad for the Amalgamated Vaudeville Agency at 729 Seventh Avenue at Forty-ninth Street (New York City), B. S. Moss, President. M. D. Simmons is listed as "General Booking Manager."[18] In any event, this agency is hardly a major player in the vaudeville world.

Some other features of this photograph are worth noting, although they say

HAPPY NEW YEAR

SEVEN KINGS OF RAGTIME

NEW ORLEANS CREOLE BAND

W. M. JOHNSON, Mgr.   Booked Solid

We stop 'em every show.   Western Representative, SIMMONS AGENCY

6.3 This photo, printed as an ad in the 1917 Christmas issue of *Variety*, was something of a fiction, since Baquet left the band ca. May 1916 and Norwood Williams left for California in April 1917. And why was this copy inscribed on the snare head by Baquet to his friend George Landry on February 18, 1915? [*Variety*, Dec. 28, 1917]

nothing about the band's current status. First, the photograph is not the well-known version with background detail masked out. Second, the name of the photographic studio (Empire / Los Angeles) usually cropped, is plainly evident. Third—and perplexingly—written on the snare drum head is "Compliments of Geo. F. Baquet to my friend G[eorge?] Landry, Feb. 18th, 1915." No matter whether Bill Johnson or the Simmons agency placed the ad, isn't it strange that the copy of the photograph they came up with was one that had been inscribed by George Baquet? Perhaps it was inscribed but never sent; perhaps Bill, lacking a copy himself, dashed off a letter to Baquet requesting one.[19]

The last stop on their trip around the W.U.B.O. theatres was at the Palace in Danville, Illinois, for the second half of the week of January 14, 1918. The Friday mini-review singled out the "music of the 'darky' band lined up in front of 'quarters' on a southern plantation," presumably a reference to the drop— if not an actual cabin set piece—that the group had used since 1915.[20]

At this point, they began their last group of appearances at theaters booked out of the W.V.M.A. office in Chicago's Majestic Theater building, beginning as the headline act (of six) at the Majestic in Springfield, Illinois, a large house of some 1,700 seats. This tour was to last until their last known appearance, at the Virginian Theater in Kenosha, Wisconsin, some eight weeks later. They received the usual praise, with one paper adding a detail, once again attesting that they were still using both the old special set and the old routine: "The act . . . is a fetch down from the time the moon rises on a serenade before the old preacher's cabin to the time he is teared out of a sermon into a darky show-down and jig."[21]

The known appearances of the band in their terminal phase are as follows:

week of Jan. 21	Springfield, Majestic
	Chicago, Wilson Avenue
Jan. 28	Chicago, Kedzie
	Davenport, Columbia
Feb. 4	Waterloo, Majestic
	Dubuque, Majestic
Feb. 11	Lincoln, Nebraska, Lyric
	Sioux City, Orpheum
Feb. 18	St. Paul, Palace
	Duluth, New Grand
Feb. 25	Minneapolis, New Palace
	[probably a full week]
March 4	Madison, Orpheum
	Milwaukee, Palace
March 11	Rockford, New Palace
	Kenosha, Virginian
March 18	
March 25	
April 1	[St. Louis, Grand Opera House]

The band was scheduled to appear in Evansville and Terre Haute, Indiana, sometime during the two weeks between March 18 and April 1, but, despite an advance blurb in the *Terre Haute Sunday Star* of March 24, they evidently did not show up as planned. Nor is there any evidence that they made it to St. Louis.

Their notices showed no essential changes in the act, although occasional piquant details pop up here and there. In Sioux City, the reporter noted that the band "gave several 'Blue' numbers and sang two or three selections in a manner that won hearty applause." Whether this means literally that they played pieces with "blues" in the title, or which were "blues" in harmony and melody must remain an open question; evidently they did offer instrumental selections without singing. Oddly, H. Morgan Prince was stated to be the comedian of the company.[22]

The reviewer in St. Paul, in addition to mentioning their elaborate scenery, thought the act included an old "mammy" in addition to "Uncle Joe." Did this unique mention indicate that one of the members of the band gave a female impersonation from time to time?[23]

More interestingly, perhaps, the Creole Band during this St. Paul engagement was in competition with Sophie Tucker, who with her Five Kings of Syncopation could be seen at the Orpheum. She even contributed a small newspaper item in which she explained "jazz" to the uninitiated. That the uninitiated might require explanations is amply demonstrated by a sizeable article (with a photograph) on a South St. Paul jazz band, comprising seventeen kindergarteners all under five years of age, playing patriotic airs with drums, cymbals, woodblocks, and kazoos.[24]

Their days in Madison elicited several notable remarks in the local press, as well as a spectacular letter from the band to the *Chicago Defender*. The reviewer for the *Wisconsin State Journal* found:

> The New Orleans Creole rag band had the feet of half of those in the audience itching to try the "chicken-wing" clog. The setting is clever and a quartette makes a little harmony, but the feature is the jazz music of the players, with the real ragtime swing of way-down-South darkies.[25]

Thoroughly exceptional—because of the source, not the content—is the brief review by the "staff correspondent" of the *Madison Blade*, an African-American weekly paper. Not only did they receive continuous rounds of applause from the large audiences, but "their act of comedy singing, dancing and eccentric orchestra playing is sure to please the most critical vaudeville fan." Reference is made to an earlier, undocumented visit: "The Blade and all Madison heartily welcome the boys back. They are old paid subscribers to the Blade."[26]

The theatrical reporter and critic for the *Chicago Defender*, Tony Langston, received the most unusual and unique—and in some ways most informative—document bearing on the career of the Creole Band: a letter from Madison dated March 8 and presented as coming from the entire group.

The following letter hit the Old Roll Top Desk a little late for publication last week; it is so enlightening that we run it in this issue and we hope the world will appreciate all it says. Read:

Madison, Wis. March 8, 1918.—Dear Friend Tony: Just a few lines from the Original Creole Band: we are all well and hope this will find you the same. Tony, we have been out five years and have only laid off five weeks, and we think that that is going some. It has been hard for us, as there were six Creole Bands out last year trying to do what we have done. We refused to work for Harry Weber for small money; he wanted us to play the Orpheum time and said that we would not play New York, but we did. We will use this act for the rest of the W.V.M.A. for the time this year; after that we go over the Orpheum. We are closing every bill that we work on. Leonard Scott, our comedian, knocks them off their seats, and all is well. Regards to all friends. Your friends,

ORIGINAL CREOLE BAND[27]

One detail is a trifle exaggerated: the band could only be thought of as "out five years" if one simply totted up "1914, 1915, 1916, 1917, 1918"; in fact they had been on the road for some three and a half years only. There are other perplexing details: one would be hard pressed to identify more than a couple of groups called "creole bands" on tour in vaudeville in 1917. One might be the New Orleans Jazz Band that accompanied Mabel Elaine briefly and rather unsuccessfully. Another could be the act "Maxine and her Creole Band," which played McVicker's Theatre, Chicago, in April, 1918, but which probably existed prior to that date. But conceivably the writer or writers of the letter also had in mind one of Charles Elgar's bands, one of which was probably playing at the Fountain Inn on Chicago's South Side in 1916—but not, to my knowledge, in vaudeville.[28]

The most intriguing remark concerns their refusal to go along with Harry Weber's offer, a defiant act that must be regarded as exceptionally foolhardy. Weber was by 1915 an extremely well-known and powerful agent, both in Chicago and in New York, and well positioned to make his threat stick. Speaking against this, however, is the fact that the band's placement in New York was stated to have been while under the management of the Simon agency, whose head, John Simon, was something of a crony of Weber's.[29] Not only that, Jelly Roll Morton recalled them as having been under Weber's management.[30]

The pride expressed in this remarkable letter can't fail to strike us. That it might have stood in the way of vaudeville success seems obvious. The grand pooh-bahs of vaudeville were intolerant enough of "uppity" performers of white (or pink) complexion. Imagine their attitude toward African-Americans who didn't behave with the proper respect! however it may be, there's nothing to suggest that the group was about to play its final vaudeville date; they even were set to go on the Orpheum circuit for the 1918–1919 season. This would have been their first serious engagement with vaudeville's big time; the Pantages, Loew, Butterfield, "Junior Orpheum" and W.V.M.A. engagements were, while not negligible, still small-time, or perhaps, "small big-time." A projected tour around the Orpheum circuit receives some support from Bill Johnson's recollection in his interview with Bill Russell in the fall of 1938; he recalled that they still had 25 contracts unfilled at the end.[31]

From Madison, it was an easy 80-mile jump to Milwaukee, where the band appeared for the second half of the week of March 4. It was hard work at the Palace Theater: on weekdays there were six acts crammed into four shows a day (2:00, 3:30, 7, and 9), with a fifth show added at 5 p.m. on Saturday and Sunday, virtually "continuous vaudeville." We learn from the *Free Press* that the band "was such a success here early in the season that it has been secured for a return engagement."[32]

The band went to Rockford, Illinois, for a Sunday opening at the New Palace, where the bill attracted a large business, then on to Kenosha, Wisconsin's Virginia Theater for the end of the week. In the Thursday ad they were billed as "the Original New Orleans Ragtime Band," but on Friday as "The Original Jazz Orchestra." As earlier, they seem to have been operating in somewhat reduced circumstances, with a five-act bill and four shows a day.[33] This is the band's final verified appearance.

While there could be any number of reasons for the band to have broken up, the proximate cause was quite possibly a medical one. According to Sidney Bechet (as reported by Mary Karoley in 1940) "The Original Creole Band was stranded in Chicago at that time with their trombonist Venson [a common misspelling of Vincent] recuperating from an appendectomy; so the Deluxe band was able to get Freddie Keppard, the Creoles' star cornet man, to take Sugar Johnny's place."[34]

BY THE MIDDLE OF May, Keppard, described as "formerly cornetist of the New Orleans Creole Band," was playing at the Royal Gardens, although he was stated as slated to go on the road with "Madame Sherry," a big review.[35] The recovered Eddie Vincent, and also possibly Bill Johnson, began playing in the burgeoning jazz scene of the wartime South Side. That story, however, belongs in another chapter (or another book?).

Finally, there's the strong possibility that, as George Baquet suggested to

Danny Barker, there was more money to be made by playing in the South Side cabarets, once jazz bands had become a national fad. More money, without the constant hassle of traveling.[36] Surely, too, the romance of the theater world must have become threadbare after four years, especially if they'd just finished a series of small-time engagements.

It would be pointless as well as wrong to lament the end of the act in vaudeville. Much as we may understand why the Creole Band presented itself as a traditional plantation act, painting a blithesome image of darkeydom "befo' de war," we don't like it much and can't help thinking the demise of these last traces of blackface minstrelsy as a step forward.[37] The discovery that a New Orleans musician could earn an excellent living in Chicago and be lionized by other musicians, white as well as black, must have been welcome and highly gratifying.

Not only that, but via Keppard, Noone, Vincent, and Johnson a tangible link was forged to one of the most appreciated strands of the history of jazz, that leading to Joe Oliver's Chicago recording band of 1923–1924, and the many New Orleans–flavored ensembles of the later 1920s, such as the 1926–1927 Hot Five, the New Orleans Wanderers / Footwarmers and the bands led by Johnny Dodds just before the onset of the Great Depression.

Of course, the lack of phonograph recordings by the Creole Band allows only speculative conclusions regarding the manner of playing. One suspects that the New Orleans–based South Side Chicago style of the 1920s was rather different in some respects, given drastic changes in dancing style between 1914 and 1924, as well as in the move to the cornet-led ensemble. On the other hand, the persistence of warm and expressive melody, coupled with vital swinging rhythm so characteristic of southern dance music in general and New Orleans in particular, is something I believe could survive transplantation to Chicago.

Brian Rust, the eminent discographer of jazz and entertainment, has long been a vehement advocate of the Original Dixieland Band's priority in the history of jazz, most recently in the pages of *Jazz Journal International*.[38] His concluding paragraph closely mirrors the views of Nick LaRocca, the band's cornetist and Rust's chief informant:

It has often—too often—been claimed that the Original Dixieland Jazz Band were not the originators of jazz, that there were other (mainly black) bands playing that idiom before them. If that were so, is it not strange that these allegedly superior bands were not noticed by an alert-eared impresario[?] That the bands existed is not in doubt; what they played was probably a form of ragtime, and if the survivors whose resurrection in the 1940s is any yardstick, it is not surprising that they did not make some deep, indelible impression that the ODJB did.

J. Russell Robinson, who played piano with the ODJB for some months in 1918 and 1919, is reported to have said that when he heard the records of the band he knew what it was: ragtime played by ear. And there is ample testimony that early practitioners of what we would call jazz thought of their music as ragtime. Of course, there is the position of Jelly Roll Morton, that there was some kind of fundamental change in the beat that differentiated ragtime of the Joplin variety from jazz — as invented by Morton.

With the passing of the years, ragtime feeling retreats more and more from popular dance music and jazz until finally it can't be heard. But so far as what the ODJB played is concerned, from the standpoint of 1926, it was ragtime. Rust suggests that if there had been bands playing "that idiom"—undefined except as designating the sound of the ODJB—it would have been noticed. One observes that the ODJB was playing (presumably "that idiom") in Chicago for some ten months without any "alert-eared" impresario noticing and recording them. (Of course, dance music was not recorded in Chicago at that time.)

I take it as definite that the Creole Band received an offer from Victor to record, almost certainly in early 1916. If so, then the La Rocca / Rust position can be turned on its head: the Victor company's taste for "that idiom" had been so stimulated by the Creole Band that, as soon as they heard something resembling it in the music of the ODJB, they snapped it up. At the risk of over-simplification, let's simply say that the Creole Band had done all they could do in the vaudeville framework, especially with their moribund and hackneyed plantation material. An alternative might have been to add a couple of attractive women and a "dancing director" in the style of the Tennessee Ten, but even they drew on the traditions of the plantation act. Finally, maybe they were simply tired of playing together and saw no obvious future possibilities for musical renewal.

7 Life and Music after the Band

AN OBSESSION WITH symmetry might here demand an attempt to parallel the kind of detail found in the earlier biographies of Chapter 1. Two reasons speak against this: first, while documentary sources for New Orleans are concentrated in a handful of archives and libraries in New Orleans itself, this no longer holds once the various members of the band settled down in California, Chicago, or Philadelphia; second, the available information in standard reference works is reasonably reliable. Nonetheless, one point in particular justifies some biographical explorations, namely, the sound recordings made during the 1920s by Johnson, Keppard, Noone, Baquet, and possibly Vincent, and the 1940s recordings by Louis Delille. They truly are the only extant audible evidence for any speculations we might have regarding the sound of the Creole Band. Strangely enough, for the most part they haven't been taken seriously.[1]

BY THE TIME the band played its last known engagement at Kenosha, Wisconsin's Virginia Theater, the commercial possibilities for jazz bands in Chicago, especially New Orleans jazz bands, had mushroomed. The Original Dixieland Jazz Band had come and gone; Tom Brown and his band was still around with a band different from his Lambs' Café group, along with other "white Dixieland" musicians from New Orleans. In 1917, there were two principal venues where they might be heard: Mike Fritzel's Arsonia on the West Side and Al Tearney's Grand Auto Inn on Thirty-fifth Street on the South Side. In point of fact, things were not so segregated as they might seem, since, disappointed in his efforts to attract the Creole Band, Fritzel hired a group led by Manuel Perez. As Ed Garland remembered it, there were two bands at the Arsonia in early 1917, the other led by "Red Nichols."[2] Perez's band grew larger and had migrated to Dan Jackson's Pekin on the South Side by 1918.

Lest it be thought that the entire city of Chicago was saturated with the sounds of New Orleans jazz whether "black" or "white," one has to admit that in this first wave there were relatively few bands, perhaps several dozen musicians in all, which circulated among a handful of dance halls and cabarets outside of the Loop. In a few years, they either enlisted the musical help of non-New Orleanians, or found jobs in large bands, such as those led by Charles Cooke or Charles Elgar.

Norwood Williams

Norwood Williams didn't participate in Chicago's enthusiasm for hot music for the excellent reason that he seems never to have returned to the city. After arriving back in Los Angeles, Williams and his wife Maude operated the Elite Hotel at 1217 Central Avenue. Perhaps to gain additional income or to avoid being drafted into the armed forces, Williams stated at the time of his selective service registration that he was employed in the pipe department of the Los Angeles Shipbuilding Company in San Pedro.[3] Any further involvement with professional music-making has left no trace, thus strengthening our suspicion that his tenure with the Creole Band was a matter of happenstance.

Additionally, after touring with the band Williams used his savings to buy a filling station, perhaps the very filling station and garage in Watts, near 116th Street where Bill Russell spent a few hours with him around 1940. When he died of a heart attack early in 1943, the place of his death was at the location of the Elite Hotel. Whether it was still operating as a theatrical lodging house isn't known. He was survived by his wife, Maude; the death notice mentions no children.

It's really a shame that William Russell gleaned no information about how Williams's guitar operated in the Creole Band—or in any other band for that matter. One is inclined to assume that in the absence of a piano or drum set that the guitar would have to stick to business, emphatically marking the beat. On the other hand, Johnson was such a powerful bassist that perhaps that assumption doesn't hold. The more general question of how emphatic a beat—whether four-four or two-four—was laid down by early New Orleans bands remains unanswered to this day.

Henry Morgan Prince

Although Morgan Prince certainly shouldn't be thought of as a lesser member of the band, nonetheless as a non–New Orleanian who was an all-around en-

7.1 Aboard the S.S. Shinyo Maru: photographic evidence of a tour to the Far East and beyond that Morgan Prince made with Wilbur's Blackbirds beginning in April 1928. The trumpeter is Buddy DeLoach, and Prince is holding the guitar. [Prince scrapbook; information on the tour from Mark Miller]

tertainer rather than a musician (although he was in fact experienced on a number of instruments), we think of him in rather different terms. This kind of parochial attitude is endemic in jazz history; I hope I've managed to avoid it.

His career in the twenties and thereafter is regrettably obscure. Among the photographs from his memorabilia is a group shot taken aboard the S.S. *Shinyo Maru* with Prince holding a guitar. This was probably during a tour to the Far East with Wilbur's Blackbirds that started in April 1928, and further memorialized by a feature article published in a local newspaper in 1962. There Prince claimed—and I see no reason to doubt him—travels to "Japan, China, the Philippine Islands, Java, Batavia, Singapore, Bankok Siam [*sic*], Ceylon, the Isle of Penan [*sic*] Rangoon and Mandalay Burma." In the attached photo, a beaming and natty Prince is holding a framed photograph of himself taken at the "Kings Tombs" in India.[4]

Also included among his papers was a still photograph of a movie set, perhaps for "The Queen of Sheba." Prince appears as an extra at the extreme left. Also on the set are two unidentified musicians in "Egyptian" costume, one with a trombone, the other with a drum set. Possibly he put in an appearance in other movies.

Prince's show business career was decidedly sporadic after this point. He'd been dropped from membership in Local 648 of the American Federation of Musicians (the Oakland black local) in 1926. One isolated entry from the San Francisco city directory for 1930 lists his occupation as actor, otherwise he's called a "car washer" or something of the sort. In the 1962 newspaper article he stated that he'd worked on the Golden Gate Bridge, which would bring his residence in the Bay area to the mid-1930s.

There's a sizeable gap between this and his last known public appearance: a tap dancing and singing act in 1954 for the American War Mothers in Santa Cruz, California—for which he garnered a first place trophy. Thus came to a close a half-century in show business, unless one would include his later vocalizing at the Four Square Church in Compton.

When Prince died of a heart attack—he had had a stroke, paralyzing one side—on Christmas Day 1969, he was still living in Compton with his wife Edna Hood Prince. The death certificate gives no hint of his theatrical career, merely stating his occupation for the past thirty years as a service station mechanic.

Jimmy Palao

Surely the most unlucky of the core members of the Creole Band, Jimmy Palao owed his floundering career to a combination of factors: first of all, no doubt, his state of health, which was eventually to result in an early death at age 46 (he was the first band member to pass away); second, the decline in the popularity of the violin, particularly in a jazz context; finally, a move to Milwaukee, which, for all its proximity to Chicago, was still out of the loop (forgive the pun).

The Palao family had moved from California to New York City around 1916 and lived there for some two years. This suggests that Jimmy had some notion, perhaps due to the "Town Topics" tour and the many Winter Garden Sunday concert appearances, that New York would be a good base of operations. Clotile Palao recalled some involvement with Bob Slater and the CVBA [Colored Vaudeville Benevolent Association]. Slater was one of those who played an engagement with an ersatz Creole Band at Gibson's Standard Theater after the break-up in Boston. Once the band reorganized in the fall of 1917, there would have been little reason for the family to stay in New York, so they returned to Chicago.

Lil Armstrong remembered that Palao had worked with the Lawrence Duhé band in which she also earned her jazz wings (so to speak). The well-known photograph of this band as it was constituted at the DeLuxe cabaret doesn't show Palao.[5] In his draft registration of September 12, 1918, he calls himself a "vaudeville actor" in the employ of Dan Jackson at the Pekin Theatre. His name was written by the clerk as "James Falarest Palao," with the middle name partly confirmed by the signature. A year later, he was shown in a band at the World Series in Comiskey Park, holding a tenor sax.[6]

In its issue of December 27, 1919, the *Chicago Whip* published a photograph of a nine-piece orchestra, Jones' Dreamland Band, "The Jolly Jazzing Jeopards." In an associated article, the band is further identified as Clarence Jones's, but under the leadership of "Senor E. S. Washington." Be that as it may, Lil Armstrong is at the piano and Jimmy Palao is standing in front with a tenor sax. This is hardly visible in the Whip's halftone but amply clear in the large-format print given by Lil to John Steiner and now held at the University of Chicago. She dated the photo incorrectly as 1921, and I believe it has been dated as late as 1924.

Clotile Palao Wilson remembered that the family moved to Milwaukee at some point, in part due to the race riots of July–August 1919, but just when this was was not entirely clear. It might not have taken place until Palao's return from California after leaving Joe Oliver's band.

In any event, as is well known, Palao went with Oliver's band on their trip to California, beginning probably in June 1921.[7] At some point during the year that followed, Oliver decided to let Palao go. Jimmy, nevertheless, appears in the only known photograph of the band on the coast.[8] This must have been taken prior to the replacement of drummer Minor Hall with Baby Dodds, which probably took place late in the year.[9] Minor Hall recounted the story a couple of times with varying detail, but in one version he said, "Maybe the people didn't go for 'Dixieland' so good in a dance hall, like they did, so Oliver wanted to lay off one man." But instead of letting go saxophonist Dave Jones, who had been the last to join the band, Oliver picked on Palao.[10]

Ed Garland remembered that Minor Hall resigned in protest because of Palao's being let go "at the end of the Southern Pacific Line" and then having to play his way back to Chicago. Hall then went to Local 6 (San Francisco) and pressed charges because Oliver had sent to St. Louis for Baby Dodds. The union forced Oliver to pay two weeks wages to Palao and to Minor Hall as well and also fined him $200. When Oliver returned to Chicago for a job at the Plantation at Thirty-first and Cottage Grove with a twelve-piece band he told the proprietress, told Miss Barnett, that in addition to the $200 he already owed

7.2 This photo is on the back of a publicity card advertising Dave & Tressie. Palao is third from the left, performing an old trick in which one musician fingers the instrument of another. We have to wonder whether this eight-piece ensemble really used four saxes! [Palao family scrapbook]

Local 6, each of the men in the band would have to pay $100. This appears to have been a deal-breaker since, as it turned out, the Oliver band was advertised at Lincoln Gardens in the *Defender*, June 17, 1922.

It's not clear when the Palao family left Chicago for Milwaukee. Possibly it was as early as the fall of 1919. The only document I've seen bearing on the question is a postcard from a friend postmarked Chicago, July 5, 1922, and addressed to 517 Cherry Street, Milwaukee.[11] It's possible that Jimmy worked mostly in Milwaukee during this period, although time must be found for a stint with Erskine Tate's Vendome Theater orchestra recalled by his daughter Clotile.

By mid-1923, Jimmy had probably joined the "Syncopated Ginger Snaps," the band accompanying the song and dance duo of Dave & Tressie. The *Defender* of November 10, 1923 noted the personnel of this group, then working various midwestern theaters: Stanley Wilson and Jimmy Palo, sax; Porter Lamont (or Lamont Porter?), clarinet; Ed Williams, banjo; Ray Green, drums; Anthony Spaulding, piano; and Bill Johnson, bass.[12]

Although Bill Johnson may have temporarily left the band,[13] he appears to have rejoined it, since it was he who informed Palao's wife of her husband's ill-

ness and the need for him to return home to Chicago. His major illness was tuberculosis, that scourge of nineteenth-century New Orleanians, particularly
the black population. The illness was so far advanced by the time Palao returned to Chicago that he had to be transferred to a sanitarium then transferred on New Year's Day to Cook County Hospital, where he passed away on
the morning of January 8, 1925, little more than a month short of his forty-
sixth birthday. Four days later he was buried in Mount Olivet Cemetery.[14]

I PREPARED A TAPE of several violinists of different styles for Clotile Palao.
Included were Al Jockers, widely recorded between 1915 and 1925; the West
Indian violinist, Cyril Monrose; Stuff Smith perhaps; and finally, Michael
Gusikoff, a specialist in the light classical whom we would find today rather
syrupy, albeit very skilled. It was Gusikoff that Clotile thought sounded most
like her father. But perhaps that was just the way she liked to think of him. If
I had had my wits about me, I would have prepared a saxophone tape inas-
much as her father was primarily performing on sax in the last years of his life.
Clotile recalled that Palao disapproved of her listening to blues records. On
the other hand, she accompanied him in duets—the family "always had a piano"—in pieces such as *Humoresque* and *Fleur de Lis*. I assume the piece was
Beethoven's "Für Elise."

As to Palao's composition, his piece dedicated to George Baquet from 1911
is a modest yet interesting work, with a piano part that is somewhat amateur-
ish. It was published by a notorious song shark, H. Kirkus Dugdale of Washington, D.C., who undertook to print pieces for hundreds of aspiring composers
about this time. From time to time after her husband's death, Armontine Palao
heard pieces that to her sounded like Jimmy's. Accordingly, she corresponded
with the copyright office, which told her in a letter of June 24, 1966, that while
"O You Sweet Rag" had indeed been registered "following publication
December 11, 1911," it had not been renewed and was therefore in the public
domain.

Another index of her continued interest in her husband's work was her be-
lated submission of an unremarkable patriotic piece (surely written around the
time of World War I) "Upon the Field of Battle," with both words and music
by James Palao.[15] One wonders whether there were other compositions in a
trunk.[16] Perhaps so, but the only one that could be shown to me was a short
(33 measures without repeats) piece in three sections for unspecified, but
probably for C melody saxophone and piano, titled "Echo of India." The piano part is simple accompaniment, perhaps destined for an amateur, as note

7.3 a–c According to Palao's daughter, this brief piece—in Palao's own musical hand—dates from the end of his life, therefore at the end of 1924. The piano part for the coda is notated on the reverse of page 2 of the piano part, which I failed to photograph through inadvertence. Since the separate sax part is in the same key as the full score, it seems that it was written for C melody saxophone.

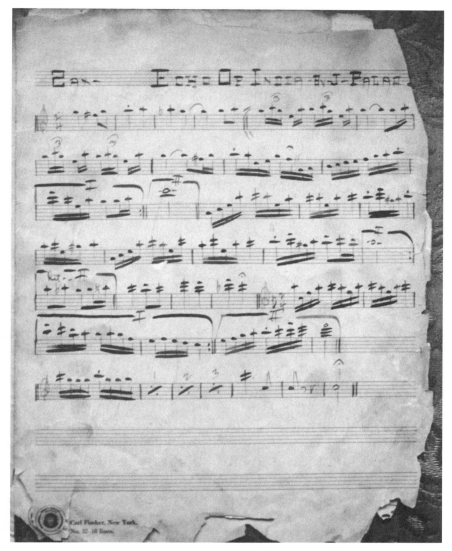

7.3 (continued)

letters are written in next to the lower right-hand pitches. The saxophone part stays almost entirely in the upper register—with a big finish on high F—and is unchallenging. The copying hand is practiced, although not always clear, and omits some important instructions, su7.3 a–c ch as a *dal segno* at the end. While Jimmy's violin fell apart, his tenor banjo and saxophone were shown to me in 1979. They were subsequently donated by the family to the Chicago Historical Society.[17]

7.3 (*continued*)

Eddie Vincent

After the breakup of the band in Boston, Vincent clearly returned to New Orleans, where on June 6, 1917, he married Amelia Richardson (or Richards; the records are discrepant). Confirmation can be found in the 1920 Federal Census: Eddie was enumerated with his wife, Amelie, at 3124 South Park, Chicago, on January 3.[18]

7.4 The band at the Royal Gardens, Chicago, ca. mid-1919. This priceless photograph shows three members of the Creole Band, Eddie Vincent (trombone), Jimmy Noone (clarinet), Bill Johnson (double bass), plus Paul Barbarin (drums), Joe Oliver (cornet), and Lottie Taylor (piano). [Timme Rosenkrantz Samlingen, Odense Universitets Bibliotek, Denmark]

Although a brief item in the *Defender* of November 2, 1918, refers to a band of Eddie Vincent's at the Royal Gardens, it seems probable that the group was in fact operated by Bill Johnson. There were three or four bands composed of black New Orleans musicians working in Chicago around this time, trading personnel, and also working after-hours jobs in addition to their regular gig. Remarkably, the Johnson band was photographed playing on the stand—one assumes at the Royal Gardens—and indeed shows a trombonist who surely is Vincent, along with Paul Barbarin at the drum set, Joe Oliver, Jimmie Noone, Bill Johnson and pianist Lottie Taylor. A likely date for the photograph is between May and July 1919.[19]

Perhaps Vincent again returned to New Orleans. Lee Collins mentioned that sometime around 1920 he worked a job at Butcher Hill's Lawn Party uptown with Big Eye Louis Delille and Eddie Vincent [as Vinson].[20] Quite incidentally, Louis Armstrong said that he was playing a funeral for Vincent's father when he received the invitation to join Oliver's band in August 1922.[21]

According to Albert McCarthy, perhaps basing his statement on a well-known photograph showing Tommy Ladnier in front of the band, Vincent was playing in Milton Vassar's band in 1922; this was probably at the Lincoln Gardens, shortly before Joe Oliver returned from California to take up his accustomed post. Mentioned as members of the band, besides Vincent and Ladnier, were Jerome Pasquall, Willie Lewis, and Eddie Jackson.

Glover Compton loaned a photograph of Ollie Powers's Harmony Syncopators to *Jazz Information*, in which it was reproduced in volume 2, no. 8. The band was playing at the Dreamland at the end of 1923 and beginning of 1924, recording "Play That Thing" and "Jazzbo Jenkins," ca. September 1923. The trombonist clearly appears to be Eddie Vincent [spelled "Venson" in the caption]. The Powers band recorded six (!) takes—of which four were issued—of cornetist Tommy Ladnier's solo specialty, "Play That Thing." Vincent is very much in the background in all takes, although he can be heard best on the fifth. I can find very little to say about his perfectly competent playing, except that at one spot in the first chorus he plays a kind of stuttering double-time measure (takes 3, 4, and 6).[22]

Two photographs of bands under the leadership of Everett Robbins were loaned by Milwaukee saxophonist Jimmy Dudley to *Record Research* and published in July 1964. One is of a six-piece group playing in a Milwaukee club named the Blue Chip; the other is of eight pieces in an unnamed locale. Although the former is dated in 1922, this may be too early. The Pittsburgh *Courier* of February 21, 1925, lists the band at the Blue Chip Cafe as Everett and his Syncopated Robins. Be that as it may, Eddie Vincent is identified as the trombonist in both, although the images are really not very clear.

It seems reasonable to assume that Vincent is present on an extremely rare recording made by the Everett Robbins band for the Autograph label in mid-1924—if a trombonist is present at all. Alas, the only copy I have of this is of such miserable fidelity that no conclusions can be prudently drawn from it. Vincent is alleged to be the trombonist on Paramount 12279, a recording of "Old Steady Roll" and "Homeward Bound Blues" by Jones's Paramount Charleston Four. What the authority for this is, I don't know; the Paramount ad in the *Defender*, June 13, 1925, states the instrumentation as "two banjos, cornet, and jazz horn." Be that as it may, it remains unreissued to the best of my knowledge.[23]

Another recording that is alleged to demonstrate Vincent's trombone playing was made for the Paramount label under the leadership of Keppard, the quite well-known and often reissued "Stock Yards Strut" and "Salty Dog." When the jazz magazine *Jazz Information* issued it in 1940, they asked percussionist Jasper Taylor, the listed composer of the former piece, about the identity of the musicians, besides himself, Keppard, and Papa Charlie Jackson (given label credit as the singer of the latter tune). His response was ambiguous, suggesting either Jimmy O'Bryant or Johnny Dodds as the clarinetist, Eddie Vincent or Honore Dutrey as the trombonist. Confusing the two clarinetists may seem to us today as implausible, but we speak with sixty years of additional experience. But the identification of the trombonist, recorded in any event at some distance from the recording apparatus, is not easy. Certainly, he is someone with a sure and quite "clean" technique and an excellent low register. Besides that, his style is a varied mixture of legato and staccato and works well with Keppard. Even assuming that the identification with Vincent holds, this hardly allows any far-reaching conclusions as to how a trombonist wanting to recreate the Creole Band, however hypothetically, should play, except that it should *not* be a conventional "tailgate" Dixieland line, more or less continuous in texture and mixing a bass part with countermelody.[24]

One suspects that a very careful sifting through the black newspapers of the late 1920s and early 1930s would turn up some references to Vincent; whether much would be gained from this is doubtful. Eddie's end was particularly sad, if not ludicrous. Jack Ellis wrote in his orchestra column in the *Defender* of November 2: "Eddie Vincent, sax and trombone, met with a fatal accident Wednesday (23rd) at his home, 29th and Vernon. Eddie was returning from work and while going up the winding stairs he dropped his horn over the banister and reaching for it, he became unbalanced and fell. The remains are at James Hall, undertaker, 4031 South State Street. Sympathy to the bereaved family." The Palao family remembers that he had borrowed Jimmy's sax and was in the process of returning it when, having had too much to drink, he lost his grip on the instrument, his balance, and his life. A sorry ending for the last of the Algiers musical buddies to die!

George Baquet

The details of Baquet's separation from the Creole Band are muddled. His story as told to Fred Ramsey in 1940 passes over the "Town Topics" tour completely and appears to blend together his linking up with Oma Crosby with an incident that took place on that tour. His 1948 address to the New Orleans Jazz Club, however, refers to "being placed" in the show and mentions the stars, Bert Leslie and Trixie Friganza, as well as her replacement, Sophie Tucker.

In 1959 Bill Johnson remembered that Baquet was "with a woman" and didn't

Special to The Freeman.

One of the biggest hits, and one of the prettiest up-to-date acts opened at the Strand theater, Hoboken, N. J., a few weeks ago that has been seen in the metropolis for many moons, stopping the show on a bill with six standard white acts at their first performances. This is the first colored man and woman team to produce and present something entirely new and different from all their predecessors and were an immediate hit. The theme is "The Baquets," George F. and Oma. The theme of the skit—Ragtime Sam with his clairionet flirts with a soubrett. Mr. Baquet was the original clarionet player with the famous Creole band, touring the country last season with the great Schubert production of "Town Topics." This famous band was the biggest hit on Broadway (colored) since Williams & Walker. It is an undisputed fact that Mr. Baquet is the greatest rag-time clarionet player of the present day, while Oma Crosby Baquet is too well known by all theater going people of the United State and abroad as one of the most accomplished refined and talented little actresses of her race. Having always been the acme of perfection in any artistic line she has ever followed, theatrically, and we have seen Mrs. Baquet in every role from a dancing pony to a stately queen in "Queen of the Jungles," way back in Peken Stock Company days. To say this little lady is versatile is putting it mild, and to say that we see Mrs. Baquet at her best in this beautiful act is also too mild. She just seems electrified with life sparkle and her charming personality and her dainty work leaves the audience screaming for more. Mrs. Baquet quit the Elite Amusement Company to join hands with her husband after playing various roles in most of their leading dramatic and musical productions. Managers are negotiating with this clever team to come west and they have promised to come as soon as they can get some open time. We claim this clever duo in the west as Mr. Baquet is a French Creole from New Orleans, and Mrs. Baquet, our own Oma Crosby, of Indiana. So we anxiously await your coming, success and congratulations to you, our talented friends, "The Baquets."

7.5 This review could hardly have been better if paid for. In any event, the comparison of the Creole Band to Williams & Walker is remarkable; it would have been more gracious to write that the band was still touring. [*Indianapolis Freeman*, January 13, 1917] for that reason make the the second Pantages tour. Jimmy Palao's daughter believed (as did Norwood Williams) that an affair with Trixie Friganza was the proximate cause of Baquet's leaving the band.

In any event, four months after *Town Topics* closed the columns of the *Freeman* for September 30, 1916, note that Baquet had recently married Oma Crosby, describing him as "a genial young clubman and also well known to the stage." Oma and George put together a vaudeville act which was very favorably reviewed by the *Indianapolis Freeman* in the January 13, 1917 issue and a number of times thereafter. George apparently impersonated "Ragtime Sam"—with his clarinet and in blackface—who flirted with soubrettes. In 1940, George remembered the title of the act as "Irresistible Rag" in which he "played a sort of Pied Piper who charmed all those who threatened him in a series of pantomime adventures with his clarinet . . . There was a girl in the act."[25]

Their act was momentarily interrupted when Oma was called to her ailing mother's bedside in Richmond, Indiana. Here she contracted diptheria but without lasting consequences. Perhaps a desire to remain close to her mother resulted in bookings over the WVMA and Gus Sun circuits in the Middle West. In any event, the last known mention of the act comes from December 1917.

October 1919 found Baquet in Philadelphia, as orchestra leader at the Waldorf Cafe. A look at Oma Crosby Baquet's biography suggests that Philadelphia was chosen by George as home because his wife lived there: in 1912 she had moved her family from Indiana there, where she ran a theatrical boarding house at 1431 South Street. How long the union lasted is not known, but Baquet remained in Philadelphia until moving back to New Orleans at the end of the 1940s.[26] According to the 1920 Census, George and Oma were living as man and wife at 3625 Walnut Street, but in 1930 he was counted as an unmarried lodger at 1241 South Nineteenth Street.

TESTIMONY TO BAQUET's musicianship can be found in three pieces submitted for copyright in 1923. In addition, Tom Lord's *Clarence Williams* (Chigwell, Essex: Storyville Publications, 1976) lists as Baquet compositions "Bessie's Got the Blues," "I've Got Those Shooting Blues" (misprint for item 3 above?), "My Music Man," and "New Orleans Cow Cow Dance." The last two have Clarence Williams as co-composer. In my estimation, none of these works show unusual traits or any special merit,[27] although it's interesting enough that Baquet should have committed them (or had them committed) to paper. One has to wonder what there was about 1923 that led him to send them to the copyright office or enter into some kind of relationship with Clarence Williams. Possibly it was a housekeeping operation in which some older works were collected together; possibly he was going out again around the vaudeville circuits. The standard discographies don't list recordings for any of them, nor have I seen printed editions.

When it comes to recordings, however, there's a good deal more to say. In July 1929, Jelly Roll Morton, after a recording hiatus of some six months, entered Victor's Camden recording studio and during the week of July 8 produced four piano solos and eight orchestra tunes. Despite describing Baquet as "just a corn-fed player in a Philadelphia movie house" in conversation with Alan Lomax in 1938, Jelly Roll had seen fit some nine years earlier to use Baquet in a quite prominent role in his recording band.[28]

It's impossible to know what instructions Morton may have given to Baquet, but surely, in view of the other aspects of these up-to-date performances, he didn't deliberately seek an "archaic" sound. Nevertheless, that's what he got. Baquet plays with an exceptionally "straight" tone, only occasionally using an almost imperceptible vibrato. Otherwise, he plays either with extreme legato or disconcertingly abrupt staccato articulation. In a few instances—and here I suppose that Morton wanted the effect—he uses flutter tongue and slap tongue, techniques that some might classify as vaudeville or minstrel band hokum. My general impression is that Baquet was somewhat out of practice both digitally and to judge by occasional reed squawks, with respect to his embouchure. He nonetheless seems able to play effectively in the high range of the instrument (concert high C and above) that Morton demands of him. The only other clarinetist that I can think of who sounds a bit like Baquet is Big Eye Louis Delille as recorded in 1940, 1944, and 1949. This is hardly unexpected since they are very close in age and grew up in the same musical environment.

Of the eight tunes with Baquet, one might suggest listening first to his playing, both ensemble and solo, on "Burnin' the Iceberg" (in part a version of the standard, "Weary Blues"), then at a slower tempo, "Courthouse Bump," and finally the intensely brooding "New Orleans Bump" (alternately titled "Monrovia"). The last-named is especially remarkable for Baquet's growl and fluttertongue. All of these confirm, I think, his belonging to the same musical generation as Big Eye, as well as the impression of a highly competent player, seriously out of practice.[29]

Other evidence pretty much rules out that the 1929 Baquet was following Jelly Roll's instructions, since by fortunate happenstance there have been preserved informal private recordings made in Philadelphia in June 1940. Baquet is heard in a solo blues and in a duet blues with Sidney Bechet. In both we hear the same "straight" tone, the same general style of articulation, although with a few instances of note bending not present in the 1929 recordings. There's also a bit of growl, or maybe a light flutter tongue, on one of the selections. Another trait might be mentioned, especially as something similar is heard in the other two early New Orleans players for whom we have recorded evidence: the occasional recourse to rather abrupt rapid arpeggios as introductory phrases.

As to the rhythmic style, while clearly not redolent of jazz, or even ragtime as known from such a New Orleans player as Alcide Nunez, there is a kind of liveliness, a kind of overall "hopping" motion (i.e., dotted eighth plus sixteenth, slightly offset from the pulse) that may define what was current in the late 1880s and early 1890s. Those who are eager to find traces of West Indian music in New Orleans might well point to this kind of rhythm as major evidence. In my opinion, it would also fit rather well with Keppard's manner of playing.[30]

I think it's worth quoting at some length Sidney Bechet's understanding of Baquet's musicianship (the ellipses are in the original):

> Baquet was a hell of a fine musicianer; he played awful fine. But he wasn't exactly a real ragtime player. What he played it wasn't really Jazz . . . he stuck real close to the line in a way. He played things more classic-like, straight out how it was written. And he played it very serious. He was much more that way than Big Eye Louis. When Baquet played it, there wasn't none of those growls and buzzes [actually belied by Baquet's recordings with Jelly Roll Morton] which is a part of ragtime music, which is a way the musicianer has of replacing different feeling he finds inside the music and inside himself . . . all those interpreting moans and groans and happy sounds. There wasn't none of that in the way he played. I don't know if it was that Baquet *couldn't* do it, all I know is that he *didn't* do it . . .[31]

Baquet mentioned to Frederic Ramsey making Bessie Smith's acquaintance with the Lafayette Players at the Dunbar Theatre. Indeed, one finds him listed in a 1921–1922 directory of musicians mostly from Philadelphia, "Banquet, Geo., Dunbar Theatre, Philadelphia, Pa."[32] It's been asserted that Baquet at some time in the 30s played in the pit orchestra at the Earle Theater in downtown Philadelphia.[33] I asked the late clarinetist Billy Kretschmer, who was in the Earle orchestra in the late 1930s, about this, but he didn't think that Baquet ever played in it.

Baquet began playing at [George] Wilson's Cafe by 1937 at least. In his 1948 talk to the New Orleans Jazz Club, he said that he had had his own orchestra there for some fourteen years, and had been living in Philadelphia for twenty-nine years. The latter date is correct, so perhaps his tenure at Wilson's goes back to 1934.[34] To judge from two of the selections recorded in 1940, Baquet as a bandleader had kept up with the times: the style is that of a typical "jump" band of the era. He was still playing there in 1944. The *Music Dial*—a little-read monthly—noted in its column devoted to news from Philadelphia: "George Baquet is still beaming at Wilson's. George, a member of the old school of jazz, has been at this spot for seven years."

According to a letter from George Wilson, the owner of the lounge, Baquet suffered a stroke in 1945 but remained in Philadelphia for about two more years. This is confirmed by an appearance by Baquet at a jazz concert in the foyer of the Philadelphia Academy of Music on the afternoon of October 15, 1947. Among the featured musicians were Wild Bill Davison, Baby Dodds, Bunk Johnson, and Sammy Price, who in addition to playing piano, promoted the concert, perhaps in partnership with Al Rose. Several photographs were taken, including one of Baquet, Johnson, and Price.[35] Although the writer of these words believes he was there, alas, he has no recollection whatever of Baquet!

By early 1948, Baquet had moved back to New Orleans, living with his sister, Mrs. Paul Gross, at 213 North Roman Street. With her husband, she operated a restaurant called the "Chicken Coop" at the corner of North Roman and Bienville Streets. He had recovered sufficiently from his stroke to write Dr. Edmond Souchon on March 3, offering help to the New Orleans Jazz Club. Six weeks later, in fact, he spoke briefly to a meeting of the club. According to Danny Barker, he owned a bar at the corner of South Rampart and Erato Streets, entrusting its management to Ernest "Nenesse" Trepagnier. According to his death certificate, he passed away in the evening of January 14, 1949, at Flint-Goodridge Hospital. [36]

Louis Delille and Jimmie Noone

The substitution of Louis Delille for Baquet probably made little difference in the overall sound of the band. They were of the same generation, although Delille was probably somewhat lower in social status and doesn't appear to have had the same kind of legitimate training that Baquet had known, and therefore for him there was no great drama in adapting to the new hot style that came in around 1905. In point of fact, Big Eye is often given much credit for an innovative way of playing the clarinet, "putting the crying in," as some would have it.[37] Accordingly, although the overall operation of the band may

7.6 Sammy Price, George Baquet, and Bunk Johnson on the stage of the foyer (a small recital hall) of the Academy of Music, Philadelphia, in 1947 or 1948. Price collaborated with Al Rose in bringing musicians from New York for Sunday afternoon concerts. Just what point Baquet is attempting to make is a mystery. Bunk seems skeptical. [Courtesy of Hogan Jazz Archive, Tulane University]

not have changed much, surely it would have been hotter and more bluesy than with Baquet.

Noone was much younger, of course, and had begun to play professionally about the time that Keppard and company left New Orleans for California. As some of my readers surely know, of all of the members of the Creole Band Noone was the most frequently recorded, often under quite favorable circumstances. As a member of Doc Cooke's band, he even can be heard with Keppard in several quite successful recordings. Besides that, of course, there are many dozens of recordings by bands with Noone as leader and as most prominent musical voice from 1928 until his death on April 19, 1944.[38]

The difficulty in attempting to draw any conclusions about the effect of his arrival in the Creole Band is that in the early 1920s Noone is believed to have embarked on some formal study of the clarinet, obviously taking it very seriously, as his technical facility and tonal control is far superior to other New Orleans reed players of his generation. He can be heard on some recordings of 1924 with Doc Cooke to quite good effect, and it's my belief that results of his formal studies are already quite audible. Still, his melodic sweetness—some have termed it overbearing sentimentality—was quite possibly part of his fundamental musical voice and must have significantly altered the overall impact of the Creole Band.[39]

Despite the relative brevity of his stay with the band, Noone would surely have had some interesting things to say about the experience, including some details about who was actually in the band, but a handful of interviews are all quite brief and unenlightening with respect to his early career. When Noone died in 1944 rather unexpectedly he was probably regarded as a contemporary figure who would always be there to talk with, even while the living fossils of New Orleans such as Bunk Johnson had been debriefed many times over.

Not that there is that much more surviving interview material from Big Eye, but one source is really quite remarkable and valuable with respect to his career with the band. During a two-month stay in New Orleans in 1944, Belgian poet Robert Goffin clearly took advantage of the opportunity, and much of what he wrote about the Creole Band came from the clarinetist. (This interview has been discussed above in chapter 5.) So far as one can tell, Big Eye spent the rest of his life between leaving the Creole Band in Boston in 1917 and his death on August 20, 1949, in New Orleans. The frequency with which he's mentioned in the Russell-Allen interviews indicates that he was far from forgotten, and he appears to have been quite steadily employed as a musician even in the Depression years.

While it would take us too far out of the way to discuss all of the recordings made by Big Eye during the 1940s, one demands mention since the tune "Egyptian Fantasy"—or, correctly, "Egyptia"—was part of the Creole Band's stage routine, played as the curtain was going up. It was the work of Abe Olman and published as an intermezzo by Will Rossiter in 1911. (I know it from the orchestration.) Sidney Bechet recorded it for Victor in 1941—incidentally claiming copyright, along with John Reid—at a rather stately tempo in the original key of G minor, but omitting one of the three sections of the original. In the recording made in New Orleans in 1944 all three sections are present and the key is F minor. Most strikingly different, however, is the tempo, a quite lively *vivace* (forgive the redundancy) which seems more appropriate as the opening to a vaudeville turn than the moody Bechet approach.[40] It's a bit difficult to distinguish between the two clarinetists present—Alphonse Picou in addition to Big Eye—but the one I take to be Delille plays with the distinctive dotted eighth-sixteenth patterns mentioned above.

Delille and Picou had appeared together a few years earlier, in the recordings made by Heywood Broun for his Delta label. They were the oldest musicians at the recording session and their work is the only good evidence for New Orleans jazz-ragtime clarinet style of the first decade of the century even though it was preserved forty years after the fact. Big Eye also was recorded in 1949, shortly before his death. Between the recordings made by Baquet in 1929 and 1940 and those by Big Eye, we have a lot of information that could be used to re-create a hypothetical Creole Band.[41]

While his elegant musicality would have been ample to guarantee him respect, Big Eye's prestige could only have been increased by his season on the road with the band. One gathers that he was amply aware of this, always carrying himself as something of a big-timer. In photographs from the '40s taken during the height of summer, Big Eye is always wearing a necktie, if not a jacket, where the other musicians are sensibly dressed for the subtropical weather.

Fred Keppard

Of all the members of the band, Fred Keppard[42] is the one who managed to carve out for himself the largest place in jazz history. In my opinion, this is less because of his relatively few recordings than for his becoming part of a jazz mythology based on a kind of relay race of cornetists: Buddy Bolden to Keppard to Joe Oliver to Louis Armstrong (to Roy Eldridge to Dizzy Gillespie, etc.).

Keppard was located in Chicago for all but a brief period between the breakup of the band in 1918 and his death a mere fifteen years later. Since he played important solo roles in a variety of prominent bands, large and small, he attracted attention and consequently is mentioned in a good many of the interviews with musicians who were on the Chicago scene during the 1920s. Because of his prominence and the remarkable force and individuality of his playing, he must have exerted a strong influence on young cornetists, black or white, whose style was being formed during the half dozen years after the close of World War I. My ears keep hearing in some of the older players basic tone production and articulation that's strongly reminiscent of what we can hear of Keppard on record. Unfortunately, this was not a line of inquiry that appears to have been pursued by jazz writers and historians. They asked about King Oliver often enough, and about Armstrong, once his way of playing began to be widely copied, but Keppard is for the most part ignored as a kind of musical dinosaur whose records, so the early and oft-repeated legend would have it, show him to be much diminished as a player. Even though, as early as 1940, the speciousness of this notion was recognized by some, it still pops up.[43]

Only two months elapsed between the Creole Band's last vaudeville engagement on March 16, 1918, and Freddie's first mention as a new star in the Chicago scene. The *Freeman* reported: "Fred Keppard, formerly cornetist of the New Orleans Creole Band, will probably go out with 'Madam Sherry' a big review. He is at present at the Royal Gardens." The first advertisement for the Gardens known to me is from a month before, although apparently there had been cabarets at the same address before. Be that as it may, the show *Madam Sherry* was a hit of 1910 but had a number of road companies subsequently. Perhaps further research can establish that a full-scale revival was planned.[44]

In these first few years during and just after the war, New Orleans jazz was a novelty on the South Side, with perhaps twenty to thirty players in various combinations rotating between the handful of cabarets that welcomed their music (chiefly the Royal Gardens, DeLuxe, Dreamland, and Pekin). Before Joe Oliver arrived in town, Keppard pretty much had the South Side sewed up. There was Thomas "Sugar Johnny" Smith in Lawrence Duhé's band and briefly after his death, Mutt Carey. There was also Manuel Perez playing at the Pekin, in a band that must have been rather different that the hotter and rougher bands in which Keppard could be heard. Once Oliver had arrived, it certainly would have been good for business to foster rivalry between the two cornet kings.[45]

Violinist Juice Wilson recalled a band at the DeLuxe with Tony Jackson, Keppard, Tio [probably Lorenzo, Jr.], Wellman Braud, and "Baby" Hall [presumably Tubby Hall]. He also worked in a band led by Keppard at the Entertainer's at Thirty-fifth and Indiana, as one of two violinists alongside a very young Eddie South.[46]

Keppard continues to pop up in news items through 1919, but it must have been around this time that he decided to pay a visit to the East Coast.[47] It's perhaps too much to expect to know why he did so. Hyperimaginative jazz historians might suggest that Joe Oliver was beginning to cut into his business. Alternatively since Philadelphia appears to have been his first stop in the East, George Baquet might have made Fred an attractive offer. Be that as it may, all of the information we have on this comes from Charlie Gaines, not necessarily an unreliable source but impossible to verify from independent testimony.

According to Gaines, Philadelphia violinist and bandleader Charlie Taylor, working at Danceland at Twentieth and Montgomery Streets, wanted to liven things up and accordingly sent for Keppard. His presence had the desired effect and Taylor's group moved to the Roseland Dance Hall—a dime-a-dance place in fact started by the proprietor of New York's Roseland—at Twelfth and Chestnut Streets, in the center city.[48] Still according to Gaines, by the time he left to join Charlie Johnson's band in Atlantic City, Keppard had gone back to Chicago. According to an earlier interview, Gaines and Keppard worked together in a band at La Vida dance hall, where Keppard took all the hot solos since he couldn't read music.[49]

But there are indications that Keppard played with Wilbur Sweatman's band at the Brighton Beach Hotel in Coney Island,[50] and another source says that he played with Tim Brymn's orchestra at the Cocoanut Grove in Times Square. This latter engagement would have startled Keppard, since the Cocoanut Grove occupied the premises of Doraldina's Montmartre, where the Creole Band had played in March 1917. Another item placing him in New York City is Sidney Bechet's assertion that Keppard played on a "good many" recordings by Wilbur Sweatman.

To take up the last point, Sweatman was at the end of his recording career for Columbia in early 1920, with only two issued titles. When he resumed recording in 1924, Keppard was firmly ensconced in Chicago, although it has been often stated that Keppard can be heard on a rare Edison by Sweatman of "Battleship Kate." For myself, I'm not so ready to dismiss the idea that the strong cornetist on the two 1920 Columbia Sweatmans might be Keppard.

I also have the eccentric notion that one of the cornetists on the recording of "Dance-O-Mania" by the Happy 6 (Columbia A2949, recorded May 18, 1920) could be Keppard, which then opens the door to the possibility of his presence on other issues of this often-recorded band, as well as with other groups. One is less inclined to dismiss this notion knowing that the trombonist of the Happy 6 was fellow New Orleanian Tom Brown.

This is all something of a tangle. Yet Tim Brymn's orchestra was mentioned in *Variety*, on June 11, 1920, as opening at the Hotel Shelburne at Brighton Beach. In point of fact, we have really no idea as to Keppard's location in 1920 or early 1921. The *Defender* prints no mentions of his presence either in ads or in various news items from Chicago, but one of the sporadic reports from Local 208 printed in the *International Musician* of April 1921 lists Fred Keppard as a new member. These reports are usually a couple of months late, which would approximately date Keppard's arrival back in Chicago around February 1921.

Sometime in 1921 or 1922 would be a good date for a quartet that played at the Lorraine Gardens: Buster Bailey, clarinet; Lil Hardin (or Johnson as she might have been known at the time), piano; Keppard, cornet; and Jimmy

Bertrand, drums.[51] The usual pattern for most of the musicians on the South Side was to work in a large band for the first part of the night, often in a large dance hall, then in a small combo for the wee hours. The important thing is that Keppard, like many another, would have had ample exposure to white pleasure-seekers and musicians, since most places he played were "black and tans"—that is, white clientele and black staff (including musicians).

I hear echoes of his sound in, for example, Louis Panico—usually only linked with King Oliver—and the rarely recorded Al Turk, perhaps even Ray Lopez and Frank Quartell, although Lopez, as a contemporary New Orleanian drank from the same musical springs as Keppard. And Bob Pope on the Coon-Sanders recording of Deep Henderson from 1926 is a near replica of Keppard.

The most detailed and interesting recollection of Keppard during this period comes from clarinetist Garvin Bushell, who was on the road with Mamie Smith in early 1921, with a week at Chicago's Avenue Theater from February 27 through March 6. He heard both the Oliver band and a twelve-piece band at the Sunset with Keppard and Fats Williams as the two cornets.[52] Williams played lead and Keppard played the jazz, but Bushell found them enormously exciting as a team, although quite different from the far-better-known later team of Oliver and Armstrong. "Joe Oliver never had the power of Freddie Keppard. Freddie could make the glasses on the bar move—they'd bet money on that. Freddie was more exciting than Joe. He played spells of intricate passages. High notes. Screams. Tongue flutters. But Joe was gutbucket jazz and blues. He played things that hit you inside."

The first firm date for Keppard after that comes from 1923 in a mention in the *Defender* of Erskine Tate's band, along with Ollie Powers, Glover Compton, and Jimmie Noone; the occasion was of the grand opening of the Paradise Gardens.[53] Next came the June 23, 1923, session for Okeh records of Erskine Tate's orchestra: "Cutie Blues" and "Chinaman Blues," often reissued. This would be the first appearance of Freddie on record, to be followed seven months later by six tunes recorded for Gennett under Doc Cooke's leadership.[54] Both of these sessions involved two cornetists, respectively James Tate and Elwood Graham. This creates some problems in distinguishing Keppard from his section mate (more on this below).

For the next two years or so Keppard probably worked with Doc Cooke at Paddy Harmon's Dreamland Ballroom on the West Side for his early job. For his after-hours stint he began a long association with Bert Kelly, whose Stables at 431 Rush Street constantly featured some excellent New Orleans players, such as the Dodds brothers and Natty Dominique.[55]

I find utterly convincing the description of the situation of Keppard with the large Doc Cooke band given by Jerome "Don" Pasquall, who was a bandmate over the entire period of Keppard's tenure: "We depended upon Freddie Keppard mostly to give the band the lift . . . Cooke would never write any parts especially for Keppard. He just said, "Give Keppard his head," see, and while we were playing, Keppard would do practically anything he wanted to do . . . he'd sing out above the band and just drove the fans wild . . . Keppard came in a little late because Elwood Graham was doin' what Keppard was doing—trying to do what Keppard was doin', but he didn't have the power, see, so Keppard came in a little late . . . so soon as Keppard came in it gave the band lift, and the band just really went to town."[56] Of the numerous examples, I'd single out "Here Comes the Hot Tamale Man" (the big band version for Columbia) and "Spanish Mama." Particularly the first demonstrates his power in the lower register.

This powerhouse role was not really required in the recordings from the small band drawn from the big band, Cookie's Gingersnaps, which show a greater variety of tone and contrast between muted and open playing, as well as sensitive responsiveness to others in the band. Also, there is no problem with sorting out Keppard from Graham.[57] While these recordings are relatively well known, students of early jazz have mostly depended for their knowledge of Keppard on the superb recordings made under his own name—Freddie Keppard's Jazz Cardinals—made for the Paramount label circa August or September 1926.[58] The band's name may be only a *nom de disque*, but it may also mark Keppard's exit from the Doc Cooke band. Possibly his proverbial and deeply ingrained willfulness had become magnified by his alcoholism to the point that a leader might be reluctant to hire him, no matter how dynamic a contribution he could make to a sluggish band.

KEPPARD'S RHYTHMIC STYLE

It's here that the present-day listener may have the greatest difficulty in evaluating or appreciating Keppard's playing. This is largely due to the overwhelming influence of Louis Armstrong's approach to the cornet, with its lazy triplet feel and pervasive delaying tactics. Keppard, on the other hand, is frequently on top of the beat or anticipates it and his phrasing is excitable, even tense. Also, where Armstrong seems to favor extended four or eight-measure structure, Keppard builds his units out of shorter modules. The way in which vibrato is used underscores this: Armstrong notoriously developed a prominent but rather slow terminal vibrato to articulate his phrase endings; Keppard uses a much more rapid vibrato, more like an ornament, that could be used anyplace in a phrase. A cornetist who is apt to be known by aficionados of the old New Orleans style and who most remembles Keppard in many, but not all, respects was, I think, Thomas "Mutt" Carey. One who did not resemble him was Willie "Bunk" Johnson. Both are from the same musical generation as Keppard. (I take a musical generation to last no longer than ten years.)[59]

Be that as it may, his subsequent career left no recordings.[60] A 1928 or 1929 photograph with a small band led by Lil Armstrong (or possibly Don Pasquall) shows an obese Keppard sporting a tiny moustache and a "long model" cornet.[61] He was nevertheless enough of a name on the South Side to be cited as one of the reasons for the success of a gig played by the Erskine Tate band in April 1930, and at the end of the year he led the house band at the Zeppelin Inn.[62] His last appearance in the press seems to be at another new venue—the Club Congo in the Arcade Building at Thirty-fifth and State—in Clarence Browning's band. 1932 is a blank—possibly Keppard was playing only "casual engagements" as the expression would have it, getting sicker by the week until he became unable to work. (His death certificate stated that he had been unable to work since December 1932.) Trumpeter Bob Shoffner recalled that when the Louis Armstrong band was leaving Chicago in a bus in 1931, Armstrong told the driver to stop in front of Keppard's apartment, whereupon the entire band trooped upstairs to greet the old-timer.[63] When he passed away on July 15, 1933, the attending physician cited acute pulmonary tuberculosis and chronic nephritis as causes.

It strikes me that many of the tales of Keppard in Chicago being "past his prime" originate from this rather lengthy period—some half-dozen years—of physical decline and spotty "work record," rather than from the truly excellent recordings from 1926.

Bill Johnson

The 1920 Federal Census enumerated Bill Johnson twice. First, he was found living at 3920 Indiana Avenue on January 13, with his thirty-year-old wife, Ada. Bill's identity is unambiguous as his occupation and employer are given as "Plays Bass Violin / Orchestra and his birthplace as Alabama. There were five boarders in the house with Ada designated as keeper of a lodging house.

He was enumerated a second time on January 16 rooming at 220 31st Street, designated as a forty-year-old mulatto working as a musician at the "Royal Garden." His wife was Mrs. Josie Johnson, a mulatto 25 (or 28) years old born in Missouri, employed as a dressmaker for a private family. The only hitch is that

Johnson's birthplace (and that of his parents) is given as California, but it's easily understood considering how much time Bill had spent in California and his lack of a southern accent, that his wife or other residents of the house would think of him as coming from there. I should add that his 1939 application for a Social Security account listed a Josie Love as his spouse.

At the Royal Gardens Bill would have been playing with Joe Oliver, but may have left sometime prior to Oliver's departure for California in May 1921 when the bass player was Ed Garland. After the end of the Pergola job and a brief vaudeville tour, Oliver and at least some of the San Francisco band, including Garland, went to Los Angeles. After this, Garland decided not to return to Chicago.

The *California Eagle*, full of West Coast but especially Los Angeles news and ads, began to advertise at the end of 1921 "Johnson's Southern Cooking," a restaurant at 811 Central Avenue. Various members of the Johnson family were at one time or another in the restaurant business: Dink, Bessie (i.e., Anita Gonzales Ford), and Bill himself in Chicago in the 1930s. It's my guess that this was a kind of family trade passed on to them by their mother, Hattie. Be that as it may, in January 1922, a front-page article went on at some length about William Johnson, "a Real Business Man," who was making a success of the restaurant after having a cafe and lunch counter on East Ninth Street. In February, however, an ad for the new management of the restaurant mentions that William Johnson had put (past tense) Southern cooking in vogue there; the same issue advertises the opening of Johnson Bros. pool hall. In March and April, Joe Oliver was still in Oakland, playing with Kid Ory at a Mardi Gras ball or on his own, so there's no exact correspondence between Johnson getting out of the restaurant business and Oliver leaving the Bay Area. At the end of April, however, Oliver was in Los Angeles, playing at Wayside Park with, among others, Jelly Roll Morton and at the Hiawatha Dancing Academy.[64]

While we can't assume that Bill Johnson went back to Chicago with Oliver, there's no reason to doubt that soon after Oliver's return he took up his post in the band at the Lincoln Gardens. Although I'd like to believe that Johnson was the manager, the band was clearly linked with Oliver's name. Although Bill's principal instrument had been the bass for some years, he had played guitar in his youth and it surely was no problem for him to switch to the tenor banjo that is visible in the three known shots from the Daguerre photo studio: in one we see him playing the banjo with the bass leaning against the backdrop; in another he's holding both instruments; and in the third he's holding the bass with the banjo on the floor in front.[65] In any event, it is generally agreed that it was Johnson's banjo that was heard on the band's first recording session at the Gennett studios on April 5 and 6, 1923, and the famous vocal interjection to Dipper Mouth Blues ("Oh, play that thing") is also Bill's. This is substantiated by comparison with the several 1929 recordings on which his voice is also heard.

In 1959 Bill recalled that 35 years earlier he had taken sick at the Gennett studio in Richmond and went back to Chicago all by himself. This may be at the root of the remark made in Laurie Wright's biodiscography of Oliver, when he wrote: "A number of authorities have believed that both Bud Scott and Bill Johnson, who were both members of the band, were used on what was then thought to be two sessions, but Baby Dodds has confidently identified Johnson each time he was asked and Johnson himself claimed to have played banjo on the first Gennett session rather than his usual string bass."[66]

A noteworthy contribution made by Johnson to the Oliver band was as collaborator in a novelty routine for J. Russell Robinson's (b. 1892) popular rag, "That Eccentric Rag"—usually known to jazz players as simply "Eccentric." Louis Armstrong tells us that for the last chorus of the tune, Joe Oliver and Bill had an act in which Oliver would make his cornet sound like a baby crying and Bill would make the bass sound as though it was a nurse calming the baby in a high voice. "Finally, this musical horseplay broke up in a wild squabble between nurse and child, and the number would bring down the house with laughter and applause."[67]

The banjoists heard on the later recording sessions of 1923 are—or at least strong discographical or biographical evidence suggests—Arthur "Bud" Scott or Johnny St. Cyr. Finally, by the end of the year, Oliver appears to have begun to use bass sax instead of banjo. It's also unclear how long the Dodds brothers stayed in the band. The generally accepted notion is that they moved over to Bert Kelly's Stables for an after-hours job, where Bill Johnson and Keppard were also playing. Possibly so, but at some point Bill began to play with Wycliffe's Ginger Snaps, or the version that became the back-up band for vaudevillians Dave & Tressie. The best we can do at the moment is to say that probably Bill Johnson stayed with Oliver in Chicago for about a year, then moved on. Although there is considerable vacillation with regard to the band's name, it seems that the original title as seen in advertisements and record labels of 1922 and 1923 is "Joe (or King) Oliver's Creole Jazz Band," which by May and June of 1923 had become "King Oliver's Jazz Syncopators" or "King Oliver's Jazz Band" (except for the Gennett company, which may have had a contract with the "Creole Jazz Band" name on it). It makes sense to me that Bill Johnson would have felt that he had a proprietary interest in the name "Creole Band" or variations thereof. Thus, he might have taken the name with him when he left the band.[68]

Back in California by the summer of 1926 (if not before) until the end of the year, Bill Johnson organized and led a band with his brother Dink on drums; Andrew and Margaret Kimball, both New Orleanians, playing cornet and piano, respectively; and Leo McCoy Davis, tenor sax. It worked for about three months, perhaps mostly at the Bronx Hotel, Seventh and Pedro [or San Pedro?], Los Angeles. Davis described it as not a good band.[69]

A year or two later, Bill was back in Chicago. Doc Cooke had lost the job at Paddy Harmon's Dreamland, and in 1928 clarinetist Clifford King led the band there. The extant photograph shows fourteen pieces with two bass players, Walter Wright and Bill. (The cavernous Dreamland could no doubt profit from doubling up the bass, as well as the keyboards.)[70] This band made no recordings, and King left for Europe fairly soon after. Not to despair, however: over an approximately one-year period, from June 1928 through July 1929, Johnson's bass can be heard with great clarity on some sixty-four issued recordings (not counting alternate takes). The best known of these are surely those with large and small groups under the leadership of Johnny Dodds made for the Victor company. Also in 1928–1929 he was used by Tampa Red on about a dozen Vocalion records intended for the race trade, and he even recorded two tunes under his own name, as Bill Johnson's Louisiana Jug Band.[71]

The most striking aspect of his playing, apart from his quite powerful sound,[72] is the manner in which he mixes arco and pizzicato and two- and four-beat playing. It's rare to hear him play more than eight measures with the same rhythm and articulation. Additionally, Johnson uses a fair number of smaller note values, both triplets as well as (approximately) dotted eighth plus sixteenth-note beats. He's also quite fond of anapest patterns of two eighths and a quarter, often in groups of two or four. Another favorite rhythmic phrase on up tempos is two quarter note beats preceded by a shorter pickup note.

It was during these years that the late Milt Hinton, one of the most highly regarded jazz bassists of recent years, heard and was mightily impressed by Bill's playing. According to Hinton, "Bill Johnson was *very* famous in Chicago during the 20s. He was the leading bass player . . . [he'd] pull his strings directly out from there and they'd snap back and it was just amazing to watch him play and see him work." Hinton gave a demonstration of how Bill would alternate picking and snapping and how he'd play triplets using the side of his hand. Perhaps some such tricks lay behind Dave Peyton's characterization of Bill in the *Defender* as "an eccentric bass player."[73]

The implications for the sound of the Creole Band are important. What Bill would not have provided, on the basis of his 1928–1929 recordings, is a driving and incessant beat. Rather he'd have moved in and out of the melodic texture as he saw fit, perhaps doing tricks, such as spinning the bass around and chiming in with vocal encouragement. Possibly this is a style developed in playing in the small three- and four-piece "string bands" of his youth, in which a more or less incessant two- and four-beat pulse would have been rather tiresome. Continuing in the speculative line, maybe this is what's behind Bill's statement to Bill Russell at the end of the 1940s that he'd like to record in a trio of guitar and concertina.

It seems to me that Bill's manner of playing may be most varied in his many accompaniments with Natty Dominique as cornetist. Although Dominique is clearly not as aggressive or virtuosic a player as Keppard, there are nevertheless resemblances between the playing of the two men, not limited to the obvious point that Dominique doesn't copy Armstrong in tone, phrasing, or overall rhythmic approach. Continuing this line of speculation, I'd ask interested readers to listen to how Johnson plays in the February 11, 1929, recording of "Boot That Thing" with Junie Cobb's band. (The same remarks apply to the other three tunes with Cobb.) Here the context is more up-to-date than in the various Dodds and Dominique combinations, not to speak of the "skiffle" bands with Tampa Red; cornetist Jimmy Cobb is quite strongly Armstrong-influenced. Bill plays bass lines that are mostly straight ahead four-beat without resorting to his usual repertory of rhythmic tricks, and sometimes not bowing at all.[74]

The recording industry was about to collapse, so perhaps it's little wonder that Bill Johnson is not to be heard on subsequent recordings. On the other hand, he may have gone back to California for a while, since an alternation between Los Angeles—where, after all, his mother, brother (or brothers) and sister lived—and Chicago forms the framework of his life from ca. 1920 to 1950 or thereabout.[75]

BRIEF NOTE ON THE RECORDING OF STRING BASS

Some of the impact of Jelly Roll Morton's 1926 recordings for Victor was surely due to the new electrical recording technology that made it possible for the string bass to be heard in a New Orleans jazz band. Consider for a moment how many great recordings of early jazz there are in which the bass part that was always there in a New Orleans dance band was absent. To name the salient examples: Original Dixieland Jazz Band, New Orleans Rhythm Kings, King Oliver's Jazz Band, Clarence Williams's Blue Five, Armstrong's Hot 5, New Orleans Wanderers (or Bootblacks). The changeover to electrical recording, beginning in March 1925, for

Victor and Columbia, didn't happen overnight for all labels. Surely the Dixie Stompers (a *nom de disque* for the Fletcher Henderson band) recordings made for Harmony are a poor reflection of how these players sounded. There is also the matter of the continued use of the brass bass (call it tuba or sousaphone), either because the public had become used to it or because many of its players were not that skilled as string bassists. And even Jelly Roll Morton "reverted" to the brass bass for his band recordings after 1926.

Bill was back in Chicago in 1932 playing in a group known as Jack Ellis's Wildcats. In fact, an item in the *Defender*—which apparently foisted the wildcat onto the band as a kind of publicity stunt—lists Bill with one of his several nicknames, "Jumper Hair." Actually, this ought probably to be spelled "Jump a Hare," [cf. the blues verse, "blues jumped a rabbit, rode him for a solid mile"] possibly with reference to Bill's readiness to enter into intimate relationships. Another nickname, reported to me with more than a bit of embarrassment by Armontine Palao, was "Sweet Dick." Finally, there's the decidedly uncomplimentary "Louse," which may have been used only in New Orleans in the old days.

Bill may have played with this band for much of the decade. In 1940, *Down Beat* gave a 1931–1937 roster of the band with Bill Johnson on bass. On the other hand, it's during this period that Preston Jackson reported to the readers of the French magazine *Jazz Hot* that Bill was playing Michigan with the Smizer Trio.[76] Around the end of 1936, the monthly report from Local 208 (Chicago) stated that "William Bill Johnson" was on the trial board of the local.[77]

In the many titles recorded by "Half-Pint" Jaxon later in the 1930s, he used other New Orleans bassists, such as John Lindsay and the younger Ransom Knowling (Chicago) and Wellman Braud (New York). You'd think that Bill might have been used; one wonders if Bill had hung up his bow in favor of the small Thirty-first Street restaurant that he was running in 1938 (apparently located behind the musicians' union headquarters and having as a motto "Pig's Feet with that Old Fashioned Flavor," as Bill Russell's 1938 notes would have it). On the other hand, Decca made quite a few blues records in its Chicago studios during the 1930s, and it's conceivable that Bill's unmistakable bass can be heard on some of them.

Bill was still in Chicago in 1946. Adrian Tucker wrote to Bill Russell on June 8 that Ollie "Dink" Johnson had gotten his brother to come to Los Angeles from Chicago, to be a front man in getting a beer license for Dink, who was *persona non grata* to the authorities, due to his having once been arrested for

7.7 Bill Johnson was still playing bass in the late 1940s when this photograph was made. The truncated pianist is Little Brother Montgomery, the others (from left to right) are identified as Lonnie Johnson, Bill Johnson, Oliver Alcorn, Pork Chop Smith, and Lee Collins. Preston Jackson is cut off at the right. [R&S, p. 171]

bootlegging. This never happened, since Bill's wife telegraphed him from Chicago that she was ill, and he had to leave before the application process was completed.[78]

During the first part of 1947, Johnson was announced as playing at least three concerts, one on March 23 at the Twin Terrace Room in a band billed as the New Orleans Wanderers with Lee Collins as trumpet, another at the same location on April 27, in Bunk Johnson's backup band. He may also have played behind Bunk on May 11, then been in a band at the end of June which featured four trumpeters: Bunk, Lee Collins, Jimmy McPartland, and Doc Evans. According to John Schenck, he still had a "terrific beat."

On May 11 Bill Russell talked to him at a concert at the Twin Terrace cafe.[79] Russell found that Bill had aged greatly; Bunk opined that he really was 75 years old. It was then that Johnson—Bill, that is—talked about wanting to record in a trio of piano and concertina, or perhaps guitar and concertina. If he played in public after this date, we don't yet know about it.

Bill Russell thought that he had last seen Johnson around 1950. News that

Bill had moved to Texas around that time and might even have been earning a living by smuggling items across the border from Mexico—one wonders what—trickled back to Russell in New Orleans. Later in the decade Russell set jazz promoter and historian Al Rose, who was then living in New Orleans but who traveled widely in the South as an itinerant caricaturist, the task of locating Bill if possible. A letter survives giving some details of Rose's fruitless search.

This was just about the time that another would-be interviewer was trying to locate Johnson, eventually succeeding with the help of a Chicago contact. In a letter dated November 6, 1958, Johnson included an explanatory postscript: "One reason you had such difficulty reaching me with your various letters was the fact I spent about four years in Mexico beginning with 1954, and did considerable moving around."

In a radio interview for station KFMV, Los Angeles, in 1950 or 1951 Bill's half sister Anita Ford said he was in Mexico City, playing bass violin in a band, a "jazz band" in fact.[80] In San Antonio, Texas, Bill appears to have been employed by Miriam Monger—perhaps also a dear friend—whose acquaintance with Bill went back to Chicago in the 1940s, at least, when her conversations with him resulted in the absurdity of *Tales from Toussaint*. Actually, the relationship was explained by Johnson in a letter of July 9, 1959. He said that he had lost a great deal of money in the stock market—perhaps even as early as the October 1929 crash—and was obliged to go back to work. "I became the chauffeur for the family of this author and have always kept up connections with the family. I drove her down to Mexico lately with her sister and drive her about town, as she hates driving" [the car was a Chrysler].

The decade of the 60s is a blank; if Brooks Kerr's recollection of 1962 is accurate, maybe he had returned for a while to Mexico. Other than that, there's no reason to believe that Bill was doing anything other than what he had been doing in the preceding decade, acting as driver and general man-of-all-work for Monger.

Miriam Monger, Bill's patron for so many years, was pronounced dead on arrival at Robert B. Green Memorial Hospital, San Antonio, on January 5, 1971; the only cause mentioned is "arteriosclerotic vascular heart disease." The box for the name of the informant is filled in as "William Monger," but the writing is actually that of Bill Johnson as nearly as I can tell. Is this not astonishing?[81] At the very least it's testimony to the closeness of their relationship. She was buried on January 7 in Roselawn Memorial Park.

It must have been very little time after this that Harry Carley found Bill wandering around in San Antonio in the vicinity of an apartment house Carley

7.8 Bill Johnson in San Antonio, July 1959. He seems a quite vigorous octogenarian.

owned, subsequently placing him in a nursing home in Pleasanton, Texas. William Everett Samuels, a well-known Chicago musician on the board of directors of Local 10–208, heard about this from an unknown source and sent a money order in the amount of $100 for Bill's birthday on August 10. This was celebrated at the nursing home in Pleasanton, Texas, with an 18 by 24-inch cake and three gallons of ice cream shared by all in attendance. The local paper was there and took photographs.

In a letter of September 2, replying to one from Samuels dated August 28, Carley wrote: "At the present time Bill spends most of his time in a wheelchair just sitting aroud [*sic*] doing nothing which is not good . . . At times Bill is very alert and talks very understanding about things around him, and then at other times, he does not remember from one minute to the next . . . Bill is diabetic and we have to watch what he eats and drinks but other than that he is doing

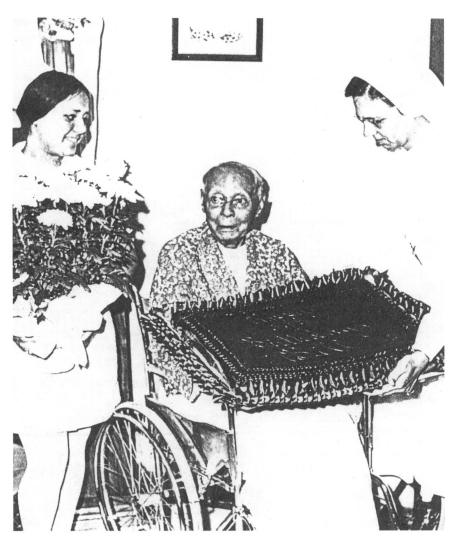

7.9 Bill had been placed in a nursing home in Pleasanton, Texas. When William Samuels of Local 208 (Chicago) learned about this he sent a money order for $100 for Johnson's (alleged) 100th birthday on August 10, 1972. While 1872 is quite possibly too early for his year of birth, all sources known to me agree on the month and day. [Courtesy of William Everett Samuels]

very well for his age." Carley had apparently tried to locate any relatives but without success, asking about a son and daughter that Samuels's letter must have referred to.[82]

Shortly after the birthday party, Carley had Bill moved to Colonial Manor in New Braunfels, the town where the Carleys resided; and in fact Carley's oldest daughter worked there and cared for Bill. Bill's death occurred at 11:20 a.m., Sunday, December 3, with the funeral taking place at Comal Cemetery on the following Tuesday afternoon, complete with flowers on the coffin from Local 10-208. On December 26, Samuels wrote a letter of thanks to Carley, recalling that Bill had been "one of the first musicians to come to Chicago from New Orleans. He preceded Joe Oliver, Louis Armstrong, Honore Dutrey, Dominique and many others." He also said that a death benefit check in the amount of $1000 would soon arrive.

Whether Bill was depressed or upset after hearing of the deaths in 1949 of the last surviving members of the band—George Baquet and Big Eye—we will, of course, never know. We may want to regard it as a great irony that the founder of the band, who probably learned his first tunes in the 1880s, well before anyone had ever heard of jazz or ragtime, was still alive to hear, if he'd been so inclined, not only revival Dixieland and New Orleans bands but bebop and its descendants, "free jazz," jazz-rock, and fusion. While over the years he was willing enough to talk to those few who were interested—Paul Eduard Miller, Bill Russell, among others—and also seemed quite cognizant that he and his band had been true pathfinders, he neither claimed nor was given the fame that surely was his due.

Of the other members of the band, only George Baquet seems to have shared with Johnson both the personal modesty as well as the perspective to recognize his place in history. Noone was only with the band for some six months, during its undeniable decline; Big Eye seems to have been a disappointed and even angry man who might have had an interesting axe to grind had anyone been able to pursue the subject of the Creole Band with him at length.

Of all the members of the band, only Freddie Keppard and Jimmie Noone had what could be called important careers, in part due to their staying on in Chicago. One can only guess that Palao, who was of course also rooted in Chicago, might have made a dent in the 1920s jazz scene with his saxophone, despite his relatively advanced age. Norwood Williams appears to have done little or no performing, although he kept in touch with show business via the Elite Hotel. Baquet had settled down to an honorable but purely local career in Philadelphia—with a style that was as quaintly archaic as Big Eye's. Morgan

GREETINGS

The New Offering in White
and Black

MABEL ELAINE

AND HER

Ragtime Band

Late Feature, "TOWN TOPICS" and
NEW YORK WINTER GARDEN

In "A Scene on the Levee"

SPECIAL SCENERY
PLAYING U. B. O.

7.10 This ad from *Variety*, December 15, 1916, speaks volumes in the contrast between the hoyden in blackface and the demure lady in pearls. Just which "ragtime band" was backing Mabel up is a matter for further research. [Courtesy of Variety, Inc.]

Prince, never quite part of the New Orleans clique, although he may indeed have been responsible (or shared the responsibility) for the band's vaudeville career, seems to have regarded his three seasons with the band as only one of the episodes, albeit an important one, of a varied show business career.

Finally, we shouldn't forget Mabel Elaine, that sprightly black-face tap dancer whose success in "Town Topics" surely must have been in large part due to the music provided by the Creole Band. Presumably still under contract to the Shuberts, Mabel was placed in the fall 1916 Winter Garden "Show of Wonders" but didn't survive long enough to be mentioned in the *Variety* review.[83]

Her attempts to continue in an act backed by a jazz band misfired. For instance, her offer to the ODJB to be in a "big time vaudeville act" for $200 a week plus transportation derailed since the band was already earning $200 a week at the Casino Gardens.[84] She must have found another band, however, since she inserted an ad in the December 15, 1916 issue of *Variety* for "A New Offering in White and Black, Mabel Elaine and her Ragtime Band," supposedly booked into U.B.O. theaters. (I've not been able to trace it.) On the left we see her in antic burnt cork, on the right with a stylish bob and pearl necklace.[85]

Beginning in mid-April 1917, she put together a vaudeville act with "The New Orleans Jazz Band," led by violinist Herb Lindsay and managed by guitarist Louis Keppard (Fred's brother), but it was not well received, lasting only some five weeks. [86]

For the season of 1919–1920 she was with the musical "Hello, Alexander,"

along with her old mentors McIntyre and Heath, and Gilda Gray. Although not a success, there was apparently a touring company. Other shows with Mabel Elaine in the cast were "Red Pepper" of 1922—again with McIntyre and Heath
—which lasted only twenty-two performances. But "Lovely Lady" of 1928 did reasonably well with 164 performances.

Her last known appearance may have been with the show "Boom Boom," which had some 72 performances at New York's Casino Theater in early 1929. If her obituary in *Variety* is to be believed, she continued in show business until 1937. This may have coincided with her marriage to Hughie Fitz[patrick] "an oldtime circus clown with Barnum & Bailey." Her daughter, Josephine, was married to William W. (for Wally) Byrne, a movie projectionist.[87]

Mabel's career after "Town Topics" seems little blessed by coherence or success. Though that could be said of thousands of show people, she was still enough remembered to receive an obituary in *Variety*. Her skills derived from the old-time minstrel stage and one wonders how they could have found a place in a more up-to-date show business.[88]

Of the New Orleans natives in the Creole Band, only Louis Delille returned home. Three stayed on in Chicago, one went to Philadelphia, one to Los Angeles. With the exception of Norwood Williams, they remained active as professional musicians, but mostly not in the context of bands identifiable as New Orleanian in style. For some, this may have been because their musical skills were of an order that allowed them to play up-to-date music. Their grandest moments, in terms of recognition, surely were reached during their nearly four years in vaudeville, when they presented New Orleans ragtime / jazz to thousands of Americans for the first time and rubbed shoulders with some major and still-remembered vaudeville stars.

THE ACCUMULATION OF evidence here presented will convince the reader, I sincerely hope, that the credit for the first jazz band to carry the gospel of New Orleans jazz to the heathen—as it were—must go to the Creole Band. This is not because they were African-American, but because of the duration and geographical scope of their nearly four years in vaudeville, as well as what we know of their individual musical style in later years.

If by some miracle we were to hear them today, we might find their ensemble and rhythmic style unlike what we know of African-American jazz bands from New Orleans in the 1920s. The differences between Kid Ory's Sunshine Orchestra, Joe Oliver's Creole Jazz Band, the Original Tuxedo Jazz Orchestra and Piron's New Orleans Orchestra, Johnny DeDroit and his New Orleans Jazz Orchestra and Johnny Bayersdorffer and his Jazzola Novelty Orchestra—to name the earliest groups made up entirely of New Orleanians (oh, well, with a couple of exceptions)—are quite substantial and should put us on guard against generalizations.

But some would say there's a core that we could call New Orleans style, or New Orleans style between 1922 and 1925. But the recordings made only a few years earlier of the ODJB, the New Orleans Jazz Band with Achille Baquet, and the recordings of Alcide Nunez and Tom Brown by themselves or together, are also quite disparate and in any event rather different from the 1922–1925 group.[89]

The reconstruction of a style on the basis of later recorded evidence is a not uninteresting undertaking, and I can even imagine good music resulting from the experiment. But it should not be made a major issue, for there are larger and more significant historical questions.

There's a kind of fundamental struggle in matters of history between two contrasting points of view: either that the course of human history is largely accidental and unpredictable *or* that things happen because they have to happen. My ingrained tendency when presented with a dichotomy is to squash it and suggest that maybe there's another possibility (or several).[90] In this case, it's a question of levels. I admit some degree of large-scale determinism: that a combination of forces meant that some southern band would come north and make a hit, but it was unpredictable which one would succeed.

The large-scale force was economic: the South, then as more recently, was an enormously rich reservoir of idiosyncratic and orally composed and transmitted music—I avoid the term "folk music," but if you care to use it, be my guest. Already in 1890 New Orleans composer W. T. Francis pointed to a kind of economic pressure, by which poorly remunerated southern music would, in the course of time, migrate northward. One might also observe that the internal migration of southern African-Americans to the West Coast and to the larger northern cities, particularly Chicago, is a major dynamic force in U.S. history between 1900 and 1930 and carried entertainers along with it.

In show business, there had been an important presence of African-American entertainers reaching far back into the nineteenth century, but my impression is that the southern presence was minor. After the turn of the century a great many entertainers from New Orleans, Memphis, Atlanta, and Birmingham worked the numerous theaters all throughout the South that catered to a black clientele. In fact, they probably could make a decent living doing so. In the course of time, and especially in the 'teens many large northern cities saw the opening of such segregated theaters—often, however, with white ownership.

The Creole Band might have, had they been willing, worked as a sideshow band for one of the major national circuses, or in one of the surviving, if moribund, minstrel or Uncle Tom shows. But they were not at first show people of that sort, they were dance band players. It might be said that their entry into show business had two root causes: first, the fact that Baquet, but especially H. Morgan Prince, knew show business and probably had a good idea of what it took to succeed in the larger entertainment world; second, however, Alexander Pantages was both highly competitive in having to make a place for himself in the West Coast circuits dominated by the Orpheum and Sullivan & Considine time, as well as favorably inclined toward African-American performers. Also, as a recent Greek immigrant and a resident of the West Coast, he was possibly more inclined to experiment.

Once launched, however, the band had to, or was supposed to, play by the same vaudeville rules as everybody else. In this scheme of things, the performers were at the bottom of a hierarchy of major and minor circuits, bookers, agents and theater owners in which vociferously expressed audience opinion could make you or break you. On the one hand, the vaudeville life had much to offer: pretty decent salaries, travel all around the country, a certain glamour and status. On the other hand, the seeming freedom of the show business life was a hoax. You were incessantly on the road, according to the rigorous itineraries concocted by agents and bookers, adhering to a code of proper stage deportment, and loving the audience in order to be loved in return. Black performers might have the admiration and respect of fellow entertainers, but once out of the theater, there were constant reminders of where they belonged in American society.

The story of the Creole Band is in part one of ambiguity. So far as the southern, "plantation" theme went, the act had very long whiskers, two or three generations old, but this served as a pretext, allowing them to play their own up-to-date, if very southern, music. It was good enough to carry them all over the United States and Canada for nearly four years. Unfortunately, they didn't deal with the "power structure" gracefully or with cleverness. To go up against an agent as major as Harry Weber was surely risky business, and failing to honor the Portland, Maine, engagement was probably a near-fatal blow to their reputation.

The "loan" by the Shuberts to Marcus Loew was, I think, short-term. Af-

ter Portland, they might have been brought back to New Y
ther at Doraldina's or another cabaret that would have gua
dancers prolonged exposure to their variety of New Orlea
"jazz," as it was henceforth to be known. At this point,
bia, which also seems to have been on the lookout for e
dance music—could well have offered them a second cl
between the ODJB and the Creole Band might have been playcu
playing field.

But of course it wasn't. As matters worked out, in 1922–1924 it took an unlikely coalition between the Melrose Bros. music publishers and the Gennett
record label to bring some of the greatest New Orleans players to the attention of the record-buying public, but it was too late for the Creole Band as
such. Only a few years later, the major New York–based labels saw that there
was money to be made by recording in Chicago, and it was a different ball
game, not least because of the advent of electrical recording in 1925.

It's notable how many of the band's engagements were either in Chicago or
in Illinois, Iowa, and Indiana—something like a third, close to one-half if
Michigan and St. Louis are included in the tally. While it's clear that the southern component in the new music was crucial, maybe this early exposure to
Chicago and the cities within an approximate radius of 170 miles habituated
"middle Americans" to this odd new music, and has something to do with the
subsequent history of jazz, especially as played by Americans of European descent.

One might fantasize that the old gang could have been reunited for some
recordings in Chicago: but between 1924 and 1928 Bill Johnson seems to have
been in California; Palao had passed away at the beginning of 1925 and Norwood Williams seems to have been out of music. It's true that Keppard, Vincent, and Noone were firmly entrenched in Chicago, and a few recordings may
preserve echoes of the Creole Band.

But another ten or twelve years had to pass before it was realized that a very
special kind of music was on the verge of dying out yet could perhaps be saved
in the nick of time: thus the recordings from 1939 and 1940, not only of Jelly
Roll Morton and Sidney Bechet's band but of some of the oldest old-timers
there were, with recordings involving the deans of New Orleans ragtime clarinet: Picou and Delille. But while a few individuals had some inkling of how
special the adventure of the Creole Band was—surely Bill Russell and, possibly, Paul Eduard Miller and Fred Ramsey—it had become the stuff of legend.
What a shame that Bill Johnson wasn't asked to revive the sounds of his youth.

hope is that this narrative has not so much rescued the Creole Band from the legend as it has shown —despite their all-too-human sins of vanity, drinking to excess, and short-sightedness in business matters—how pioneering, meritorious, and, I think, brave their accomplishment was and how deserving they are of the title of "Pioneers of Jazz," the initial link in a chain of musicians and bands that brought New Orleans music (both sweet and hot) to an as yet unhomogenized America, and had momentous effect on the subsequent course of jazz.

Bibliographical Note

PASSING IN REVIEW the books and articles on jazz that mention the Creole Band is something of a comedy of errors, at least from hindsight, which, as we know, is always 20/20. Virtually none of the early accounts should be read today by a person seeking accurate information; they nonetheless contain nuggets of truth that can't be ignored by the historian. In fact, the Creole Band is cited—as the first band to leave New Orleans—in one of the earliest attempts to sketch the history of jazz.

This early mention comes from the second chapter of Marshall Stearns's "The History of 'Swing' Music," which *Down Beat* began publishing in serial form in 1936.[1] Stearns identified Chicago trombonist (although born in New Orleans) Preston Jackson as his informant. The only known photograph of the band accompanied the article (with no source stated). Jackson surely knew Bill Johnson, the manager and bassist with the band, who lived in Chicago for most, if not all, of the thirties and we can presume that both photograph and information came from him.

The name of the Creole Band also surfaced in the October 1936 issue of *Orchestra World* in an interview with Clarence Williams in which he stated: "The first hot band to leave from the South and introduce swing music was the Creole Jazz Band . . . Following was the Dixieland Jazz Band which recorded Livery Stable Blues and Tiger Rag which swept the country. The Creole Band was colored and the Dixieland Band was white and they used to play across the street from each other and used to sit in for each other during rest periods."[2]

Paul Eduard Miller, a noted, if eccentric, writer on jazz during the 1930s and 1940s, showed an awareness of the importance of the Creole Band in a curious *Down Beat* article from September 1937, the point of which is made clear in the headlines, "Was Importance of First Jazz Soloists Exaggerated by Records? / Many Musicians More Responsible for Development of Swing Forgotten Because They Didn't Record."[3] A year or so later, he produced

Down Beat's Yearbook of Swing. It contained a lengthy paragraph on the Creole Band, which, although riddled with chronological errors, is otherwise remarkable for depth of detail, particularly when compared with many subsequent publications.[4]

In the same year there appeared *Jazzmen,* an epoch-making history of jazz under the editorship of Frederic Ramsey, Jr., and Charles Edward Smith.[5] There were in fact ten authors, most notably for our purposes here, William Russell, erstwhile avant-garde percussion composer and Chinese musical instrument demonstrator (in vaudeville). Russell coauthored (with Steven Smith) the crucial first chapter on black New Orleans music, and had full credit for chapters on Louis Armstrong and boogie-woogie.[6]

The editors claimed in their introduction that "one or another of the authors has interviewed every living jazz musician who could contribute factual material." Why Jove didn't unleash one of his thunderbolts as this phrase was being written I'll never understand. It was nevertheless the case that an effort was made—seriously limited by a lack of funds and the very accelerated schedule of book production—to seek out some surviving witnesses to the early days in New Orleans and Chicago, to cross-check the information with other sources and re-interview if necessary, and to exchange drafts with other authors of the book for comment. Fortuitously, in the fall of 1938 Russell was in Chicago and in a position to do some research.[7] Here he spoke with Bill Johnson and collected important information about the Creole Band, which, together with an important passage from Jelly Roll Morton and tidbits from a variety of other sources, were distilled in some two and a half pages of the book.[8] Johnson also contributed a photograph of the band and a business card, both from Los Angeles, and from trumpeter Sidney Desvigne there came two marvelous portraits of clarinetist George Baquet and "star cornettist" Fred Keppard.

Little more than a year later, Ramsey published in two successive issues of *Down Beat* the results of an interview with George Baquet.[9] These articles were chock-full of otherwise unknown details regarding Baquet's career in general and the Creole Band in particular, although not lacking in some quite misleading errors.[10] The much consulted compilation of excerpts *Hear Me Talkin' to Ya* drew on Baquet only for one remark concerning Buddy Bolden, completely passing over the wealth of material on the Creole Band.[11]

Russell, meanwhile, found himself in Los Angeles in 1940 and sought out, among other California old-timers, Norwood Williams, the band's guitarist. The notes he took were sparse, hardly enough to permit expansion into even a modest article. In subsequent years Russell retained his interest in the early history of jazz, the Creole Band and Bill Johnson, and at the end of the 1950s made a serious but unsuccessful attempt to locate the bassist.

The next major effort to collect information about the Creole Band was made by the Belgian poet and essayist Robert Goffin, who spent several months in New Orleans in early 1944, primarily working on his biography of Louis Armstrong, which appeared in 1947. After working on this in the morning, he'd go with photographer Scoop Kennedy in search of others who might cast light on the beginnings of jazz. Accordingly, he spoke at some length with Louis "Big Eye" Delille who had played clarinet with the band for the 1916–1917 season. Big Eye also recounted events that he couldn't have witnessed directly but surely heard about from the other band members.[12]

In 1946 there appeared the first number of *Jazzways*, a periodical not destined to have another. Among the contributions was an important essay on the beginnings of jazz in Chicago by Frederic Ramsey, "Going Down State Street," which reprised much of Ramsey's 1940 article on Baquet, blending it with items evidently drawn from Bill Russell's interview notes with Bill Johnson. More importantly, perhaps, the *Esquire Jazz Book* for 1946 brought to the attention of a wider readership the work of Paul Eduard Miller and George Hoefer, which attempted in eight large-format pages to synthesize "Chicago Jazz History."[13] It repeated in abbreviated form the information published by Miller in 1939, so it might be considered a step backward. In any event, the band is given much credit in the beginnings of jazz (or ragtime-jazz, to use the nomenclature of Miller and Hoefer).

The many small collectors' and jazz fans' magazines of the late 30s and 40s, published not only in the United States but also abroad, are full of references to some of the musicians associated with the Creole Band or active during the same time period. Some of them are now extremely rare, but thanks to the Institute of Jazz Studies whose library has the best collection in the world of these periodicals, including the ones from Europe originally acquired by Harold Flakser, I can hope that I've not missed any truly important sources. These will be found cited in the text as the occasion presents itself.

Jelly Roll Morton's words on Bill Johnson and the band recorded for the Library of Congress in 1938 saw the light of day with the 1950 publication of Alan Lomax's *Mr. Jelly Roll*. It was a great boon to have some comment on the band and its music by a musician fully qualified to hear and to judge—it was a shame that only some of the remarks dictated to a stenographer by Morton simultaneously with the recordings were published. Would that the topic had been pursued in even greater depth, since Morton was amorously connected with Johnson's sister, Bessie, and knew his brother Ollie (or Dink, as he was known familiarly); he was also present at the band's first appearance in Chicago in 1915 and heard them in Detroit in 1916.[14]

1962 marked something of a breakthrough, with the publication of Samuel Charters and Leonard Kunstadt's *Jazz: A History of the New York Scene*.[15] Its fourth chapter was titled "That Creole Band" (borrowing the phrase from a 1915 review). The breakthrough was neither in length—the band was discussed in a mere two of the chapter's twelve pages—nor in accuracy, but in quoting from two reviews of their appearances in New York theaters. For the first time a link to a specific and verifiable time and place was made.

Five years later, Martin Williams, a noted jazz critic, published his *Jazz Masters of New Orleans*.[16] His treatment of the Creole Band—much of it relying on Charters's and Kunstadt's work—was embedded in a chapter on Freddy Keppard, presented as the musically most authoritative figure in the group. This view allowed Williams to sidestep any questions regarding the music produced by the group, as well as details of their lengthy touring in vaudeville. This could only have irritated him as did the vaudeville element in Jelly Roll Morton's recordings.

In 1978 Williams, then associated with the Smithsonian Institution, asked me to write liner notes for a reissue of recordings by Keppard.[17] For this I did a good deal of reading, not only of the existing publications by jazz writers but also of the theatrical trade papers of the time. These excavations in *Variety*, the *New York Clipper*, and the *Indianapolis Freeman* provided a basis for a broad outline of the chronology of the group's vaudeville career. I had a lot to learn, as the subsequent years were to demonstrate, but managed to steer clear of out-and-out misstatements—with one major and a number of minor exceptions.

My fascination with the group continued throughout the next decade and in 1988 I contributed a brief article on the beginnings of the band to *Black Music Research Journal*.[18] In this essay, I profited greatly from my obsessive reading of IF, as well as access to notes of a 1959 interview with Bill Johnson. Once again, however, despite the wealth of new information regarding the band, it turned out that there was a good deal more to be learned.

I had one major advantage over all other writers on the topic: a position at a university that expected and provided the opportunity for research. Perhaps a long habituation to microfilm reading machines should also be cited. Finally, research trips to San Francisco, Los Angeles, New Orleans, and New York were funded by a fellowship from the Guggenheim Foundation in 1983. The upshot of this phase of my interest in the band was the article in *Black Music Research* cited above.

Oral Histories and Interviews

This brief summary of prior work on the band would be incomplete without mentioning the hundreds of oral histories collected in New Orleans by William Russell and Richard B. Allen, and now one of the treasures of HJA. The archive has over the years indexed the interviews so that the researcher can readily locate interviews in which a particular musician or venue is mentioned. There are many entries for the Creole Band and its musicians, but one soon learns that the folks back home, while well aware of the band's success, knew little to nothing of the particulars. There are indications that various members of the band sent letters, postcards, and photographs to their good friends in New Orleans, but these have not escaped—with the exception of several photographs—the ravages of time. Possibly this history will shake loose some additional material still in private hands in New Orleans and California.

The Russell-Allen interviews for the most part took place at the end of the 1950s. Even then, many of the direct witnesses to the band and its musicians had died. Fortunately, another researcher who had long been fascinated with the band's story, had the ambition and the energy to seek out Bill Johnson— whom Russell surely would have brought to New Orleans had he been able to locate him—and Henry Morgan Prince. The only obvious person who was never, as it were, debriefed was the dancer Mabel Elaine, who had passed away in New York City in 1955.

Acting on a tip from Dick Allen, in 1979 I sought out James Palao's daughter, Clotile Palao Glover, in Chicago. She had important memorabilia that she generously shared with me, but she was really too young to recall much about the time her father had been with the Creole Band. Amazingly—or so it seemed to me—her mother, Armontine Carter Palao, was still alive and willing to speak with me. In both cases, it was as much a matter of deriving inspiration and a feeling that the research was worth doing, as garnering facts.

Newspapers and Theatrical Papers

One might think that the activities of the Creole Band would have been amply documented in African-American newspapers, particularly the *Indianapolis Freeman*, the *Chicago Defender*, and the *New York Age*. But these weeklies evidently saw it as their principal mission to cover black entertainers working before black audiences in black theaters, since these engagements were not covered by the "mainstream" theatrical press. And the Creole Band traveled the white vaudeville circuits. There are nonetheless crucial documents from these sources, but not many. Nevertheless, there was no substitute for reading every line of the pages devoted to theater, week by week, during the period 1914–1918.

There were in the 'teens three principal "mainstream" theatrical weeklies: *Variety*, *Billboard*, and the *New York Clipper*.[19] The first and third of these produced a number of important reviews, but most of all they served to establish the detailed itinerary of the band. They also were required reading to gain a sense of the now long-vanished world of vaudeville. For Chicago, an obscure local theatrical weekly was quite important, the *Missouri Breeze*, but, operating apparently with a staff of two or three at most, even the Chicago coverage was sometimes woefully incomplete.[20]

One might hope that other African-American papers would take note of the band as it passed through their city of publication. But although such a paper as the *California Eagle* turned out to be of some importance, a depressingly large number of papers paid no mind to their exotic visitors from New Orleans. One could go into possible reasons for this, but suffice it to say that a great many African-American papers were shoestring operations, consisting mostly of boilerplate, church news, and local social notes with little or no entertainment coverage.

The daily "mainstream" papers of the hundreds of locales where the band played during its four-year career were of enormous importance: first, to verify that the band actually showed up when *Variety* said it was going to; second, to demonstrate the advance publicity and billing that the band received; and finally, for the occasional review that was a personal reaction to the band's performance rather than a rehash of material from the booking office. Contrary to expectation perhaps was the scarcity of pay dirt from the daily papers in the largest cities: San Francisco, Chicago, New York, and so on. This had a number of causes: first, the larger cities had so many theaters that it couldn't possibly devote space to all of them, particularly if they were not the top-flight Keith or Orpheum venues; second, in Chicago and St. Louis many of the band's appearances were in suburban theaters that didn't advertise and were not reviewed.[21]

Miscellany

I might mention here my efforts some twenty years ago, to write to the locals of the American Federation of Musicians in cities where the band appeared, in hopes of locating old-timers who were either in the pit band or the audience. I often received no response at all, but when I did it was negative. Were I to do it over again, I might have pursued this line of inquiry with more intensity and ingenuity.

There are many collections of theater programs in local and state historical societies. I've looked at such collections in a few places, particularly Chicago. My impression is that the persons who saved programs were for the most part patrons of legitimate theater, not vaudeville (or, for that matter, burlesque).

The importance of photographs, especially in the absence of recordings, is very great. Unfortunately, many of the photos in published collections are without indication of the original source, and even more unfortunately are cropped so that many names and addresses of photographers are removed. There is no really good or systematic way to go about locating a given image, except to go to the major public collections, list in hand (IJS, HJA), and the largest private collections, notably that of Frank Driggs. Duncan Schiedt also has a very large collection but is not strong in the period prior to 1920. My suspicion is that there are as many photographs still in private hands — scrapbooks of an illustrious musician ancestor — as have been published or have found their way to the known collectors.

I've thought that there might be copies of popular songs of the 1914–1918 period with a photograph of the Creole Band (most likely, the well-known one from the Empire Studios, Los Angeles). None have so far been identified. I do know of an edition of Shelton Brooks's "Walkin' the Dog" with a portrait of Mabel Elaine on the cover. This type of source, quite important for the 1920s, I have not explored.

One more point: operating with Stratman's magisterial bibliography of theatrical periodicals, I made a survey of most state historical societies and major libraries with a view to finding the more obscure publications, which hadn't wound up in the research libraries or the National Union Catalog. This was nearly entirely unproductive. I particularly regret not having found any extant issues of the *Seattle Critic*, which might well have had good coverage of the activities of the Pantages office.

Appendix 1:
Billing Names

VAUDEVILLE BILLINGS FREQUENTLY offer a title for an act in addition to the names of the performers. In the case of a band it becomes a bit more complicated; just how complicated can be easily seen from the list below. Be that as it may, there were only four titles for the act itself, as distinct from the names for the band: "Southern Reverie," which was used only once; "Plantation Days," which seems to have been first used for the new season in the fall of 1915 and lasted until some time in 1917. (Once it was called "Old Plantation Days.") After the second Pantages tour, the title "Uncle Joe's Birthday" is commonly used (with the variation of "Uncle Eph's Birthday" at the end of 1917). These phrases, along with the panoply of ensemble names, were quite likely set by the language of the band's contracts, or were sometimes inventions of the home office's publicity machinery.

What follows is a listing, in roughly chronological order, of these "inventions." Parentheses sometimes indicate variations in the form of the name when advance publicity, advertisements, and reviews are compared.

Original New Orleans Orchestra and Ragtime Band
  L. A. Times, August 17, 1914
Original Creole Orchestra and Ragtime Band
  L. A. Examiner, August 17, 1914
New Orleans Creole Ragtime Band
  reviews from August 1914
New Orleans Ragtime Band
  This is very common for the first Pantages tour.
New Orleans Creole Orchestra
New Orleans Creole Musicians

Original New Orleans Creole Band
    advance puff: *San Francisco Chronicle*, December 6, 1914
Original Creole Band / featuring H. M. Prince
    ad in *Defender*, January 30, 1915
Creole Band
    reviews in *Defender*, *Missouri Breeze*
Creole Rag Time Band
    more or less alternates with "Creole Band"
Famous Creole Band
    review *New York Evening World*, December 7, 1915
(Seven) Creole Serenaders
    in Pittsburgh
7 - Original Creole Ragtime Band - 7 / W. M. Johnson, manager
    New York Morning Telegraph, January 23, 1916
Creole Ragtime Band
Famous Creole Band
Wonderful Creole Band
    on tour with Town Topics and at Winter Garden concerts
Johnson's (Original) Creole (Ragtime) Band
    for the second Pantages tour
Alabama Jazz Band
    Cedar Rapids *Gazette*, December 20, 1916
Creole Ragtime Band
Original New Orleans Creole Rag Time Band
    Peoria, December 24, 1916
Original (New Orleans) Jaz Band
    Chicago, McVicker's Theater, February 5, 1917
Creole Band
    at Doraldina's, March 1917
Morgan Prince and his Creole Band
    Springfield, Massachusetts, *Daily News*, April 21, 1917 [But Prince not with
    band?]
Creole Band / Sometimes called the Jazz Band
    Portland, Maine, *Daily Eastern Argus* ad, August 26, 1917
(New Orleans) Jazz Band
    Advance ad in *Detroit News*, October 28 and 29, 1917
. . . and finally, just to come full circle . . .
Original New Orleans Creole Ragtime Band
    Davenport, Iowa, *Democrat & Leader*, February 1, 1918

Appendix 2:
Repertory

THE TUNES THAT a band chooses to play or that make a band famous are bound to interest us.[1] And sometimes it seems that such choices go deeper, that is, play an essential role in the sound image we have from the recordings a jazz band leaves behind. What would the New Orleans Rhythm Kings be without "Shim-Me-Sha-Wabble" or "Tin Roof Blues"? What would King Oliver's Jazz Band be without "Snake Rag," "Riverside Blues," or "Mabel's Dream"?

Exactly what relation a band's recordings had to what they normally played is something not always easy to state. Fletcher Henderson's band didn't record the waltzes and tangos that surely they provided for the patrons at Roseland; Jay McShann's band recorded mostly blues for Decca, which wasn't interested in the more "advanced" numbers in the book.

Until such time as some eager beaver goes through all the interviews with the older musicians (say, those born before 1895) at Tulane, there's little we can say about what the common repertory of New Orleans ragtime bands was—although it's probable that "High Society," "Panama," and "Tiger Rag" (under various titles) were played by everybody from ca. 1910 on. Nor are we well informed about the special repertory of particular bands.

I know of one instance when such information was systematically collected: at one point in the 1950s Marilyn Fletcher sat down with her father, clarinetist Gus Mueller, and his old friend and bandmate cornetist Ray Lopez to collect their memories. Among other things, she asked about the tunes they remembered playing with Brown's Band between 1911 and 1915 approximately. They managed to recall fifty-eight titles, ranging from "Blue Danube"—presumably the famous waltz—to "Put on Your Old Gray Bonnet" to "Too Much Mustard." But they prefaced the list with the statement "Dozens of tunes floated around New Orleans which didn't have names—blues, rags, "stomps" and "struts." Most musicians and bands had their own numbers. Rarely did anything go down on paper: a new tune would go from band to band and soon become New Orleans music."

So far as the Creole Band is concerned, we need to consider, first, that their act, as most acts in vaudeville, was relatively brief, with time for perhaps six or seven tunes at most; second, while it might please us that they played some of the good old New Orleans tunes for the folks in Ledbridge, Alberta, what would be the advantage—from the vaudeville point of view—of playing tunes nobody would recognize?

We probably should assume that they might play—if not on stage, at least at any extra engagements—hits of the day lending themselves to a raggy performance. That they would have been approached by Chicago or New York song pluggers I'm inclined to doubt, since so far as we know Morgan Prince limited his vocalism to the Stephen Foster songs that were a constant part of the act, and to a plugger instrumental numbers were secondary.

Since we've broached the topic, let's look through reviews of the band's appearances for "plantation songs." "Old Black Joe" and "My Old Kentucky Home" were mentioned at their initial engagement in Los Angeles. In Edmonton, Alberta, some weeks later, the reviewer substituted "Massa's in the Cold, Cold Ground," for "Old Black Joe." For the remainder of the band's stage career, virtually the only one of these "southern" or "plantation" songs to be mentioned was "Old Black Joe." (Stephen Foster's name never appears; such is fame.) This might be due to the most prevalent title for the act, that is, "Uncle Joe's Birthday." Both solo and quartet performances of "Old Black Joe" are mentioned; sometimes it was danced to. In this case, I assume that a raggy, uptempo version was played by the band.

Shelton Brooks's big hit of 1916, "Walkin' the Dog," was clearly in the band's repertory, both in "Town Topics" and in vaudeville. An earlier hit dance song, Chris Smith's "Balling the Jack," is mentioned as having been played in Detroit in February 1915, and it's likely that it was done in "Town Topics" as well.

Mabel Elaine had two big numbers in "Town Topics." The first, in which her character was Gertie Gorgonzola, was to the song "I Want Someone Who's Lonesome." The second was the transformation scene, with the levee turning into a plantation set and Elaine (with chorus) and the band. The tune listed in the programs I've seen was "Cotton Blossom Serenade." It never achieved any notoriety although it was listed as having been published by G. Schirmer, along with sixteen other numbers composed for the show. (Some were apparently not used.) However, in the Conductor's Score folder for the show (at the Shubert Archive) a detailed listing of all the musical numbers calls for "Cotton Blossom Time," a song published by Leo Feist in 1914 with words by Jack Mahoney and music by Percy Wenrich. The cover shows a stylishly dressed woman perched on a cotton bale and holding a cotton plant, with a levee and steamboat traffic in the background.[2] Surviving orchestra parts don't resolve the issue.

The *Freeman* in reporting Leonard Scott as a member of the group in October 1917 says that he was going to introduce a piece by Charles Warfield, "From Now On, Let Me Miss You." This was published by Frank K. Root, Chicago, in that year. It's possible that there exists an edition of the song with Scott's photograph, maybe even one of the band.

The band probably played various blues written or published by W. C. Handy. In a 1941 publication he wrote:

> It was this tune [Memphis Blues], and later "St. Louis Blues," which ushered in the jazz era; and it was James Reese Europe, heretofore mentioned, along with his jazz band, who were the first to make a recording of "Memphis Blues." Soon the Creole Band of New Orleans featured "blues" in vaudeville. Other bands quickly got in line and copied their style.[3]

In an interview with Bill Russell, Dink (Ollie) Johnson, Bill's brother, maintained that his tune "Animal Ball" was used by the Creole Band. I don't know if it was ever published, but as "Animule Ball" it was recorded by Dink and issued as NOLA LP12. Whether this is related to the tune recorded by Jelly Roll Morton, or to the one often cited as popular in New Orleans in the 'teens, I also don't know.

In his interview with Bill Johnson in the fall of 1938, Bill Russell noted down the following as tunes played by the band: "The Gypsy," "Steamboat Bl[ues]," "Roustabout Shuf[fle]," "Pepper Rag"—Joplin, "Midnight Dream."[4] Following Gushee's Law No. 1: No New Orleans musician ever gives a song title correctly, we could make these out to be

Egyptia: Intermezzo (1911, Abe Olman)
Steamboat Bill (1911, Ren Shields and Leighton Bros.)
Roustabout Rag (1897, Paul Sarebresole)
Red Pepper (1910, Henry Lodge)
Mississippi Dream

The last of these didn't make it into the version of Johnson's information published in *Jazzmen*. And the attentive reader will note that I ride roughshod over Johnson's association of "Joplin" with "Pepper Rag." (There is no work of that name by Joplin.) There is a 1914 "Steamboat Rag" by Ernie Burnett that might be substituted for "Steamboat Bill"; I chose the latter because of its great popularity.

It's probably worth pointing out that a phrase in Russell's first notes and the typed "processed" version was significantly altered in *Jazzmen*. The manuscript notes: "Played real N. Or. music"; typed notes: "Said they played real N.O. music"; *Jazzmen*: "Everywhere they played the old New Orleans standby tunes." Was Johnson talking about repertory or style?

In his interview from 1959, Bill recalled these tunes (unprompted, according to the interviewer): "Old Black Joe," "Swanee River," "Gipsy" (the opening tune), Scott Joplin tunes, "12th Street Rag," "Beale Street Blues," and "Rooster." Given the importance of the trained chicken to the act—almost an eighth member of the troupe—some kind of chicken or rooster piece was certainly in order. I have a note to myself (no source indicated! shame!) that Keppard liked to play "Chicken Reel." Rather than the well-known "Chicken Reel" (by Joseph Daly, 1910) I'd prefer "King Chanticleer" (from around the same time) just because I'm fond of the piece.

Norwood Williams mentioned that the band jazzed up "On Wisconsin," the well-known college fight song from 1909.[5] It strikes me as odd that this is the sole piece he cited to Bill Russell. The section with lyrics is actually the trio of a three-strain march.

In a letter to the magazine *Jazz* for May 1943, Eugene Williams cited "Livery Stable Blues" as a freak specialty number of Fred Keppard and Louis Delille. The first recording of this piece comes from April 1917 (and published forms thereafter), the very month in which the Creole Band with Delille as clarinetist broke up in Boston. Skepticism is in order, therefore, although it's perfectly possible that this routine was in common circulation among New Orleans musicians prior to the ODJB recording. In fact, the copyright litigation between Ray Lopez and the ODJB from October 1917 claiming infringement of a piece from Brown's Band, "More Power Blues," by "Livery Stable Blues" (or, as it eventually was titled, "Barnyard Blues") lends support to the idea.

Darnell Howard, in speaking with John Steiner about hearing the band in Milwaukee in late 1917 or early 1918, remembered them as playing "Panama," the 1911 piece by William Tyers. The earlier "Panama Rag" was also played in New Orleans, but this is probably not what Howard meant. Howard also recalled that Keppard had told him that he had originated the high cornet part that's usually played in the last strain of "Panama."

Howard also mentioned to Bill Russell in 1957 that one of Keppard's sweet specialties at the Deluxe, Chicago, was "Only a Rose." This is but one of a number of tunes cited (without much rhyme or reason) as being favorites of Keppard, such as Joe Jordan's "Sweetie Dear," "Panama," and one or another operatic selections. But with the exception of "Panama," there's no clear association with the Creole Band, much as I'd like the New Orleans Feetwarmer's 1932 recording of "Sweetie Dear" to embody a routine invented by the Creole Band.

More than one musician has had the idea of "reviving" the Creole Band. Choosing a play list from the tunes mentioned above is only a faltering first step. A far more important step is to rid oneself of preconceived notions as to how a jazz or New Orleans ragtime band should play, how the various instruments should relate to one another on the basis of the Hot Five, say, or the New Orleans revival bands of the 1940s. But most difficult of all is to devise an appropriate rhythmic style that's more than an unthinking adoption of the alternatives known from recordings of the 1920s and after. Finally, there surely is room for more than one "solution" to these problems.[6]

Appendix 3:
On the Word (and Concept) "Creole"

WHY WAS THE Creole Band called the Creole Band? A simple enough question but one that has both simple as well as complicated answers. The simple answer is that it was named after an earlier band, such as the quintet that traveled to California in 1907–1908 or the Creole Orchestra of Oakland, California, discussed above. But even if that were true, it's only putting off the day of reckoning.

The next simple answer is that a Creole is a light-complected person of mixed European and African ancestry, roughly equivalent to the terms "mulatto," "quadroon," and "octoroon." In such a person European physical characteristics outweigh the African ones: thus, straight hair, aquiline nose, relatively thin lips, light complexion.

When the notorious impresario Sam T. Jack opened his theater in Chicago in the early 1890s, he staffed his company with very light-skinned African-American women who were called Creoles but who could have been called "quadroons" and "octoroons." In other words, it was not just a matter of mixture of phenotypes but of privileging European ancestry.

There's a nasty side to all this, to be sure. The extramarital sexual desire of "white" men for "black" women was perhaps regarded as more tolerable the more a woman had European features. This lands us in antebellum New Orleans, with its "quadroon balls" and its liaisons between white men and "free women of color."

The term "free person (or man, or woman) of color" is a translation of the French "personne (homme, femme) de couleur libre" a term necessitated by the existence in colonies of the New World of a class of persons who, despite their African ancestry, had been liberated from slavery—in a variety of ways and for a variety of reasons that won't be gone into here. People are sometimes startled to learn of the size and importance of this class (or caste) in nineteenth-century New Orleans and other cities in which slaves and free colored persons coexisted (Mobile, Charleston).

Of course, the mere fact of being free didn't mean that a person was light of complexion, but since it was common that the offspring of a white colonial and a slave woman were made free, there's some correlation. Still, some free persons of color were very black—indeed, more than some slaves. Consequently, legal status and appearance were two separate but related questions.

The complete story of the etymology and earliest usages of the term has yet to be told and can't be attempted here.[1] Nevertheless, there is evidence that in the beginning it did refer to a slave born in a colonial household rather than one imported from Africa. With the passage of time the word was laundered (so to speak) to mean a white person born in the colonies.

A similar laundering took place in the second half of the nineteenth century, when some influential New Orleans writers such as G. W. Cable and Grace King attempted to limit the term to white persons, particularly those who were Roman Catholic and French-speaking. This is the reason for the expressions "colored creoles" and "creoles of color," which might otherwise be viewed as redundant.

But the entrepreneurs of feminine pulchritude and the writers of the theatrical press in fin-de-siècle America were neither etymologists nor persons with a New Orleans axe to grind. To them "Creole" meant a light-skinned African-American. Was this meaning appropriate to the "pre–Creole Band" of 1907–1908? It certainly was to William M. Johnson, often cited for his light complexion and un-southern speech, and cornetist Ernest "Nenny" Coycault was sometimes called (or called himself) "Johnson" because of his resemblance to William Manuel. (Extant photographs indeed show a person of quite light complexion.) Since there are no photographs known to me of the other three members of the band (Paddio, Washington, and Ferzand), the point can't be pursued.

But if it can't be pursued, no one has offered evidence to contradict my notion that this 1908 group was called a "Creole Band" because all or most of its members were light-skinned. At least it helps answer why the 1914 "real" Creole Band was called that despite the fact that while Johnson, Baquet, Palao, and Keppard were light-skinned in varying degree, Vincent, Williams, and Prince were rather dark and "African" in appearance.

Finally, it's possible that for these New Orleanians, "creole" conferred some degree of musical status. While I don't want to perpetuate the melodramatic myth of light vs. dark, Downtown vs. Uptown, that has been one of the conceptual engines of works on jazz[2] it is true that among the free persons of color in New Orleans—and the group that after the Civil War continued their way of life—there was not only a desire to cultivate formal study of language, literature, and art but often some modest disposable income to permit that study. So to say "Creole Band" might be to say that this was not just a bunch of illiterate country blacks only a generation removed from slavery, but, rather, a group that comprised some "real musicians." Not that this kept them from having to exploit (and be exploited by) the plantation stereotype.

Appendix 4:
On the History of the Word "Jazz"

JUST AS THE PATHS of the Creole Band and Brown's Band ran parallel in 1915 and early 1916, so too did those of the Creole Band and the Original Dixieland Jazz Band at the beginning of 1917. All three terms, "original," "dixieland," and "jazz" deserve some investigation and this seems like a reasonable place to attempt it.

"Original"

We recall that in the Los Angeles photo of the band from 1914, Dink Johnson's bass drum head read "Original Creole Orchestra," an inscription that must have been added after the fact according to our arguments in the section that discusses this document. Were there other "creole orchestras" in the area? A news item from 1907 referred to the Creole Orchestra from Oakland, California, and another, from the *Clipper* in February 1914 mentions a Creole Orchestra from McAlester, Oklahoma. In 1916, the *California Eagle* informs us that there was a Creole Orchestra in San Diego. I assume that there may well have been another "Creole Orchestra" in or around Los Angeles in 1914 that neither advertised nor received mention in the press but convinced Bill Johnson to distinguish his group as "Original." It's possible that Ernest Coycault, the cornetist who had come west with the 1908 band and remained in California, had something to do with this group.[1] Recall that the Creole Band's Los Angeles business card reads "The Famous Creole Orchestra from New Orleans, Louisiana," another way, possibly, of distinguishing them from some upstart California band that used the name "Creole."

Fast-forward to Chicago in 1915–1916: Brown's Band didn't call itself "original" in 1915, nor did Johnny Stein's group that opened at the Schiller

Cafe in March 1916. It was billed as Stein's Band from Dixie, then Stein's Dixie Jass Band. But when Tom Brown returned to Chicago from New Orleans in April, 1916, his group was called "Original Brown's Jass Band from Dixieland." It could well be that when four of Stein's musicians left him, eventually to open at the Casino Gardens in July, they were unwilling to let Brown claim the laurels and so used the term "original." One might suggest that perhaps they also felt the Creole Band breathing down their collective neck.[2] In any event, there were quite a few groups jockeying for position in the "inventors of jazz" sweepstakes in late 1916 and 1917.

Dixieland

Here is not the place to recapitulate the history of the word "Dixie" from the time of Dan Emmett's super-hit to the present, nor that of the derived "Dixieland," except to observe that in the 1861 Firth & Pond sheet music, the cover title reads "I Wish I Was in Dixie's Land," but that in the lyrics it's "Dixie" or Dixie Land.[3] In the first decade of the twentieth century the word Dixieland crops up in a variety of contexts. In 1909, there was a large spectacular show, *Dixieland*, with a cast of over 100 African-American entertainers. In late 1910 or early 1911 the popular theatrical duo of Charles King and Elizabeth Brice recorded "Let Me Stay and Live in Dixieland" (from the *Slim Princess*) for Victor. Around 1913, Conway's Band recorded a "Dixieland" turkey trot (or one-step) for the same company.

But credit for using the term as an adjective in a band's title was claimed by trombonist Eddie Edwards, who prior to his entry into the U.S. Army in 1918 was the band's manager. In a letter written to *Esquire*, dated January 17, 1946, Edwards said that the name "Original Dixieland Jazz Band" was his own idea and, further, that other members of the band had suggested "Louisiana" or "New Orleans." These were rejected because they were "too sectional."[4]

That the words "Dixie" and "Dixieland" were considered equivalent at the outset seems demonstrated by the band's first record, Victor 18255-A, which was first issued as "Dixieland Jass Band One-Step." Later pressings had "Dixie Jass Band One-Step / Introducing 'That Teasin' Rag,'" and even later ones reverted to "Dixieland."[5]

The subsequent history of the use of the term to designate a particular style or way of playing is too complicated to go into here. Suffice it to say that Jelly Roll Morton labeled Freddie Keppard's band ca. 1908—a bit too early—as the "first Dixieland combination" because of the reduced instrumentation of cornet, clarinet, trombone, piano, and drums (poor business had forced the owner or the leader to drop the violin, bass, and guitar that were in the original seven-piece band, substituting a piano).[6]

Jazz

First, to clear up a misunderstanding: the first thing that people often learn about the history of the word "jazz" is that in the beginning it was spelled "jass." That's true . . . but the spellings "jazz," "jaz," "jass," "jas," and "jasz" appear more or less simultaneously in the course of 1916–1917. Since it was a word new to the written language, there was no "proper" or "official" spelling; neither do we have a record of the different pronunciations there may have been, which might in part account for the panoply of different spellings.

Second, it's important to avoid reifying [please excuse this quasi-philosophical term] the word, that is, assuming that the word unequivocally designates a particular kind of music. Some of the music that was called "jazz" between 1915 and 1925 would be found bizarre and not jazz by listeners today, so that the term these days functions more like a value judgment than a historically based description. To be kept in mind is that the great majority of older New Orleans musicians born prior to the turn of the century agree that the word wasn't applied to music in their native city and they didn't hear it so used until they came north.

While it seems pretty clear that "jazz" was synonomous with sexual intercourse around the turn of the century, it's not at all clear that this was the first or only usage, or that, as sometimes happens with matters etymological, there wasn't a sound-alike with a different origin or meaning. Neither is it known how regional the word was.

San Francisco. Thanks to the interest in the etymology of slang words by the late Peter Tamony and the further researches of Richard Holbrook, it's been established that some San Francisco sportswriters (and a columnist) used the word "jazz" in San Francisco newspapers in 1913. Furthermore, if the memories of one of them can be relied on, the music of drummer Art Hickman's small dance band at the San Francisco Seals training camp in the same year was considered to be jazz.

It now (May 2004) appears that San Francisco was not the first place where this novel term appeared in print. In its edition of April 2, 1912 [part III, p. 2] the *Los Angeles Times* offered a small item headlined, "BEN'S JAZZ CURVE" in which pitcher Ben Henderson is quoted as saying, "I call it the Jazz ball because it wobbles and you simply can't do anything with it."

From my experience with some new terms describing dancing, it wouldn't surprise me to find even earlier newspaper mentions—from the West Coast or elsewhere. There's no way short of a systematic reading of every newspaper and humor or social commentary magazine to determine this, bearing in mind that a writer who knew the word as obscene—in the year 2002, it's necessary to add "by the standards then prevailing"—would not have written it for publication except perhaps in a pornographic novel.[7]

It's worth pointing out that Art Hickman in 1920 distanced himself from jazz. Stating that his band was not a jazz band he went on to say that "Jazz is merely noise, a product of the honky-tonks, and has no place in a refined atmosphere. We have tried to develop an orchestra that charges every pulse with energy, without stooping to the skillet beating, sleigh bell ringing contraptions and physical gyrations of a padded cell."[8]

Vaudeville. It seems clear that by 1915 the term jazz was part of the vernacular of the theater. See, for example, the citations from Sam Kahl above. But there's some theatrical testimony from a few years earlier. In 1968 vaudevillian and eventually television actor William Demarest (1892–1983) wrote to Richard Holbrook that he had learned the word from his older brother George when they worked as a double act at the Portola Theater, San Francisco, in May 1910. In that context it meant to put some pep or energy into the music they were playing on stage. Holbrook is not as careful as one might wish: he appears to identify the attested uses of the verb jazz with the noun jazz, meaning a kind of music.[9]

Brown's "Jad" Band; Bert Kelly. The reader may recall the quaint anecdote stemming from Ray Lopez as to the term "jad," used in an ad rather than the tenderloin word "jazz." Lopez stands in opposition to Tom Brown, who maintained that at Lamb's the band had been called "Brown's Original Dixieland Jazz Band" and perhaps was even in lights as such on Lambs' sidewalk sign. Another story from Brown was that Lipschultz, the leader of the small concert orchestra at Lambs', applied the term as an insult to the upstarts from New Orleans—who were not members of the musicians' union—even going so far as to instigate a "knock" in the newspaper hoping to drive the public away by saying that the music at Lamb's was "Jazz Music."[10]

Bert Kelly made repeated claims to have been the first to use the term jazz for music. One instance was in a caption for a movie taken at a fancy ball given at the College Inn on Washington's Birthday 1915; another was its use on tent cards on the tables of the Hotel Morrison's Boosters' Club in September of that year. Neither document has survived. The context of Kelly's claims has to be taken into account: the true jazz, according to him, was that produced by his quartet of banjo-mandolin, saxophone, piano, and drums. The claim is undermined by an item in the "Hotel Notes" of the *Chicago Examiner* for February 3, 1915: "The most recent acquisition of the College Inn is the "Frisco Ragtime Four," which furnishes fox-trot music on banjos." This must, in my opinion, refer to Kelly's band. As the months passed, he began to expand his activities, placing a number of "Bert Kelly bands" in Chicago hotels and cabarets, some of them using New Orleans musicians playing in a manner that would have made the term "jazz band" reasonable.

The recent availability of on-line full text databases for some important newspapers has borne unexpected fruit. The *Chicago Tribune* of July 11, 1915, had a relatively lengthy item associating jazz with blues and also with the saxophone: "The blues are never written into music, but are interpolated by the piano player or other players . . . The trade name for them is "jazz." . . . Saxophone players since the advent of the "jazz blues" have taken to wearing "jazz collars," neat decollate things that give the throat and windpipe full play. . . ." One recalls not only that Bert Kelly's College Inn quartet had a saxophone, but that as soon as clarinetist Gus Mueller joined him in late 1915, he took him to Lyon and Healy to buy a saxophone.

Published Music. In a remarkable and very occasional periodical, "La Gidouille," appeared a compilation of titles using the word "jazz" (and variations) from the Library of Congress *Catalogue of Copyright Entries*, plus gleanings from record catalogues and newspapers.[11]

Relatively few compositions from 1916 are known. A fox-trot for piano by Arthur S. Shaw, "Jazbo," was copyrighted on January 3 and 7 by Chicago music publisher F. J. A. Forster. No recordings are known, but two piano rolls were made in early 1917, perhaps in reaction to the burgeoning interest in this new music. Next in line chronologically was "When I Hear That Jaz Band Play," with words and music by Eddie Gray (Chicago: Frank K. Root, copyrighted May 18, 1916), then a hiatus of some months until the appearance of Gus Kahn and Henry Marshall's "That Funny Jas Band from Dixieland" (New York: Remick, copyrighted November 8 and 13, 1916). Recordings were made by the very well-known team of Arthur Collins and Byron Harlan for both Victor and Edison, then by Collins alone for Operaphone. An otherwise unknown Tom York wrote an unpublished piece, "The Jazz Rag," arranged by Lewis J. Fuiks (better known by his pseudonym, Victor Arden), deposited at the Copyright Office on November 21. To close out the year came "Ephraham's Jazbo Band," with words and music by Jack Smith, also apparently un-published and deposited on December 9. It was recorded for the extremely obscure label Par-O-Ket, by Arthur Collins and by George O'Connor for Victor, both in early 1917.

With 1917 came a veritable flood—close to forty—of pieces with "jazz" or a variant in the title, thus ratifying the passage of this new music from a Chicago novelty to a national fad. This does not count the increasing frequency of pieces with a generic designation, for example, "a jazz song," "jazz novelty" and the like.

Appendix 5: Jelly Roll Morton on Freddie Keppard and on the Creole Band

EACH OF THE FOLLOWING excerpts merits annotation, especially regarding chronology: many of the dates are several years off the mark. For example, Fred Barrasso of Memphis began his career of entrepreneurship in 1909 in a small way, then linked up with William Benbow, eventually owning half a dozen theaters and fielding three or four stock companies in 1910. So, instead of 1908 as the date of Keppard's arriving in Memphis, 1910 might be suggested as more plausible.

FROM NOTES OF an interview of Bill Russell with Morton in 1937 or 1938, written down from memory in 1944 and copied by me in 1983. I suppose the original is in *HNOC, WRC,* but I haven't located it yet:

WR asked about the CB and their style:

The Creole Band was *tremendous.* They really played *jazz,* not just novelty and show stuff. The reason Baquet played rather straight at times was because he was the only one who could read and they had him play the lead for this reason. He would play the tune rather straight, down low (in vocal register). Jelly demonstrated at the piano just how the Creole Band played a piece. He took a tune and played it straight, and then added the high trumpet part of Keppard above the clarinet lead. Keppard's part was more like a clarinet part or an obligato to the melody. In the Creole Band Keppard played the variations or embellished part. (WR jazz not the same as ragtime.)[1]

Jelly said he never heard a man that could beat Keppard. His "reach" was very exceptional, both high and low, all degrees of power, more tone than anybody, great imagination. Manuel Perez was the only one that could compare with Keppard, but Perez did not arouse the enthusiasm that Keppard did, making people stand up and yell and really get them excited. Perez was the perfect player. Jelly never heard him make a mistake, never heard him crack a note. Oliver cracked lots of times, Keppard too. (Bill Johnson told WR that FKs tone was so big people couldn't stand to sit in the front rows of the theatre and would have to move back after the first number . . . and he played a lot of fancy and high stuff away back before Louie was playing high.

THE FOLLOWING EXCERPT from Dave Stuart's short biography of Jelly Roll:[2]

That [New Orleans Blues], by the way, was the first blues the city of Memphis had ever heard, and that wasn't until 1908, when an excursion band with Freddie Keppard, who I consider to be the greatest of the jazz trumpeters who ever lived, came to Memphis and played. I happened to be playing there in a colored theater circuit which was just organized by Fred Barrasso. It just happened that, during my stay there, Keppard came to town with the band and I asked Freddie to play the entire blues with the band. As the people of Memphis had never heard a band play blues, they went wild with joy and Keppard was mobbed every place he played. He would simply put the band in a wagon and ride around town and advertise a dance he was playing and the place would be overflowing with people. Soon as he put his horn to his lips the people would crowd around. He would often stand in front of the Monarch Saloon in Memphis and play. Freddie could play as soft as a violin and loud as anything. The only trouble, though, is that he couldn't be depended on and usually went his own way. He was hard to control because of that and also because he started drinking heavily.

The following is a transcription from the 1938 Library of Congress interviews, record no. AFS-1652A. It begins with Morton playing "Salty Dog" for 2 minutes and 12 seconds, with a certain amount of give and take between Alan Lomax and Jelly Roll. The second half of the record takes "Salty Dog" as a jumping-off place and continues with some words about the Creole Band. There are a few trivial differences between this and Mike Meddings' transcription at <www.doctorjazz.freeserve.co.uk>.

That's the way Bill Johnson used to play, him and his three-piece organization. Bill Johnson's a brother-in-law of mine, and he's older than mine [sic]. Very, very good lookin' boy in those days, and my, how did the girls take to him and those bad chords on the bass fiddle. My, they really taken to him, I'm tellin' you. [Q from Lomax: Was he the one brought the first jazz to New York?] Yeh, Bill Johnson was the first one that taken the first jazz band into the city of New York; they played the

Palace Theater. Well, I'm a little bit ahead of my story. Bill . . . Bill wanted to come to California and in the meantime he wrote my wife a letter and she financed the trip. He had a band and he composed his band formerly of some of the Tuxedo orchestra which was Freddy Keppard's old original orchestra, which was the first combination of what is known now as the Dixieland combination, but of course this band was augmented a bit—from the Dixieland combination, they had added then the guitar and the bass fiddle. Of course, Bill seen the opportunity so he got into the band and got the bass fiddle and got the band for himself. So he . . . we financed the trip and came to Los Angeles. On entering Los Angeles, they made such a tremendous success that the Pantages circuit signed 'em up immediately—that was the year of 1913, and they made the trip throughout the country of the Pantages Circuit, which was the largest circuit at that time in the world. And through this trip they came East. And they came into Chicago in early 1914. I happened to be there myself with a similar combination of what Freddie Keppard used to have, which was considered a Dixieland—which is considered *now* a Dixieland combination. They came to Chicago and turned the town upside down, caused my trumpet player to quit, which was considered the best trumpet player in Chicago at the time—his name was Armstrong—but not Louie Armstrong—was *John* Armstrong of Louisville, Kentucky, and John couldn't play that kind of trumpet. And I had been teachin' him a little bit, and he was a little stubborn, and when Freddy played, he wanted to hit me with a rack.

The attentive reader of *Mr. Jelly Roll* will see that the account on p. 142 ff (of the paperback edition), takes elements from the recording and blends them with others from the steno notes below. In the editing process—presumably by Lomax—some details drop out, others are altered in meaning.

IT'S WORTH CITING at length Morton's remarks on Keppard from the Library of Congress steno notes, item 10.[3]

Freddie Keppard—greatest hot trumpeter in existence—more numerous ideas—lowest and highest notes in history—very fine fellow when he wasn't drinkin', always after goodlookin women—spent every dime he could get—died broke in Chicago. Had the first Dixieland Combination—piano, clarinet, trumpet, trombone, and drums around 1908. It was created by the place they worked—business got bad, had seven pieces—bass violin, viol, drum, guitar, trombone, trumpet, and clarinet. On Franklin Street between Custom House and Brenville [Bienville], big dance hall in tenderloin district. Had to cut two pieces instead cut off three and stuck in a piano with Buddy Christian—fair pianist—no good piano player would fake a job like that—reason, J. R. quit guitar. F. K. was working for $1 a night—the lower classes went to the dance halls, all the rich trade went to sporting houses. These places had 4 or 5 parlors and you could go from one to the other.

The following is from the steno notes, item 33:

Freddie Keppard—1907. He thought my playing was different than anybody elses's; he liked it. I wrote the Indian Blues and he was crazy about it. This tune enticed him to play like I did. Keppard born in New Orleans. He wasn't well known because he wasn't in the district. In a year he had a big reputation. The women were swelling his head. He had the most wonderful ear I ever heard. Had a beautiful tone, marvelous execution. No end to his ideas, could play one chorus eight or ten different ways. He had formed a little band. This was just before the Tuxedo organized. Freddie Keppard had plenty of cheap notoriety. Bolden was as popular as Freddie in a year's time [order reversed?].

After the killing of Billy Phillips, the Tuxedo Band was cut down and a piano was put in. The piano player was Buddy Christian. Keppard made a big hit in the Tuxedo.

1908—Freddie Keppard went to Memphis and this was the first time they played the blues in Memphis. Keppard made records with Erskine Tate and Charley Cook between 1923 and 1924. (Tate and Cook are not good jazz men—just like Paul Whiteman. Good men but they don't know much.)

1914—Freddie Keppard was still around New Orleans. At this time Bill Johnson had taken over Freddie.

1923—Freddie was tops. You could hear at this time only Keppard and King Oliver. King had a band and worked at Royal Garden. Keppard started playing with Charley Cook at the Dreamland. This was in Chicago around 1923 and 1924. Oliver and Keppard were rivals—the two best trumpeters in the world. Buddy Petti [Petit] was a good player—better than King Oliver but not better than Keppard. Freddie was in a class by himself. He liked to drink a lot and talk big. A lot of people misunderstood and thought he was egotistical. He died in Chicago about 1930 or 1931. He had become very fat, almost as wide as he was tall. He could make the highest notes clear as a whistle; first to start the high note business. There was no limit to how he could go. Louis Armstrong is not in his class. Keppard used only a metal mute. There was no mutes but one.

Keppard was a Creole boy, about my color. Always had a Creole accent. Women would hang around him all day long. He did things in a king [sic] of big way. I presume he made a lot of money. He was a good spender and wore plenty nice clothes. Occasionally he had a nasty disposition.

King Oliver was the cause of mutes to come into existence. He would hit the notes up in the air with those mutes. It gave the instrument a different flavor. He (Oliver) mad [*sic*] his first recording with Erskine Tate. Recorded for Brunswick.

Before Freddie Keppard, there was Manuel Perez. He was like Buddy Bolden. They played strictly rag time. Perez was classified as the best trumpet player in New Orleans before Keppard. Perez is a Creole; had a little band.

Keppard and Perez came from good families. Don't know about Bolden. He came from uptown section of town. Kind of loose section.

[re King Oliver] He played hot, but he couldn't play as much as Freddie Keppard. This style was going around like wild fire.

THE FOLLOWING IS from item 37–38:

Freddie Keppard was one of the greatest hot trumpet players ever lived. Made high C, high G, high F, could make a high note on the trumpet as well as the trombone.

John Armstrong [typed over an erasure] was turning to hit me with a rack. He thought I had a big pistol. I used to carry a 45 and he had seen it. It was almost legal at that time to carry a pistol in the city of Chicago. He took a second thought and decided not to hit me with the rack. John Armstrong played pretty good trumpet in the style they played all over, which in my mind was not very good. It was considered the best in Chicago. Well, the Creole Band [written in] made a smash hit at the Grand Theater in Chicago in 1914; Dave Payton was conductor in the pit.

WILL JOHNSON AND HIS CREOLE BAND

They were on their way East. When they played Detroit I was there. This combination consisted of bass violin played by Will Johnson, violin—Jimmy Palao, guitar—GeeGee Williams, clarinet—George Bakay, at that time the first great hot clarinet player. Freddie Keppard first greatest jazz trumpet player. Eddie Vincent—trombone. They left the drummer in California. His real name was Ollie Johnson, a brother of Will, he liked to be called by his nick-name, Dink. Will Johnson is now about sixty years.

[excursus on Tony Jackson and Bob Caldwell omitted]

The Creole Band continued on its way to New York on its agency planned trip. In New York they played the most prominent spot in 1914—the Palace Theater. It was known that no acts played the Palace Theater more than a week. They played the first week to standing room only, and they held them for a second week, breaking all box-office attendance of the Palace Theater. They were booked by the Weber Simon Agency, with offices in the Palace Theater Building. After this two week engagement, the town admitted it was the most exciting type of music ever heard in New York.

During this time there was a show, considered the greatest show, entitled "Town Topics." The trip was ended there but the agents hired them for this show for another act and the [*sic*] stole the whole dog-gone show.

In this band there was a comedian, Morgan Prince and his trained chicken. He lives in Tacoma, Washington, if he is still living.

Everyone of the bunch drank up everything they could find, including the leader. There was hardly a day but what almost all of them was late. They started to break up when they arrived back in Chicago because of arguments. There was an argument all the time with Keppard's big talk. He was mostly kidding all the time. Morgan Prince from a different section, took Keppard seriously and always thought Freddie wanted to break up the band. He [Keppard? Prince?] would always say, "Let them wait for me, the band can't play until I get there." Through these arguments in the City of Chicago, Morgan Prince hit Freddie Keppard across the head with a cane—that started breaking up the band. I don't know when they disbanded but it was beginning to end.

Jelly Roll was generous to musicians he admired—for example, Tony Jackson, Sammy Davis—but there's no musician he admires so much and at such length as Keppard.

Notes

Abbreviations

DB	*Down Beat*
Def	*Chicago Defender*
e.d.	Enumeration District (in the Federal Censuses)
EJB	*Esquire's Jazz Book*
HJA	New Orleans, Tulane University, Hogan Jazz Archive
HNOC	The Historic New Orleans Collection, Williams Research Center
IJA	Newark, Rutgers University, Institute of Jazz Study
IF	*Indianapolis Freeman*
MJR	Alan Lomax, *Mr. Jelly Roll* (1950 Grove Press paperbk. unless otherwise stated)
NYT	*New York Times*, Oral History Project
RC	*The Record Changer*
R&S	Al Rose and Edmond Souchon, *New Orleans Jazz Family Album* (1st ed.)
TSA	New York City, The Shubert Archive
WRC	William Russell Collection (at HNOC)

Preface

1. "How the Creole Band Came to Be," *Black Music Research Journal* 8:1 (1988): 83–100.

Introduction

1. Appendix 5 brings together the quite copious remarks made by Morton about the band.

2. The question is discussed in some detail in Hans Nathan's *Dan Emmett and the Rise of Early Negro Minstrelsy* (Norman, Okla.: University of Oklahoma Press, 1962), chap. 11.

3. Singing, understood as a more natural and direct expression of emotion (or passion), was something the African, as "child of nature," was widely thought to be capable of, where the more cerebral manipulations of violin, piano, and wind instruments were closed off to him. The question is inextricably bound up with musical literacy: where we all can sing naturally, instrumental performance—at least as understood in the context of European "classical" music—requires instruction, partic-

ularly in the difficult art of deciphering the arbitrary signs of musical notation. Thus the well-known legend of the requirement that the pit orchestra members of the 1921 African-American production of "Shuffle Along" memorize their music, because they were supposed to play entirely "by ear" and not by training.

4. *La Tribune de la Nouvelle-Orléans*, Wednesday, February 10, 1869. The term "nos cousins" is not just humorous writing but literally true, given the common ancestry of many Caucasians and "free persons of color" in New Orleans.

5. "Buck and wing" has become a catch phrase pretty much devoid of meaning. In fact, a modest amount of research may convince one that it never had a very specific meaning.

6. *Jazz Dance* (New York: Macmillan, 1968), p. 50.

7. *Chicago Daily News*, March 6, 1916, p. 6.

8. There's a natural tendency to focus on theater, dance hall, and cabaret, but an important component of the complex of interacting institutions was high school and college dancers. The *Seattle Sun* reported in 1914 the denunciation by university administrators of the style of dancing at the University of Washington. The entire article is interesting, but I cite here only the last paragraph: "The music is played in such a way that the old waltz and two-steps cannot be danced to it. I have cautioned the freshmen girls as to their dancing and their dress and in the women's assembly I advised the straight-arm hold as one remedy against the loose style of dancing" ("'U' dance Warning Has Quick Effect," Sunday, October 24, 1914, p. 2).

9. There's a tendency to see any kind of lively or rhythmically complex movement as practiced by African-American dancers as seductive or sexy. This reaction may well be one of our inheritances from the New England Puritans, if not other Protestant sects.

10. Despite the fact that movies were one of the sources that rendered vaudeville obsolete, some of the best performers in movies and radio had learned their skills in vaudeville: Milton Berle, W. C. Fields, Fred Allen, Eddie Cantor, Burns and Allen, to name just a few who may be remembered. I'm not old enough to have experienced vaudeville when it was in full bloom. But I was able to see during the 1940s remnants of a great tradition in the appearances of big bands, usually accompanied by a few solo acts, together with movies in a major central city theater in Philadelphia. Also, burlesque survived in a more traditional form until the 1950s.

11. The reader who would like an enlightening reading list can scarcely do better than the short "bibliographic essay" in Robert W. Snyder's *The Voice of the City: Vaudeville and Popular Culture in New York* (New York: Oxford University Press, 1989). The entire book (short as it is) will amply repay the reader.

12. Managers in the local vaudeville theaters would often—perhaps were obliged to—submit reports of how an act performed and how they went over. Some of these, from Keith-Albee theaters, survive at the University of Iowa Library, Special Collections. Alas, there are none of the Creole Band.

13. H. Morgan Prince, the singer and dancer, appeared in blackface. Whether the others did is not clear.

14. I've addressed this issue in some detail in "The Nineteenth-Century Origins of Jazz," in *Black Music Research Journal* 14:1 (spring 1994): 1–24.

15. Many of the early writers on jazz are now seen, with twenty-first-century lenses, to have had an "agenda," or, as someone once said, to have been "Ivy League Marxists."

16. The oral histories on file at the Hogan Jazz Archive of Tulane University, as well as most autobiographies of jazz musicians, are so anecdotal that the least reference to a concrete musical fact or phenomenon is cause for celebration. There are a number of reasons: first, there really isn't a commonly agreed on vocabulary for a lot of the things that go on in jazz; second, many musicians work instinctively without reflecting much on what they do; third, musicians, interviewers, and readers alike love good stories. Finally, it's very possible that we remember things, especially our own personal history, as a bunch of anecdotes, often shakily dated. It then falls to the historian's lot to put these anecdotes together in an often deceptively continuous history.

17. We should also bear in mind that prior to the 1950s, African-American musicians were barred de facto if not de jure from existing locals of the American Federation of Musician—with a few noteworthy exceptions. Accordingly, they formed their own locals within the A.F.M. Thus in Chicago, there was Local 10 (white) and Local 208 (African-American), not to speak of for a time a separate Polish musicians' union.

18. Someday the questions of when a player's characteristic musical voice is formed and to what degree it remains unchanged for the rest of a career will receive adequate treatment.

19. Perhaps Lindsay was the leader because, as was normal in New Orleans (and perhaps elsewhere), the fiddle player was automatically the leader. But he went home and some form of the original group began playing in South Side cabarets, supposedly under the leadership of Laurence Duhé. I believe that guitarist Louis Keppard was the original manager, again as was common in New Orleans.

20. Much of what has been said about phonograph records applies to piano rolls, which were an important factor in the music business until approximately 1930. At first, the rolls were punched by machine according to a score in front of the puncher —which didn't preclude some changes or additions. Finally, around 1910, so-called hand-played rolls appeared: the pressing of the keys by a live pianist made marks, which were then punched. Although such rolls still might have a published edition as their guide, the deviations could be great; more important, there didn't need to be a published original.

21. Reprinted in *Talking Machine Review* 10 (June 1971): 53–60.

22. There are a large number of good dance music recordings from late 1914 through 1916 and beyond by (Fred) Van Eps's Banjo Orchestra. Although the U.S. public had long been familiar with the sound of Van Eps's banjo, they still merit some attention.

23. It deserves to be more widely known that pianist Clarence Williams made a trial cylinder recording of his new song hit "Brown Skin, Who You For?," in 1916, that it was sent to Columbia in New York, then recorded for that label by their in-house studio band. Why Williams, Georgia Davis, and A. J. Piron weren't invited to New York to make the record is a question we can't answer, except that it would have been a real "stretch" in terms of what was usual for the time. And maybe it wasn't that good a trial recording.

24. Largely neglected for decades was a huge number of recordings made for sale to the European "ethnic" communities of our larger cities. See Richard Spottswood, *Ethnic Music on Records* [Music in American Life] (Urbana: University of Illinois Press, 1990).

Chapter 1

1. I had the privilege of many conversations with Clotile Palao Wilson, Jimmy's daughter, whose memories were vivid and consistent. I also spoke with his widow, Armontine, who also answered questions addressed to her by Clotile at my behest. Both helped me to imagine a living person in a way neither press clippings nor photographs could.

2. Felix Palao and Rebecca Spriggs were married October 19, 1878, at the Holy Name of Mary Church in Algiers. The family bible gives October 18 and St. Mary's Church in the French Quarter, the archbishop's church.

3. It is customary to refer to jazz musicians by a nickname, no doubt because it seems to fit the informality of the music. As a matter of historical methodology, it is always important to record the full name of a person, including middle initials, but this doesn't oblige us to use it. The family bible in question was a wedding gift from Felix Palao to his son and his wife, Rebecca Spriggs. The baptismal register entry from Holy Name of Mary Church for James gives the form (in the margin) of James Florestan, where the bible has Florestan James.

4. The card gives 5485 Woodlawn Avenue, Chicago, as his home address and lists his instruments as "jazz violin," tenor banjo, C melody and tenor saxophone. A copy can be found in HJA. According to my understanding of the Palao family's various moves, this card must date from shortly before Jimmy's death in 1925.

5. (1870 FC, New Orleans, 5th District, dwelling 1164) As is often the case with census data, this information is somewhat at odds with that provided by the 1880 census, when James was recorded as a 42-year-old railroad cook, Clara 46, Rebecca 21, Harriet 17, M. Louisa 12, Clara 8, and Ernestine 6 (1880 FC, 15th Ward, enum. district 89, p. 2).

6. The accuracy of a diagnosis of epilepsy more than a century ago is surely to be questioned and more particularly that one might die from the condition. Of course, the condition might have resulted from a brain tumor, concussion, meningitis, or a similar disease. In any event, the chance that someone with epilepsy will have an epileptic child is thought to be very slim.

7. It is possible that the mother of some of these children was someone other than Madeleine Perrault (probably more completely Marie Madeleine Perrault), a question that is in principle resolvable by delving into baptismal records.

8. John McCusker, "The Onward Brass Band and the Spanish American War," *The Jazz Archivist* 13 (1998–99): 24–35.

9. Felix's interest in his son's education can't have involved much ordinary schooling. Surviving postcards from Jimmy show him to have had little grasp of conventional English spelling and grammar.

10. Alternatively, Palao might have started Albert out on a widely distributed publication entitled "The ABC of music, or, Easy solfeggi, to which is added a short and easy method of vocalization," issued by a wide variety of publishers during the later nineteenth century. (See OCLC WorldCat.)

11. This could have been the proximate cause of Armontine Palao's deciding to leave New Orleans for Los Angeles. In his interview of September 25, 1959, Albert

said that Joe Palao, in addition to working at the funeral home since he (Joe) was a boy, also played the trumpet and lived on St. Peter Street. I've not made the requisite city directory and phone book search.

12. Cornetist Johnny Lala, born in 1894, stated that the prohibition against brass instruments in the District lasted only three years. Alas, he didn't state the years [HJA interview]. Marquis, in his biography of Buddy Bolden, cites a 1907 police report in which the proprietors of Nancy Hanks's saloon at Marais and Iberville (Ada Hayes and John Exnicious) had been issued a permit allowing singing with cornet and band, also for electrical piano (Marquis, *In Search of Buddy Bolden,* p. 59). Given the deterioration in Bolden's mental state by 1907, it seems unlikely that he would have been playing there then.

13. HJA, Interview of August 11, 1959.

14. This locale was known variously as the 101 Ranch, then the 102 Ranch, after being taken over by Billy Phillips. At some point it was also called The Entertainers, and I believe that as early as 1896, if not before, it was called—after its street number— The 28 or possibly Big 28. On this last point, there's some unclarity, with R&S locating it between Custom House and Canal Streets.

15. The instrument would be more properly called an E-flat alto valve trombone, to judge from the illustrations from a Lyon & Healy instrument catalogue of ca. 1912–1914. One roster for the Pacific Brass Band as given by Charlie Love comprised Joe Lizard, Bobo Lewis (married to Love's cousin Henrietta) on bass horn, George Hooker (cornet), George Sims (baritone), Buddy Johnson (trombone), George Davis (bass drum), Duke Simpson (snare drum), Dude Gabriel (clarinet), Palao (alto), with Vincent joining them occasionally as a substitute. A more detailed roster of this organization, said to date from the 1880s, appears in an interview with Milton Martin from 1964 (HJA). Tom Albert, present during this interview, stated that Vincent was at first a routiner (i.e., playing by rote or ear), then taught by Albert to read music, and further that Vincent would accompany Nootzie Reuben to the latter's lessons with a musician from the French Opera and thus gain free instruction—until the teacher caught on.

16. Johnson mostly appears with his unhelpful nickname of Buddy, but by putting together clues from various sources, it seems that his given name was Edward, that his barber shop was at 1204 Teche and his home at 1405 Nunez, both in Algiers and only two or three blocks apart.

17. Armontine Palao recalled an incident when Jimmy told her to wait outside a dance hall while he went in to speak to Bolden. Clotile Palao assured me that her mother had not read any New Orleans guide books or works on jazz history. There are indications that Bolden's first instrument was the accordion, so it's conceivable that when he wanted to pick up the cornet he would have sought some instruction in (at least) basic fingering and embouchure, which Palao as a sometime brass player would have been equipped to provide.

18. Sidney Desvigne contributed two important photographs to *Jazzmen,* reproduced after p. 32. One of Keppard in a jauntily cocked derby is inscribed "Compliments of Fred Keppard, Star Cornettist Creole Ragtime Band" (see fig 1.8). The other is of George Baquet, inscribed "With sincere good wishes to Emanuel Perez From

George F. Baquet, Aug. 20, 1915" (see fig 1.5). Desvigne was the source of some of the most important New Orleans–related photographs in *Jazzmen*. Where are they now?

19. HJA has an invaluable collection of 4 x 6 note cards gleaned from reading the *New Orleans Item*, which includes a number of references to bands at District dance halls during the first decade of the century. They are predominantly small bands of about four players.

20. R&S, p. 147. On a Man Creole Cato, see HJA, Tom Albert interview, September 25, 1959. The second document accompanying the photo gives the circumstances of a break-in during which the photograph was torn, unfortunately mutilating the image of Palao's face.

21. The photograph is from HJA, cataloged as Buddy Johnson's band, but its rather poor condition precludes reproduction.

22. Although one is justified in thinking that African-American performers might earn perhaps one-half the wage of "mainstream" musicians—something that seems to have been true in the '20s and '30s, for example—this may not have been true in New Orleans. One notes bitter complaints in the 1920s from white musicians in the musicians' union that black bands were being hired in preference to their own.

23. See Lawrence Gushee, "The Nineteenth-Century Origins of Jazz," *Black Music Research Journal* 14:1 (Spring 1994): 1–24. In this article, I failed to point out—indeed I didn't know—that the Sanborn fire insurance map for 1896 (sector 124) showed *three* "Negro Dance Halls" at the intersection of Custom House (now Iberville Street) and N. Franklin, with another only one house removed.

24. The couple had evidently separated, since Armontine recalled storing the furniture in one room while she lived with "an old lady." A James Pelayo, musician, probably to be identified with James Palao, is found in Soards's 1913 city directory living in the Seventh Ward at 2204 Annette Street (at about Miro Street). The information for this would have been collected in late 1912 or early 1913 (after his wife's departure for Los Angeles).

25. The publisher, H. Kirkus Dugdale, of Washington, D.C., was in effect a vanity publisher, responsible for an enormous number of copyrights around this time. Although he probably deserves the derogatory epithet "song shark," it's possible that in 1911 New Orleans, an African-American musician would have found it extremely difficult to be published by one of the local music houses (Werlein, for example).

26. We here give him for the first and last time the correct accents that his name would have in French.

27. The instructions to census enumerators read "Be particularly careful in reporting the class *mulatto*. The word is here generic and includes quadroons, octoroons, and all persons having any perceptible trace of African blood. Important scientific results depend upon the correct determination of this class in schedules 1 and 5." See *Twenty Censuses: Population and Housing Questions, 1790–1980*, U.S. Department of Commerce, Bureau of the Census, October 1979. One observes that this instruction is not matched with one applied to persons "having any perceptible trace of White (or Chinese, etc.) blood."

28. *IF*, December 31, 1898. The instrumentation of the orchestra was a bit odd,

with ten violins, one each of viola, 'cello, and contrabass, three cornets, one clarinet, a trombone, piano (Nickerson's young daughter, Camille), and drums. No names of compositions were given.

29. Why did he return? Let it be duly noted that in the 1910 census (taken on April 21) Baquet was living at 1325 St. Peter Street with his 24-year-old wife, Agnes, born in New Orleans of a father from South Carolina and a mother from Virginia. They had been married four years. Agnes's niece, Mrs. George Henderson Jr. (see HJA, interview with Geo. L. Henderson, Jr., May 3, 1961) asserted that George deserted her aunt, who "died of grief" around 1915.

30. The item reads "George Baqie sends regards to Roscoe & Holland's Minstrels (an alternative name for Richards & Pringle's Georgia Minstrels) and Frank Clermont." Moret's band may have been the continuation of the Excelsior Band.

31. *DB*, December 15, 1940, pp. 10, 26. This passage appears in Marquis, p. 99, as a quotation but is inexactly transcribed.

32. *La Nouvelle Orléans, Capitale du Jazz* (New York: Editions de la Maison Française, 1946), p. 140. Clarinetist Emile Barnes (1892–1970) also maintained that he had been offered and turned down the job.

33. The title was expanded for the Fourth of July all-night ball to "Johnson's Imperial Band of Los Angeles and New Orleans." That Baquet recalled an exact date suggests that he had a scrapbook or date book at hand when preparing his talk. It's also possible that the new name was chosen at a time when cornetist Emanuel Perez was expected to join the group.

34. *Jazzmen*, section of photographs following p. 33. On August 15, 1915, the band was opening the season at the Columbia Theater, Davenport, Iowa. The photo is drastically cropped, so that information regarding the photographer is missing. Others were photographed at other times wearing a tie pin of the same design, for example, Fred Keppard and Louis Delille. See photographs in the liner notes to Smithsonian Collection R020, "The Legendary Freddie Keppard," and below.

35. For a reason I cannot devine, John Steiner, the eminent jazz historian and collector, always wrote Vincent's name as "Vinçon."

36. E.D. 141, sheet 3. Vincent's death certificate confirms his father's name as Henry Vincent, and his date of birth as July 25, 1883. The 1880 census identifies Henry, age 42, and Caroline, age 45, and the infant, Edward, 10 months of age, born in September.

37. Vincent's World War I draft registration gave his date of birth as July 3, 1879, listing Amelia Vincent as his wife. At the time (September 12, 1918—thus after the breakup of the band) they were living at 3516 Wabash Avenue, Chicago. Vincent listed his occupation as "musician & actor" and his employer as Vergil Williams, 521 East 31st Street. Since this date was provided directly by the registrant, I believe we should accept it, barring further research.

38. "Gigi" was pronounced with hard *g*'s according to Bill Russell. Apparently, Russell wrote down his notes only in April 1944, which could account for their disjointed and highly incomplete character. Disconcertingly, he pops up in a few sources as "Leon Williams." There was such a person in show business between the late 1890s and 1918 at least, but he's clearly not the New Orleans guitarist.

39. This information comes from his death certificate and from his World War I draft registration. The former gives 1885 as his date of birth, the latter is a year earlier. Bayou Sara—which appears to have disappeared from official road maps and authoritative atlases—was on the Mississippi, very close to St. Francisville in West Feliciana Parish.

40. String bassist Steve Brown, in an interview of April 22, 1958 (HJA), thought that a member of the Creole Band lived around 6th and Laurel streets and held rehearsals there. This was only ten blocks from the Dryades Street address.

41. As nearly as can be reconstructed from an incomplete survey of extant records, Norwood Williams's mother, Emily, rather than the Emmaline of his death certificate, had been married for five years to Albert Wethers, a plasterer. Of her five living children, three were listed as stepchildren of Wethers: daughter Bell, born in 1875; Norwood, born in August 1884; and Maxwell, born in 1878. In 1910, Norwood was given as head of the household, although his mother was living with them, having reverted to the name of Williams. His sister, Belle Coyle, was widowed without children, and with sister Ophelia, age 26, and brother Charles, age 23, made up a family of five persons.

42. Mr. and Mrs. Williams had at various times operated the Elite Hotel at 1217 South Central Avenue in Los Angeles, advertising it as "for the profession," i.e., professional entertainers. In fact, Williams died at that address, although I don't know if he was still operating a hotel when Russell spoke with him.

43. In a 1961 interview with Louis Keppard, Bill Russell took pains to note that the name was pronounced as in French, i.e., with relatively even accentuation and silent *d*, rather than the more assertive English fashion, rhyming with "leopard." This latter pronunciation is more in line with such frequently encountered misspellings as Keppert or Keppit. Nevertheless, Louis, Jr., said that his father was a light-skinned Creole, was French, and looked Italian. Louis himself was quite dark with features that strike some viewers as a blend of African and Native American.

44. Jones is the mother's maiden name according to Fred's death certificate. Brother Louis told Andy Ridley that her maiden name was Peterson, although there were cousins named Jones (letter to LG from Ridley, September 12, 1987). "Peterson" is also the name on the birth records of the three children.

45. The 1900 Federal Census has November 1889 as his date of birth. Louis's recollection that 13 months separated the brothers must also be in error—it was two years.

46. In the interview collected by Bill Russell on January 19, 1961 (now part of HJA) Louis's birth date is given as February 2, 1889. Louis stated that all three children were born at 2007 Customhouse Street. Such a number, however, postdates these dates of birth, using the new system of house numbers that went into effect ca. 1896. City directories from 1896 and 1897 record cook Louis Keppard as living at 2026 Customhouse. For what it's worth, this should be between Prieur and Johnson streets.

47. John Keppard's occupation as a coffee house keeper can be linked to the occupation of Louis Keppard, Sr., as cook. Louis, Jr., stated that his father was the head cook at a well-known saloon and restaurant, Fred Bertrand's, at Canal and Dauphine.

48. Be it noted, as "Louis Keppler." But his occupation and place of residence leave no question that he was the father of Fred, Mary, and Louis.

49. This was actually the house of Martin Joseph Gabriel, father of Martin Manuel Gabriel (1898–). Martin Joseph played accordion, at first, then cornet, and founded and led the National Jazz Band (unattributed memoir in the New Orleans Jazz Club Collections of the Louisiana State Museum). After 1903 (approximately) the Gabriels moved to Miro Street between Conti and St. Louis, with Fred Keppard playing violin in Martin Joseph's band at a place on Franklin St. run by a man named Kizer (Kaiser?). Kizer wanted Martin Joseph to play cornet, in emulation of Emanuel Perez, so he took some lessons with Alcibiades Jeanjacques, who also gave some lessons to young Keppard. See Larry Gabriel, *Daddy Plays Old-time New Orleans Jazz* [published by the author, 1987], p. 21.

50. "Old man" doesn't seem like a particularly apt designation for the Adolph Alexander, Sr., recorded by the 1910 Federal Census, at 1839 St. Peter Street, as a thirty-four-year-old shoemaker. Charters, *Jazz: New Orleans*, devotes a paragraph to him as "an early orchestra musician"—on cornet and baritone horn—who played with the Golden Rule Orchestra and sometimes with the orchestras Superior and Imperial, in addition to the brass bands Excelsior and Onward. He is also said to have arranged two tunes for a 1927–1928 Papa Celestin recording session. He died in 1936.

51. Louis Keppard's memories are inconsistent on a number of points, particularly the question as to which were Fred's beginning instruments. In the 1961 HJA interview, he states at one point that accordion was first, then corrects himself and says it was first a harmonica, then mandolin. Also, old man "Ba-Boy" (or "Bour-Boy," see above) who elsewhere is mentioned as giving Keppard pointers on violin, is especially credited with helping the youngster out on accordion. "Ba-Boy" ought eventually to be identifiable, in that he walked with a crutch and played cornet as well as accordion.

52. University of New Orleans, Special Collections. The year 1907 is mentioned by Eddie Dawson as the date when Keppard organized the band (Bechet, *Treat It Gentle*, p. 115; see also *Footnote* 4:2, p. 30f).

53. Except perhaps this: when Keppard left for California in the spring of 1914, his place in the Olympia was taken by Joe Oliver. It was probably this band that played the so-called scrip dances—the admission could be paid in student body scrip—held in the Tulane University gymnasium. Dr. Edmond Souchon recalled their great success, so presumably their music was in tune with what college undergraduates wanted. Although the exact dates are unknown, the time must have been ca. 1915–1916. See Bechet, *Treat It Gentle*, passim, and Charters, *Jazz: New Orleans*, s.v. Keppard, Oliver, Piron, Steve Lewis.

54. Ralph Collins, *New Orleans Jazz: A Revised History* (New York: Vantage Press, 1996), p. 195. While this agressively revisionist and quirky work is sometimes resoundingly wrong either in its facts or interpretations, the author, nevertheless, was close to Manetta and is not to be automatically dismissed.

55. Lee Collins, *Oh, Didn't He Ramble* (Urbana: University of Illinois Press, 1974), p. 40, remembered the name of Fred's girlfriend, when he was playing in the District, as Albertine McKay. There exists a death certificate (no. 149,638) for Thelma Keppard, 1813 St. Ann Street, 27 days old, who died of cerebral meningitis on May 24, 1910. (The census enumeration began on April 15.)

56. Arthur Briggs, who would have heard Keppard in Chicago or New York prior to his leaving for Europe in 1919 (undated interview with James Lincoln Collier for the Smithsonian Institution on file at IJA) emphasizes some of these technical points. It strikes me as possible that Fred's practice of hiding his valves with a handkerchief while playing parades, mentioned by Armstrong (typescript for *Satchmo*, IJS) might have been designed to conceal his half-valving. This may well be a pervasive myth: it is said that the klezmer clarinetist Naftule Brandwine turned his back to the audience so that other players couldn't pick up on his special fingerings.

57. Alan Lomax, *Mr. Jelly Roll* (New York: Grove Press, 1950), p. 116: "He became to be the greatest hot trumpeter in existence. He hit the highest and the lowest notes on a trumpet that anybody outside of Gabriel ever did. He had the best ear, the best tone, and the most marvelous execution I ever heard and there was no end to his ideas; he could play one chorus eight or ten different ways." See Appendix 5 for more on Keppard from Jelly Roll.

58. *Mr. Jelly Roll*, p. 144 f.

59. Much of the information on which this sketch is based comes from an interview conducted in the summer of 1959, with supplementary data gleaned from *IF*.

60. Prince still had a 1907 or 1908 photograph of Fer-Don's 10–piece band led by cornetist George Bryant, taken in Eureka, California. Prince is holding what appears to be a mellophone.

61. My guess would be that the principal reason to rehearse was to make the "Uncle Joe" or "old man" routine that Prince would surely have known from his time with Mahara's or the Black Patti show work with the music provided by the band. Also, the ensemble singing by the band might have needed some polishing.

62. She apparently married violinist Jimmy Bell at some point and was known on occasion as Princess Bell. An item from the *Def* of January 29, 1921, datelined Vancouver, British Columbia, shows her billed at the Lodge Cafe as "Olive Bell."

63. *Def* of June 25, 1921 tells us that Mrs. Madeline Prince, wife of Henry Morgan Prince, was much improved after a serious illness requiring hospitalization and was back at the Elite Hotel. This hotel, by the way, was operated by Norwood Williams and his wife.

64. The 1900 Federal Census declared him to have been born in August, 1876 while his World War I draft registration (Federal Archives and Records Center, Atlanta, GA, Record Group 163, Local Board Division no. 3, Chicago) gave August 10, 1874 as his birthday. Bill registered at the final registration of World War I, September 12, 1918. He would not have had to register at all if he had been born in August 1872. His 1939 application for a Social Security account initially had had August 10, 1876, as Bill's date of birth, but the the year was corrected to 1872, which would have qualified him for a pension somewhat earlier. Taking everything into account, I believe that 1874 is the most reasonable date. The 1920 Federal Census, however, lists him as 40 years old (City of Chicago, e.d. 122, at 3920 Indiana Avenue and e.d. 59 at 220 31st Street), but I assume this might have been carelessness on the part of the census enumerator, or else an attempt by Bill to make himself not quite so much older than his 30-year-old wife Ada.

The Chicago musicians' union, local 10–208, was sufficiently convinced that in

1972 Bill had reached one hundred, as they sent him a bonus check, then a death benefit. The former presumably helped pay for an elaborate cake as seen in the photograph, figure 7.9 above.

65. For the 1880 census, see Alabama, Montgomery Co., e.d. 130, p. 49. For the Social Security information: Form SS-5, Application for Social Security Account Number, for William Manuel Johnson, SS no. 328–14–4426, May 23, 1939.

66. James was known as "Uncle Bookie" to Bessie's family and lived in Los Angeles. David's full name was probably Tunney David Johnson, and during the '50s he, Martin, and Robert appear to have lived in Portland, Oregon.

67. See Louis Armstrong, *Satchmo*, p. 238: "Bill Johnson had the features and even the voice of an ofay, or southern, white boy at that, with an unlimited sense of humor." In a letter of Jan. 1, 1959 Bill wrote: "I had a white and very prominent father. My mother being also very light, I turned out a 'white man.' the rest of the family were dark, tho Anita [i.e., Bessie] was light-skinned to a degree, though not like me."

68. The William Johnson listed in the 1894 CD as residing at Camp Nicholls, Bayou St. John near Esplanade, is not our quarry. The biennial report of the camp—which served as the Soldiers' Home of Louisiana—for 1894–1896 lists a William Johnson of the C.S. Navy, who entered on February 15, 1889, and died on February 9, 1895.

69. See *EJB* 1945, s.v. Bill Johnson. My supposition is that the information in these capsule biographies came from questionnaires circulated by Paul Eduard Miller, perhaps even interviews. It is further stated that Bill began playing bass in 1900, and played in a trio at Tom Anderson's Annex between 1903 and 1909.

70. See *IF*, December 17, 1898, and the *New York Clipper* of December 10, in the "Miscellaneous" column. The Puggsley group received brief mention in the notes by Doug Seroff to "Gospel Arts Day" at Fisk University, June 19, 1988. My thanks to Lynn Abbott for sending me a copy.

71. *IF*, July 11, 1908, p. 5, "A Successful Orchestra of Hattiesburg, Miss."

72. One can't be dogmatic about the exact date when Johnson changed over from guitar to string bass. In any event, in his conversations with Bill Russell in 1938, he said his adoption of bass pizzicato was the result of a happy accident. One night in Shreveport, his bow broke, forcing him to pluck. In expanding his notes, Russell added—presumably filling in a detail which he hadn't been able to write down—"The effect was so novel and added so much more swing and flexibility to his playing, that he took to slapping his bass entirely thereafter." To be sure, slapping isn't the same as picking.

73. *EJB*, 1945 (based probably on information given by Bill to Chicago jazz writer Paul Eduard Miller) gives 1903 to 1909 as the dates. The 1903 date presents no problem, as Tom Anderson's Annex opened in 1901, but 1909 contradicts much other information on Johnson's early career. We learn from Charters, *Jazz: New Orleans*, p. 10, that valve trombonist Ed Jones also sat in with this band. Jimmy Palao's widow and daughter state that Palao taught Johnson to play the double bass in California, but this may simply refer to some lessons in note-reading.

74. Charters, *Jazz: New Orleans*, p. 33. Several books (R&S, *EJB* 1945) mention that Bill also played with such brass bands as the Peerless, the Excelsior, the Uptown, and the Eagle. This seems rather careless as the Peerless and the Eagle are not known to

have been street bands (there is an early Eagle band from the 1890s—see William J. Schafer, *Brass Bands and New Orleans Jazz* [Baton Rouge: Louisiana State University Press, 1977]—but there is not known to be a link between this and Dusen's band) The Uptown is recorded only in the brief biographies of Bill Johnson in the sources above.

75. R&S, p. 64.

76. Although it was designated a "tonk" by Pops Foster's autobiography, p. 19, this derogatory term doesn't fit the rather elaborate establishment for which a construction contract and architectural drawings were filed by Anderson's notary.

77. The 1900 census is a bit at odds with this, assuming that the black male musician Thomas Brown at 334 South Liberty Street is the same person. He was born in July 1869, had been married twice, and was living with his wife Amelia and his son Mouton [*sic*].

78. A connection between Washington and Johnson is demonstrated by a request in the January 30, 1915 issue of *IF*, that Charles Washington of New Orleans wanted to hear from William Johnson of the "New Orleans Orchestra."

79. Preston Jackson, "Chicago News," in *Jazz Hot*, no. 5 (September–October 1935): 15; the passion for concertina reported in a box of typescript notes from Bill Russell, formerly kept at HJA.

80. R&S, p. 90.

81. Lawrence Gushee, "How the Creole Band Came to Be," *Black Music Research Journal* 8:1 (1988): 94.

82. The Main Event was advertised in weekly issues of the *Referee* in October and November, 1909. The Oakland city directory for 1910 lists the business as North and Johnson, cigars, with Johnson living at 1669 Tenth Street. A year later the business is listed in the name of Gaston E. Durggan. Remarkably, Durg[g]an's home address is the same as Johnson's in the previous year. Not incidentally, the coproprietor of the business is Robert "Kid" North, a character in the sporting life who figures in Jelly Roll Morton's biography.

83. "End of 1912," Gushee, "How the Creole Band," p. 94.

84. In a letter from 1959 Johnson very strongly asserted his role in starting Keppard out in 1906, perhaps because of the tendency of jazz history to give to Keppard the credit for leadership or management of the Creole Band.

Chapter 2

1. The dating of these photographs has been a matter of much discussion. The Bolden orchestra, originally thought to be from 1895, has been moved up to ca. 1905. (See Alden Ashforth, *Annual Review of Jazz Studies 3,* "The Bolden Band Photo—One More Time.") It is also believed that he normally had a violinist in the band, DeeDee Brooks or another (see the tentative discussion in Donald Marquis, *In Search of Buddy Bolden* [Baton Rouge: Louisiana State University Press, 1978], p. 78).

The Robichaux orchestra photograph has also been incautiously dated to 1896. The style of dress makes me think it should be later. (Extant manuscript orchestrations at HJA are for a smaller ensemble.) We know that John Robichaux received regular mailings from the principal publishers of dance orchestrations and that, consequently, his band consisted of a minimal force required to give them justice. For example, orchestrations often have two violin parts and two cornet parts, thus Robichaux's roster had pairs of violins and cornets. On the other hand, many published orchestrations of the time are written so that some subset of the full complement will be able to produce an acceptable rendition.

On either side of 1900, orchestrations are often advertised as being for ten (or eleven) instruments plus piano, with the piano part available for an additional fee. So the avoidance of pianos in New Orleans may merely reflect common American practice.

2. This group might conceivably be what Joe Mares, Sr., had in mind in a letter he wrote to *Jazz Journal*, December 1953, as cited by Roy Carew in the same periodical in December 1957. According to Mares, around 1885 Negroes formed "combos" of clarinet, cornet, trombone, and bull-fiddle, which jazzed up popular tunes of the day.

3. Here the race of the musician would quite likely play a role. Would African-Americans have been welcome at the Colonial, the McVickers, or the North American Hippodrome, to mention three vaudeville theaters in the Loop where the Creole Band played, not to speak of the smaller neighborhood houses such as the American, Lincoln, Wilson Avenue, Logan Square, Windsor, and so forth?

4. Frederic Ramsey, Jr., "Baquet and his Mob 'Carved' King Bolden!" *DB*, January 1, 1941, pp. 6, 19. This is the second part of an article that had begun in the previous issue. Much of this chapter is taken over directly from my article, "How the Creole Band Came to Be," *Black Music Research Journal* 8 (1988): 83–100. One might incautiously think that Baquet was talking about the 1908 band firsthand. This wasn't so; quite possibly he was simply repeating what Johnson had told him.

5. *IF*, July 11, 1908, p. 5.

6. Hattiesburg *Daily News*, April 4, 1908. *IF* for April 18 reported that the band had just finished a three weeks' engagement at the store, additionally singling out Prof. W. B. Jones as the manager.

7. *IF*, July 1 and July 15, 1911. It seems likely that the Mrs. Johnson is Hattie Johnson and her son, Robert.

8. The two interviews, from December 5 and 15, 1958, are held at HJA. The verbatim transcript was published in *The New York Times Oral History Project: New Orleans Jazz*, reel 2. It seems that no one thought to go to Pass Christian to speak with Handy's father.

9. In a postcard from George Blacker to me, dated November 13, 1987, the highly regarded expert on cylinders stated that a home-recorded cylinder could withstand frequent playings.

10. Al Rose, *Miss Lulu White de Basin Street, Nouvelle Orléans* (Paris: Gaston Lachurié, 1991), p. 153, reproduces the record of purchase of the lot on which Mahogany Hall was constructed, dated July 3, 1897. The three-story mansion of thirty-seven rooms (to accept Al Rose's figure) was already built. Johnson might have been referring to Lulu's earlier establishment at 166 Customhouse Street, opened in 1891.

11. Jelly Roll Morton recalled that when playing for "naked dances" at Emma Johnson's Circus House, a screen was placed "around the players to satisfy guests." But Morton foiled the scheme by making a hole in the screen with a knife (Jelly Roll Mor-

ton: Miscellaneous Manuscript Materials, Library of Congress, Music 0332 [microfilm]).

12. Edited by Paul Eduard Miller (New York: A. S. Barnes, 1945), p. 197.

13. R&S, 1 ed., p. 21; Samuel B. Charters, *Jazz: New Orleans, 1885–1957* (Belleville, N.J.: Walter C. Allen, 1958), p. 10. According to the 1910 Federal Census, Thomas P. Brown, "Musician / String Band," was 44 years old, born in Pennsylvania (e.d. 34, sheet 1B). The most tantalizing recollection in the HJA interviews came from guitarist (later bassist) Eddie Dawson (b. 1884), who remembered playing at Tom Anderson's with Brown on mandolin, C. C. Washington on a second guitar, George Jones on bass, and Frank Keeling on cornet. This would have been in all likelihood around 1910 or 1911.

14. At one point, Bill recalled that his cousin was in Los Angeles.

15. For a detailed and lively account of the excursions along the Gulf Coast operated by the L&N, see R. J. Carew, "New Orleans Recollections," *Record Changer*, December 1943, p. 14f.

16. The somewhat garbled form of the story that Frederic Ramsey, Jr., published in *Jazzways*, p. 36, includes some details found nowhere else: "A New Orleans newspaper threw a big party for publicity men in that year, and in the group there was a promoter from up north."

17. Frank J. Gillis and John W. Miner, eds., *Oh Didn't He Ramble* (Urbana: University of Illinois Press, 1974), p. 4 f. The information in this work is at odds with the 1900 census, Bay Saint Louis, Miss., Ward 3, Hancock Street. It might take a lot of investigation to resolve the issues.

18. The Tramps Social Club is mentioned a goodly number of times in the pages of *IF* from the end of 1907 through 1908. In February 1908, they published a roster of 33 members, and describe themselves as an organization of performers. As a working hypothesis, S. Moran may well be the Samuel Moran, musician, listed in the 1913 city directory at 204 South Franklin St., and E. A. Jones may be the valve trombonist mentioned in Charters, *Jazz: New Orleans*, p. 10, as sitting in with the string trio at Tom Anderson's led by Tom Brown.

19. The adjective "obscure" is justified, I think, by the absence of any mention of the Hattiesburg excursion either in John Chilton's much consulted *Who's Who of Jazz* or *The New Grove Dictionary of Jazz*.

20. Not in the *Hattiesburg Daily News* which began publication on May 1, 1907, or the *Times-Picayune*, the supposed sponsor of the trip. The Great Southern Hotel was finished in 1902 (or 1903). It was situated at the base of a mile-long pier, and had some 300 feet of frontage on the Gulf. A handsome brochure published in 1903 shows rail connections, not only from Chicago via the Illinois Central but also from Boston, New York, Philadelphia, and Washington. Since apparently through sleepers from Memphis to Gulfport were in service from 1904 on, perhaps the event in 1907 was inauguration of Pullman service from the East Coast. This would have linked with the G & S I at Hattiesburg. According to timetables ca. 1911, the trip from Jackson to Gulfport, although only some 160 miles, took more than seven hours, indicating a roadbed not permitting higher speed.

21. In an interview with Bill Russell, Ollie "Dink" Johnson, Bill's half brother, stated that Coycault was already in California and joined the band there. Another complica-

tion is that during repeated questioning in 1959, Bill insisted that the cornetist's name was Carquet, not Coycault. (The interviewer spoke French fluently.) Neither the given nor the family name of Patio are certain, but for consistency's sake I'll use "Harold Patio," unless in a quotation.

22. Bisbee was the center of intense copper mining activity. Much mining also went on in Yuma and surrounds: gold, silver, and to a lesser extent lead and tungsten.

23. Jazz Oral History Project, sponsored by the Smithsonian Institution, now on file at the Institute of Jazz Studies, cassette 5, p. 18. A parallel version was collected by Tom Stoddard from Spikes in 1972 and was published in his *Jazz on the Barbary Coast*, p. 56f. (In 1907 and 1908, Spikes was living in Los Angeles but paid his brother, Tom, a visit of several months.) This version doesn't mention Keppard and is more accurate with regard to the trombonist: "They had a valve trombone player named Padio and he came from New Orleans with them. He went to Vancouver, British Columbia, and I hear he died there." Admiring words were bestowed on Padio by Jelly Roll Morton. When he needed a trombonist for a gig in Vancouver in 1920, he sent to Oakland for his friend Patio, *MJR,* p. 159. My thanks to Mark Miller for providing a full given name (Harold) for him, from the Vancouver Musicians' Union ledgers.

24. Local Board for Division no. 3, Chicago, Serial no. 4494, September 12, 1918.

25. Horace Eubanks and Horace George are known jazz clarinetists and poor candidates for Mayme's memories. I mention as a long shot a Horace G. Woodward, trap drummer, whom *Def,* Dec. 22, 1917, reported as having died during the year (in Macon, Ga.).

26. At the time Russell spoke with her, she was operating a one-girl brothel on Third Street close to the train station. Johnson's draft card gives her address as Clyde Street, a block away from Third Street and even closer to the station. This suggests that the Mamie Johnson found by the 1920 census enumerator at 276 Ritch Street—close to the two addresses just mentioned—is the same person. She was a Louisiana-born mulatto, 38 years old, serving as housekeeper for William Foster.

27. The publisher was Bruce Humphries, Inc., in Boston, with a copyright date of April 25, 1945, under the registration number A187568. There was, apparently, no renewal. The book was announced in *Publishers' Weekly* for June 16, 1945, p. 2385. No reviews have been located.

28. He also used "William Monger" when he rented a post office box in Marble Falls, Texas, ca. 1958.

29. Not as the crow flies, but going west to Gulfport, then north to Hattiesburg.

30. Perhaps the most comprehensive source is the database of some two million U.S. place names <http://geonames.usgs.gov/>, although I did locate a listing for New Mexico that purported to include "cities, flag stops, post offices, settlements, towns, villages, trading points" past and present.

31. In his *Jazz on the Barbary Coast,* p. 134, Tom Stoddard cites this item, but with an unfortunate typographical error: "1917" for "1907." The holdings of this paper are extremely fragmentary, making any investigation of other related items from 1907–1908 impossible.

32. On the mixing of races: Oakland *Tribune,* October 5, 1920; Tom Stoddard, *Jazz on the Barbary Coast* (Chigwell, Essex: Storyville, 1982), p. 81.

33. *California Eagle*, October 9, 1915, January 29, 1916, and other dates around this time.

34. *International Musician*, issues of February and September 1920. The four musicians in common between the two lists are William Hoy, Oscar Holden, H. Patio, and Sydney Kelland. An entry from the ledger for Local 145 communicated to me by jazz writer and historian Mark Miller of Toronto reads "Harold Patio." Oscar Holden and Hoy's careers intersect with Jelly Roll Morton during his stay in the Pacific Northwest. A musician named Albert Paddio is listed in the 1899 New Orleans city directory at 3214 Saratoga Street, identical in name according to IF, December 27, 1919, with the trombonist playing at the Patricia in Vancouver, B.C., in 1919. I suspect that they are one and the same, also that further research will show that Harold and Albert are the same person.

35. *The Referee* 2:19 (October 1909): 12. The only run of this periodical is found in Special Collections of the University of California at Los Angeles library. It began publication in San Francisco in 1907 and after merging with a similar paper called *The Announcer* appeared at least until 1917. The coverage was strongly slanted toward boxing, and at least some weekly issues contained inserts of prizefight programs. Additionally, both papers included a lot of news of San Francisco and Oakland cabarets and dance halls and many ads. Finally, Los Angeles events receive notice.

36. Regarding the Arcade, see Phil Pastras, *Dead Man Blues* (Berkeley: University of California Press, 2001), pp. 39–43, complete with a photograph of the saloon.

37. One should probably say "half sister" and "half brother" for "sister" and "brother."

38. The Chinese lottery was a kind of variant of policy or "the numbers game," at the time enormously popular in California, if not elsewhere.

39. Frank Amacker recalled playing with Palao on the night of the Billy Philips-Harry Parker fracas, which would place Palao as still in New Orleans in April 1913. There's nothing unreasonable about this, although it's been observed that so many New Orleans musicians placed themselves in proximity to the gun battle that it must have been barely possible to move in the street.

40. Armontine Palao recalled that Williams was in Los Angeles when she came from New Orleans. In fact, city directories attest to his presence there from 1911. Norwood Williams in his 1940 interview with Bill Russell didn't mention Palao as a member of this group. For him the trio consisted of the Johnson brothers, Bill and Dink, along with Williams. He also stated that this trio (or quartet) played in the ring between boxing bouts.

41. There are indications that other musicians, for example clarinetists Emile Barnes and Louis Delille (who was later to join the band for the season of 1916–1917), cornetist Emanuel Perez, and trombonist Cornelius "Zue" Robertson had been asked to come to California before Baquet, Keppard, and Vincent. An account given by Jelly Roll Morton (Lomax, 1950, 116f. and 143f.) states that Bill Johnson, bankrolled by his sister Bessie, took over the band that Fred Keppard had organized for the Tuxedo dance hall after the killing of saloon keeper Billy Phillips in March 1913 (the actual date, not that given by Morton) and took it to California. According to Morton, the members of that band—which had been reduced from the usual seven pieces to five

for economic reasons—were Keppard, Baquet, and Vincent, accompanied by pianist Narcisse "Buddy" Christian and drummer Didi Chandler. While Morton may have been in New Orleans for brief periods between 1912 and 1914, his home base appears to have been Texas for much of the time, and his knowledge of events was probably secondhand at best or thirdhand.

42. Ramsey, "Baquet and His Mob."

43. "George Baquet . . . Address before the N. O. Jazz Club, April 17, 1948," *The Second Line*, September-October, 1965, p. 134 f. There are differences, mostly minor but some important, between the holograph draft of the speech, now in the N. O. Jazz Club collection at the Old Mint and the published version. Thanks to the curator, Steven Teeter, for sending me a copy of this. Such precise recall of the date makes one think that Baquet had brought a scrapbook along with him from Philadelphia. In any event, it parallels the account constructed by Goffin (*La Nouvelle-Orléans*, p. 139 ff.) on the basis of an interview with Big Eye Louis Delille. According to Delille, Jimmy Palao sent a telegram in care of Big 25, the musicians' hangout on Franklin Street, requesting that Keppard, Vincent, and Delille come to fill an engagement he had set up to play at the Rivers-Cross fight. Since Delille was then entangled with "une voluptueuse créole" he decided to stay in New Orleans, thus suggested Baquet as a replacement.

44. Bill Grauer, "Dixieland Clarinet," *RC*, August 1948, p. 11.

45. Would that matters were so relatively uncomplicated! Guitarist Norwood Williams claimed to be de facto business manager despite what was stated on the sole surviving business card, since he was the only member of the band who didn't drink a lot. He also claimed that a trio composed of himself and the Johnson brothers played at prizefights and that, hearing them, vaudeville magnate Alex Pantages asked them to send for additional musicians from New Orleans. The more usual story is that Pantages or his agents didn't hear the band until the August 11 Rivers-Cross bout. But he may have heard them more than once. The Williams interview is found in a transcription of miscellaneous materials collected by Bill Russell, no. 149 of the *NYT* microfilm, and also at HJA.

46. Beginning with Stearns, "The History of 'Swing' Music" (chap. 2), *DB*, August 1936, p. 6; this was republished, credited to *DB*, in their issue of August 15, 1940, p. 17. In between, it appeared in *Jazzmen*, between pp. 32 and 33 (JM); then Grauer & Keepnews, *Pictorial History of Jazz* (New York: Crown Publishers, 1955) PHJ, and R&S, p. 162. There are many other sources by now.

47. It's of course normal for the snare to be set up to the left of the bass drum and tilted inward so as to make it easily playable. Such tilting would make it effectively unplayable if by some extremely peculiar chance Dink Johnson placed his snare to the *right* of the bass drum. But this is shown to be clearly impossible, since the horizontally mounted cymbal would then be unplayable.

48. Landry is a quite common family name in New Orleans and the 1913 Soards' city directory lists three George Landrys. The handwriting seems close to that of the photograph inscribed by Baquet to Emanuel Perez published in *Jazzmen*.

49. The band may not have played loud, but other testimony, notably from Bill Johnson, tells us that Keppard was capable of exceptional volume, for example, in the-

ater engagements he could be so loud that the audience members in the first rows were prompted to move further back.

50. Howard's memories are found (among other sources) in an interview by Bill Russell of July 31, 1969, and in an oral history collected on May 8–9, 1978, by Patricia Willard and Buddy Collette for the Smithsonian Institution. A transcript is on deposit at IJS. The actual title—usually cited incorrectly—of the piece in question is *Egyptia*, an intermezzo written by Abe Olman in 1911. In the orchestration published by Will Rossiter, Chicago, and arranged by Harry L. Alford, the melody of the first strain is indeed allocated to clarinet in the low register. The piece is best known from Sidney Bechet's 1941 recording of it as "Egyptian Fantasy"—for which he claimed copyright, along with his friend John Reid.

51. December 1931, pp. 4 and 6. My thanks to Doug Caldwell, who passed on to me photocopies he had obtained from Lance Bowling.

52. Stephenson Avenue is today's Traction St. and 716 would be just past the intersection with Hewitt Street. This, in turn, was about a block away from Alameda and two blocks from Central Avenue and Third Street. Steve Isoardi, in his *Central Avenue Sounds* cites an article from the *California Eagle* for August 28, 1931, p. 10, which mentions four cabarets from ca. 1908, including the "Golden West . . . at Third street opposite Rev. Hill's church." (My thanks to Phil Pastras for directing my attention to this.)

53. See Phil Pastras, *Dead Man Blues*, Berkeley: University of California Press, 2001, pp. 89 f. and 121 f.

54. In an interview with Flournoy Miller in Los Angeles, February 8, 1965, conducted for the book by Marshall and Jean Stearns, *Jazz Dance*, we read the following: "Florence Mills had been with the Panama Trio and Johnson's Creole Band was playing out here. First time I ever saw a guitar in a band. I came back and told Weber it was the best band. They were picking the bass also—this was at the Santa Fe Café in L.A. Weber finally got them to come to New York. They had to get a girl to go with it. U. S. Thompson directed the band in this act—comedy. The show was called Tennessee Ten." [the interview is found among the miscellaneous papers assembled by the Stearnses for their book, now at IJS.] This passage seems to apply more to the Tennessee Ten and not the Creole Band, however. [See below in the discussion of the Creole Band's breakup in April–May 1917.] Be that as it may, the Santa Fe is mentioned in both *Def* and the *California Eagle* for February 1914 as managed by Rufus Hite and located at 733 East Third Street, or the corner of Third and Rose. This was only a block away from the Golden West. By November the cafe had been renamed the Cosmopolitan, still under Hite's management. In any event, it would have been easy for Miller to confuse the Santa Fe and the Golden West; or quite possibly the Creole Band played in both places. Miller's act started out at least by early 1911. In early 1914, they were in the East, but after an appearance at the Majestic, Chicago, in August, they wound up in California in September when they might conceivably have overlapped with the Creole Band.

55. WRC, Jazz Files, CA Notes, Folder 18.

56. *Los Angeles Record*, Saturday, July 25, 1914, p. 7.

57. *Record*, August 12, 1914, p. 9.

58. This contradicts the account constructed by Goffin (*La Nouvelle-Orléans*, p.

139 ff.) on the basis of an interview with Big Eye Louis Delille (or Nelson). According to Delille, Jimmy Palao had sent a telegram in care of the musicians' hangout, Big 25, requesting that Keppard, Vincent, and Delille come to Los Angeles to fill an engagement he had set up to play at the Rivers-Cross fight. Since Delille was at the moment entangled with "une voluptueuse créole" he decided to remain in New Orleans, thus suggested Baquet as a replacement. The problem with Goffin's account is characteristic of his entire book: while it conveys often exceptionally important information from a host of interviewees, it is obvious that in stitching together a full-fledged account from the data in his notes, Goffin constantly introduced errors and misleading assumptions—not to speak of mishearings of names, such as "Pantages Circus" for "Pantages Circuit."

59. Doubly interracial, perhaps, since Leach Cross, "The Fighting Dentist," was one of the best-known of a horde of Jewish boxers ca. 1910. His "real" name was Louis Wallach (1886–1957).

60. *The Announcer* 8:219 (January 31, 1914): 3.

61. Ramsey, "Baquet and His Mob," *DB*, January 1, 1941.

62. George Baquet, "Address to the New Orleans Jazz Club, April 17, 1948," *The Second Line* (September–October 1965). The collections of the club now are preserved at the Louisiana Museum's branch at The Old Mint, New Orleans, and have Baquet's autograph notes for his talk as well as his letter of March 3, 1948, offering Dr. Edmond Souchon his assistance in the activities of the club. These notes are nearly identical. One crucial point is different: the piece that Keppard played is called "in Mandalay" and not "Mandalay" as in the published version.

63. Fred Ramsey, Jr., "Vet Tells Story of the Original Creole Orchestra," *DB*, December 15, 1940, pp. 10, 26.

64. Harry Carr, "Disgusting Exhibition," *Los Angeles Times*, August 12, 1914, sec. 3, p. 1.

65. H. M. Walker, *Los Angeles Examiner*, August 12, 1914, sec. 2, p. 2.

66. Page 9 in the *Record*, and p. 12 in the *Tribune*, both on August 12.

67. Monday, August 17, 1914, p. 5.

68. The Moreland Motor Truck Company, founded around 1911, indeed had its base of operations in Los Angeles. Some intrepid researcher should have a look at the Society pages of various Los Angeles daily newspapers or a weekly such as *The Graphic*.

Chapter 3

1. This embroiders only slightly on George Baquet's story recounted above. It's important to observe that the plantation material came only after this addition, and that it was the music that captured Pantages' enthusiasm.

2. *California Eagle*, January 31, 1914.

3. This can be clearly seen only in the copy used for advertising in the December 27, 1917 issue of *Variety*.

4. *Los Angeles Times*, July 25, 1914, 2:6.

5. It's interesting that Trixie Friganza—of whom we will hear more later—was playing that week at the Orpheum.

6. *Los Angeles Tribune*, August 17, 1914 (Monday), p. 5.

7. *Los Angeles Tribune*, August 19, 1914 (Wednesday), p. 13, and *Oakland Enquirer*, September 10, 1914 (Thursday).

8. *Examiner*, Wednesday, August 19, 1914, 2:4; *Evening Herald*, Tuesday, August 18, 1914, 2:10; *Graphic* (a weekly), Saturday, August 22, 1914, p. 9.

9. The clipping was deemed good enough to keep. A question of some interest is the identity of Steve Corola. One plausible guess, but still a guess, is that he was an agent, either independent or in the Pantages office. This review also confirms the names of the others on the bill, viz. Cooper & Ricardo, character singers and entertainers; The American Newsboys' quartet; the Hendricks and Belle Isle company in "The Schoolmaster"; the Standard brothers, strong men; and "the usual comedy pictures." The ad for Pantages adds Lillie Jewell's Manikins who were not reviewed.

10. Letter of Clotile Palao Glover to the author, September 3, 1979.

11. "The week of ..." begins on a Sunday. It should be kept in mind, however, that many cities did not permit theatrical performances on Sunday. For split-week performances, the "first half" goes from Monday (or Sunday) through Wednesday, the second from Thursday through Saturday.

12. The "Harvard" and "Yale" were operated by the Los Angeles Steamship Company and presented a somewhat more luxurious and not significantly slower option than the train for going between Los Angeles and San Francisco. The trip would have taken the better part of a day in any event.

13. Tom Stoddard, *Jazz On the Barbary Coast* (Chigwell, Essex: Storyville Publications, 1982), p. 31. Stoddard in editing LeProtti's reminiscences from the recording, made all kinds of small changes not affecting the meaning and here and there a few large ones that introduce errors of some consequence.

14. The LeProtti band with Pete Stanley and the others mentioned can be seen in the background on a small stage in two movie stills, with Nettie Lewis Compton and Pet Bob Thurman dancing in the foreground (John Steiner Collection, University of Chicago).

15. I draw chiefly on an account written more or less from the inside: Joe Laurie, Jr.'s *Vaudeville: From the Honky-Tonks to the Palace* (New York: Henry Holt, 1953). Pantages's doings were grist for journalistic scandal: he had, it is said, a Negro mistress; and in later life was involved in a then notorious rape accusation and a hit-and-run accident.

16. September 17, 1915.

17. November 12, 1910, p. 5 in "Los Angeles News."

18. *Missouri Breeze*, December 19, 1913, 8:21 (no page numbering).

19. *Variety* of September 5, 1913, p. 16, has a lengthy review of what may well have been a rather similar act, there titled "Just Kids." Laurie, 1953, p. 234 describes, "flash acts" consisting of "a two-man act (with their own vaude material), a singing and dancing soubrette, a prima donna in the lead, and a line of six to eight girls." Clare and Rawson's act appears to be an economy model of this pattern. In Vancouver it was described in the ads as "the girl show beautiful." Mark Miller kindly directed me to Clare's obituary in *Variety*, August 30, 1923, at the age of 38. With her husband, Guy Rawson, she had considerable success for several seasons on the burlesque wheels, managing to successfully make the transition to vaudeville.

20. According to the description in the *American Newspaper Annual and Directory* of N. W. Ayer for 1915.

21. *Missouri Breeze*, October 3, 1914.

22. *Edmonton Daily Bulletin*: Tuesday, September 29, p. 3, and Thursday, October 1, p. 3. *Edmonton Daily Journal*: Tuesday, September 29, p. 3.

23. *Seattle Post-Intelligencer*, Tuesday, October 27, 1914, p. 12, and Thursday, October 29, 1914, p. 7; and the *Seattle Star*, Thursday, October 29, 1914, p. 6. These Seattle reviews might be considered especially telling, since the city was the headquarters of Alexander Pantages.

24. Tuesday, November 3, 1914, p. 2.

25. *News*, Tuesday, November 17, p. 9; *Ledger*, the same date, p. 6.

26. *Daily Oregonian*, Sunday, November 22, 1914.

27. November 24, 1914, p. 12 (buried in the Empress review).

28. November 26, 1914, p. 4. The story regarding the upcoming "jinks" printed in the same paper on the day before does not mention the band, so the word "surprise" seems to have been meant literally. H. Morgan Prince didn't save all that many clippings, but one, from an indeterminable and undateable Seattle paper, documents the band's appearance at an "old clothes social" sponsored by the local Elks' lodge; there aren't any details, however.

29. San Francisco papers examined were the *Bulletin*, *Call & Post*, *Chronicle*, and *Examiner*. I was unable to consult the *News*.

30. *Times*, Tuesday, December 22, 2:6; *Tribune*, same day, p. 13; *Examiner*, same day, 1:9; *Record*, Wednesday, December 23, p. 3; and *Variety*, January 1, 1915, p. 41. Since all of these sources use "New Orleans Ragtime Band," surely that must have been the principal billing of the group, as opposed to "New Orleans Creole Musicians," which seems to have been used through Canada. Could it be that Pantages was passing them off as a new act?

31. *Ogden Standard*, Friday, January 15, 1915, p. 3.

32. *Music and Rhythm*, June 1941, pp. 13–17. About this same time, Spencer, according to John Steiner, a hanger-on on the South Side, contributed several articles to *DB*. This pretty story fails an important test: according to Orleans Parish death records, Emily Keppard passed away on August 6, 1916 at the age of 67. At the time, the band was in Alberta and Montana, where it seems unlikely that the mercury dipped below freezing.

33. Friday, November 17, 1916, p. 2.

34. In its listing of routes ahead, *Variety* had the band at the Empress Theater in Cincinnati, but close reading of the Cincinnati papers does not show their presence.

35. *Missouri Breeze* (December 19, 1913): 8:21, Christmas Issue, under the rubric "Chicago Theaters."

36. Charles A. Sengstock, Jr., *Jazz Music in Chicago's Early South-Side Theaters* (Canterbury Press of Northbrook, 2000) gives the address of the old Grand as 3104 and includes on p. 36 a photograph of the new Grand just prior to its demolition in 1959.

37. *Def*, February 6, 1915; *IF*, same date.

38. *Missouri Breeze*, February 5 and 12, 1915. It's not impossible that they remained at the Grand longer than this one week. On February 19 the *Missouri Breeze* observed

somewhat ambiguously (p. 3): "the Creole Band which has been seen at the Grand since it got to Chicago . . ." This doesn't mean that they were there all the time, nor would an extended stay preclude appearances elsewhere.

39. *Def*, June 8, 1929, p. 10. The outlines of Peyton's account are reasonably accurate. Inaccuracies include the date of arrival—1915, not 1910—and the deformation of George Baquet's name. Also, only Palao had died by 1929. The context of Peyton's foray into musical history is his admiration for the originality of Southern musicians: "The southern boys of melody seem to have it on the northerners when it comes to theory and versatility. New Orleans has produced many of the standout musician players of today and more especially in the field of modern syncopation. Many of the noted musicians are Creoles . . . The New Orleans musicians are noted for their peculiarity in playing. Each of them has a different style on his respective instrument that attracts attention. In the present day jazz field the New Orleans musicians stand in the spotlight of popularity and are invaluable to the present day dance orchestra."

40. In conjunction with the famous recordings of Jelly Roll's reminiscences made by Alan Lomax in 1938, Morton either dictated additional memories to a stenographer or in some cases may have written notes out himself. The brief passage concerning the Grand can be found in Item 18 (according to my inventory) on the Library of Congress microfilm Music-332: Collection of typewritten materials that accompany his autobiography on records. It reads, "Jelly Roll's story of Will Dorsey, the first visit of the Creole Band to the Grand Theatre in Chicago—first time the Egyptian—nJR[*sic*] nagging Will from the box."

41. The *Missouri Breeze* of February 12 published reviews of McVickers, the Great Northern, and the Grand, as well as of eleven other houses in Chicago and three in Milwaukee. The band is not recorded in any of them.

42. Maurice Samuels's real name was Sam Morris. He began in show business before the turn of the century, at first in burlesque as a comic, then to vaudeville, then back to burlesque as a producer. He died of cancer in New York City on August 10, 1928, at age 53. *Variety Obits*, August 15th, 1928.

43. *Saginaw Daily News*, Saturday, February 13; Wednesday, February 17, pages 7 and 8; Thursday, February 18, p. 10 (ad). On the thirteenth the Jeffers was cited as showing "Keith's Greater Vaudeville"—the Butterfield theater was the Franklin—but the following Wednesday there's a news item telling us that Butterfield was going to be in town Thursday to negotiate for a new theater. This struggle between the combative Butterfield and the Loew's Western Agency [was there some connection between the Keith and Loew agency in midwestern territory?] was of sufficient interest to merit a front-page story in the *Breeze* of February 12.

44. *Detroit Journal*, Tuesday, February 23, 1915, p. 4.

45. Monday, March 8, 1915, p. 10. Princess Ka, with whom they had to share honors, played Bay City for the first half of the week of March 21, then moved on to Flint for the second.

46. *Times News*, Friday, March 19, 1915, p. 9. Thanks to Jim Dapogny for copying this out for me.

47. *EJB*, 1946, p. 5 of the large-format edition.

48. All information cited here comes from various issues of the *Missouri Breeze* in 1914.

49. A search in Chicago newspapers turned up no advertisements for the North American. The obvious place for such ads would be theatre programs, but none have yet been found therein.

50. *Variety*, November 10, 1916, p. 6.

51. *Announcer*, June 20, 1914 (8:37), p. 5.

52. *Clipper*, September 18, 1915, p. 31.

53. Ed Garland was under the impression that Licalzi and Elaine were married.

54. For an account of Duhé and his band with Mabel Elaine, then on their own in Chicago, see Gene Anderson, "The Genesis of King Oliver's Creole Jazz Band," *American Music* 12:3 (Fall 1994): 283–303. Licalzi died of a "nervous breakdown aggravated by liver complications" on August 9, 1918.

55. *Missouri Breeze*, May 14, 1915.

56. *Missouri Breeze*, May 21, 1915.

57. *New York Star*, May 19, 1915, p. 18, under Chicago news. The *Star*, founded in 1906 and edited by Roland Burke Hennessey, was a relatively unimportant theatrical weekly.

58. *Champaign Daily News*, Wednesday, May 19, 1915, p. 3. The approximately 900-seat Orpheum still stands as a rare example of a small-town vaudeville house from before World War I. It is actually quite distinguished architecturally and has survived by being converted to a children's museum.

59. *IF*, May 22, 1915, p. 5, under Chicago theatrical news.

60. The band played at Champaign only for the first half of the week of May 16. On the way to St. Louis, it would have made sense to appear in Springfield, or Decatur, Illinois, or perhaps East St. Louis. Vaudeville routes, however, were not always logical, and so far no locale has been identified for the second half of the week.

61. *Indianapolis Star*, Sunday, May 30, 1915, p. 32.

62. *Star*, Tuesday, June 1, 1915, p. 17; *Times*, the same date, and Wednesday, June 2.

63. *Globe-Democrat*, Sunday, June 20, 1915; *Star*, Monday, June 21, 1915. Apparently the week of the band's appearance was the annual benefit of the Police Relief Association.

64. *St. Louis Argus*, Friday, July 2, 1915.

65. To be sure, in most theaters in the North, African-Americans would be admitted, but sometimes to a separate balcony, or separate section where there was only one balcony. Sometimes, apparently, they would have to purchase tickets at a separate box office, and climb a separate staircase to their seats. See Edward Renton, *The Vaudeville Theatre: Building, Operation, Management* (New York: Gotham Press, 1918).

66. *Alton Evening Telegraph*, Saturday, July 3, 1915. As the sole newspaper in a city of 22,000, the *Telegraph* had a verified circulation of 4,557.

67. Laurie 1953, pp. 407–09.

Chapter 4

1. It appears that African-American musicians were not welcome in the Loop. It was something of a breakthrough for Charlie Elgar's ten-piece band to back up the ballroom dancers, Mr. & Mrs. Carl Heisen, at the Stratford Hotel in 1915. It was located somewhat peripherally at the corner of Jackson Boulevard and Michigan Avenue.

Gunther Schuller in his *Early Jazz* (New York: Oxford, 1968), p. 178, rather maddeningly—because no source is given—writes, "In fact, it is reported that Tom Brown's Band from Dixieland was imported from Chicago to replace Johnson's Creoles."

2. The account given by Holbrook in the pages of *Storyville* can be controlled to some extent by a 22-page letter—on small format paper—from Lopez to John Steiner dated November 10, 1969. This is now among Steiner's as yet uncataloged collection held by the University of Chicago. The letter and Holbrook's article agree quite well, although the latter is more detailed.

3. *Davenport Democrat and Leader*, Tuesday, August 17, 1915, p. 3.

4. Monday, August 16, 1915, p. 16. The ad for the Columbia on p. 5 lists the band first, as "7 Dark Complexion Folks in Plantation Days," an unusual billing for them.

5. Terre Haute *Star*, Friday, August 27, p. 6. The *Star* for Sunday, August 15 had already announced that the band had been booked for the new vaudeville season at the Hippodrome. On Saturday, Aug. 28, Simmons paraphrased his Friday review, concluding: "The Creole Band always will be welcome in Terre Haute" (p. 10).

6. *Terre Haute Tribune*, Friday, August 27, p. 4.

7. This is a minimum list. The *Clipper* of February 13, 1915, adds a Palace in Rockford; a Varieties in Terre Haute (perhaps this is where the band actually was, but unadvertised); the Chatterton O.H. in Springfield, Ill.; the Illinois in Urbana. The Christmas issue of the *Breeze* (December 24, 1915) added the Regent and the North Shore in Chicago, the Orpheum in Duluth, and an illegible theater in Terre Haute besides the Hippodrome. One suspects that ownership and management agreements were volatile, changing, if not week to week at least season to season.

8. *Decatur Herald* (the morning paper), September 6, 1915, p. 3; September 7, 1915, p. 3. The *Review* (evenings), September 6, 1915, p. 10. *Breeze*, September 10, 1915, p. 6.

9. *Clipper*, September 18, 1915, p. 31. On the same page, the paper observes that the WVMA booked 1,111 acts during that week. One wonders whether it was at the American that an incident recalled by George Baquet in 1940 occurred: "Another Chicago theater was the scene of a bitter dispute over billing. A rival act was given the most prominent display; the sign announcing its attractions was turned towards the corner where bigger crowds walked by, while the sign for the Creole Band faced the other way. There was nothing the men could do about it, until one night an ape in the rival act jumped from the stage into the lap of a girl in the front row. She sued; so the ape had to go away, and the Creole Band sign was quickly put up in its proper position." Fred Ramsey, Jr., "Baquet and his Mob 'Carved' King Bolden!" *DB*, January 1, 1941, p. 6.

10. *Missouri Breeze*, September 17, 1915, p. 1.

11. Ibid.

12. Advertisement from the *Chicago Examiner*, May 22, 1915, 17:5, found by a researcher in 1959 and verified by me some 35 years later. The ad was tiny and not on the theatrical page. (The *Examiner* is at the time of writing the sole Chicago daily not microfilmed and perhaps not filmable with very yellow and exceptionally fragile paper.) So far as is known, this is the only ad to use the word "jad." A few days later, the group is advertised only as "Brown's Band / Direct From New Orleans" (*Examiner*, May 26th, 15:4).

13. *Missouri Breeze*, September 17, 1915, p. 3.

14. The polarity between Chicago and the rest of the state of Illinois ("downstate") is a remarkable and enduring condition of its political existence. One could contend, by the way, that East St. Louis was tied for second place; speaking against this is its proximity to St. Louis.

15. *Peoria Transcript*, September 21, 1915, p. 10. One wonders, nonetheless, whether the fine hand of the WVMA publicity writers may have guided the local scribe.

16. *Bloomington Bulletin*, Friday, September 24, p. 3: "Japanese Singer at the Majestic."

17. *Danville Commercial-News*, Saturday, September 25, 1915, p. 5, and Tuesday, September 28, p. 2. For the other Danville paper only a few scattered issues survive. By chance, one of them is for September 28 but has apparently been misplaced in the University of Illinois library.

18. *Missouri Breeze*, October 1, 1915, p. 3.

19. *Quincy Daily Herald*, puff on Saturday, October 2, 1915, and review on Tuesday, October 5, 1915, p. 12.

20. *Missouri Breeze*, October 15, 1915, p. 4.

21. Bert Kelly, *I Created Jazz*, pp. 61–63. My thanks to Bert's son, Albert R. Kelly, Jr., for communicating the typescript to me. Kelly mentions that Castle, an enthusiastic and apparently skilled amateur drummer, often sat in with the College Inn band.

22. There were ads in the *Galesburg Evening Mail* for Thursday, October 7, 1915, for the Elite, Empress, New Colonial, West, Princess, and 5¢ Kozy 5¢ theaters. Although the band is not mentioned in any of them, there was also in Galesburg a Gaiety Theater on the Thielen circuit [*Missouri Breeze* December 24, 1915].

23. *Rock Island Union*, Friday, October 22, 1915, p. 10.

24. *Dubuque Daily Times-Journal*, October 24, p. 10, and October 25, p. 5.

25. *Waterloo Evening Courier & Reporter*, Friday, October 29, 1915, p. 6.

26. *Sioux City Journal*, Monday, November 1, 1915, p. 8.

27. Their advertising, however, was sometimes decidedly minimal, not bothering to mention the week's featured acts. This was the case, at least, in the daily ads found in the *Chicago American*, ca. 1916–17.

28. *Cedar Rapids Evening Gazette*, puff, Wednesday, November 10, 1915, p. 5; review and cartoon, Friday, November 12, pp. 3 and 18, respectively.

29. The three extant issues of this interesting weekly are at the Chicago Historical Society. It's printed on green paper, perhaps a sign that the contents are addressed to the sporting world, broadly understood. The *Breeze* published a brief article about and photograph of Hendrick in the April 23 issue, p. 4.

30. *MB*, November 19, 1915.

31. *Variety*, November 19, 1915, p. 34. This item easily escapes notice. How many more like this are waiting to be discovered?

32. "Lightning Strikes Twice" in *Jazz Forum* 5 (Autumn 1947), p. 16 f. Smith was the "West Indian" who made Jelly Roll Morton's musical and business life difficult in the early 1930s—see Alan Lomax, *Mr. Jelly Roll*. The biggest inaccuracy in this quotation is that the band made an Orpheum tour, something that never happened so far as I can tell. A possible source for the confusion is that the Bushwick Theater, Brooklyn,

could be thought of as an Orpheum house, as it was booked out of the U.B.O. (United Booking Office). The band did, however, tour on the so-called Junior Orpheum circuit in 1917–1918. Also, the date of 1918 for their big-time start is three years too late, and "Town Topics" certainly did not play on the Century roof. Nevertheless, the context Smith establishes for the band might have been expected by someone who was deeply experienced in the ways of the music and show business, something decidedly not true of most writers on jazz history.

33. *Star*, November 21 and 26, 1915, pp. 14 and 4, respectively; the brief notices in the *Times* and the *News* come from the 26th as well. One might have expected that *IF* would have had something to say about the band beyond the bare notice that they were at the Lyric theater. We should remember, however, that their coverage of black acts in "mainstream" show business is quite sporadic.

34. *New York Clipper*, Saturday, December 11, 1915, p. 12. There were two shows at the Columbia, a generous serving of nine acts of vaudeville—the usual number for an all-vaudeville house—and movies besides. One wonders whether they used their special set for this engagement; it would be normal for the *Clipper* to mention its presence.

35. *New York Evening Journal* and *Herald* (p. 8), December 5, 1915; *Evening World*, Tuesday, December 7, 1915. *Variety* reviewed the Tuesday night show on December 10, so one might suggest that perhaps they had played just the first show on Monday. Two facts stand in the way of this notion: first, the travel time to Pittsburgh was too long for them to have arrived for an evening show; second, the *Clipper* reviewed the Monday matinee on Saturday, December 11.

36. *Dispatch* (bill for the week), Sunday, December 5, 1915, V:4; review (14 words), Tuesday, December 7, p. 11. *Post*, December 7, 1915, p. 8. *Leader*, review (5 words), December 7, 1915, p. 6. *Gazette Times*, Tuesday, December 7, 1915, p. 9. *Press*, Tuesday, December 7, 1915, p. 6. *Sun*, review (9 words), December 7, 1915, p. 10.

37. Announced bill in the *Clipper*, December 18, 1915; local advertisement in the *Jersey Journal*, Thursday, December 17. Only two of the six announced acts actually were advertised.

38. *New York Herald*, Sunday, December 19, 1915. When the band played the Winter Garden Sunday concert on January 30, 1916, it maintained its favorable position. The initial ad for *Town Topics* on Sunday, January 23 found the band singled out by type as large as that given to Wellington Cross and Lew Hearn, but also at the end of the cast list, centered and consequently very prominent. I hope my readers don't find these typographic matters trivial. Stage artists then and now are enormously sensitive to position and size of their billing.

39. *Morning Telegraph*, Wednesday, December 29, 1915, p. 4; *Variety*, Friday, December 31, pp. 15 and 17.

40. *New York Evening Journal*, special Dramatic, Vaudeville, and Photo-Play Christmas Number, under rubric "Zit's Headlines That Tell a Story." Bohm, who came to New York from Hungary at age 4, had an agency in the Putnam Building, 1493 Broadway, and was principally a booker for the Loew's circuit. He died sometime during 1916. Barring additional confirmation, my inclination is to dismiss this as a misunderstanding on Zit's—C. F. Zittel, a well-known vaudeville writer—part. Perhaps he meant Harry Weber or John Simon?

41. Needless to say, perhaps, I've made reasonably serious attempts to place them at the Palace in this decidedly confused period. My efforts have not, alas, met with success. Jelly Roll Morton, in my opinion, is really a reliable witness to most of the events he mentions—with the exception of a few evidently sensitive topics—and his remark should be taken seriously.

42. *Gus Hill's National Theatrical Directory . . . 1914–1915* (New York: Hill's National Theatrical Directory, Inc., 1914), p. 561

43. This thumbnail description is drawn from the summary history, including excellent photographs, in Nicholas Van Hoogstraten, *Lost Broadway Theatres* [New York: Princeton Architectural Press, 1991], pp. 116–21; a descriptive blurb included in the program of *Town Topics*; and the description in Cahn-Leighton, *Official Theatrical Guide*, v. 16 (1912–1913), p. 397f. Repeated desperate remodelings to make the theater profitable meant that the number of seats, location of boxes, number of balconies, and disposition of the peripheral space frequently changed.

44. All of this taken from the program of the premiere, Thursday, September 23, 1915. Naturally, in a show this large, complicated, and expensive there would be many alterations of cast and sequence of scenes during the two runs. While the ridiculousness of this extravaganza is patent, I can't resist citing the exotic note added by Trixie Friganza in a "Brazilian Jubilee," the Misses Cameron in a Barcarole, and a Siamese Dance by the Carbrey Brothers.

45. *Variety*, October 1, 1915, p. 13; *New York Evening Journal*, September 24, 1915 (from a clipping file, thus no page).

46. Most of the glass photographic plates taken by the White Studios—a major theatrical photographer—were destroyed, or rather melted down for optical glass during World War II. The studio, however, had made so-called key books—now in the possession of the Theater Library of the New York Public Library at Lincoln Center—consisting of drastically reduced prints taken from the original plates. The steamboat/levee scene from *Town Topics* is on p. 115, photo 165 of shelf-number MWEZ, n.c. 16,541. Examination with a magnifying lens of the tiny print reveals no useful detail.

47. From the Ned Wayburn scrapbooks at the NYPL (MWEZ, +n.c., 21,063/4).

48. November 12, p. 11; November 19, p. 5. These and other business details are included to give the reader a sense of the power of the Shuberts and the manner in which they controlled the hapless (or unwitting) players who found themselves under contract to them. Let it be said, however, that without Lee and J. J. *Town Topics* might well have sunk without trace. Perhaps theatrical production should be added to the list of things one is better off not seeing as it is being made (traditionally, laws and sausage).

49. None of the reviews in the three Hartford dailies mention the band, but the *Post* at least cited "Mabel Elaine, a little girl who revels in eccentric dances." The review in the *Hartford Times* was exceptionally sarcastic, ending with a listing of only the first names of the 50 women in the cast!

50. On the Hartford opening, letter from J. J. Shubert to Mort Singer, January 5, 1916, TSA, General Correspondence, folder 484.

51. Puff and display ad on p. 50f. It's worth mentioning, just to establish context, that

Sarah Bernhardt was at the Bijou, Montgomery & Stone were with *Chin Chin* at the Colonial, the famous female impersonator Julian Eltinge was about to leave, and Bud Fisher, creator of the comic strip "Mutt & Jeff" was at a Sunday concert at B. F. Keith's. Given the extreme novelty of featuring a band of African-Americans on stage, it's also possible that during the single Hartford appearance and the Boston run, the Creole Band was "on probation," as it were, and consequently received no billing. A program for the performance of Jan. 17, 1916 in Boston gives for Scene 7: Transformation to a Cotton Plantation, "The Colored Band." The eleventh musical number (performed during that scene), "Cotton Blossom Time," is listed as performed by "Miss Mabel Elaine, Plantation Band, and Chorus" (Theater Collection, Princeton University Library).

52. A small item in the *Globe* stated that the show needed ten freight cars to move its equipment. I'm not surprised.

53. *Herald*, Tuesday, January 25, 1916, p. 13 (review); *Tribune*, same date, p. 9. One suspects some kind of boycott by the *Times* of Shubert productions—or vice versa—since there is no advance publicity, advertising, or review.

54. Both on Tuesday, January 25.

55. Paul Eduard Miller has them at the "Eighth Street Theater" for four months—and with *Town Topics* for one year. But Peck Court is simply an older name for East Eighth Street, and must be what was meant, as there was no Eighth Street Theater in Chicago. These time periods are all drastically inflated. The Chicago stay was five weeks, and the time with *Town Topics* was five months.

56. Consultation of a nearly contemporary Sanborn fire insurance map doesn't settle the issue of whether the stage door in the background is indeed that of the Chicago Theater. One notes from the heavy overcoats worn by passersby that the time was winter or early spring. There may well have been other shots from this occasion; one may hope some of them will turn up.

57. No record of their playing is found in the Indianapolis dailies.

58. Copies of letters and telegrams concerning *Town Topics* are found in TSA, Folder 108 (Reed Correspondence).

59. Wednesday, April 12. Although all indications are that Elaine was from Louisville, it's conceivable that before the family went to Chicago it spent some time on the other shore of the Ohio River.

60. *Columbus Evening Dispatch*, Saturday, April 15, p. 10. The *Ohio State Journal* of the same date was also full of praise: "The dances and songs of Mabel Elaine won her tumultuous encores, particularly in her role as blackface minstrel with the Creole Rag Time Band, also a distinct hit" (p. 10).

61. Surprisingly, because in connection with a report in *Variety* in April 1915 that Tucker was contemplating going with the Shubert show "Maid in America," Mort Singer, the general manager of the WVMA, wrote to J. J., "She has played all the cheap theatres in America and therefore, would be no high class attraction." J. J. replied two days later, "I have your favor of the 26th inst., and note what you say in reference to Sophie Tucker. I did not have, and have no intention of ever engaging her." TSA, General Correspondence, Folder 484.

62. Letter of J. J. S. to Jack Reed, April 13, 1916, TSA, General Correspondence, Folder 108.

63. Memo from J. J. to Jules Murry, dated April 4, 1916: "You had better see me about "Town Topics." Miss Friganza has handed in her notice so I might not be able to go to the Coast after all, so you had better hold off the contracts until you see me." TSA, General Correspondence, Folder 72.

64. Monday, March 6, 1916, p. 6. Guy F. Lee, in the *Tribune* was grumpy: "And there is Mabel Elaine, whose knockabout dancing would be more appreciated if she didn't make faces; the Creole Ragtime band, which supplies the syncopation for her clogging, and Mehlinger & Johnson, who come in often and cavort." Wednesday, March 9, 1916, p. 13.

65. *Chicago Examiner*, March 6, 1916, p. 8. The word "wonderful" appears in a handsome four-page flyer for the Chicago Theater (Theater Collection, Princeton University Library).

66. A letter from JJS to Reed dated April 13, 1916, discusses changes to be made once Sophie Tucker has joined the show. "Cut out the Indian Suffragette entirely and open up on Newport, making Newport Scene five, thus eliminating the Prairie drop. Scene Six and One Half—the Cotton Plantation is OK."

67. *New York Clipper*, May 13, 1916, p. 9.

68. TSA, Western Union telegram, dated Philadelphia, May 18, 1916. A note in as yet undecipherable Pitman shorthand probably indicates the reply.

69. TSA, General Correspondence, File No. 108. The holdup mentioned is probably that Elaine and the Band demanded pay if they were to play the Winter Garden concert on Sunday, May 21—which they did in fact play according to the ad in the *Times* on that day, Section 3, p. 9. Also featured in this rather incredibly rich potpourri were Sophie Tucker, Al Jolson, and Doraldina and her Hawaiians.

70. *Variety*, June 16, 1916, p. 7.

71. Although not all Omas were necessarily Oma Crosby Browne Baquet, it's at least worth citing in passing the dispatch from Mahara's Minstrels published in *IF*, August 23, 1902: "Morgan Prince used to tell us about his 'Castle on the Nile', but has changed to 'Oma, let me hear from you.'" *IF* published her photograph in its issue of Sept. 25, 1909.

72. *Def*, June 5, 1916, p. 6: "Tobe Brown and Myles Harris of the Grand Orchestra leave for Detroit Monday on an extended contract, the engagement being in the American room of one of the big hotels there."

73. *Buddy Bolden and the Last Days of Storyville*, p. 135. This is the only expression of this view I've seen, but we should remember that Barker was the only African-American writer besides Harrison Smith to deal with the Creole Band.

74. P. 22.

75. P. 6. The passage concludes with the obligatory irony of the ODJB being the band that made records (and history).

76. *Sidney Bechet* (London: Macmillan, 1987), pp. 290–92.

77. The ODJB's first Victor recording from February 26, 1917, did not lead immediately to more, because copyright litigation afflicted both sides of the record. The one Columbia recording from May 31 and June 1, 1917, was something of a flash in the pan not followed up by the company. Finally the Aeolian-Vocalion vertical cut records from sessions of August through November 1917, while no doubt available in most major cities, were sold in quite small numbers and acoustically unsatisfactory to boot.

It's my opinion that the real impact of the band on a nationwide, if not European basis, should be traced to the latter half of 1918, not January 1917, the date of their opening at Reisenweber's.

78. The matter of a "Mandalay" song as having been played at the Cross-Rivers bout in 1914 is discussed above in chapter 3.

79. A footnote seems to be the appropriate place for several other versions, such as that of Marshall Stearns's *The Story of Jazz*, p. 117: "One legend says that Keppard didn't want his style copied; another legend insists that the record executives decided that Keppard played too "hot and dirty" for the family trade. Both could be true." Or false. Onah Spencer asserted that the problem was that Freddy didn't show up at the recording session [*Music & Rhythm*, June 1941, pp. 13–17]. John St. Cyr as reported by Alan Lomax [*MJR*, p. 145] thought that the band held out for a flat fee instead of a percentage deal. It's noteworthy that most of what has percolated into jazz history (or quasi history) puts Keppard in the foreground, under the impression that he was the leader of the band.

80. *Jazz Records* (New Rochelle: Arlington House, 1978), p. 359, and letter to author.

81. In answering Barker's question as to the reasons for the breakup of the band, Baquet suggested that imitators took away the band's novelty. This part of the interview as transmitted by Barker has more than a few errors: Dink Johnson is mentioned as a member of the vaudeville band whereas he stayed behind in California when the band began touring in 1914; Norwood Williams is renamed Leon Williams and is said to have left for France (he went to California); Jimmy Palao is not mentioned at all in the band's roster; George was supposedly on the Orpheum Circuit with the band when Storyville was closed down by the Navy (Jimmie Noone was touring with the band then); the importance of the Orpheum circuit in the band's vaudeville career is vastly overstated; and finally, the band did not break up in New York.

Chapter 5

1. There are several different ways of spelling this name. In this book I've opted for "Delille" following the 1913 New Orleans city directory, which has a number of "Delille" listings as well as "Delisle" and even four "Del'Isle"—no "Delile," however. A business card (at HJA) reads "Louis Delile, Clarinetis, Now with Superior Orchestra" (therefore ca. 1907 or 8) and a 1910 marriage license, "Delisle." His uncle Albert spelled his name either "Delille" or "Delisle." Finally, his World War I Selective Service registration card reads "Delile"—written by the clerk—and is signed in a very awkward hand I assume to be his, "Louis Delile."

2. *Jazz Information* 2:11 (December 20, 1940), p. 6 ff. Accompanying the article may be the first publication of the photograph of Big Eye with a saxophone (C melody?) and Keppard with a slide trumpet.

3. *La Nouvelle-Orléans* 1946, p. 142, my translation.

4. Folder 49, Jazzmen files, page headed "Bill J."

5. *Shining Trumpets* (repr. DaCapo 1975), p. 366. Note that this passage is not to be found in the first edition, although Big Eye—who died in 1949—is credited in the acknowledgements.

6. Notes of an interview between Russell and Johnson, seen at Russell's apartment in New Orleans in 1983 and now undoubtedly at HNOC.

7. It was originally planned that *Town Topics* would travel to the West Coast, but this tour was canceled once Sophie Tucker replaced Trixie Friganza in the show. All it would have taken was a phone call from one of the Shuberts to the Pantages organization to set up this new trip around the circuit for the Creole Band.

8. The production was not unlike *Town Topics* in its Brobdignagian size: 20 scenes, 200 people including a "chorus of 100 beauties of striking loveliness" [four-page flyer for the production in the author's possession]. Billboard, October 14, 1916, p. 4 in a short piece datelined October 8, mentions Mabel Elaine along with the other principals. But neither the review in *Variety* of November 3, nor that in *Billboard* of November 4, mentions her.

9. *Manitoba Free Press*, July 18, 1916.

10. Respectively, *Town Talk* (a weekly), October 7, 1916, in the advance puff; *Call & Post*, October 19, 1916; *Chronicle*, October 9, 1916.

11. July 28, 1916. While the *Breeze* was wont to follow acts around the Pantages circuit, its remarks were usually limited to several words, sometimes only one.

12. Both from the July 18 issues. My wild speculation is that "old circus bands" may have played much of their music by ear, or at any rate in a less housebroken fashion than the elaborate bands that came after them.

13. *Edmonton Morning Bulletin*, Wednesday, July 26, p. 3; *Journal*, July 25, p. 14.

14. Undated clipping from the Prince scrapbook. Perhaps he kept it because it designated him the "head of the troupe."

15. *La Nouvelle–Orléans*, p. 142 f. My translation.

16. Index to Orleans Parish Death Records, vol. 166, p. 1137 (consulted on the ancestry.com web site).

17. For the Majestic, see *Gus Hill's National Theatrical Directory*, 1914–1915, p. 489, which doesn't list the others.

18. Goffin's important but infuriating work is replete with details that he could not have invented, but which he often carelessly records.

19. *Lethbridge Telegram*, August 3, 1916, p. 8. In this, as well as in the *Daily Herald*, there's confusion regarding which theater offered the Pantages acts, the Orpheum or the Empress. A small question, to be sure.

20. These details are from the April 7, June 2, 9, and 23, 1916 issues of the *Breeze*.

21. *Great Falls Daily Tribune*, Thursday, August 10, 1916, p. 8. The other stops in Montana were verified in the *Anaconda Standard* and the *Daily Missoulan*. It's interesting that the advance publicity emphasized the "Society Buds" ensemble with virtually no notice of the band.

22. *Daily Province*, Tuesday, September 5, 1916, p. 3; *News-Advertiser*, same date, p. 5.

23. September 7, 1916, p. 3.

24. *Victoria Daily Colonist*, Tuesday, September 12, 1916, p. 8.

25. *MJR*, p. 144 f.

26. Prince may have traveled with his wife at some point during his tenure with the band. In any event, in early 1918 she was playing in Los Angeles at the Waldorf Cafe as "Miss Ollie Fitzsimmons of Australia" (*Def*, March 2, 1918, p. 4, col. 3).

27. *Tribune*, Monday, October 16, 1916, p. 5. Such a comment makes one wonder whether the band had replaced the "Egyptia" opening with a fast ragtime number.

28. *Examiner*, Tuesday, October 24, 1916, p. 7. The memory that Shelton Brooks had a major hit with this dance song seems to have been more or less effaced by his even more successful "Darktown Strutters' Ball."

29. *Deseret Evening News*, Thursday, November 9, 1916, p. 14.

30. *Ogden Examiner*, Friday, November 17, 1916, p. 9.

31. September 29, 1915, p. 2.

32. *Rocky Mountain News*, Sunday, November 19, 1916, p. 8, and Tuesday, November 21, 1916, p. 7. Perhaps there was a newspaper war on in Denver. The *Post* carried no ads for the Tabor.

33. *Denver Times*, Tuesday, November 21, 1916. The *Times* was a lively, small-format paper, startlingly modern in makeup and headlines; it also carried Italian news items on the back page.

34. Morrison is noteworthy for his claim that around 1911 he put a sign on his Model T Ford reading "George Morrison and His Jazz Orchestra." His statement of the composition of his band in Denver around 1916—which he described to Schuller as being composed of three pieces: violin, piano, and drums—can be amplified by an ad in the *Star* of January 6, 1917, giving the personnel as Morrison, violin; William Kelly, saxaphone and trombone; Miss Jessie Andrews, piano; Gener Montgomery, traps.

35. A front page story in the weekly *Rocky Ford Enterprise* noted that "the Grand Opera House was packed with the largest crowd in many years." *Kansas City Thespian*, December 9, 1916, p. 5

36. *Sioux City Journal*, Monday, December 11, 1916, p. 8.

37. *St. Joseph* (Missouri) *Gazette*, December 15, 1916.

38. These details are taken from the Omaha *World-Herald* of December 17 and 18, 1916.

39. The Majestic showed vaudeville exclusively and was managed by Victor Hugo —yes, that's correct—with 1,500 seating capacity divided between the orchestra floor, a balcony, and a gallery.

40. *Cedar Rapids Evening Gazette*, December 20, p. 8 (advance ad for Thursday afternoon); December 21, p. 3 (additional puff); December 22, p. 6 (Slattery), and p. 9 (review).

41. P. 3. This was half the space devoted to the Majestic show. The other four acts had to be satisfied with a couple of lines apiece.

42. The reviewer of the Erber's appearance stated that the band was "the late feature of 'The Passing Show'" (*East St. Louis Daily Journal*, January 2, 1917, p. 3). Could the band have been briefly placed in *The Passing Show of 1916* that opened on June 22, 1916? If so, it would have been for a very short time.

43. January 12, 1917, p. 6. The selfsame item appeared eight days later in *IF*!

44. *IF*, October 25, 1919, and *Def*, December 11, 1926, p. 8.

45. Why Prince would have wanted or needed such a certificate is something of a mystery. Presumably it would attest to the fact that during World War I he was employed in essential industry and not a draft dodger. But in 1942 he would have been 57

years old and not subject to the draft. My hypothesis, from city directory entries listed below under the later biography of Prince, is that this would either qualify him for employment in wartime industry or gain him seniority by union rules.

46. *Times*, Saturday, Tuesday, and Thursday, January 20, 23, and 25, 1917; *News*, Monday, January 22; *Star*, Sunday, January 21, 1917.

47. *Indianapolis Star*, January 26, 1917, p. 7. This was the very week that the Original Dixieland Jazz Band opened at Reisenweber's in New York.

48. IF, February 3, placed them at the Lincoln and Kedzie "last week" and speaks of them as opening at McVicker's on the Loen [*sic*, no doubt "Loew's"] time booking east. The *Freeman* was a bit premature: although published on Saturday, February 3, it wouldn't have hit the stands until the following Sunday or Monday.

49. *Variety*, July 7, 1916, p. 6.

50. February 7, 1917, p. 4.

51. February 9, 1917, p. 3.

52. *Breeze*, February 2, 1917, pp. 1 and 3. This could have been the band that replaced the ODJB at the Casino Gardens. Further, it's mentioned in a front page article that "jaz bands are having their inning in Chicago vaudeville this week." In addition to the Bennets, Sophie Tucker was backed up by a "regular" jaz band at the Palace.

53. *Breeze*, September 1, 1916, p. 8.

54. The designation "five white men" is easily explained. For more than two years, vaudeville audiences had seen dozens of "society" dancing couples accompanied by an onstage band of black musicians to the extent that white musicians in such a capacity had become out of the ordinary.

55. *Cleveland Plain Dealer*, Sunday, February 18, and Tuesday, February 20, pp. 6 and 7. It's perhaps worth mentioning that the advance puff in the Sunday *Leader*, Dramatic section, p. 3, sees fit to mention the "inevitable chicken [which] plays a prominent part in the proceedings." Evidently, Morgan Prince passed along his chicken-wrangling skills to Leonard Scott.

56. *Times*, Tuesday, February 27, 1917, and *Free Press* of the same date.

57. Mary C. Henderson, *The City and the Theatre* [Clifton, N.J.: J. T. White, 1973], 282.

58. Documents concerning Dance Palace Company and Clifford C. Fischer, Inc., are found at TSA, Group IV, no. 1, and Group II, no. 109a. It's possible that there was a cafe on the ground floor. TSA, Group II, No. 88, has a letter from the police department to Palais de Dance Co. regarding disorderly and irregular conditions at Monaco Restaurant: "Many undesirable characters and women of shady reputation resort to your restaurant and at times behave themselves in a very unseemingly [*sic*] manner. It has also been noticed that the 2 o'clock stipulation has been habitually violated most flagrantly."

59. TSA, Group II, no. 88, contains a letter from H. Robert Law Scenic Studios regarding the Persian motif decoration for the "Cabaret Winter Garden Roof."

60. That is according to one source. Maurice's autobiography *cum* dancing instructor states that after the death of his first partner, Leona, in Paris, he linked up with Madeleine d'Arville, who arrived with him in New York on October 14, 1910. While they were appearing in *Over the River*, d'Arville eloped with a young Englishman, and Maurice replaced her with Florence Walton. (See *Variety*, March 2, 1912, p. 5.) Thus far

Maurice. But *Over the River* did not open until January 8, 1912 (per Kinkle I, p. 56), leaving plenty of room for a short-lived alliance with Maurice.

61. I follow here Julie Malnig *Dancing till Dawn* [New York: Greenwood Press, 1992], who also offers, p. 69 (from TSA) a photograph of the Persian Room, ca. 1914, in which one can see in the background a staircase to the upper floor.

62. TSA, Letter of Clifford C. Fischer to J. J. Shubert, December 27, 1915, announcing his intention to open the new place on Friday, New Year's Eve, as "Joan Sawyer's."

63. If I am not mistaken, the Montmartre was renamed the Folies Bergère—an old name in Times Square but a new location—where the Original Dixieland Jazz Band appeared after their return from England. Subsequently (by 1923, if not before) it became the Plantation Club, in which a number of African-American groups were to appear. In 1983 it was a tropical theme restaurant called Hawaii Kai—at least the ground floor was.

64. *Variety*, January 7, 1916, p. 13, somewhat snidely observed: "If she didn't come all the way from Honolulu that won't interfere with her as a cooch dancer."

65. To cut off a possible blast from the Danish embassy at the pass, let me say that no doubt there is little or no humor to the name in Denmark, which was, I believe, Worm's birthplace, and that only an American Philistine such as myself would find it amusing.

66. TSA, General Correspondence 1910–1926, File no. 76. Webb and Goodwin were in the cast of *Love o' Mike*, which opened on January 15 for a run of 192 performances.

67. This is from the slightly longer version of March 17.

68. Wednesday, March 14, 1917.

69. Portland, Me., *Daily Eastern Argus*, Thursday, April 26, 1917, p. 4.

70. For a good summary of the White Rats, and the general climate of acrimony involved in relations between managers and performers, see Snyder, *The Voice*, chap. 4.

71. The White Rats declared the strike over on April 9 for patriotic reasons, the United States having declared war on April 6.

72. *Orchestra World*, October 1936, p. 13: "From Honky-Tonk to Swing." The photocopies and LaRocca's note are found in File 11, folder 5. My surmise that LaRocca learned of the Creole Band from Williams rests on the fact that in a typically enraged letter to Marshall Stearns from June 1936, LaRocca said nothing about them. The detail in Williams's communication regarding them subbing for each other is more than peculiar; perhaps he was thinking of another pair of bands.

73. Including the photograph of the band published in the back pages of *Variety's* December 28, 1917, Christmas issue.

74. HJA, LaRocca Collection: part II, file 2. The excerpt from *Variety* is misdated March 10, 1917.

75. Thanks to Bruce Raeburn, curator of HJA, for having verified the location and wording of these documents.

76. April 15, 1940. Wiedoeft would probably have been able to continue with the show and play at the Montmartre. An item in the *New York Musician & Knocker* for May 1917 suggests, however, that he left the show prior to its closing "to devote more of

his time to vaudeville and the phonograph" (p. 11). He was replaced by Sig Neuman, who had been playing at Rector's.

77. See *International Musician*, reports from Local 6 (San Francisco) in October 1916; Local 47 (Los Angeles) in November 1916; Local 60 (Pittsburgh), 210 (Fresno) in January 1917 and several entries for E. Arnold Johnson in reports from Local 10 (Chicago).

78. Two tunes ("Johnson 'Jass' Blues" and "Night-time in Little Italy") are now available on CD, Timeless CBC 1-035, *Ragtime to Jazz I*. The titles of the Columbia tests are not known. Neither Sudhalter's compendious *Lost Chords* nor Alyn Shipton's "revisionist" and very lengthy *New History of Jazz*, nor even the revised and expanded *New Grove Dictionary of Jazz* deign to mention the Frisco Jazz Band. If pressed, the authors might say that what the Frisco Jazz Band played was ragtime, not jazz. Perhaps the problem is partly that Rudy Wiedoeft is not considered to belong to jazz—in part, perhaps, because of his statements distancing himself from jazz. These need to be placed in the context of the early 1920s, when "jazz" had come to designate for many noisy and corny music, full of instrumental tricks and "effects."

79. *New York Clipper*, April 4, 1917, p. 21. Could the reviewer have mistaken a clarinet for a flute? Or was Big Eye temporarily replaced by an unknown flutist . . . or, might he have been playing flute? (No one has ever suggested that he could.)

80. *Variety*, April 6, 1917, p. 30. The *Morning Telegraph* review—on Wednesday, April 4, p. 14—mentions, for the first time in a long while, a "little man who shifts from singing 'Old Black Joe' effectively to dancing with the animation of a pickaninny."

81. Given the unsettled character of Loew bookings at this time, it's always possible for the band to have made an unscheduled appearance. I doubt that the *Age* would have made up this detail, perfectly logical in view of their next recorded appearance in Springfield, Mass. Gordon's Olympia in Scollay Square would perhaps have been the largest theater in which the band ever played. *Variety* of November 11, 1913, describes it as a two-million-dollar building with 3,200 seats (without a post) and an 800-foot artesian well for cooling water.

82. *Springfield Union*, Tuesday, April 24, 1917. Other mentions are found in the *Republican* and the *News*.

83. Thursday, April 26, 1917 and Friday, April 27, p. 13. The *Daily Eastern Argus*, Portland's morning daily, used virtually identical language although the two papers don't seem to have been under the same management. The Thursday ad read: "Here's the Big Shubert Management Act that has made New York sit up / The Creole Band / Sometimes called the Jazz Band. A Troupe of Wonderful Creole Musicians . . ." (p. 4).

84. Orin Blackstone, "Big Eye Louis," *Jazz Information* 2, no. 11 (December 20, 1940), p. 6 ff. In my estimation, Big Eye was one of those informants who could be sometimes exceptionally precise, at others would fabricate. For example, he would have us believe that *he* missed the opportunity to make a recording, when the offer came before he had joined the band . . . unless there were *two* offers, one in 1916, the other in the following year.

85. My translation from *La Nouvelle-Orléans*.

86. The Simpson and Murdock Directory for Boston, 1919, lists Lydia Wood, lodg-

ing house, 9 Worcester Square. Worcester Square was an extension of Worcester Street, between Washington and Harrison Streets, not far from the boundary between Boston and Roxbury.

87. HJA, as written up by Bill Russell from his notes. Bill Russell also read his notes to me at his house in April 1983. The rough notes are now in WRC, Jazz Files, CA Notes, Folder 18. On one detail, Williams's memories appear to have been confused, or perhaps became so when Russell wrote up his notes in 1944 after an interval of four or five years. Williams thought that Big Eye was sent for, and the band kept on going. In Bill's transcript "At that time, perhaps for the last year, Big Eye Louis had replaced Baquet already by that time." He appears to have confused Big Eye with Jimmie Noone.

88. Two agents, Max Hart and Marvin Welt, competed to bring the ODJB to New York City, with Hart winning out. It is said that Hart took no commission for his efforts regarding whatever he did for the band as a "hobby" [typescript by Edwards dated November 9, 1955, in the possession of the Edwards family]; in any event, existing correspondence between Reisenweber's management and Eddie Edwards indicates that Hart had little or nothing to do with the band's working conditions and salary. On the other hand, he seems to have played a role in the publication by Leo Feist of tunes by the band.

89. *La Nouvelle-Orléans*, p. 137 f.

90. In his definitive biography from 1994, Edward Berlin doesn't mention Big Eye's story.

91. *La Nouvelle-Orléans*, p. 145 ff.

92. Trow's New York City Directory for 1918.

Chapter 6

1. *IF*, October 27, 1917: "Leonard Scott, formerly of the Dahomian Trio, is now with the Creole Band, where he will introduce Charles Warfield's song "From Now On, Let Me Miss You."

2. The published rosters for the Tennessee Ten are few; they indicate that up until the Orpheum tour, their clarinetist was Blaine Gaten.

3. Wesley M. Neff (with help from Mr. and Mrs. Noone), "Jimmie Noone" in *Jazz Information* 2, no. 6 (October 4, 1940).

4. See Kenney, *American Music* 4:2 (1986) with particular emphasis on the so-called classical or legitimate features of his technique and concomitant deemphasis on those that link him directly to other New Orleans jazz clarinetists of the generation of the 1890s—especially his vibrato and portamento. The article presents no new biographical information to add to the (exceptionally scant) earlier sources.

5. *NYT*, reel 2, chap. 59 (Maurice Durand).

6. Barnes's statements come from the typed summary of reel 4 of the interview conducted by William Russell on July 27, 1960, on deposit at HJA. It is also available in a microfilm edition, *NYT*, reel 2, chapter 16. However much Barnes's style may have become more idiosyncratic and rougher in his later years, it nevertheless seems that he would have given the Creole Band a hotter and wilder sound than Noone. Barnes ad-

mired Noone but several times comments on his lack of nerve, going so far as to say that Noone had "a lot of chicken in him" and could be run off an advertising truck by just looking at him.

7. *Variety*, October 5, 1917, p. 46 (Chicago column).

8. October 5, 1917, p. 46, and January 31, 1919, p. 35.

9. *Billboard*, October 20, 1917.

10. All of this was reported in *Variety*, issues between October 12 and November 2.

11. *South Bend Tribune*, Saturday, November 24 and Friday, November 30.

12. *Def*, December 1, 1917.

13. *Indianapolis News*, Saturday, December 1, 1917.

14. *Lafayette Journal*, Tuesday, December 11, 1917, p. 10, and the *Purdue Exponent* for the same date, p. 2.

15. *Kalamazoo Gazette*, Sunday, December 16, 1917. The headline read "New Orleans Creole Band in Real Jazz Music . . ."

16. Saturday, January 5, 1918, p. 6.

17. *Saginaw Daily News*, Friday, January 4, 1918.

18. I wondered whether Simmons could be a typographical error for "Simons," i.e., the band would still be represented by John Simon, as it had been beginning in the spring of 1915. But I'm inclined to think that someone at *Variety* would have caught such an error.

19. We know that Baquet inscribed at least one photograph to an old New Orleans friend, Manuel Perez (see above chap. 1, n. 18). Landry is a reasonably common name in New Orleans—the 1913 city directory notes three George Landrys—and Edna Landry Benbow, from New Orleans, was a star in black vaudeville of the time.

20. *Danville Commercial-News*, Friday, January 18, 1918, p. 11.

21. *Springfield State Journal*, Monday, January 21, 1918, p. 9. Possibly the details about a preacher and a sermon refer to a variation by Leonard Scott on the Uncle Joe act as conceived by Morgan Prince.

22. *Sioux City Journal*, Friday, February 15, 1918, p. 6. The reporter felt it worthy of note that the house was filled, despite a "near blizzard."

23. *St. Paul Pioneer Press*, February 19, 1918, p. 5.

24. The article on the juvenile jazzers can be found in the *Pioneer Press* for Thursday, February 21, 1918, p. 3.

25. Tuesday, March 5, 1918.

26. March 7, 1918, p. 4. The paper is quite unpretentious and while it does give some coverage to African-American performers, it is usually rather brief and unexceptional. As to when the earlier visit might have been, my guess is sometime in November 1917, when there's a one-week gap in the band's itinerary.

27. *Def*, March 16, 1918, p. 6.

28. The term "Creole" did not usually excite any comment, but on this tour a writer for the *Duluth News-Tribune* thought "the members are darkies, not Creoles in the true meaning of the word, and they will get out and shake themselves just as the colored folks did on the antebellum plantations." Thursday, February 21, 1918, p. 5.

29. *Missouri Breeze*, Dec. 10, 1915, p. 3.

30. Jelly Roll Morton, "I Created Jazz in 1902," *The Needle* 2:1 (1945), reprinted from

DB, September 1938. However, Morton also recalled that they played the Palace, New York, for two weeks while under Weber's management. There is no record that the band ever worked at the Palace, however. Given the depth of coverage of the Palace shows by the theatrical weeklies, it seems unlikely that any act working there would escape notice.

31. WRC, General Correspondence & Working Files, Jazzmen, folder 50. Russell noted down that the band had broken up about 1923, possibly a confusion with the date Johnson left Joe Oliver's Creole Band.

32. *Milwaukee Free Press*, pt. 3, p. 3.

33. *Kenosha Evening News*, March 14 and 15.

34. Mary E. Karoley, "New Orleans Clarinets: 7. Sidney Bechet" in *Jazz Information* 2:10 (December 6, 1940), p. 12. Vincent's illness may well account for the statement that Eddie Atkins, then no doubt in Chicago, played with the Creole Band for a while.

35. *IF*, May 18, 1918. "Madam Sherry" was a very well-known show from 1910, so much so that no fewer than five road companies went out in 1911.

36. The economics of vaudeville worked against anything other than solo or duet turns. For these a salary between $50 and $100 a week would be quite normal. The Creole Band appears to have earned between $70 and $80 a week per man—a quite substantial sum, except for the most sought-after headliners. To this might be added additional fees for playing parties, dances, or even parades. The jazz craze would have made it easy for them to earn $100 a week or more playing the South Side cabarets. This was harder work, but New Orleans musicians were not unaccustomed to playing seven- or eight-hour jobs when working in a dance band.

37. Not that "plantation" routines and stereotypes didn't persist, or were transmogrified into the stereotyped images that populated movie screens and radio until mid-century or even later. It could even be argued that the expectations of the mainstream audience for "hot" music played by African-Americans were hardly less expressive of a conviction that black "children of nature" weren't capable of "higher" forms of creativity. But this topic has been explored by many others.

38. 54:12 (December 2001), pp. 12–17.

Chapter 7

1. I include information regarding CD reissues, in full and apologetic awareness that some will be out of print, others only available by special order, sometimes from abroad.

2. Interview with Burt Turetsky, January 1977. My guess would be that this was a group led by clarinetist Red Rowland. Garland recalled that after the vaudeville engagement with Mabel Elaine accompanied by Lawrence Duhé's band came to an end, he worked for Izzy Shaw [surely Izzy Shore] at the Luncheonette for a while, then joined Perez. The chronology is not entirely clear: when Louis Keppard registered for the draft on June 5, 1917, he still listed as his employer Mitchell Licallza [recte Licalzi] at the Wilson Theater, who managed the Duhé band. On the same date, Lorenzo Tio, Eddie Atkins, and Frank Ahaynou listed themselves as employees of Mike Fritzel at Madison and Paulina streets (the Arsonia).

3. Los Angeles, Local Board 11, registration of September 12, 1918, serial number 1860.

4. *Compton Westside Herald American*, Thursday, September 27, 1962, Mary Ellen Perry, "Compton Resident is Originator of 'Rock-Roll' Craze." As though this claim were insufficient, Prince also claimed that he was the "father of jazz bands." More believably, he mentioned visiting in India, the Taj Mahal, Madras, the Great Caves of Qualumpa, Fort Goldcanga, and the Nazam Palaces in addition to performing for the Rajah Bendehara.

5. Both the versions in Blesh, *Shining Trumpets*, after p. 256 (from Frederic Ramsey, Jr.), and in Grauer & Keepnews, *A Pictorial History of Jazz*, p. 34, come from the same source print and are cropped, showing neither the guitarist nor violinist who ought to have been there.

6. There are at least two different poses of this, one loaned by Frederic Ramsey, Jr., to Rudi Blesh for *Shining Trumpets*, after p. 256, the other by William Russell for Frank Driggs and Harris Lewine, *Black Beauty, White Heat*, p. 55. The latter shows Palao much more clearly. Just for the record, four games were played in Chicago, on October 3, 4, 6, and 9.

7. The report from Local 208 (Chicago) in the *International Musician* for July 1921— which usually was at least a month or two after the fact—mentions transfers issued to Joe Oliver, Edward Garland, Minor Hall, James Palao, Honore Dutrey, Lillian Hardin, and John Dodd [*sic*]. Either Hardin did not make the trip or else returned to Chicago soon after arrival.

8. This photograph has been very frequently reproduced and can also be found on postcards. It even served as endpaper (both front and back) to Ole Brask's *Jazz People* (New York: Harry N. Abrams, 1976). The musicians are all clad as rustics, therefore the photograph was probably made during the vaudeville tour that followed the band's six-month contract at the Pergola on Market Street.

9. *Jazzmen*, p. 68, quotes from Oliver's contract with the Pergola Dancing Pavilion, which was for six months. Whether it actually lasted that long is not known. Baby Dodds recalled (Larry Gara, *The Baby Dodds Story* [Los Angeles: Contemporary Press, 1959], p. 32 f.) that he and Armstrong had left Fate Marable around the first of September 1921. Dodds said additionally that he was in New Orleans when the call from Oliver came. The description of his first job seems to fit the Pergola ("a jitney dance hall where everybody paid to get in the ring and dance"). At the beginning of 1922 Oliver and Kid Ory joined forces and played in Oakland, then Oliver proceeded to Los Angeles.

10. Garland's version is in an interview with Burt Turetsky, done for the Smithsonian Oral History Project and on file at IJS. Hall's reminiscences come from "Minor Hall Speaks," *The Record Changer*, August 1947, and an interview with Bill Russell, September 2, 1958, now held at HJA. It occurs to me that Palao's usefulness would be mostly for playing tangos, waltzes, and the like at the Pergola, and that when the six-months contract was at an end, he was no longer needed. The *International Musician* in April 1922 reported that Joe Oliver had been reinstated in Local 208.

11. The card is signed "Bo," who states that he's working at Riverview. The Riverview Park summer gig was frequently played by Doc Cooke's band, once the

Dreamland ballroom had closed down. Perhaps the card was from Jimmie Noone, known by some as "Jimbo."

The following comment deserves not to be buried in a footnote. However it may be despite Armontine Palao's continued bitterness at her husband's extramarital adventures when I spoke with her around 1985, it's possible that these took place mostly in the early years of their marriage. In a profession not known to foster marital stability, Jimmy Palao appears to have kept his family together, not only providing them with a living but with a memorable presence. While other members of the band may have fathered children—most notably Bill Johnson—they seem not to have taken their paternal role very seriously.

12. Dave (Stratton) and Tressie (Mitchell) had been a team from 1921 on; they announced their intention to add a jazz band to their act early in 1923 (Billboard, January 7, 1923). This may not have happened until six months later, when an ad in *Variety* referred to Wickliffe's Gingersnaps as their seven-piece jazz band.

13. He was present at a wedding reception for Lil Hardin and Louis Armstrong, which took place on February 7, 1924, in Chicago at a time when Dave & Tressie were either on the east coast or traveling there (*Def*, Feb. 16, 1924; *IF* Feb. 2, 1924). Two photographs from the same session published in *Storyville* 67 (October–November 1976, p. 16–17) show a band "believed to be of The Syncopated Gingersnaps," one of them with Dave & Tressie themselves, and both with Palao. In the one of the band by itself, Palao is shown holding a tenor sax and with a banjo on the floor in front. Neither this six-piece band nor the seven-piece band in the next photograph show Bill Johnson.

14. The guitarist Johnny St. Cyr recalled that it was extremely cold on the day of Palao's funeral. He, Jimmy Noone, and Freddie Keppard went there in an open car but mistakenly joined another cortege and wound up at a different cemetery two miles short of their goal. It was so cold, however, that they decided not to go to the interment (Bill Russell, *New Orleans Style*, p. 67).

15. A copy was received at the Copyright Office on July 9, 1942, and registered as E unpub. 301875.

16. A trunk—I was tempted to write "the proverbial trunk"—was remembered by Clotile Palao as containing publicity slides for the band and possibly the band library—or parts of it—and some original compositions. Armontine Palao kept taking the trunk along on her various moves around Chicago until she moved away from St. Lawrence Ave. (The copyright certificate for the patriotic song was sent to her at 4715 St. Lawrence Ave.) To the best of my knowledge only two items of the trunk's contents survived: the front cover of a music folder of heavy black paper, inscribed "Creole Band," and the "Echo of India."

17. Photographs can be seen at <www.chicagohs.org/treasures/music2.html>.

18. Index to Orleans Parish marriages, vol. 39, p. 859. 1920 Federal Census, enumeration district 76 (Cook Co.), sheet 2B, l. 63.

19. The photograph has by now appeared in three published sources: (1) *Storyville* 136 (December 1, 1988), after p. 139; (2) accompanying Gene Anderson "King Oliver's Creole Band," *American Music* 12, p. 291; (3) Frank Büchmann-Møller, *Is This to Be My Souvenir?* (Odense University Press, 2000), p. 140. The original—never properly described—is in deplorable condition. Of the published versions, the third is preferable.

20. *Oh, Didn't He Ramble*, p. 28. Lee also recalled going with Vincent to visit the seriously ailing Freddie Keppard in 1932. Shortly thereafter Vincent telephoned him that Keppard had died (p. 55).

21. According to the index to Orleans Parish death records (vol. 184, p. 1079), Henry Vincent (colored), age 68, died on July 2, 1922. The date of Oliver's telegraphed invitation to Louis is often given as July 22, although Louis himself sometimes gave August 8.

22. All extant takes were most recently reissued on the CD King Jazz KJ170, "Play that Thing," although in the improbable key of A major.

23. With the exception of an English LP reissue from the late 1960s, Audubon AAQ, available by subscription. It might be easier to find the original Paramount. Recent diligent efforts have failed to turn up a copy, either an original or a reissue.

24. The discussion regarding the identification by Jasper Taylor can be found in *Jazz Information*, vol. 2, no. 16. It's worth remembering that the reviewer in Salt Lake City in November 1916, was moved to mention the "dusky trombonist of Arthur Pryor ability."

25. *DB*, January 1, 1941, p. 6.

26. Oma Baquet's career has an interest all its own. She had apparently been, as Oma Browne, one of John Isham's Octoroons prior to 1900. She then teamed up with Harry "the Squirrel" Crosby, a ragtime piano player from Detroit. They toured together in vaudeville for a few years, then by 1909 Oma had her own act, Oma Crosby and her Kinkies, presumably having separated from Harry. A wedding with actor Will H. Brown received mention in the theatrical columns of the *Freeman*; this presumably was dissolved by the time of the marriage with Baquet in 1916. Oma was touring in 1921 as "Orma [*sic*] Crosby's Cubanolas," but nothing more is known of her after that. Oddly, perhaps, H. Morgan Prince was apparently an acquaintance of hers shortly after the turn of the century; one wonders whether he might have introduced her to Baquet.

27. These are: (1) manuscript lead sheet of a song "What'll You Do When Your Daddy Says 'Good-bye'" E555301; (2) another manuscript lead sheet of the same song, professionally copied, with the lyrics typed on a separate sheet, E569025, received September 5, 1923. The claimant was Clarence Williams Music Publishing; (3) manuscript lead sheet for "I've Got Those Shouting Blues," arranged by Ellis H. Reynolds, E558796, received March 22, 1923. This is in the same hand as item 1 above; (4) manuscript piano score of "R-C-O-Band, March," E568413, received August 11, 1923. The musical hand is different from items 1–3.

The handful of compositions copyrighted by George's younger brother Achille a few years earlier show both originality and what may be idiomatic New Orleans traits lacking in George's works.

28. It's been suggested that Baquet is present in several Bessie Smith blues accompaniments from September and October 1923. Or at least so he claimed in the interview with Frederic Ramsey, Jr., published in *Down Beat*. Yet the clarinetist on the tunes in question, issued as Columbia 13000-D, is certainly not the Baquet we hear in recordings of 1929 and 1940. I believe that the explanation is this: the two tunes were recorded—four and three takes respectively—on September 27 with Baquet, but

these were rejected. The issued versions come from October 15, 1923, as takes 7 and 6 respectively, using a different clarinetist. See Rust, *Jazz Records*, p. 1439 f.

29. All of Morton's Victor recordings are available as of writing (January 2003) on the English 5 CD set, JSP 903. Some may prefer the sound on the complete works issued on the French "Masters of Jazz" label, but these will be more difficult to find (and considerably more expensive). The 1940 recordings are available on American Music AMCD-44, "The John Reid Collection, 1940–1944."

30. Although not in the way suggested by the headline writer in the December 15, 1940 *DB* article, viz. "Baquet Played Hot Counterpoint to Keppard's Torrid Cornet Solos!"

31. Sidney Bechet, *Treat It Gentle* (New York: Hill & Wang, 1960), p. 79.

32. *The American Musician and Sportsman*, a rather rare African-American periodical published in Philadelphia.

33. Al Rose, *I Remember Jazz* (Baton Rouge: Louisiana State University Press, 1987), pp. 126–27. For all his deep and abiding interest in New Orleans jazz, Rose didn't always check his facts carefully. It may be that Baquet played in the pit band of one of Philadelphia's black theaters, for example, the Pearl on W. Market St. Rose also has Baquet playing on a quite possibly apocryphal cylinder recording by Buddy Bolden's band.

34. The 1937 date comes from *Music Dial* 1:12, June 1944, p. 30 (Philadelphia news).

35. Another one of Baquet with Bunk and his entire band, captioned "Philadelphia, Pa. c. Dec. 1945," can be found in the booklet accompanying the CD "The John Reid Collection, 1940–1944, American Music AMCD-44. Clarinetist George Lewis grins shyly, if not obsequiously. Perhaps he was very conscious of Baquet's status as a real, note-reading musician. In any event Baquet appears to be in poor health, a far cry from the Baquet pictured with Sidney Bechet a few pages later in the booklet.

36. Much of this account is drawn from information provided by Paul A. Larson of Lakewood, New Jersey, to Alan Barrell, for the latter's articles in *Footnote*, viz. "B is for . . . Baquet" 17:3 (February–March 1986), p. 4 ff., and "The Baquets—some concluding notes" 18:2 (December–January 1987).

37. Alan Lomax interviewed Big Eye in the late 1940s for his book on Jelly Roll Morton and quotes him as saying "Happen sometime you can put some *whining* in the blowing of your instrument. There are a whole lot of different sounds you can shove in—such as *crying*—everywhere you get the chance. But you gotta do that with a certain measurement and not opposed to the harmony. Don't play like you're at no funeral" (*MJR*, p. 85).

38. The six 1924 Doc Cooke recordings have been reissued as a group on King Jazz KJ111 FS, as also the eight from 1926. Noone's recordings under his own name from 1928 are widely available. Some of his best playing from this period is with Louis Armstrong, accompanying Lillie Delk Christian. These recordings are available on Document DOCD-5448.

39. Actually, it doesn't take much stretch of the aural imagination to hear in Big Eye's manner of dealing with a slow, melodic number (e.g., "You Made Me What I Am," recorded in July 1949 and newly available on American Music CD AMCD-7) the roots of Noone's syrupy melodic style.

40. Two takes are included on American Music AMCD 44, "The John Reid Collection, 1940–1944."

41. The Broun recordings have been reissued as American Music AMCD-41, "Prelude to the Revival, vol. II"; the ones from 1949, as AMCD-7, "Big Eye Louis Nelson Delisle."

42. Although jazz writers appear to prefer "Freddie," rather than "Freddy," or "Fred" (or, for that matter, "Frederick"), on what authority do they do so? A surviving photograph inscribed by him (*Jazzmen*) reads "Fred," and so do a number of references in *IF* from the time of the Creole Band.

43. One point should perhaps be made: much of Joe Oliver's success seems to depend on his businesslike and serious attitude toward running a band. Keppard appears to have been not only a lone wolf, but alcoholic and a skirt chaser to boot, neither of which is conducive to the self-control needed to keep a band together and musically effective.

44. *IF*, May 18, 1918. On the earlier history of 459 East Thirty-first Street, the locale of Royal Gardens, see William Howland Kenney, *Chicago Jazz* (New York: Oxford University Press, 1993), p. 19. One wonders just how Keppard would have been featured in *Madame Sherry*. Would he have been a solo cornet foil to a singer, as Ray Lopez was to Blossom Seeley between 1917 and 1920? See also the reasonably well-known photograph of Keppard and Sidney Bechet, probably dating from the summer of 1918, to judge by the straw boaters that both are wearing. (Bechet had left Chicago by the summer of 1919.) See fig. 4.7.

45. Keppard may have had the royal title bestowed on him prior to Oliver's arrival in Chicago. Cf. *Def*, November 2, 1918, p. 6: "King Keppard, the great jazz cornettist, is at the DeLuxe Cafe, and Ed Vincent, member of the Original Creole Band, is at the Royal Gardens, and both doing great work." Vincent's band probably had Bill Johnson as manager and was the one Joe Oliver and Jimmie Noone were soon to join.

46. Alec Boswell, "Juice Wilson," *Storyville* 75 (February–March 1978), pp. 90–94. According to the article, the two young violinists were known as the "Golders Twins." This surely must be "Gold Dust Twins." The dates given are in 1918, but this seems a year or so too early.

47. In the 1920 Federal Census, Keppard was enumerated in Chicago at 52 East 50th Street on January 3, 1920 (enumeration district 288, sheet 3A, line 8).

48. Taylor inserted a listing in the musicians' directory published in *The American Musician* in early 1921. He and his wife, Nettie, a banjorine player, lived at 1214 Montrose Street, Philadelphia.

49. Thurman and Mary Grove, "Charlie Gaines," *Jazzfinder*, December, 1948. Russ Shor, "Charlie Gaines," *Storyville* 68 (December 1976–January 1977), pp. 44–49. Keppard played in Chicago for a New Year's party thrown by club owner Izzy Shore for his employees. This was on December 28, 1919, so provides an anterior limit for the trip to Philadelphia.

50. Sweatman showed to publisher, record dealer, and jazz historian Leonard Kunstadt a cancelled check written to Keppard.

51. The Lorraine Gardens was at Thirty-fifth and Prairie, and may have been called the Paradise Gardens, either before or after it was called Lorraine Gardens. A band led

by New Orleans trombonist George Filhe was working there at various times in 1921 and 1922, as well as groups with drummer Ollie Powers.

52. This fits with Keppard's joining the musicians' union. Just whose band it was is not clear to me. My guess would be that the band was led by Carroll Dickerson, who was perennial at the Sunset and often employed Bobby Williams (who was poisoned and died in 1923). Bushell also recalled reed player Norvel "Flutes" Morton as being in the band. Hentoff, "Garvin Bushell and New York Jazz in the 1920s," *Jazz Review* 2:2 (February 1959), p. 9 ff. and Mark Tucker, *Jazz from the Beginning* [Ann Arbor: University of Michigan Press, 1988], pp. 25–26.

53. Issue of March 3, 1923. Noone is spelled "Moone," and Keppard "Kepper."

54. Cooke's name is often spelled "Cook," but on the basis of printed music and the ASCAP biographical dictionary, I assume that the "Cooke" is correct.

55. Between the opening of his club in 1921 and 1923 Kelly employed white New Orleans musicians such as Ragbaby Stevens and Alcide "Yellow" Nunez. His policy appears to have changed around the end of 1923.

56. From a 1953 interview with Frank Driggs and Thornton Hagert, published in *Jazz Journal* 17: 4–5 (1964). All of the recordings mentioned may be found on King Jazz KJ111 FS. An exceptionally valuable discussion of Keppard's recordings is Englebert Wengel's in *Doctor Jazz* (October–November 1970), pp. 2–5.

57. This problem is accentuated by Keppard's propensity to play a rather free second part in the middle or low range, leaving the straight lead to his fellow cornetist. While I can't assert that this is an old-fashioned trait, it's worth observing that the notion that in a New Orleans ragtime or jazz band the lead is always allocated to the cornetist is a relatively recent one. Furthermore, one supposes that in the Creole Band, where the violinist probably had primary responsibility for the melodic lead, interesting combinations between the clarinet and cornet must have been worked out.

58. Both the label as well as Paramount ads from *Def* read "Freddie," which some would take as justifying that spelling.

59. I discussed a number of these matters of style in the notes to the LP "The Legendary Freddie Keppard, New Orleans Cornet," The Smithsonian Collection R020, © 1979.
Some of the most eloquent praise and knowledgeable description of Keppard's style come from Jelly Roll Morton, in steno notes he dictated at the Library of Congress in 1938 and available on the Library microfilm Music-332 and included in appendix 5 below.

60. The LP anthology, Smithsonian R020, included two selections by Jasper Taylor and his State Street Boys from 1927 on which the cornetist is NOT (I'm almost certain) Keppard.

61. It's truly sad to see how the young and handsome Keppard changed over the years to the jowly, glowering, and seriously overweight person he became in the 1920s. The process was already beginning by the middle of 1918. The small band was drawn from Pasquall's ten-piece "World Wonder Orchestra," playing at Harmon's Dreamland. Keppard observed Pasquall's refusal to permit drinking and according to the leader was playing "at his very best" (from interviews with Pasquall by Thornton Hagert).

62. See *Def*, May 3, 1930, p. 20: "Freddie Keppard, the wizard cornetist, better known as 'King Keppard,' is back in the Limelight again. He was one of the reasons why the International Harvester's Dance was a success last Saturday night." For the Zeppelin Inn on Indiana Ave. (perhaps quite short-lived) see the same paper, November 15, p. 11 and November 22.

63. This story comes to me from James Dapogny, who got it from Shoffner.

64. *California Eagle*, October 1, 1921 (referring to September 13); January 14, 1922 (front-page article); January 28, 1922; February 18, 1922 (pool hall and new management of restaurant). Morton was actually the manager of Wayside Amusement Park, according to *Def*, April 22, 1922. The presence of Oliver there comes from Marshall Stearns's article (based on Lowell Williams's research) in *DB*, January 15, 1938. It couldn't have lasted very long,

In 1959, Johnson recalled that when Oliver went to California he played in a trio with Ed Wyer, violin, and Leon Smizer, guitar. But in 1935 Preston Jackson reported in the pages of *Jazz Hot* that Bill was playing in Michigan with the Smizer trio. Perhaps these were two separate episodes fourteen years apart.

65. All three are published together in Laurie Wright, rev., *"King" Oliver* (Chigwell (Essex): Storyville Publications, 1987), pp. 17–19.

66. Ibid., p. 20. The famous "Dipper Mouth Blues" on which Bill cried out "Oh, play that thing" was the antepenultimate tune of the Friday recording session. Consequently, if Bud Scott is to be heard, it would be on "Froggie Moore" and/or "Snake Rag."

67. *Satchmo*, p. 239 f.

68. Notwithstanding that there were many bands that used the name "Creole" in their title (even in 1918), including "Oliver and Ory's Celebrated Creole Orchestra" in the *Western Appeal* of March 8, 1922. However, in two advertisements from around the same time we read "King Oliver's Aces of Syncopation" and "King Oliver's Jazz."

69. Information passed on to me by Karl Gert zur Heide, who had it from Frank Driggs, June 14, 1977.

70. See *EJB* 1946, opposite p. 54.

71. Many thanks to Steven Lasker for compiling a tape of some 49 recordings involving Johnson and making it available to me.

72. Of course, this is in part due to choices made in the recording studio as to how far away from the microphone Bill was placed. Certainly, his strength on the Dodds Victors seems to be in part due to placement.

73. June 8, 1929, p. 10. Perhaps only "eccentric" compared to what younger or less enterprising bassists, such as Wellman Braud, Pops Foster, and Steve Brown played. Hinton's remarks are from a lecture on "Early Slap Bass" given at Schoenberg Hall, UCLA, on August 23, 1988 and passed on to me by Alden Ashforth. Although a questioner from the audience attempted to elicit more detail, Hinton pretty much limited himself to a demonstration of how Johnson would stomp as he played.

74. We should allow for the possibility that Bill just forgot his bow, or had taken it to the repairman to be rehaired. Or maybe he left his rosin at home. The excellent bassist in my band of the mid-1980s constantly forgot his rosin. But in this case I suspected he just didn't want to use the bow. (You know who you are!)

75. The Federal Census of Chicago for 1930 doesn't seem to have found Bill, unless he was the 47-year-old "Fiddle-Musician" born in Alabama and living at 715 East Fiftieth Street (a black neighborhood). Other difficult details are a wife, Virginia, and a 6-year-old daughter, Gloria.

76. *DB*, May 15, 1940; *Jazz Hot* no. 5 (September–October 1935), p. 15.

77. *International Musician*, February 1937.

78. WRC, Correspondence (Dink Johnson), F. 45.

79. The Twin Terrace Concerts were under the auspices of the Hot Club of Chicago. Whether Johnson might have been playing steady jobs around this time is not known. John Chilton, *Who's Who of Jazz*, 4th ed. [London: Macmillan, 1985], 168, has him still playing in the 1950s, giving up playing in the early 1960s without indication of where this might have been.

80. The interview was with Bob Kirstein, alias "Dr. Jazz." A tape of the interview is in my possession. The pianist, Brooks Kerr, recalls having met Bill in Mexico City around 1962 (personal communication, March 26, 1997).

81. Bill Russell received a SASE dated June 30, 1958, from Will McClain, Johnson's next-door neighbor in Chicago, with the following new address: "Mr. Wm. Monger, Post office Box 122, Marble Falls, Texas," with the further instruction, "write in care of this box number above, c/o Mr. Wm. Johnson" (WRC, Bill Johnson files, F. 2).

82. Letter from Harry F. Carley to William Everett Samuels, dated September 2, 1972.

83. November 3, 1916, p. 16. If she had, she would have been reunited with her old mentors, McIntyre and Heath.

84. Her telegram of November 25 and Eddie Edwards's letter of the same date are in a scrapbook in the possession of the Edwards family. It's true that Elaine did not state explicitly that the band was to accompany her, but there is no reason to think that she ever was a booker.

85. P. 123. Her affiliation with "Town Topics" was important enough to mention. The name of the act, "A Scene on the Levee" and the indication that it used special scenery, may mean that she already was using the drop known from the photographs with the Duhé (or Herb Lindsay) band.

86. Clarinetist Laurence Duhé kept a copy of the contract dated April 13 among his memorabilia. Elaine and her band may have opened April 9 at the Grand, the stamping ground of the Creole Band, proceeding then to the Kedzie and the Windsor, and capping their Chicago engagements with an appearance at McVicker's. They played the Palace in Danville, then went to Cedar Rapids, Iowa, for the first half of the week of May 14. One photograph of the act, in front of a steamboat drop, has been reprinted a number of times. Another photograph from the same session was used for advance publicity in the *Cedar Rapids Gazette* of May 12. The usual copy of the photograph—of which Duncan Schiedt gave me a copy—has written on it in a crude hand "Chicago, Ill. May 15/17," but clearly this is impossible in view of the use of a photo from the same session on May 12. Even at the Grand, the band was found to lack pep. The Kedzie review suggested that since Elaine was "corked up" and "surrounded by a bunch of darkies" she should "uncover" (i.e., remove her makeup) lest people suspect she was "high yellow."

87. *Variety*, June 22, 1955, p. 71, and the *New York Times* of that date. Mabel Elaine's

daughter continued living for several years at 356 West Forty-fifth Street, New York, after the death of her husband in 1957. She may have died in December 1976 at the age of 63 or 64.

88. In an undated press release—misfiled, and the only contents of the Mildred Elaine file at TSA—publicizing the appearance of the "dainty little dancer" Mabel Elaine in the Shubert show "Boom Boom," there's an interesting concluding paragraph that not only explains how she might have updated her act but how she managed to fit in with a rowdy bunch of New Orleans ragtimers: "Miss Elaine has one ambition in life and that is to play 'boy' parts. Come one of these fine days she plans to journey to England and sign up with an English producer of pantomime, in which, as a rule, the principal 'boy' is always portrayed by some fascinating girl."

89. I believe, however, that if I'm given a "blindfold test," I could do rather well in identifying a clarinet player from New Orleans, and with less certainty, a cornetist. And there are others whom I'd trust to make the same kind of identification.

90. These are deep philosophical waters in which I'm not really qualified to navigate. I'll simply mention that there is a "hard" determinism that admits no role at all for free will, and a "soft" one.

Bibliographical Note

1. *DB*, August 1936, pp. 6–7. This chapter makes much of the role of riverboats in moving jazz from New Orleans to Chicago, something that Stearns in his 1956 book *The Story of Jazz* (New York: Oxford Univesity Press) describes as an inadequate cliché of jazz history. The magazine kept the photograph in its files, using it again in its issue of August 15, 1940, p. 17, repeating the erroneous identifications of the players as in the 1936 caption.

2. "From Honkey-Tonk to Swing," p. 13 f. It seems doubtful that the two bands ever played in such proximity or that they sat in for each other. It may be that LaRocca learned of the Creole Band from this source. As with other bands who seemed to him to infringe on the priority of the ODJB, refuting the claims Williams made for them became an unshakable obsession.

3. *DB*, September 1937, p. 15. In the April 1937 issue, p. 5, Miller claimed that "Roots of Hot White Jazz Are Negroid," crediting as initiators of the second major period, "the Chicago period (1918–1925)," King Oliver and Freddie Keppard, who "after touring extensively with the Original Creole Band, formed a group of his own in Chicago."

4. Chicago: Down Beat Publishing Co., 1939, reprint: Westport, Connecticut: Greenwood Press, 1978. The nature of the details indicates that they must have come from a member of the band. Of the six surviving members (Prince, Johnson, Williams, Baquet, Noone, Delille) only Jimmie Noone and Bill Johnson lived in Chicago and only the latter would have known about the period prior to 1917.

5. New York: Harcourt, Brace. It remained in print throughout the war, and the copy I won by doing well on the Time magazine Current Affairs Contest in 1946 was a 1945 printing. It also appeared in a paperback edition for the U.S. Armed Forces. Stearns's book-length history was not to appear until 1956.

6. Smith's contribution was minimal. See the valuable account of the inception and writing of *Jazzmen* in Bruce Boyd Raeburn, "New Orleans Style: The Awakening of American Jazz Scholarship and Its Cultural Implications." Ph.D. dissertation, Tulane University, 1991.

7. HNOC, WRC, General Correspondence and Working Files, letter of Frederic Ramsey to Bill Russell, dated October 25, 1938. John Hammond and Wilder Hobson were lined up for the book, and Ramsey's draft of an agreement was in the hands of Harcourt, Brace. "I think it will be safe for you to stay on and look around Chicago, etc., as things look pretty certain now." Ramsey asks in a letter of May 2, 1939, whether the "Chi exam came out all right," and two days later writes, "I hope you are now a Ph.D., and feeling fine."

8. Russell took down the information in a small black two-ring binder about 3.5 by 6 inches, now HNOC, WRC, General Correspondence and Working Files, Jazzmen, folder 50. These rather telegraphic notes were then fleshed out in a three-page type-script contained in folder 28. Some important information never made it into the book, including details regarding the 1907–1908 band that traveled to California.

9. *DB*, December 15, 1940, p. 10, "Vet Tells Story of the Original Creole Orchestra," and January 1, 1941, p. 6, "Baquet and his Mob 'Carved' King Bolden." Ramsey must have taken a short jaunt to Philadelphia, where Baquet led "George Bakay's Swingsters" at Wilson's night club.

10. Examples are the mention of a 1908 Creole Band of which Ramsey states Baquet was a member—there was such a band but not with Baquet—and a cartoon in the *Los Angeles Times* showing him playing clarinet. Bill Russell searched diligently in the *Times* for this, rather than in the *Examiner* where it actually was published. Baquet had a chance to speak for himself in a talk given to the New Orleans Jazz Club on April 17, 1948. This was belatedly published in the *Second Line* (September–October 1965) and adds a few details to the 1940 account—for example, Keppard's use of an "egg mute" and a derby in playing "Mandalay" at the Leach Cross and Joe Rivers bout.

11. Nat Shapiro and Nat Hentoff, New York: Rinehart, 1955 and as a paperback, New York: Dover, 1966. Mentions in the book of the Creole Band by Wellman Braud and Jelly Roll Morton don't even merit an entry in the index.

12. *La Nouvelle-Orléans, Capitale du Jazz,* New York: Editions de la Maison Française, 1946. This work has been quite unjustifiably neglected, as much due to the linguistic chauvinism of Americans as to a small press run. Of course, it would be pointless to translate it now without extensive commentary distinguishing Goffin's active imagination from the core of fact.

13. New York: Smith & Durrell, 1946. A similar attempt to synthesize the history of jazz in Chicago was made in 1959 by John Steiner—in Nat Hentoff and Albert J. McCarthy, eds., *Jazz* (New York: Holt, Rinehart & Winston, 1959; paperback: Da Capo, 1975), pp. 137–169 but is comparatively standoffish about the role of the Creole Band, partly due to a muddled chronology (not that earlier attempts were all that clear!). See also Steiner's notes to the Columbia LP set, C3L32, *Jazz Odyssey* (v. 2): *The Sound of Chicago.*

14. The most recent edition is the fourth: Alan Lomax, *Mister Jelly Roll* (Berkeley: University of California Press, 2001). Information on the band and some of its musi-

cians appears on pp. 124–26 and 153–55. The process of giving continuity to Morton's oral history—and blending it with some material dictated to a library stenographer—results in some egregiously false or misleading statements—for example, that Bill Johnson took over the band at the Tuxedo dance hall and, on hearing about California from Morton, took it west (p. 153) Further, Morton's words on the band's manner of performance appeared only in an as yet unpublished interview conducted by Russell in the winter or spring of 1937–1938 and written down by him in 1944.

15. New York: Doubleday, 1962. The vast wealth of data had been collected by Kunstadt in his capacity as editor and publisher of *Record Research*. Charters took "the responsibility for the organization, interpretation, and writing" (p. 7).

16. New York: Macmillan, 1967; repr., Da Capo Press, 1978.

17. *The Legendary Freddie Keppard, New Orleans Cornet*, Smithsonian Collection R020, 1979.

18. "How the Creole Band Came to Be," *BMRJ* 8:1 (1988), pp. 83–100.

19. One should perhaps add the *Dramatic Mirror*, although it was interested primarily in legitimate theater, and the *Morning Telegraph*. I confess that the latter has been read by me only selectively.

20. I didn't pass up the opportunity to look through any lesser periodicals, such as the *New York Star* and *Review*, as well as the local *Kansas City Thespian*. One soon learns that many theatrical weeklies are not extant, at least in public collections; one that might have been of very great help, the *Chicago Saturday Evening Telegram*, exists in only three numbers at the Chicago Historical Society.

21. It's amazing how many daily newspapers have made it through to the age of microfilm. I'd say that at least three-quarters of the dailies listed in the *Ayer American Newspaper Annual and Directory* are accessible. (The occasional holding library will not loan even a microfilm, but these are fortunately few.) With a very few exceptions, I did not look at the many weekly papers that existed in the United States around the time of World War I, nor the profusion of papers in foreign languages.

Appendix 2

1. "Chooses"? Well, not always, since it's been quite common for publishers to use a band as a vehicle for pushing an item from their catalog.

2. On the cover is printed "Dolly Connoly's [married to Wenrich] Big Rag Song Success" and it seems likely the person depicted is she.

3. "A Panorama of Negro Music" in *Who Is Who in Music, 1941 Edition* (Chicago: Lee Stern Press, p. 566 f). Actually, Europe is said to have featured "Memphis Blues" when his band accompanied Vernon and Irene Castle during their so-called "whirlwind tour" of Spring 1914. A group led by Europe didn't record the tune until 1919, by which time it had been recorded by a Columbia studio band.

4. WRC, General Coll., Working Files, *Jazzmen*, folder 50, for the MS notes, somewhere else [forgive me!] in the Russell papers for the typed version.

5. "Jazzed up" is what Bill Russell wrote in his interview notes.

6. There's interesting testimony from Roy Carew, Jelly Roll Morton's friend and publisher in the late 1930s but living in New Orleans during the first two decades of the

century. In a letter to Morton dated July 9, 1941, Carew relates how he has just bought the reissue of the Keppard Jazz Cardinals recording (of Stock Yards Strut and Salty Dog). He writes, "They sound like old New Orleans, very natural." *Oh, Mr. Jelly!*, p. 304.

Appendix 3

1. An excellent summary, although in a work with limited distribution, is to be found in Lester Sullivan's contribution to *Guide to Arc Light*, New Orleans: Amistad Research Center, ca. 1983, but almost any discussion of New Orleans history in the nineteenth century comments on these issues. Some of the ins and outs as applied to the history of jazz are reviewed in Jerah Johnson's "Jim Crow laws of the 1890s . . ." in *Popular Music* 19:2 (2000), 243–51.

2. See especially Alan Lomax, *Mr. Jelly Roll* (Berkeley: University of California Press, 2001).

Appendix 4

1. Coycault was apparently called Ernest Johnson by some of his contemporaries, supposedly because of his resemblance to Bill Johnson. But perhaps it was not just a matter of a near-Caucasian complexion (Coycault's features are rather unlike Bill's) but also of their association in the 1908 band. One imagines them being asked, "Are you two fellows brothers?"

2. The Creole Band often used the term "original" in the thirty or so variants of their "nom d'affiche," but not always. In any event, this goes back to Los Angeles in 1914. The "Original Brown's, etc." designation comes from a unique 1916 flyer for the North Star Inn sent by Tom Brown to a private collector.

3. For a detailed discussion of the various titles and lyrics of early editions, see James Fuld's *Book of World Famous Music*.

4. From a scrapbook in the possession of Edwards's descendants, Portsmouth, Rhode Island.

5. See *Horst H. Lange's The Fabulous Fives*, revised by Ron Jewson et al. (Storyville Publications: Chigwell [Essex], 1978), p. 11. "That Teasin' Rag," a piece by Joe Jordan, was at first used without acknowledgment. As I write these lines, I'm looking at a copy of Victor 18255-A with "Dixie Jazz Band One-Step." The piece became a jazz standard as "Original Dixieland One-Step."

6. *MJR*, p. 116. This is on p. 126 of the most recent edition from University of California Press. The seven-piece instrumentation (without piano) is of course that of the Creole Band, as well as many another New Orleans dance band.

7. It might not be uninteresting to examine dirty books and pamplets published between 1890 and 1920 for uses of "jazz" and other vernacular terms pertaining to music, such as "rag" and "blue."

8. *Talking Machine World*, July 15, 1920, p. 6. The road from the baseball training camp of 1913—hardly, one imagines, "a refined atmosphere"—to the high-class St. Francis Hotel where Hickman played in 1914 led steeply upward. Hickman's band could play, nevertheless, quite raucously in its 1919 recordings, especially of the blues,

although without resorting to the noisemakers of the contemporary trap drummer's kit (Hickman was a drummer). This sounds very much like the point of view of Bert Kelly.

9. Dick Holbrook, "Our Word Jazz" in *Storyville* 50 (December 1973–January 1974), pp. 46–58.

10. It's difficult to reconcile these conflicting claims. At first glance Lopez seems more judicious, Brown rather angry. Clearly the internal dynamics of the band come into play. My opinion is that Brown was anxious to back up his claim to priority with a misdated document. He wrote, for example, "The sign in front of Lamb's cafe read, 'Added attraction—Brown's Original Dixieland Jazz Band Direct from New Orleans—Best Dance Music in Chicago.'" ("Chicago's First Jazz Band? Tom Brown's Story as told to J. Lee Anderson" *The Record Changer*, March 1951.) I've seen a flyer from the North Star Inn for April 27, 1916 that was in Tom Brown's possession. The billing reads "Original Brown's Jass Band from Dixieland." This was nearly two months after Johnny Stein's band (later to be the ODJB) began playing at Schiller's and used the word "jass" in at least one ad.

The related discussion in Sudhalter's *Lost Chords* relies almost entirely on Lopez and not at all on Tom Brown.

11. *La Gidouille/CMH-Info*, August 1987, no. 4. Only 100 copies were reproduced, with 90 distributed.

Appendix 5

1. The famous comedian (and erstwhile ragtime pianist) Jimmy Durante is quoted as saying: "In some of the bands in those days, the cornet player played the melody, in some others, the clarinet player played the melody. In our band, nobody played the melody." Samuel B. Charters and Leonard Kunstadt, *Jazz: a History of the New York Scene* (Garden City, NY: Doubleday, 1962), p. 80.

2. See William Russell *O, Mister Jelly* (Copenhagen: JazzMedia ApS, 2000), p. 130ff.

3. This and other item numbers are from my personal inventory of the microfilm. I've indulged in no editing other than the selection itself.

Index

Page numbers in *italics* indicate illustrations.

Gabriel, Albert, 27, 44
Gabriel, Manny, 49, 317 n.49
Gabriel, Martin Joseph, 317 n.49
Gaines, Charlie, 50, 256–57
Garland, Ed, 213, 235, 239, 261
Gennett records, 275
George Richards & Co. (act), 128
Gibson, Mr. (theater operator), 216, 238
Gibson Theatre (Phila.). *See* Standard
    Theatre
"Gidouille, La" (publication), 301
Gillespie, Dizzy, 255
"Gipsy," 290
Giuffre, Santo, 16
"God Gave Me More Than My Share," 195
"Go Down Moses" (spiritual), 6
Goetz, Coleman, 195
Goffin, Robert, 41, 179–80, 183–84, 254
    on Creole Band breakup, 211, 214, 215,
        217
    on Creole Band hiatus, 217, 219
"Going Down State Street" (Ramsey), 64
Goldberg, Jack, 135
Golden, Billy, 109
Golden Horse & Lady, The (act), 119
Golden West (Los Angeles hotel and
    saloon), 85–87, *85*, 326 n.52
Gonzales, Anita, 77, 83
Goodwin, Gloria, 204, 208
Gordon's Olympia Theatre (Boston), 210,
    212
Gorham, Joe, 134
Graham, Elwood, 258, 259
Grand Opera House (Great Falls, Mont.),
    184
Grand Opera House (St. Louis, Mo.), 229
Grand Theater (St. Louis, Mo.), 52, 197, 198
Grand Theatre (Chicago), 118–19, 120, 121,
    133, 134
Gray, Eddie, 301
Gray, Gilda, 272
Gray, Nan, 188
Gray, Thomas J., 157
Great Fer-Don Medicine Show, 51, *52*
Great Northern Hippodrome Theater
    (Chicago), 121, 145
Great Southern Hotel, 322 n.20
Greeley, Horace (drummer), 72
Green, Ray, 240

Griffin, Prentice, *52*
grizzly bear (dance), 9, 33
Grofé, Ferde, 95
Groshell, Eddie, 32
Grove, Thurman and Mary, 351 n.49
G. Schirmer (publisher), 288
Guiguesse, Alphonse, 39
Gunn, Earnestine, Jr., 226
Gusikoff, Michael, 241
Gus Sun theater chain, 10, 126, 130–31, 249

Hagert, Thornton, 352 n.56
Hall, "Baby," 256
Hall, Minor, 239
Hamilton Theater (St. Louis), 130
Ham Tree, The (show), 8, 158
Hancock (Mich.) Evening Copper Journal, 123
Handy, John ("Captain"), 67
Handy, W. C., 51, 289
Hanley, Peter, 54
Hannan's saloon (New Orleans), 28
Happy 6 (band), 257
Hardin, Lil, 257
Harlan, Byron, 301
Harmon, Paddy, 258, 263
Harrah, Roy and Anna, 104
Harris, Skinny, *52*
Hart, Max, 344 n.88
Hattiesburg Daily News, 70
Hattiesburg Excursion Band, 68–71,
    322 nn.19–20
Hawaiian Butterfly, 138
Hawkesworth, Margaret, 143
Haymarket Theater (Chicago), 121, 127
Hearn, Lew, 157, 160
Heimann, Jim, 88
Heisen, Mr. and Mrs. Carl, 121, 331 n.1
"Hello, Alexander" (musical), 271–72
Helstein, I., 154
Henderson, Ben, 299
Henderson, Charles C., 65, 66, 68, 69, 202
Henderson, Fletcher, 15, 265, 287
Henderson, Mary C., 341 n.57
Henderson, Nannie, 66
Hendrick, Z. A., 147, *148*
Henshel, Jimmie, 125
Herbert, Victor, 157
"Here Comes the Hot Tamale Man," 259
Hickman, Art, 20, 299, 300, 358 n.8

Hill, Murray K., 141
Hinton, Milt, 263
Hippodrome theater (Kansas City, Mo.), 117, 118
Hippodrome theater (Terre Haute, Ind.), 136
Historic New Orleans Collection, 64, 180
historiography, 4, 13–19, 172, 273
"History of the Band and Orchestra Business in Los Angeles" (Bagley), 85
Hoefer, George, 80, 81, 124
Hoffman brothers, 224
hokum, 140–42
Holbrook, Richard, 135, 138, 299, 300, 359 n.9
Holly, Emanuel ("Manuel"), 66
"Homeward Bound Blues," 246
Hot Five (jazz group), 233, 264
Howard, Darnell, 290–91
Howard, Ed, 101
Howard, Paul, 63, 84, 326 n.50
"How the Creole Band Came to Be" (Gushee), 64, 79
"How to Train a Chicken" (Breland and Bailey), 96
Huddleston, George, 102
Hugo Brothers Minstrels, 51, 53, 95, 145
Humphrey, James, 63, 223
Humphrey, Willie, Jr., 50, 239
Humphrey, Willie, Sr., 28, 29
Huntz and Nagel's Casino (New Orleans), 28
Hutchinson (theater manager), 211
Hyatt's Minstrels, 107
Hyer sisters, 109

Illinois State Register, 137
"I'm on My Way to Mandalay," 91, 100
Imperial Band of New Orleans, 41, 78–79
Imperial Orchestra, 28, 30, 31, 82, 93
improvisation, 14, 16
Indianapolis, Ind., 129, 150, 162, 163, 198–99, 225–26
Indianapolis Freeman, 39, 107, 119, 128, 179, 181, 216
    on Baquet/Crosby act, 168, 249
    Creole Band prehistory and, 65–66, 68, 69–70, 75
    on Keppard and Chicago scene, 256

on Pantages, 103
on Scott, 289
Indianapolis News, 150, 162–63, 199
Indianapolis Star, 129, 150, 199
Indianapolis Sunday Star, 97
Indianapolis Times, 129, 150, 198–99
"In Far Off Mandalay," 91, 100
"In Mandalay," 89, 327 n.62
instrumentation, 5, 17, 18–19, 31, 61–62, 177
    Creole Band and, 62, 138–39
    Dixieland and, 298–99
    early jazz and, 301
International Musician (periodical), 209, 257
"In the Footlight Glow" (Marmaduke column), 107
"I've Got Those Shooting Blues," 249
"I Want Some One Who's Lonesome," 158, 288
"I Wish I Was in Dixie's Land," 298
"I Wonder Who's Kissing Her Now," 157

Jack, Sam T., 293
Jackson, Dan, 235
Jackson, Eddie, 246
Jackson, Papa Charlie, 247
Jackson, Preston, 57, 265, 266, 320 n.79
Jackson, Tony, 256, 308
Jake Wells theater chain, 126
Jaxon, "Half-Pint," 265
"Jazbo," 301
jazz
    African music and, 4–5
    band repertories and, 287–91
    beginnings of, 3, 13–19, 219
    Chicago late-teens scene of, 235–36, 297–98
    copyright and, 301–2
    craze for, 219
    Creole Band's historical significance in, 13, 272, 274–76
    dances and, 4, 5, 8–9, 20
    historiographic approaches to, 4, 13–19, 172, 273
    history of word "jazz" and, 138, 297–302
    improvisation and, 14, 16
    instrumentation of early, 17, 18–19, 31, 61–62
    New Orleans brass bands and, 17

Mahoney, Jack, 289

Main Event, The (cigar store), 320 n.82

Majestic theater (Bloomington, Ill.), 139, 197

Majestic theater (Cedar Rapids, Iowa), 145, 194–95

Majestic theater (Dubuque, Iowa), 144, 229

Majestic theater (Springfield, Ill.), 136–37, 229

Majestic theater (Waterloo, Iowa), 229

Make Me a Pallet on the Floor, 40

Malnig, Julie, 342 n.61

"Mandalay," 327 n.62

Mandot, Joe, *87*

Manetta, Manuel (Emanuel, "'Fess"), 27, *27*, 28, 29, 49, 50

Manitoba Free Press, 105, 182

Mannion's Park (St. Louis), 130

"Maple Leaf Rag" (Joplin), 214

Marcus Loew Agency, 156

Marcus Loew' theaters. *See* Loew's theaters

Mares, Joe, Sr., 321 n.2

Margaret Theater (Anaconda, Mont.), 184

Marmaduke (critic), 107, 183

Marrero, Billy, 30, 49, 82

Marrero, John, 223

Marrero, Simon, 223

Marshall, Henry, 301

Martin, Joe, 31

Martin, Louis, 203

Martin, Milton, 26

"Massa's in the Cold, Cold Ground," 106, 107, 288

Matthews, J. C., 119

Maurice Samuels & Co. (act), 121–22

Max and Mabel Ford (act), 122

Maxine and Her Creole Band, 231

maxixe (dance), 9

McCarey, Tom, 89, 90

McCarey's Arena. *See* Vernon Arena

McCarthy, Albert, 246

McConnell & Niemeyer (act), 104

McCusker, John, 312 n.8

McIntyre, Jim, 8

McIntyre and Heath (minstrel team), 8, 158, 181, 272

McNeil (booker), 156

McPartland, Jimmy, 266

McShann, Jay, 287

McVickers theater (Chicago), 121, 197, 198, 200, 201, 231

Medlin, Watts, and Towns (act), 193

Melrose Bros., 275

"Memphis Blues," 289

Meskin, Walter, 223

Michigan Vaudeville Circuit theaters, 122

Midland Saga (Monger), 73

Miles Theater, Cleveland, 202

Miles Theater, Detroit, 122–23, 200

Miller, Flournoy, 326 n.54

Miller, Irvin, 215, 216–17

Miller, Paul Eduard, 80, 125, 270, 275

Mills, Florence, 213, 326 n.54

Milwaukee, Wis., 229, 232, 290

Milwaukee Free Press, 232

minstrelsy, 19, 41, 63, 139, 140, 142, 145, 158, 181, 216, 233, 272, 274

 Caucasian vs. African-American, 5–8

"Mississippi Days," 91

"Mississippi Dream," 289

"Mississippi Dreams," 90, 91

Miss Match Miss (act), 211

Missouri Breeze (weekly), 104, 105, 108, 118, 120, 121, 126, 128, 134, 137–39, 140, 141, 142–43, 147, 150, 158, 182, 184, 188, 201

Mitchell, Adam, 102

mixed-race ancestry, 293–95

Molyneux, Eileen, 157

Monger, Miriam, 64, 72–79, 267

Montgomery, Little Brother, *266*

Montmartre (N.Y.C. nightclub). *See* Doraldina's Montmartre

Montrose, Cyril, 241

Morand, Herb, 31

Moran, Samuel, 322 n.18

Morant, S., 57, 69

"More Power Blues," 290

Moreland Motor Truck Company, 327 n.68

Moret, George, 39

Morosco, Oliver, 162, 209

Morrison, George, 188, 340 n.34

Morton, Jelly Roll, 13, 87, 219, 261, 265, 275, 289

 Baquet's recordings with, 41, 250, 251

 on Creole Band, 3, 18, 51, 121, 154, 186, 231, 303–8

 Creole Band prehistory and, 65, 72, 76

Spriggs, James ("Jimmy"), 24
Spriggs, Rebecca, 312 n.2
Springfield (Ill.) News Record, 137
Springfield (Mass.) Union, 210
Stables (Chicago nightclub), 258, 262
Standard Theatre (Phila.), 217, 238
Stanley, Pete, 102
"Steamboat Bill," 289, 290
"Steamboat Rag," 290
Stearns, Marshall and Jean, 8
Stein, Johnny, 297–98
Steiner, John, 124, 239, 290, 356 n.13
Stein's Band from Dixie, 298
Stein's Dixie Jass Band, 298
Stephen, Hal, 91–92, *91*
Sternad, Jake, 126
Stevens, Ashton, 164–65
"Stock Yards Strut," 246
Stoddard, Tom, 65, 75, 102
Storyville (New Orleans). *See* "District"
Stratford Hotel (Chicago), 331 n.1
Strauss, Richard, 162
string bass recording, 264–65
Stuart, Dave, 304
Sugar Johnny (musician), 232
Sullivan & Considine theater chain, 103, 274
Sullivan, Lester, 358 n.1
Sumiko (vaudevillian), 139
Sunshine Orchestra, 272
Superior Orchestra, 29–30, 49, 82
"Swanee River," 105–6, 290
Sweatman, Wilbur, 142, 257
"Sweetie Dear," 291
"Swing Low, Sweet Chariot," 6
Syncopated Ginger Snaps (band), 240, 262
syncopation, 7, 8

Tabor Grand Opera House (Denver), 188
Taborn, George Leroy ("Roy"), 51, *52*, 102
"Tack 'Em Down," 176
Tacoma Daily Ledger, 112
Tacoma Daily News, 112
Tales from Toussaint (Monger), 64, 72–79, 267
Tamony, Peter, 299
Tampa Red (musician), 263, 264
tango, 9
Tanguay, Eva, 96
Tate, Erskine, 240, 258, 260
Tate, James, 258

Taylor, Charlie, 256–57
Taylor, George, *52*
Taylor, Jasper, 247
Taylor, Lottie, 245, *245*
Tearney, Al, 235
Tennessee Ten (act), 150, 212–13, 221, 234, 344 n.2
Terre Haute Sunday Star, 229
Terre Haute Tribune, 136
Texas Tommy (dance), 33
"That Eccentric Rag," 262
"That Funny Jas Band from Dixieland," 301
Theater Owner's Booking Association (TOBA), 13
Theaters, segregation in, 321 n.3
"This Is the Life," 90, 91
Thomas, G. W., 34
Thompson, U. S. ("Slow Kid"), 212, 221
"Ti" (bass player), 44
"Tiger Rag," 207, 208
Times-Picayune. See New Orleans Times-Picayune
Tinette (violinist), 28
Tio, Lorenzo, Jr., 223, 256
Tio, Luis (Louis; "Papa"), 39, 212
TOBA (Theater Owner's Booking Association), 13
toldolo (dance), 33
Town Topics (show), 13, *43*, 135, 150, *153*, 154, 156–67, 175–76, 180–81, 183, 187, 199, 220, 238, 247, 249, 271, 272, 288, 339 n.7
  Elaine's two big numbers in, 159–60, 288–89
  history of, 156–59
  listing of musical numbers from, 289
Tramps (social club), 322, n.18
  orchestra, 57, 69
Trepagnier, Ernest ("Nenesse"), 174, 252
Tribble, Andrew, 119
"Trumpeter Fred Keppard Walked Out on Al Capone!" (Spencer article), 117
"Trumpet in the Cornfield Blows, The," 107
Tuck, Tony, 140
Tucker, Adrian, 265
Tucker, Sophie, 11, 163, 168, 230, 247, 336 n.61, 337 n.66, 341 n.52
Tulane Jazz Archives, 56, 69
Tulane University, 317 n.53